Faces in the Clouds

"Couldn't be a man. Must be a god!"

Drawing by Ross; © 1989
The New Yorker Magazine, Inc.

FACES

in the

CLOUDS

A New Theory of Religion

STEWART ELLIOTT GUTHRIE

New York   Oxford
OXFORD UNIVERSITY PRESS

To my extended family
and especially to Alan,
whose young life contained much
and continues to inspire

Oxford University Press

Oxford   New York
Athens   Auckland   Bangkok   Bombay
Calcutta   Cape Town   Dar es Salaam   Delhi
Florence   Hong Kong   Istanbul   Karachi
Kuala Lumpur   Madras   Madrid   Melbourne
Mexico City   Nairobi   Paris   Singapore
Taipei   Tokyo   Toronto

and associated companies in
Berlin   Ibadan

First published in 1993 by Oxford University Press, Inc.
198 Madison Avenue, New York, New York 10016-4314

First issued as an Oxford University Press paperback, 1995

Oxford is a registered trademark of Oxford University Press, Inc.

Library of Congress Cataloging-in-Publication Data
Guthrie, Stewart Elliott, 1941–
Faces in the clouds : a new theory of religion /
Stewart Elliott Guthrie.
p.   cm.   Includes bibliographical references and index.
ISBN 0-19-506901-3
ISBN 0-19-509891-9 (Pbk.)
1. Anthropomorphism.   2. Religion—Controversial literature.
I. Title.   BL215.G88   1993   211—dc20   92-9498

4 6 8 10 9 7 5 3

Printed in the United States of America
on acid-free paper

Preface
to the Paperback Edition

Earlier writers who have seen anthropomorphism as basic to religion have disagreed about its nature and causes. Most have slighted its secular forms. My own claim is simple. I hold that religion is best understood as anthropomorphism and that anthropomorphism results from a strategy of perception.

The strategy is to interpret the world's ambiguities first as those possibilities that matter most. Such possibilities usually include living things and especially humans. Although the strategy leads to mistakes, it also leads to vital discoveries that outweigh them. We see shadows in alleys as persons and hear sounds as signals because if these interpretations are right they are invaluable, and if not, they are relatively harmless.

The strategy is involuntary, mostly unconscious, and shared by other animals. Understanding it and the anthropomorphism to which it gives rise illuminates secular as well as religious experience.

New York City
November, 1994   S.E.G.

Preface

I am pleased and excited but also a little apprehensive to be offering a new theory of religion. To offer a new theory of anything invites scrutiny, but a theory of something as important as religion may invite skepticism or outright dismissal. I fear, too, that some believers, including some of my own kin, may be dismayed. At the same time, I feel exhilaration and a culmination.

Writing about a modern Japanese religious movement some years ago, I found that the movement resembled other religions primarily in its anthropomorphism—in viewing the world as humanlike. In a later article I developed the underlying idea that all religion is a kind of anthropomorphism. Readers of various persuasions found this theory of religion provocative and wanted more evidence.

In pursuing the idea, I came to see anthropomorphism as pervading human thought and action. It ranged from spontaneous perception in daily life, to art, to science; from voices in the wind, to Mickey Mouse, to the Earth as Gaia. It also seemed central to religious belief, so much so that explaining it would explain religion.

Because the study of religion clearly needs a new theory, the enterprise has been even more exciting. Although theories abound, none is powerful and none prevails. Religious studies remains a welter of ideas and approaches.

In this confused arena, I admittedly am an outsider—not a scholar of religion but an anthropologist—emboldened, perhaps by his innocence.

I sometimes feel as though I had chanced, like a folk-tale rustic, on a pot of gold hidden unaccountably under a stone. The idea uncovered appears potent yet mostly is overlooked or dismissed.

Although I claim to explain religion, much of the book is about secular experience. This is because I want to show that religion is an aspect of something more general—anthropomorphism. And, since anthropomorphism occurs everywhere, it requires a broad canvas.

Because anthropomorphism is involuntary, knowing about it does not prevent it. The evening my publisher accepted this manuscript, a friend and I went out to celebrate despite a downpour. We held umbrellas but, as we rounded a corner, a horizontal shower struck us on the legs. I was surprised and indignant. This was unfair! Then we saw that the shower on our legs was not rain but came from a powerful lawn sprinkler. Fairness, of course, has no place in meteorology, and to expect it from the weather is to anthropomorphize.

Inevitably and automatically, we all anthropomorphize. We see punishment in accidents, faces in clouds, and purpose everywhere. Such illusory perceptions tell us more about ourselves than about the world. Most arrestingly, they tell us about the kind of thought and action, and the kind of experience, we call religion.

Boulder, Colorado
July 1992   S.E.G.

Acknowledgments

The idea for this book grew out of an earlier effort to describe and interpret a particular Japanese religious movement. The work was funded by the National Science Foundation, the Japan Foundation, and Yale University. The first published sketch of the present argument, "A Cognitive Theory of Religion" (1980), was funded by a fellowship from the American Council of Learned Societies. The writing of the present and more substantial version was made possible by a Fordham University Faculty Fellowship and by a generous additional year's leave of absence.

Various members of my family also aided me. My sister, Anne Guthrie, commented on early drafts and provided highly agreeable accommodations in Boulder. My nephew, Alan Guthrie Maecher, kept my mood elevated with long runs and rappeling off cliffs. My brother, Walter Guthrie, brought an invaluable philosophical eye to the editing. My friend and fiancée Phyllis Kaplan went through the manuscript again and again, critically and creatively, almost from the beginning, and gave vital companionship and moral support. All these, together with my sisters Janet and Margaret and my parents, set standards of enthusiasm, love, and courage.

Other readers who have improved the manuscript include my Oxford editors Cynthia Read, Susan Hannan, and Peter Ohlin; anthropologist James W. Fernandez; art historian Elizabeth Parker; philosophers Donald A. Crosby, Bernard B. Gilligan, Leonard Kalal, and Wayne Proudfoot; photographer Martha Cooper; psychologists Mark Mattson and Fred Wertz; scholars of religion Bob Orsi and Hans Penner; and my longtime friend, John Henry. Support and encouragement have come as well from other scholars and friends, especially from Keith Brown, H. Byron Earhart, Edward and Janice Goldfrank, Paul Kahn, Anne Mannion, David Miretsky, Nina Swidler, and Edward Yonan, and from the respondents to my original article. I am grateful for all the help.

Contents

Introduction, 3

1. The Need for a Theory, 8

2. Animism, Perception, and the Effort After Meaning, 39

3. The Origin of Anthropomorphism, 62

4. Anthropomorphism as Perception, 91

5. Anthropomorphism in the Arts, 122

6. Anthropomorphism in Philosophy and Science, 152

7. Religion as Anthropomorphism, 177

Notes, 205

References, 249

Figure Credits, 273

Index, 275

Faces in the Clouds

Introduction

This book holds that religion may best be understood as systematic anthropomorphism: the attribution of human characteristics to nonhuman things or events. Anthropomorphism is familiar, pervasive, and powerful in human thought and action. It often is noted in religion. Nonetheless, it has remained unexplained and hence inadequate as an account of religion. My book provides the missing explanation.

I claim we anthropomorphize because guessing that the world is humanlike is a good bet. It is a bet because the world is uncertain, ambiguous, and in need of interpretation. It is a good bet because the most valuable interpretations usually are those that disclose the presence of whatever is most important to us. That usually is other humans.

Scanning the world for humans and humanlike things and events, we find apparent instances everywhere. We later judge many of these interpretations mistaken, but those that are correct more than justify the strategy. Because betting on the most significant interpretations is deeply rooted, anthropomorphism is spontaneous, plausible, and even compelling.

Many writers, beginning at least with the early Greeks, have said religion anthropomorphizes. A recurrent quip inverts Genesis: man makes God in his own image. Yet most people see anthropomorphism as a superficial aspect of religion, not central to it. Gods, they think, have existences and reasons of their own, untouched by anthropomorphism. Religious anthropomorphism, in their view, consists of attributing hu-

3

manity to gods. My view is roughly the opposite: that gods consist of attributing humanity to the world.

Modern humanists and theologians alike tend to see religion not as beliefs or practices but as a kind of experience. Many think this experience is direct and unmediated. Some think it wholly subjective. But if the religious experience is direct and unmediated, it cannot be questioned. If it is subjective, the question of whether gods exist is meaningless.

For other scholars, the question of whether gods exist has meaning but is beyond the purview of science. Few such writers now ask about the origin or characteristic content of religious thought and action. Most social scientists, for example, deem scientific only narrower issues, such as how particular religions support or do not support particular social structures. These scholars and others give only slight attention to the questions of why religious beliefs arise and how they differ from other beliefs.

I address just these questions. I claim religion consists of seeing the world as humanlike and arises because doing so is a good bet even though, like other bets, it may fail. My account has three aspects. One is ethnographic. It shows that we find plausible, in varying degrees, a continuum of humanlike beings from gods, spirits, and demons, to gremlins, abominable snowmen, HAL the computer, and Chiquita Banana. We find messages from many of these beings, or glimpses or traces of them, in a wide range of phenomena such as weather, earthquakes, plagues, traffic accidents, and the flight of birds.

A second and central aspect of my account is analytic. It shows why such figures and messages are plausible. They are plausible for four nested reasons: our world is ambiguous and perpetually inchoate; our first need therefore is to interpret it; interpretation gambles on the most significant possibilities; and the most significant possibilities are humanlike. The third aspect of my account offers evidence for these claims, from cognitive science among other sources.

My account, then, attributes to religion a particular worldview, one in which humanlike beings are central. These beings arise, as initially unconscious but reasonable hypotheses, from our existing models of and for humans.

My claims—that our strategy is to bet on the most important possibility, and that religious belief constitutes such a bet—recall a classic argument. This is Pascal's wager regarding God. In the face of perpetual uncertainty as to whether God exists, Pascal says we should try to believe He does. If we believe and are right, we may gain eternal reward, while if we believe and are wrong, we lose little. Even if it seems unlikely that God exists, we still should bet He does, because the possible reward is much greater than the possible loss. Thus Pascal applies game theory to theism.

Whether or not Pascal persuades us to believe in God, his strategy does account for anthropomorphism. It accounts as well for animism, the attribution of life to inanimate things and events. We animate and anthropomorphize because, when we see something as alive or humanlike, we can take precautions. If we see it as alive we can, for example, stalk it or flee. If we see it as humanlike, we can try to establish a social relationship. If it turns out not to be alive or humanlike, we usually lose little by having thought it was. This practice thus yields more in occasional big successes than it costs in frequent little failures. In short, animism and anthropomorphism stem from the principle, "better safe than sorry."

In explaining religion, I shall not explore its social uses. Others have shown that these are diverse and important. Many have tried to build a theory of religion from them. Showing that religion may be useful, however, does not show why religion arises and is believed. If religion did not arise for its own reasons or were not believable, its potential social uses could not create it. The very claim is teleological and thus anthropomorphic. What makes religion possible is what makes it plausible. What makes it plausible is our tendency to find people in every scene, a tendency based on strategy. We see apparent people everywhere because it is vital to see actual people wherever they may be.

My account is somewhat like saying the clothes have no emperor. It is commonsensical yet discomfiting and is rarely advanced. Many people note anthropomorphism in religion, but few find it central there. No one convincingly explains it, there or elsewhere.

The book has seven chapters. Chapter 1, "The Need for a Theory," shows that present theories of religion are inadequate. No widely shared definition of religion exists, even within any one discipline. Theories offered by believers are unsatisfactory because they either explain only some single religion or, if general, are incoherent. Theories of nonbelievers also are unsatisfactory. The view that religion is wishful thinking, for example, fails because much religious belief is frightening.

Other humanistic theories have other flaws. Most fail to find anything universal in religious beliefs, modes of thought, or worldviews. Those theories that do identify something, such as animism or anthropomorphism, as universal in religious thought have trouble explaining why it occurs. Still other theories see some kind of action, such as ritual, or some result, such as social solidarity, as universally and typically religious. But these approaches fail to show that such actions or results actually are either universal or especially religious. They fail again to account for, or even identify, religious thought.

Although existing theories are woven from diverse materials and in diverse patterns and though they unravel under stress, some strands may be recombined. The first chapter ends by gathering these strands and suggesting a different cloth.

Chapter 2, "Animism, Perception, and the Effort After Meaning," shows that animism stems from a perceptual strategy. The term "animism" commonly is used in two ways. In religion, it means belief in spirit beings. In psychology, it means attributing life to inanimate things or events. The second meaning encompasses the first.

Animism is universal in perception. It occurs because perception is interpretive (seeing is "seeing as"), because interpretation is a choice among possibilities and thus a gamble, and because those interpretive bets that aim highest (by attributing the most organization and hence significance to things and events) have the greatest potential payoffs and lowest risks. For example, it is better for a hiker to mistake a boulder for a bear than to mistake a bear for a boulder.

Animism constitutes a class of interpretations that aims too high, attributing to things and events more organization than they have. Animistic interpretations thus are the failures of a generally good strategy. All humans and many animals display animism: mechanics see tools as rebellious, runners see distant fire hydrants as dogs, horses see blowing papers as threats, and cats see fluttering leaves as prey.

Chapter 3, "The Origin of Anthropomorphism," offers an account similar to that given for animism. "Anthropomorphism" also is used in two ways. In theology, it means attributing human characteristics to God or gods. More inclusively, it means attributing human characteristics to nonhuman phenomena. In my terms, it is the class of apparent instances of humanity that have proved illusory. Just as animism is universal in perception generally, so anthropomorphism is universal in human perception.

There are two standard explanations of anthropomorphism: that it comforts us and that it consists in using our good knowledge of ourselves to account for what we know less well. Although each explanation has some truth, neither is sufficient. Comfort does not explain anthropomorphism well because much anthropomorphism is uncomfortable. Reliance on self-knowledge does not explain it well either, because our knowledge of ourselves is no more reliable than knowledge of what is not ourselves.

Instead, anthropomorphism stems principally, as does animism, from Pascal's strategy: faced by uncertainty, we bet on the most significant possibility. If we are mistaken, we lose little, while if we are right, we gain much.

Chapter 4, "Anthropomorphism as Perception," demonstrates that anthropomorphism pervades ordinary perception and does so for good reasons. Cognitive science shows we tend to see the human form and human behavior everywhere, and again suggests, in varied ways, why this is so. Artificial intelligence, for example, shows that a predisposition to see given forms makes perception possible, and that the more organized these forms are, the more powerful perception is. Experimental, clinical, and developmental psychology show that anthropomorphism begins in infancy and lasts throughout life. Ethnography shows it occurs around the world.

Chapter 5, "Anthropomorphism in the Arts," shows that anthropomorphism pervades literature and the visual arts. Literary scholars call it personification or the pathetic fallacy, and it abounds in literature. They have no good explanation for it, however. Anthropomorphism also permeates commercial, folk, and tribal art, and it appears often in fine art and in architecture. In all art, anthropomorphism may be explicit, implicit, or both.

Chapter 6, "Anthropomorphism in Philosophy and Science," shows that anthropomorphism occurs even among philosophers and scientists, although they are its most consistent critics. Scientists in particular try to avoid it, but they must make a constant effort. Its cause here appears the same as elsewhere: we strive to understand our world by pursuing important possibilities, and humanlike forms and behaviors are the most important ones we know.

Chapter 7, "Religion as Anthropomorphism," shows that all religion is anthropomorphic in that, in postulating deities in or behind natural phenomena, religion credits nature with the human capacity for symbolic action. Some deities have animal or other nonhuman forms, but all act symbolically and hence like humans. Some theologians try to understand God nonanthropomorphically but their God either interacts symbolically with humans or cannot be understood. A few religions have parallel systems without deities, as in demythologized Christianity and in some Buddhist philosophies, but these systems are ethical, philosophical, or psychological, not religious. The presence of gods is what causes some forms of Christianity, Buddhism, and some other systems to be called religious.

Religion has much in common with other broad systems of thought and action, such as science, art, and common sense, and it is continuous with them. Even when set apart, religion interacts and intermingles. Like other such systems, religion aims to interpret and influence the world. Both religious and nonreligious interpretations of the world posit beings that are humanlike but not human. Religion differs from other schemas mainly in granting humanlike beings a central role.

Theologians and many others find anthropomorphism inevitable in, yet inessential to, religion. They see it as an unfortunate limitation of human thought and peripheral to religious experience. In contrast, I hold that anthropomorphism is the core of religious experience. I claim that anthropomorphism springs from a powerful strategy and pervades human thought and action, and that religion is its most systematic form.

1

The Need
for a Theory

Writers have speculated on the nature and origins of religion for well over
two thousand years but have not produced so much as a widely accepted
definition. Instead, there are nearly as many definitions as writers.[1] Religion is difficult to define because definitions imply theories, and no good
general theory of religion exists.

Present theories of religion comprise two broad camps, those of believers and those of nonbelievers. Believers' theories concern primarily
their own religions. Most fall short of a general theory for one or both
of two reasons: they account for the origin of the writer's own religion
but not for that of others, or they claim belief must precede understanding. These theories primarily concern some single, ostensibly true, religion, not religion in general.[2]

Even with regard to a single religion, a believer's theory has a more
limited aim than does a theory accounting for religion in general: it aims
only to say how people come to specific views and practices, the truth
and validity of which it assumes. The theory may be that people have
these views and practices because God or gods revealed them; or it may
be that people have divined them by observing the works of gods, for
example, in nature. In either case, the theory has only to say how the
truth in question came to be known. Such a theory convinces people who
already endorse the religion but, since it usually requires that religion as
a context, it does not persuade nonbelievers.

In contrast, general theories of religion must say not only how people come to subscribe to a religion but also what it is that all religions share. Because religious beliefs and practices are diverse, descriptions of what they have in common must be abstract. In the past two centuries, religious writers who have attempted a general theory, such as Friedrich Schleiermacher, Rudolf Otto, and Mircea Eliade, have argued that what religions share is not beliefs or practices but an experience.[3]

These writers say the experience in question is ineffable and autonomous. It can be neither refuted by, nor related to, nonreligious experiences. At the same time, they suggest the experience consists in apprehending something, indicated by terms such as the holy, the numinous, or the sacred. This something is transcendent and irreducible. Religious experience allegedly is "prereflective, transcend[s] the verbal, or [is] in some other way free of the structures of thought and judgment which language represents."[4]

To the outsider, these theorists must remain uniquely vague, since their religious experience, by definition, is inexpressible. If nothing essential can be said, the experience remains hermetic and inaccessible except to those who have had it. The vagueness entailed by ineffability weakens the claim by these writers that all religious experience shares something essential.[5]

Besides being vague, Schleiermacher and his successors are internally inconsistent.[6] They say religious experience is unconditioned, primitive, immediate, and prior to beliefs and concepts. At the same time, they say it is the experience of particular feelings, emotions, and sensations—such as unity, infinity, dependence, love, and awe. But such feelings and emotions do not exist in a vacuum: they implicitly are directed toward or are about something, whose existence they assume. Assuming that existence, they thus are grounded in beliefs.[7]

Emotions and other experiences also depend upon interpretations of sensations such as heat, cold, and nausea, and of such phenomena as sweating, shivering, and smiling.[8] Emotions are not primitive, but are at least midlevel models, situated above perceptions of bodily states and below broad interpretations of, for example, human relationships.[9] As such, they are based on an assumed order. In Wayne Proudfoot's example, a woodsman who mistakes a log for a bear has an experience of being frightened by a bear.[10] When his companion points out that it is only a log, he is reassured. His fear, like other emotions, occurs not in isolation but as the product of a context and an interpretation. When the interpretation changes, the experience changes. Since experience depends on interpretation, it cannot be prior to beliefs and concepts, but is generated partly from them.[11] Schleiermacher and others then cannot claim simultaneously that religious emotions are simple, immediate, or unconditioned by belief and that they constitute an experience.

Kai Nielsen also finds religious statements self-contradictory.[12] He says religious discourse not only is incoherent but also is part of a larger, shared discourse. It is not autonomous and self-sufficient but shares the categories, concepts, and syntactic structure of profane discourse. Nielsen agrees with Schleiermacher that to understand religious discourse is to grasp it as an insider. He denies, however, that to have such an understanding is to endorse it; witness people who have grown up within religious traditions and hence understand them as insiders but nonetheless come to reject them.

Even if Schleiermacher and his followers were coherent, their claim to be understandable only in their own terms still would restrict their audience to believers. To say that any alleged religious understanding *not* accompanied by belief is not an understanding is of no help to nonbelievers.

The theories of nonbelievers also must say what all religions have in common. In addition, they either must show how religion could arise and persist despite consisting of, or being founded on, mistaken beliefs and views[13] or must show that it consists of, or is founded on, something else. The resulting theories are diverse, sharing little more than claims that gods do not exist and that religion is a human creation.

Indeed, humanistic theories of religion are in disarray. E. E. Evans-Pritchard wrote twenty-five years ago that "either singly or taken together, [they do not] give us much more than common-sense guesses, which for the most part miss the mark."[14] Clifford Geertz wrote shortly afterward that the anthropology of religion was in a "general state of stagnation" and lacked any "theoretical framework [for] an analytic account."[15] Most writers still agree. Murray Wax sees continuing "theoretical stagnation."[16] J. S. Preus finds "evidence of an identity crisis" in incommensurate modern approaches to religion.[17] In short, the consensus is that there is no consensus, and little optimism.

Humanistic theories of religion nonetheless may be described in terms of three loose groups. The first, which may be called the wish-fulfillment group, holds that people create religion in order to alleviate unpleasant emotions. The second, the social functionalist or social solidarity group, views religion as an attempt to sustain a social order. The third or intellectualist group, to which my approach belongs, sees religion as an attempt to interpret and influence the world, a task it shares with science and common sense. In and around these major groups are synthesizing theories, some of them shared by believers. In the following, I review theorists from these three humanistic groups.[18] The review takes us through shoals and toward what looks like deeper water.

Theorists in the first group think religion may be understood as an attempt to allay fears, anxieties, and dissatisfaction. This idea is old and widespread and has been advanced by such disparate writers as Benedict de Spinoza, David Hume, Ludwig Feuerbach, Karl Marx, Bronislaw Malinowski, and Sigmund Freud. The notion seems plausible. Certainly, suffering and anxiety correlate with religiosity in some way. Old age, sickness, death, natural and social cataclysms, tragedy of all sorts, the unknown and the unexplainable, all have a long and widespread connection with religious enthusiasm. Shamans, for example, probably the earliest religious specialists and virtually universal among tribal peoples, largely aim to remedy or prevent illness, starvation, and other dangers. Popular religious movements—nativistic, millennial, or revitalization—also seem to spring from suffering, fear, and uncertainty. They arise typically in the wake of plague, economic hardship, foreign invasion, or genocide. The unknown and the unexplainable—the occult, the dark, and the mysterious—are common foci of religious thought and action.

Many writers have suggested that anxiety causes, or at least intensifies, religiosity. The Greek historian Diodorus Siculus wrote in the first century B.C.E. that "Fortune has never . . . bestowed an unmixed happiness on mankind; but with all her gifts has ever conjoined some disastrous circumstance, in order to chastize men into a reverence for the gods, whom, in . . . prosperity, they are apt to neglect and forget."[19] Euripides similarly writes, "The gods toss all life into confusion . . . that all of us, from our ignorance and uncertainty, may pay them the more worship and reverence."[20] Spinoza says people are religious because, "driven into straits where rules are useless, and being kept fluctuating pitiably between hope and fear [they are] very prone to credulity. . . . Superstition, then, is engendered, preserved, and fostered by fear."[21] Hume, author of the first extended account of religion as anthropomorphism, concurs:

> In proportion as any man's course of life is governed by accident . . . he encreases in superstition [including religion]; as may particularly be observed of gamesters and sailors . . . every disastrous accident alarms us. . . . And the mind, sunk into diffidence, terror, and melancholy, has recourse to every method of appeasing those secret intelligent powers . . . all popular divines . . . display the advantages of affliction, in bringing men to a due sense of religion.[22]

Hume later says, "the primary religion of mankind arises chiefly from an anxious fear."[23]

Although he has several views on religion, Freud also agrees. The gods have a "threefold task: they must exorcise the terrors of nature, they must reconcile men to the cruelty of Fate, particularly as it is shown in death, and they must compensate them for the sufferings and privations [of] civilized life."[24]

Malinowski again finds the roots of religion, and of magic, in uncertainty and insecurity. Magic concerns having to perform crucial activities beyond our complete control. In the Trobriand islands, for example, lagoon fishing is safe and hence uses no magic, while deep-sea fishing is dangerous and thus surrounded by magic. Religion concerns the overriding, universal fact of mortality: "strong personal attachments and the fact of death, which of all human events is the most upsetting and disorganizing to man's calculations, are perhaps the main sources of religious belief."[25] Religion and magic enable people to act and to live despite uncertainty, powerlessness, and anxiety. Both offer beliefs and actions which, though technically ineffective, give a sense of adequacy in crisis.

Other observations linking distress with religion are legion. From millennial movements in sixteenth-century Europe[26] and in Ch'ing China to cargo cults in Melanesia[27] after the Second World War, and from nativistic movements in North America to the Japanese "New Religions" of the nineteenth and twentieth centuries, observers have linked religious movements to unusual and widespread suffering.[28] Hegel and others say Christianity arose in part because the Roman emperors "spread misery which compelled men to seek and expect happiness in heaven."[29] Two recent anthropologists, Weston La Barre and A.F.C. Wallace, say all religions begin in social crises.[30] And a philosopher, J.C.A. Gaskin, remarks of Hume's view that religion originates in fear, "to the twentieth-century reader this may seem so obvious as to be scarcely worth insisting upon."[31]

The association of religion and anxiety, then, is broad and enduring. The question is, what underlies it? Many observe it, but few convincingly explain it. Most assume that religion is comforting and is an attempt to ameliorate stress. Secular observers usually explain this as wishful thinking, an irrational escape into fantasy from otherwise-intractable problems. Freud, for example, says religion is "born from man's need to make his helplessness tolerable." Its ideas are "not precipitates of experience or end-results of thinking: they are illusions, fulfillments of the oldest, strongest and most urgent wishes of mankind. The secret of their strength lies in the strength of those wishes."[32]

Freud thinks wish-fulfilling thought is not merely illusory but also delusional, and even mass-delusional; it

> regards reality as the sole enemy and as the source of all suffering . . . so that one must break off all relations with it if one is to be in any way happy. [Then] one can try to re-create the world, to build up in its stead another world in which its most unbearable features are eliminated and replaced by others that are in conformity with one's own wishes . . . [this] delusional re-moulding of reality [may be] made by a considerable number of people in common. The religions of mankind must be classed among the mass-delusions of this kind.[33]

Malinowski similarly thinks religion is self-delusion. In particular, it consists in denying death: religion is the "affirmation that death is not real, that man has a soul and that this is immortal, [and] arises out of a deep need to deny personal destruction."[34] Hence religion is entirely different from science and other secular thought. It is motivated not by intellectual or practical needs but by emotional ones. It is a fantasy "more akin to daydreaming and wish-fulfillment"[35] than to science. "Both magic and religion open up escapes from such situations and such impasses as offer no way out," escapes founded on the "belief that hope cannot fail nor desire deceive."[36] Religion attempts not to explain experience, but to contradict it. Empiricism and logic are not merely irrelevant, but inimical.

This irrationalist view of religion as wishful thinking prevails in many quarters. In "Western academic philosophy," Norman Malcolm says, "religious belief is commonly regarded as unreasonable and is viewed with condescension or even contempt. It is said that religion is a refuge for those who, because of weakness of intellect or character, are unable to confront the stern realities of the world."[37] Feuerbach puts the same view more neutrally: "The more empty life is, the more concrete is God . . . God springs out of the feeling of want; what man is in need of . . . that is God."[38] Marx calls religion a "universal ground for consolation and justification" and "illusory happiness,"[39] and most famously, the "opium of the people." Recent social scientists and others continue this view.[40] The idea, then, that religion consists in hoping against hope not only is old and popular, but also continues to permeate academic thought.

The wish-fulfillment or comfort view in its usual version, however—that religion consists in escaping the real world of suffering by entering an alternative and desirable imaginary world—assumes both that religious beliefs constitute a more sanguine world, and that the religious imagination is somehow unique. If religion's appeal is its hope, though, believers must think deities are protective, souls are immortal, injustice will be righted, or some such comforting thought. Freud, for example, thinks religion claims "a benevolent Providence [and] a moral order in the universe and afterlife . . . all this is exactly as we are bound to wish it to be."[41]

However, there are religions without such beliefs, or with others that seem less than comforting. Many have wrathful and capricious deities and demons. Some have neither a universal moral order nor an afterlife. Others have only a gloomy netherworld, or one or more hells. Such religions may perpetuate fear and anxiety more than allay them. In a gloomy Christian instance, John Ruskin, as the young child of Evangelical Anglican parents, lived in a world "where Damnation awaited most and Death waited for all, a world penetrated by the gaze of an immanent, punishing God who [let few] escape the pain and horror of hell."[42] Similarly, Hume grew up among "beliefs and practices of great severity and bleakness."[43] Views of the afterlife and other religious ideas, then, often threaten as much as they promise. Most promise no more certainty or happiness than we know on earth.

The lack of an afterlife, or of a happy one, found in many religions thus undermines two chief forms of the wish-fulfillment theory: that belief is motivated by desire for immortality, and that it is motivated by a desire for posthumous retribution. In addition, not only religion but also science and other secular thought and action rely significantly on metaphor, symbol, and image. Thus even if religion did consist of rosy imaginings, only its rosiness would distinguish it.

The wish-fulfillment view in its usual form, then, appears weak. As A. R. Radcliffe-Brown writes, "while one anthropological theory is that magic and religion give men confidence, it could equally well be argued that they give men fears and anxieties from which they would otherwise be free—the fear of black magic or of spirits, fear of God, of the Devil, of Hell."[44] Geertz similarly says, "The inadequacy of this 'theology of optimism' [is] radical. Over its career religion has probably disturbed men as much as it has cheered them."[45] To constitute an account of religion, wish-fulfillment theories at least have to show why religious beliefs often are uncomfortable.

Freud has two possible explanations for this. First, wishes may be disguised. In dreams, for example, the ego may protect itself from anxiety caused by the desires of the id by compromising, distorting, transforming, and otherwise hiding the wishes. Similarly religion, itself a neurotic expression of desire, may disguise or partially deny people's real wishes. A second explanation is that the wished-for relation with God replicates the infant's ambivalence toward its father. The infant loves and needs its father, but because of its helplessness and uncertainty also hates and fears him. Religion is a projection upon the world of this early ambivalence.

A skeptic, however, might still ask why, if religion is wish fulfillment in some ways, it is not in others. Why does religion not posit, for example, a more satisfactory father/child relationship between God and humans than we experience as children? Freud would answer that by projecting the unsatisfactory relationship, religion attempts to recreate that relationship so it can be renovated. One might object, again, that many religions, especially animistic and polytheistic ones, do not look like parent/child relationships; or that, as in Bali, humans may have the role of parents and gods have the role of children.[46] Freud again would reply that, like other neurotic behavior and like dreams, religions disguise their real intent. To a non-Freudian, however, the argument begins to resemble the hall of mirrors it depicts. One might say of it exactly what Freud says of religious doctrines: "just as they cannot be proved, so they cannot be refuted."[47]

Further, Freud's assertion that religious ideas are not "precipitates of experience" makes their cultural variation hard to explain. His claim that "religious ideas have arisen from . . . the necessity of protecting oneself from the crushingly superior force of nature"[48] reflects the Western view of nature as alien. It does not reflect the view of those peoples who see nature as continuous with themselves, or who aim at harmony with nature, not conquest of it.

Nonetheless, much in Freud is compatible with my account of religion. He makes clear that individuals depend on, and must attune themselves to, society; that for everyone, other human beings are important; and that we are largely unaware of how important they are. Hence we should look for the roots of our conceptions, including religious conceptions, more in our social lives (for Freud, in early relations with our parents) than in our experience of nature. Freud also shows that early childhood experience has lasting effects on personality and on worldview. Most relevantly, he makes—if briefly—the "humanization of nature" central to religion.

Unlike my view, however, Freud's view offers few links connecting religion to the general human project of interpreting the world, and none to perception and cognition in animals other than humans. Instead, Freud makes religion a noncognitive enterprise, primarily a covert attempt to divert, stifle, and control those fearful and selfish individual impulses that would undermine psychic stability and subvert social life. Nor does Freud link anthropomorphism in religion with anthropomorphism elsewhere.

Although the prevailing versions of the wish-fulfillment theory are unsatisfactory, two others do appear possible. The first depends on evidence that a tendency to look for humans in our environment is innate. Some researchers studying infant face perception and mother-infant attachment and most post-Freudian psychoanalysts of the "object-relations" school[49] suggest that this tendency to see humans is inborn. Hence any discovery of humans, real or apparent, reassuring or frightening, would gratify a universal human desire.

The second version is related to the first, but is more general and situational. It depends more on broad activities of inquiry and begins with the claim that what people desire is a plausible account of experience: not rosy but believable. What they wish to avoid is unaccountability. Such a claim is supported by recent psychology. Daniel Stern says even the youngest infants "busily embark on the task of relating diverse experiences,"[50] and Jerome Bruner similarly says humans begin at birth to develop and test hypotheses about the world.[51] Geertz's Javanese informants were willing to give up one hypothesis for another, but would not surrender one for no hypothesis at all;[52] and the philosopher and writer Miguel de Unamuno finds the idea of nothingness "more terrifying than Hell."[53] Thus humans may typically find even a gloomy interpretation of the world better than no interpretation.

This version of the wish-fulfillment theory, then, recognizes the desire for interpretation, for information and meaning, as fundamental. As a theory of religion, however, it still must show how religious accounts differ from other accounts, and what makes them both significant and plausible. If, as often is done, one simply makes *any* answer to pressing but otherwise unanswerable questions "religious," religion becomes a hodgepodge of notions, distinctive neither in content nor plausibility.

A stronger alternative is to say religion is one kind of interpretation of the world—one in which the world, in whole or in part, is significantly humanlike. Such an interpretation of the world is both plausible and

peculiarly meaningful, although the world depicted may be far from comforting. In this alternative, wish fulfillment becomes much less like irrational "hope against hope" and very much like intellectualism.

The second group of theorists, the social functionalists, holds that religion is a way to create and maintain social solidarity.[54] This theory is perhaps as old as wish-fulfillment and almost as widespread. It makes
enforced solidarity the basis of society. Structural-functionalists assume
that what solidarity preserves in a society is its social structure. Their
studies of religion usually are "symbolic." This means they think religious
beliefs and practices concern not the world in general, as they seem to
do, but only social relations among humans, especially the established
social order.[55] Religious beliefs and practices undergird the social order
by formulating and expressing it in symbols. Symbolism in this sense is
the dominant approach to religion in contemporary social science.

    The power of religious symbolism to unify has long been recognized.
In China, the founders of the Chou dynasty tapped it when, overthrow-
ing the Shang rulers around the turn of the first millennium B.C.E., they
told the Shang populace that the conquest showed they had acquired the
"Mandate of Heaven." Subsequent dynasties repeated the claim for almost three thousand years. In addition, the Han and most later dynasties,
as well as successive regimes in Korea and Japan, made Confucius a bul-
wark of the state and society, and the focus of a religion.[56] In Japan, the
Meiji, Taisho, and early Showa governments (from the late nineteenth
century to the midtwentieth) similarly made Shinto the foundation of
society and state. The Meiji ideologist Inoue, for example, wrote that
ancestor worship, in Shinto form, "unites the emperor and the people
into one family."[57]

    The social solidarity theory of religion is old and enduring not only
in East Asia but also in the West. The Greek historian Polybius wrote in
the first century B.C.E. that religion is the "principal foundation of the
power and strength of monarchies and seignories: as also for the execution of justice, for the obedience of the subjects, the reverence of the
magistrates, for the fear of doing evil, and for the mutual love and amity
of every one towards others."[58] Jean Bodin, a sixteenth-century lawyer,
diplomat, and political writer, cites Polybius and agrees religion is vital
to society.[59] Even "superstition [holds] men in fear and awe, both of the
laws and of the magistrates . . . whereas mere Atheism doth utterly root
out of men's minds all the fear of doing evil."[60] Giambattista Vico is still
more sociological: "all the virtues have their roots in piety and religion,
by which alone the virtues are made effective in action."[61] And Auguste
Comte, often called the father of sociology, finds the origins of religion
almost entirely in society, which needs it for "*regulating* each personal
life, no less than *combining* different individual lives."[62] Twentieth-
century exponents of this view include Freud and Malinowski, though
both have other views, and Radcliffe-Brown.[63]

The most influential theorist of religion as social glue, however, is Emile Durkheim, occupant of the first university chair of sociology. Durkheim, perhaps impressed by Kant on religion as an outgrowth of moral experience, sees religion as encoded morality. Always interested in how societies can cohere despite discordant individual aims, he says the central topic of religious thought is not the world in general, but human social relations. Religious thought is not belief in deities, according to Durkheim, since deities are illusions and hence cannot be the basis of anything so universal as religion. Moreover some religions, such as Buddhism, have no deities. Rather, religious thought is a division of everything in the universe into two mutually exclusive realms, the sacred and the profane.

The sacred can be anything, from gods to rocks, trees, pieces of wood, or houses. What matters is what these represent. They symbolize, or are icons of, something "set apart and forbidden." What is "set apart" actually is society, though believers do not realize this. The relation of the sacred to members of society—preceding, protecting, instructing, nourishing, dominating, punishing, and outliving them—really is the relation of society to its members. The sacred then is whatever is central and vital in society. The profane is a residual category of all that is not sacred.

The distinction of sacred and profane, and its related symbolism, are created, according to Durkheim, because they reflect a truth which people apprehend, in however refracted a form. They are maintained because they are necessary to society. They are necessary because individuals do not fully realize their dependence on society, or otherwise are unable to act socially, without a symbol of society. The sum of social relations is too manifold, abstract, and subtle to grasp directly, and the demands made of individuals by society too stringent for easy acquiescence. A society therefore must be represented to its members by some emblem of its scope and authority, such as a totem.[64] In this emblem, as Durkheim's theory often is summarized, society worships itself.

Like the wish-fulfillment theory of religion, the social solidarity theory has weaknesses and strengths. One weakness is that there are other measures of a society, and thus other claims to allegiance, than religious membership. These include kinship, and membership in residential, economic, political, linguistic, and cultural communities. Such communities may not coincide with religious communities, and their claims to loyalty may conflict. When their claims do conflict, religion is divisive, not unifying.

A related problem is that while the theory makes perpetuation of society the purpose of religion, sometimes religions have destroyed their adherents instead. The millennial movements of sixteenth-century Germany, the Christian conversions of seventeenth-century Japan, the T'ai P'ing Rebellion of nineteenth-century China, the Xhosa cattle-killing of nineteenth-century Africa, the Ghost Dance of the nineteenth-century

American West, and the Jonestown colony in Guyana in the late twentieth century, for example, all ended in overwhelming defeat and often in the virtual extinction of all involved. Such catastrophes undermine Durkheim's claim that "whatever has been done in the name of religion cannot have been done in vain."[65]

Still another problem is that religion and morality are not always closely connected, as the solidarity thesis requires. The Greek gods, for example, were fickle, vain, treacherous, and thievish. They lacked "any connexion with morality"[66] and expected none of humans. Although the religions of stratified societies often do have ethical systems, the religions of unstratified ones often do not.[67] Even within ethical religions, religious individuals and groups may be unethical and inconsistent. Some Western religious thinkers deny any intrinsic connection between religion and morality. Otto and Schleiermacher, for example, think essential religious experience is without moral content. Secular observers as diverse as Hume and Mark Twain even think religion diminishes morality. Hume writes, "the greatest crimes [are] compatible with a superstitious piety and devotion [and] encrease the religious passion. . . . *Those who undertake the most criminal and most dangerous enterprizes are commonly the most superstitious.*"[68] The view seems plausible. Torture and warfare may be carried on in the name of religion, and both sides in both world wars claimed the same god.

Nor is religion necessarily social in other ways. William James thinks true religion is individual and private. Solitary vision quests among the Plains Indians, and mysticism generally, show at least that it is not always sociable. Religious hermits in such traditions as Christianity, Hinduism, Taoism, and Japanese folk religion emphasize the role of isolation.

Again, not all religions distinguish, as Durkheim says they must, between sacred and profane.[69] Shinto and other animistic religions posit spirit beings everywhere, on a continuum from less important to more, rather than in either a profane or sacred domain. Buddhism similarly has no sacred/profane distinction. Other traditions, including Jainism and American Indian religions, may view life or the earth as sacred, but not in Durkheim's contrastive sense.

Further, Durkheim bases his claim that totemism is the origin of religion on the assertion that the simplest societies still existing are living fossils of the earliest societies, and have clans and totems. In fact, however, the simplest extant societies (those of such gatherer-hunters as the Inuit and San) have neither clans nor totems. If Durkheim's claim that the simplest societies represent the earliest is right, their lack of totemism refutes his claim that this is the first religion. If they are not the earliest, the claim that totemism is the origin of religion has no foundation. Either way, the historical component of his theory fails.

More general is the problem, common to all functionalism, of showing how a society identifies, establishes, and maintains beneficial institutions, including particular religions. Functionalists avoid such questions by imagining institutions already in existence, roughly on the model of random biological evolution. They assume that what persists must therefore be useful, since they ask only how the social organism maintains itself. This assumption depends, however, on the metaphor of societies as organisms.

This metaphor, though deeply rooted in Western culture, has two limitations. First, like other metaphors, it breaks down when pushed too far: societies have, for example, neither life cycles nor metabolisms, nor do they reproduce themselves. Hence, if pursued, the metaphor necessarily misleads. At one point, for instance, Durkheim describes societies not only as organisms but also as persons: each "has its own personal physiognomy and its idiosyncracies; it is a particular subject and consequently particularizes whatever it thinks of."[70] But societies do not really have physiognomies, nor do they think.

A second problem is that even if societies were organisms, the functionalist assumption that all their features are optimal and work to their benefit would be unsupported by current biology. Francis Crick points out that natural selection works only on materials at hand, which are chance variations in preexisting structures, themselves "selected" in some earlier and different environment.[71] Thus the materials on which evolution works are arbitrarily constrained, not optimal. Seeing evolved features as optimal depends on another metaphor, that evolution is a designer. This metaphor, though prominent in Darwin's writing, already had been criticized in his time as anthropomorphic.[72]

Most relevant to my approach, however, is that Durkheim denies deities are central to religion. He depends largely on the example of Buddhism, which he thinks is godless, and on Jainism and Hinduism, which he thinks almost, or potentially, godless. But Durkheim misunderstands all three religious traditions. His misunderstanding concerning Buddhism, widespread in the West,[73] rests on a conflation of religion and philosophy caused in part by their sharing a continuum and in part by early Western studies emphasizing the philosophical writings of Asian religions.[74] As are other major religious traditions—Judaism and Christianity, for instance—Hinduism, Jainism, and Buddhism are open-ended, varying accumulations of ideas and practices that both include, and grade into, philosophy and psychology.[75]

The mainstreams of all three, however, are well supplied with gods; indeed, they have pantheons.[76] The Buddha himself, though not a god according to canon, still has varied superhuman powers such as omniscience, and popularly often is a god.[77] Even canonically, the Buddha's separation from gods is unclear. Various marks, signs, and powers set him off from ordinary humans, and the buddhologist Charles Eliot remarks, "If a Buddha cannot be called a Deva rather than a man, it is only because he is higher than both. It is this train of thought that lead [*sic*] later

Buddhists to call him Devatideva, or the Deva who is above all other
Devas. . . ."[78] Melford Spiro also says the Buddha of canonical Theravada is "certainly a superhuman being."[79] Not only the Buddha himself,
but also persons on the way to salvation, such as an *arahat,* have attributes which Westerners usually think divine.[80]

The Buddha, then, may be ambiguous in terms of the Western di-
chotomy between gods and humans, but this seems a problem only for
Westerners. Moreover, he usually is accompanied by various lesser gods.
Spiro remarks briskly, "There are, to be sure, atheistic Buddhist philosophies—just as there are atheistic Hindu philosophies—but it is certainly
a strange spectacle when anthropologists, of all people, confuse the teachings of a philosophical school with the beliefs and behavior of a religious
community."[81]

Durkheim further says that religion may include magical elements,
such as Jewish taboos and practices to produce wind and rain, with no
connection to a deity. Magic is impersonal and its effects are automatic,
bypassing or even contravening the gods. He concludes that because religion has aspects such as this, to which gods are irrelevant, gods are not
central to religion and cannot be used to define it.

However, just as some of Durkheim's examples of "religion" actually
are from philosophy, some are from magic. His syncretism is understandable because religion not only is on a continuum with, but also is inter-
penetrated by, philosophical, magical, and other strains of thought.[82]
Despite their continuity and interpenetration, however, these strains may
usefully be distinguished. Most writers distinguish magic from religion
precisely by its impersonalism.

In any case, Durkheim's rejection of gods as characteristic of religion
leaves his conception of religion denatured and abstract. Further, central
features of his theory—most importantly the sacred/profane distinction,
religious gregariousness, and social benefit—are culture-bound rather
than universal.[83] Nonetheless, Durkheim does point out that conceptions
of the world as a society result from people's social preoccupations. Moreover, he is not wedded to his best-known view, that religious thought is
only about social relations. He also says religion and science have the same
aims (to interpret and influence the world), the same topics (nature, man,
and society), and the same logic (connecting, relating, classifying, and
systematizing). Indeed, the "essential ideas of scientific logic are of religious origin."[84] Science and religion are not merely similar, but continuous: "both pursue the same end; scientific thought is only a more perfect
form of religious thought."

Durkheim further observes that scientific ideas, as much as religious
ones, depend upon climates of opinion.[85] They do not "get their authority from their objective value. It is not enough that they be true to
be believed. If they are not in harmony with the other beliefs and opinions . . . they will be denied; minds will be closed to them." Our attitudes
toward science and religion are alike:

To-day it is generally sufficient that [ideas] bear the stamp of science to receive a sort of privileged credit, because we have faith in science. But this faith does not differ essentially from religious faith. In the last resort, the value which we attribute to science depends upon the idea which we collectively form of its nature and role in life; that is . . . it expresses a state of public opinion. In all social life, in fact, science rests upon opinion.[86]

Here Durkheim develops continuities of religion and science usually ignored by his followers. Doing so, he approaches the third group of theorists.

The third group holds that religion is more nearly what believers think it is, namely, an interpretation of, and a means to influence, the world. This group often is called intellectualist, rationalist, or (usually pejoratively) neo-Tylorian. It may also be called cognitive, a term less connoting conscious deliberation.[87]

Not wise to quote these terms ?

These theorists emphasize the task of interpretation faced by humans (as by other animals) in perceiving and acting in the world. They see the world of experience as inchoate and our first necessity as making sense of it. They make religion a particular interpretation of the world, an interpretation whose conclusions (but not whose topics or even logic) differ from those of secular thought and action. Most such theorists regard religion as having much in common with science and deny that it is peculiarly emotional, irrational, or otherwise aberrant as a form of thought and action. Some regard it as primitive science.

Fontenelle

One of the first writers to view religion as primitive science was Bernard Fontenelle, a late-seventeenth-century intellectual who saw analogy and metaphor in all explanation. The Greeks saw constellations as transformed deities, and such "metamorphoses are the physics . . . of the earliest times."[88] Explanations of new phenomena always are "copied from things better known," both in myth and in science, of which myth is the early form. Myth uses a "principle so natural that even today our philosophy has none other; that is to say, that we explain unknown natural things by those which we have before our eyes, and that we carry over to natural science those things furnished us by experience."[89] Religion started when lightning, wind, and other natural phenomena made people imagine humanlike agents, "more powerful than themselves, capable of producing these grand effects."[90] People imagine these agents as like themselves because they think analogically. Fontenelle's recognition that analogy and metaphor are universal makes possible a naturalistic and rationalistic account of religion.

Hume, who in part takes an emotionalist and even antirationalist view of religion,[91] also finds some rationality in it. He says the argument for God's existence from apparent design in nature is reasonable though inconclusive, and classical mythology is "so natural, that, in the vast variety of planets and world [*sic*], contained in this universe, it seems more than probable, that, somewhere or other, it is really carried into execution."[92]

Hume

Hume finds no evidence that the system *has* been executed on this planet, but does not find it absurd in principle. Religion's unreason is not in its earliest and most basic propositions, but in later theological elaborations.

Spencer

Rationalism blooms fully in Herbert Spencer, who explains primitive religion in *The Principles of Sociology*. Spencer's early humans reasonably arrived at a dualistic worldview by observing recurrent phenomena of weather, sun, and stars, and insect and other metamorphoses. These people required plausible links among the recurrences and assumed that what recurs is spiritual. Their dualism was reinforced when they thought about themselves and their shadows, their reflections, and especially their dreams. They interpreted sleep and unconsciousness as states in which spirit doubles, or souls, wandered. Dreams of the dead gave rise to the idea of ghosts, and the ghosts of ancestors and other prominent persons became the first gods.

Tylor

Sir E. B. Tylor's better-known version of rationalism, given in *Primitive Culture,* also begins with early humans contemplating not so much nature as themselves, and similarly ends with animism, a belief in spiritual beings. Tylor contrasts this with materialism, the belief that only material exists, and attributes animism to "two groups of biological problems. In the first place, what is it that makes the difference between a living body and a dead one; what causes waking, sleep, trance, disease, death? In the second place, what are those human shapes which appear in dreams and visions?"[93]

Confronted by death and dreams, ancient people must have explained death by the loss of some "life," and explained dreams by an image or "phantom." Both life and phantom could depart the body. The ancients combined the two, as people still do, forming the idea of the soul or spirit, a "thin unsubstantial human image, in its nature a sort of vapor, film, or shadow; the cause of life in the individual it animates." This soul is conscious and willful, and can leave the body and travel. It usually is invisible but can appear in dreams or visions. Once people formed this notion of themselves, they extended it to other living things and then to inanimate ones, crediting everything with its own spirit. Later, the myriad spirits were reduced to the gods of polytheism, and still later to a single god. Thus Tylor sees animism as a form of personalism, and hence as one form of anthropomorphism.

Often cited as the founder of rationalism in the anthropology of religion, Tylor is often criticized and has few followers today. In order of increasing validity, the charges against him are intellectualism, individualism, lack of evidence, and contrariness to evidence.

As a charge, intellectualism has meant two things: that Tylor imputed too much curiosity and concern for explanation to early humans, and that he did not account for religious emotion. The two often are combined as the accusation that he tried to make philosophers of savages.[94] Neither seems damaging, however, and both have receded in recent decades. Durkheim thought foraging peoples were too busy scrambling for a living to speculate about the dead, dreams, or much else: "intellectual weakness is necessarily at its maximum among the primitive peoples. These weak beings, who have so much trouble in maintaining life against all the forces which assail it, have no means for supporting any luxury in the way of speculation."[95] This picture of intellectual indigence, however, has long been erased by Claude Levi-Strauss, Marcel Griaule, Harold Conklin, and others who show that people in simple societies have ample intellectual curiosity, and by Richard B. Lee and others who show that they have ample time to indulge it (often more time than industrialized peoples).[96]

In fact, religious concern for explanation is widespread. Geertz, though distancing himself from Tylor, admits that his Javanese informants showed a Tylorian desire for explanations of, or at least explainability in, experience.[97] My own informants in Japan said a chief reason for joining a religious movement was to obtain the movement's explanations of events in their lives.[98] Certainly interpretation of the world, if not systematic explanation, is a fundamental human (and indeed animal) need.[99]

The charge that Tylor neglected religious emotion, made mainly in the first half of this century, persists in some textbooks today. It comes largely from writers such as Robert Lowie[100] who (probably influenced by Schleiermacher and Otto) thought religion best defined by its powerful feelings, especially of awe and dread. Several responses may be made. First, as Lowie admits, Tylor was explicitly concerned to trace an *idea,* because he thought that ideas, not feelings most distinguish religion.[101] He was aware of feelings, but found them more an effect of conceptions than a cause.

Second, Otto, Lowie, and others fail to show either that any emotion is unique to religion or that all religions share the same emotions. Lowie, for example, thinks amazement and awe in response to extraordinary events are definitively religious; yet people also feel amazement and awe in secular situations. Moreover, people do not seem to have these responses in many religious traditions. Japanese do not seem to experience these feelings for their ancestors; nor do Balinese for their gods. Robin Horton writes that the "awe and reverence . . . associated with religious situations in our own culture are replaced by some very different sentiments in . . . West Africa. A complex of sentiments and emotions common to all religions everywhere is . . . a chimera."[102] James similarly writes that there is "no one elementary religious emotion, but only a common storehouse of emotions upon which religious objects may draw."[103] Gordon Allport also says there is no specifically religious emotion and that most psychologists agree.[104] The charge that Tylor neglects religious emotions lacks weight, then, because he meant to study ideas not emotions and because there is no evidence of emotions peculiar to religion.

Durkheim's claim that Tylor is too individualistic is only slightly graver. It is true that Tylor does not depict religion as peculiarly social;

but he does depict it as part of culture, and he depicts culture as social. Further, the experiences from which he says religious beliefs arise are social: the deaths of, and dreams about, other people. His theory thus is not centered strictly on individuals. In any case, he aims "not to discuss Religion in all its bearings, but to portray the great doctrine of Animism."[105] Since he is interested in beliefs as cognition, questions about social effects and uses are beside the point.

The charge that Tylor's theory lacks evidence[106] seems stronger. Tylor does show that many cultures have similar notions of death and dreams. Death usually is the departure of something, often the breath or shadow and often with personal characteristics, and dreams often are visits from spirits. However, he shows neither that death and dreams are chief concerns of all religions nor that they cause belief in spiritual beings, nor even that spirit beings are universal in religion. His theory is plausible but neither demanded by his evidence nor unopposed by other evidence.

Opposing evidence is of two sorts. One sort undermines Tylor's evolutionary scheme, in which the objects of religious belief develop from souls to spirit beings, to gods, to a single God. This evidence shows that conceptions of souls and spirit beings may be entirely distinct, as in the Hebrew Bible.[107] Hence it seems unlikely that spirits developed from souls. The other contrary evidence concerns Tylor's identification of religion with spirit beings. Tylor calls the difference between animism and materialism the "deepest of all religious schisms," meaning the schism between religious belief and nonbelief. His equation of religion with animism, and unbelief with materialism, follows the mind/body dualism (most sharply expressed by René Descartes) of later Christianity.

This dualism seemed self-evident in Tylor's nineteenth-century Western milieu. For Tylor as for most of his European contemporaries, spirits were immaterial and separable from bodies, whereas bodies were material alone. Belief in spirits was religion, and belief in material alone was atheism. This mind/body dualism, however, does not exist in many religious traditions, including early Christianity. Andrew Lang noted this problem in Tylor as early as 1898, pointing out that gods need not be spiritual or soullike. Instead a god could be a fleshly but immortal person, a "magnified non-natural man," as Lowie puts it.

Gods and demigods may have human form, be visible at most times, and even be mortal. Among Western traditions, Homeric religion is best known for its concrete anthropomorphism, often contrasted with the spirituality of the Christian concept of God. However, until the time of Augustine, the notion of God as spiritual rather than material was virtually nonexistent in the church.[108] Augustine himself for nine years conceived God as a material substance, "an immense shining body,"[109] and thought church doctrine was that God not only is material but also has the shape of a human body. When doctrine changed, making God spiritual, Augustine struggled at length to agree. At the same time, many ordinary members of the church conceived God simply as a "very large man,"[110] a view still current among Mormons.

Non-Western religions as well undermine Tylor's claim that deities everywhere are spiritual. Lowie writes, for example, that the Dwarf of the Crow Indians shows "not the slightest hint that he is soul-like: he has all the earmarks of robust non-natural anthropomorphism, he belongs as it were to a distinct and powerful, though stunted, branch of the family Hominidae." Similarly, Biliku among the Andaman islanders "eats, drinks, sleeps, mates, and reproduces like a human being" and may be threatened with snakebite by the islanders.[111]

Lowie also says the spirit which Tylor sees wherever "inanimate reality is personified" is an unnecessary hypothesis. Lowie approves Robert Marett's distinguishing as "animatism" those cases in which people simply regard as living "what we class as lifeless." When a tribesman "yells at a hurricane, he is personifying the natural phenomenon, but we have no right to assume that he is thinking of a . . . refined bodily essence residing in and directing the storm."[112] Similarly, when a Crow says a rock can reproduce, he puts it "into the organic kingdom, but it no more follows that he attributes spirit to it than that we ascribe a soul to a cat when we describe it as animate." Lowie agrees with Marett that "both animism and animatism are essentially non-religious, or only potentially religious."[113]

Lowie's point is well taken. Biology (especially ethology) supports a view of animism as an attribution of life to the nonliving, and physics undermines the coherence of spiritual beings as a natural category. Electromagnetic waves, photons, subatomic particles, strong and weak forces, and other phenomena are, for most of us, like Tylor's spirit beings: "thin, insubstantial . . . images." These phenomena also are, as are Tylor's spirits, "capable of leaving the body far behind, to flash swiftly from place to place; mostly impalpable and invisible, yet also manifesting physical power . . . able to enter into . . . and act in the bodies of other men, of animals, and even of things."[114]

If most of us do not think of these entities as spiritual, it is because they lack such human attributes as complex organization and symbolic behavior. On the other hand G. W. Leibnitz, Herman Melville, Friedrich Nietzsche, Gregory Bateson, and others have held that all entities, including "inanimate" ones, may be thought of as having mind.[115] In any case, varying conceptions of these entities and forces remind us that such oppositions as mind/body, animism/materialism, and natural/supernatural have, at the least, fuzzy edges.

Tylor's account of religion as animism, then, though commonsensical in Western terms, seemingly applicable to a wide range of cultures, and accompanied by a wealth of illustrations, falls short on several counts. Animism, as he defines it, is dubious in its causes, its cross-cultural coherence, and its universality in religion.

Nonetheless, some important features in Tylor, as in Freud and
Durkheim, are persuasive. These include his naturalism, empiricism, rationalism, cognitivism, and reference to social experience. Tylor is naturalistic in portraying religion as the product of an evolving humanity and
as equally subject to evolution. He is rationalistic in depicting religion as
a plausible interpretation of evidence and empiricist in deriving that evidence from sense perception. He is cognitive in portraying religion as a
conception of the world (not, for example, as an emotion or a social
adhesive). Finally, he bases religion in social experience and notes that
religion attributes humanlike features, in the form of spiritual beings, to
the world at large.

Despite these virtues, Tylor has been out of favor for over half a
century, eclipsed by Durkheim, Malinowski, Freud, and Lucien Lévy-
Bruhl, and perhaps by a judgment, conscious or not, that religious ideas
could have no basis in experience or reason.[116] Many if not most humanists continue, with Schleiermacher, to see religion as an experience.
Often the experience is more or less unmediated, transcendent, or ineffable. S. J. Tambiah, for example, writes that from an "anthropological
standpoint the distinctive feature of religion lies not in the domain of
belief . . . but in a special awareness of the transcendent."[117]

In the interim, Evans-Pritchard, Levi-Strauss, and Ian Jarvie have sustained intellectualism, at least in anthropology, and Horton has taken a
major, if insufficiently recognized, step to restore it. Evans-Pritchard, for
example, portrays tribal religion as a coherent intellectual system.[118] He
shows that Azande witchcraft accounts for events, such as huts catching
fire or granaries collapsing, which otherwise would remain accidents—
that is, unexplained. Evans-Pritchard says Zande are aware of "naturalistic" causes of events also, but they find these causes insufficient explanation. By implication, the difference between tribal and modern Western
accounts of the world (as Mary Douglas and Levi-Strauss also suggest)
is not so much that tribal accounts are less critical, as that Western accounts are less comprehensive.

In *Theories of Primitive Religion,* Evans-Pritchard again endorses the
"essential rationality of [religion among] primitive peoples . . . in spite of
observations being inadequate, inferences faulty, and conclusions wrong.
The beliefs are always coherent, and up to a point they can be critical
and sceptical, and even experimental."[119] The limits implied here to scepticism and criticism, and hence rationality, in tribal religion are suggested
even by rationalists such as Horton and Jarvie. But these limits, though
sometimes invoked to explain religion's persistence, differ only slightly
for religion and other beliefs. Levi-Strauss, a more radical rationalist, asserts that all realms of thought, whether religious, magical, scientific, or
commonsensical, operate on the same logical and analogical principles.[120]
These realms differ in their assumptions and conclusions but not in their
rationality.

A contemporary philosopher, Ian Barbour, has a similarly rationalistic view of religion, which he compares to science. Barbour knows he has little company. Most writers see science and religion as "strongly contrasting enterprises which have essentially nothing to do with each other."[121] Many philosophers, for example, see the functions of religious language as subjective and noncognitive: to evoke, express, or recommend particular attitudes and values.[122] These philosophers contrast what they think is the aim of science—to predict and control nature—with that of religion, which they think is to express "self-commitment, ethical dedication, and existential life-orientation."[123] But, Barbour continues, this division means religion must relinquish any claim to truth, which in fact it typically does not.

Barbour thinks that with regard to three central issues—the diverse functions of language, the role of models, and the role of paradigms—religion and science are much alike. Both are evocative and evaluative as well as descriptive, both rely on metaphor and analogy, and both work interpretively within frameworks that are historical, traditional, and conventional. Barbour is religious and defends not only (as I do) religion's plausibility, rationality, and continuities with science and other secular thought, but also (as I do not) the probable truth of its central claims. Our positions otherwise are close; we both hold that all thought and action are alike in their need to interpret and their aim to influence.

Several eclectic and synthesizing theorists are near cousins of the intellectualists. Two of these—Clifford Geertz and Robert Bellah—think religion characteristically deals with some vision of ultimate reality. Their accounts of the content of this vision, however, are vague. After looking at Geertz in some detail, and Bellah briefly, we shall return to a final and more substantive intellectualist theory.

Geertz begins his well-known "Religion as a Cultural System"[124] with the function of religion: to synthesize a people's ethos and their worldview, by making a fit between how they think things are and how they think they should be. Religion is "a system of symbols which acts to establish powerful, pervasive, and long-lasting moods and motivations in men by formulating conceptions of a general order of existence and clothing these conceptions with such an aura of factuality that the moods and motivations seem uniquely realistic." Geertz thus defines religion by its purpose: to encourage and motivate people by making them believe in a meaningful and coherent universe.

Humans must form their conceptions of the world symbolically because, unlike bees or beavers, they have no such conceptions genetically. The sum of their symbols is culture. In every culture, people encounter gaps between expectation and experience. These gaps produce bafflement, suffering, and a sense of injustice. They undermine confidence in the order of things. They threaten "not just interpretations but *interpretability* . . . [they challenge] the proposition that life is comprehensible and that we can . . . orient ourselves."[125] The task of religion is to offer—

or promise—some framework within which the gaps and contradictions may be reconciled and ultimately have meaning, even if the meaning is not immediately apparent. When Job encounters such a gap and questions it, for example, God's reply is simply that a framework does exist.

Geertz combines Tylorian rationalism (humans must inhabit a reasonable and coherent world), Freudian and Malinowskian wish fulfillment (they must paper over contradiction and uncertainty), and Durkheimian social solidarity (construction is a group project and sustains an ethos) with Max Weber's emphasis on meaning. (Meaning is a central human pursuit.) The heart of his essay, however—that religion claims unique access to an unseen "general order of existence," and claims to show how to act accordingly—follows James's view of religion as belief that there is an "unseen order, and that our supreme good lies in harmoniously adjusting ourselves thereto."[126] Within this scheme, Geertz finds the creation and maintenance of meaning central. The purpose of the overarching framework that religion asserts is to establish and maintain meaning, which it does by positing an order and by absorbing and rendering harmless apparent breakdowns in that order.

Much of Geertz's essay, for example regarding the effects of religion, is plausible. Nonetheless, the essay does not offer a coherent theory of religion, for several reasons. First, Geertz does not take the content of religious thought seriously enough. He thinks religious symbolism simply is communication between humans and other humans. Believers may posit some "cosmic order" or "transcendent truths," but religious symbols are devised by men and "serve to produce . . . motivations in men." In contrast to Geertz, however, believers think religion is communication between humans and gods. Believers intend gods, not people, to hear them. Conversely, the messages they consider sacred, if any, are those they think come from gods. Of such a situation, Geertz can say only that people are doing something other than what they think they are doing, and that their real purpose is what would seem to them a by-product. They aim at a false target (communication with gods) and, necessarily missing, hit a real one (a synthesis of ethos and worldview).

Geertz seems untroubled by the gap between what believers think they are doing and what *he* thinks they are doing, and by their aiming at one result and achieving another. His equanimity is striking, since otherwise he insists that intention is crucial. He defines action, for example, as behavior with intention. Distinguishing motivations from moods, he writes, "motivations are 'made meaningful' [by] the ends toward which they are conceived to conduce . . . We interpret motives in terms of their consummations."[127] His believers, however, somehow achieve one thing while intending quite another.

The paradox is one which Geertz does not acknowledge, perhaps because he does not try to characterize the content of religious belief. He only describes attitudes toward, and results of, that content. The heart of religion—the general order of existence which it asserts—remains a black box. Into the box go crises (bafflement, suffering, injustice) and out come solutions. The solutions are largely reassurances that all is well on some higher level. But what, or who, is in the box so that its reassurances work? Geertz does not say.

Elsewhere he does detail several religious systems, but even there he gives scant attention to religious ontology while elaborating the ethos it supposedly affirms.[128] In "Religion as a Cultural System" he simply mentions broad and varied notions as typically religious. This mixed bag includes "an envisaged cosmic order," "a wider sphere," "gods, devils, spirits, totemic principles, or the spiritual efficacy of cannibalism," and "ultimate actuality." In a later essay Geertz says, "what all sacred symbols assert is that the good for man is to live realistically; where they differ is in the vision of reality they construct."[129] Evidently that vision of reality could be anything from a cosmic order to cannibalism, as long as people believe it ultimate.[130]

Even Geertz's clearest statement of what religion *is,* as opposed to what it does, seems blurred at the outset: "The question then comes down to, first, what is 'the religious perspective' generically considered, as differentiated from other perspectives; and second, how do men come to adopt it."[131] We have been backed away from religion to a religious perspective. But we hope he will at least say how this perspective differs from those of science, common sense, and art, and how people come to take it.

The perspective Geertz describes, however, differs not in the content of what it shows but only in its attitude toward that content. He says that whereas common sense accepts as given, and acts upon, some cultural everyday world, religion sets that everyday world in some wider world. This wider world is meant to have unquestionable authority and thus to guarantee the coherence of the everyday one. Unlike common sense in *its* world, religion does not act on this wider world but accepts and has "faith" in it. Whereas science sets the commonsense world in a wider world that is tentative and hypothetical, religion sets it in one that is to be taken as given: "Rather than detachment, its watchword is commitment; rather than analysis, engagement."[132] Whereas art suspends the question of reality in order to contemplate appearances, religion is concerned only with reality. It is "this sense of the 'really real' upon which the religious perspective rests. . . . [The] imbuing of a certain specific complex of symbols—of the metaphysic they formulate and the style of life they recommend—with a persuasive authority . . . is the essence of religious action." Religion, it seems, is any complex of symbols that appears "really real."

Just as religion consists of no particular view but only of any view taken seriously, people come to it in no particular way, but in any way taken seriously. "For it is in ritual—that is, consecrated behavior—that [religion] is somehow generated. . . . It is in some sort of ceremonial form"[133] that religious moods, motivations, and conceptions come together. Geertz gives a few examples of such behavior—reciting myths, consulting oracles, decorating graves—but does not say what they have in common apart from being consecrated and ceremonial. Nor does he say how they differ from nonreligious ceremony.

Against the distinctions Geertz offers between religion, common sense, science, and art, one may point out that religion as well as common sense has practical aims, that science as well as religion relies on authority and paradigms, and that art as well as religion is concerned with the "really real." Moreover, religion for many people is part of everyday life and is not set off from science, art, or common sense. These various systems are not, as he thinks, "radically contrasting ways of looking at the world, ways which are not continuous with each other." Rather, they are radically continuous, even though they can be distinguished for some purposes. Geertz himself recognizes as much elsewhere: in Java, the "word for 'religion' and that for 'science' are the same," and "religion . . . is ultimately a kind of practical science."[134]

In a phrase of Geertz's particularly apt for my purposes, he is trying to "stage *Hamlet* without the prince." A clue to what is missing appears in how he distinguishes religion from common sense, science, and art. Rather than detachment, he says, religion's watchword is "commitment"; rather than analysis, "encounter." Its attitude is one of "faith." But faith in, commitment to, and encounter with what? Geertz says, faith in, commitment to, and encounter with notions of what is really real—whatever these notions may be. In contrast, my suggestion is that commitment, encounter, and faith all describe *social* relationships, not relationships with notions of some "really real." The appropriate question is not commitment to what, but commitment to whom.

Barbour writes, "in its biblical meaning *faith* is not the acceptance of doctrines on authority but an attitude of trust and commitment."[135] He cites Alan Richardson's comment that the core of biblical faith is "reliability, steadfastness, confidence—usually with respect to a person, rather than a statement. It is personal trust arising in a personal relationship."[136] Barbour continues, "Faith in God is an aspect of a personal relationship, resembling . . . faith in a friend or in one's doctor, or a husband's faith in his wife." Faith is a virtue because religion is an ostensible social relationship between people and gods and because faith is necessary to social relationships. In the New Testament, for example, Thomas's fault is not that he doubts Jesus' doctrines but that he doubts Jesus. Again, when Satan dares Jesus to throw himself from a cliff to test whether God will save him, Jesus says it is forbidden to tempt God— that is, to doubt the relationship sufficiently to test it.

Just as trust can be strained or broken in purely human social relationships, so it can be strained or broken in human/god relationships. Religious faith is not necessarily unconditional or nonempirical, as Geertz seems to think. Job's wife, for example, advises him at last to curse God and die; and peoples around the world on occasion abjure or revile their gods, threaten them, or shoot arrows against them.

"Commitment" and "encounter" also are aspects of social relationships, whether among humans or between humans and gods. Like faith, they may be present in varying degrees; but if they are not present at all, there is no relationship. That is why, as Geertz says, detachment is *not* a characteristic of religion.[137] Ninian Smart similarly says that for the Christian, "God is a person with whom he can have contact; God is not like the sun, to be thought of speculatively, or to be looked at."[138]

Regarding the truth of religious beliefs, Geertz says it is "not the business of the scientist to pronounce upon such matters one way or the other."[139] However, it is not clear how a scientist engaged in theory of religion can avoid such pronouncements. Several generations of social scientists *have* avoided them, perhaps to be politic or perhaps because they were interested only in the "function" of religion, but they have produced no theory.[140] A theory of religion must include a theory of religious belief, and a theory of belief must address the source of belief.[141]

Inevitably, then, Geertz does not offer a theory of religion but skirts one, since a theory of a phenomenon is something which accounts for the phenomenon. He says not how religion arises but how it behaves, not how we come to have religion but why we might want it. He offers not a genesis of religion but a field guide to cultural systems. Although he says motives are meaningful in terms of their ends, he tries to interpret religious action without characterizing the intentions of religious actors. He identifies only what they achieve, perhaps because he thinks their intentions are too diverse to characterize.

However, as writers as different as Eliade and Proudfoot have noted, religious ontology and how people relate to it—in Proudfoot's phrase, the "intentional object of religious belief"—are just what we need to know. To ignore this is to

> lose the experience, or to attend to something else altogether. . . . If someone is afraid of a bear, his fear cannot be accurately described without mentioning the bear. This remains true regardless of whether or not the bear exists outside his mind. He may mistakenly perceive a fallen tree trunk on the trail ahead of him as a bear, but his fear is properly described as fear of a bear.[142]

Geertz's definition of religion as a system of symbols, then, describes nothing peculiarly religious. Instead, it describes equally his conception of culture as a whole. Thus his explanation does not set off religion from culture at large, or from such subsystems as philosophy, common sense, science, or art. Indeed, similar views have led to such confusions as supposing that Marxism or football is a religion.[143]

The vital feature missing from Geertz's discussion, the prince absent from his *Hamlet,* is an acknowledgment that religion everywhere does have a particular worldview, namely, an anthropomorphic one. Anthropomorphism is not central to, though it often is present in, philosophy, ideology, or science; but it is central to religion.[144] Because Geertz ignores it, he cannot adequately isolate the phenomenon he wishes to explain. Crucially, he cannot identify its characteristic cognitive content.

Geertz emphasizes meaning as central to religion—although meaning is central also to culture in general and, in a broader sense, to sentient beings. He does not say just what meaning is, or what distinguishes religious meaning.[145] Still, acknowledging the issue explicitly, he breaks a long positivistic near silence in anthropology. He describes a human as a "symbolizing, conceptualizing, meaning-seeking animal," whose

> drive to make sense out of experience, to give it form and order, is evidently as real and as pressing as the more familiar biological needs . . . it seems unnecessary to interpret symbolic activities—religion, art, ideology—as . . . other than what they seem to be: attempts to provide orientation for an organism which cannot live in a world it is unable to understand.[146]

One might add that the drive to give experience form and order is itself a "biological need," since no organism can live in a world it cannot understand enough to meet its other needs. An African wild dog could not live in Manhattan nor a city mongrel on the Serengeti, primarily because they would not understand their environments.

Bellah, who provides another well-known functionalist approach, defines religion as a "set of symbolic forms and acts which relate man to the ultimate condition of his existence."[147] This definition depends explicitly, as Geertz's does implicitly, on Paul Tillich's notion of ultimacy. Ultimacy is an idea, indeed a claim, familiar in several world religions and thus has the appeal of familiar usage. The resulting definition nonetheless is ambiguous, since it depends on some view of what our ultimate condition of existence *is*. Views of what is ultimate vary widely, opening the term religion to a hodgepodge of any and all "forms and acts" that someone takes seriously. Bellah writes, for example, of a "civil religion" in America with no center but the term God, which he admits is so diversely conceived that it is an "empty sign."[148] Bellah further admits he does not know whether this civil religion is a religion or a "religious dimension."

Moreover, many religions seem unconcerned with ultimacy. Instead they are eclectic, this-worldly, pragmatic, and immediate. Their members ask, How shall we get rain, cure the sick, and understand this earthquake? On the other hand, many atheists have concerns for ultimate conditions of existence, and relate to them in symbolic ways, but they are not thereby religious.[149]

The ambiguity that makes Geertz's and Bellah's notions of religion virtually interchangeable with notions of culture inheres in all functionalism. Functionalists try to understand organic phenomena, including social ones, in terms of their supposed ends. However, since ends are pursued by persons, not social institutions, and since the same ends usually can be reached by different means, the phenomena captured by functionalist definitions are a mixed lot. Regarding structure and function in animals, for example, Howard Margolis writes, "for any given function there will be an arbitrarily large number of particular structures that could perform the function."[150] Stated another way, trying to understand religion by its functions is like trying to understand an animal by its effects on an ecosystem: not totally unproductive, yet off the mark all the same.

Anthropologists nonetheless often try to define religion by what it does for emotions, thought, or culture. However, as Mary Douglas and Edmund Perry note, religion slips "between the meshes: on the one hand, many other beliefs perform these functions. On the other hand, this functional approach tends to leave out religion in modern industrial society, where the processes of secularization have eroded all the culturally unifying functions."[151] Functionalist students of religion might benefit from Crick's advice to biologists, who should "constantly keep in mind that what they see was not designed, but rather evolved."[152] They should mistrust discoveries of efficiency.

If functionalism were at all useful in understanding religion, it would be by pointing to the broad "function" of religion in establishing—or at least asserting—meaning. But establishing meaning is not exclusively religious, and pointing to meaning does not clarify what *is* religious. Nor does religion always function well, either in establishing meaning or in other ways.

Robin Horton sets out, in a series of articles and an edited book, a clear and substantive intellectualist approach.[153] Although a few scholars find Horton the "most thoroughgoing and explicit" intellectualist, or "important and controversial,"[154] he appears insufficiently appreciated.[155] Two of his articles are especially relevant.

The first, "A Definition of Religion, and its Uses" (1960), reviews anthropological definitions of religion and offers a new one. Horton points out a difficulty, mentioned above, in Tylor: that whereas his religious beings are incorporeal, the beings in some religions are corporeal. Nonetheless, Tylor usefully implies an "analogy between human beings and religious objects generally."[156] Building on this, Horton defines religion as "the extension of the field of people's social relationships beyond the confines of purely human society."[157] That is, religion is an assumption that part or all of the nonhuman world has a social relationship with humans. Humans thus model their relations with the world on their relations with other people.

Horton suggests that people turn to relationships outside "purely human society" when relationships within human society fail to meet their needs. The unmet needs vary with the society. Societies that are small, simple, and low in technology are good at creating intimacy and friendship, but not at material control and prediction. Large, complex, and technologically advanced societies can predict and control the physical world but their members are individualistic, alienated, and lonely. Accordingly, people in small, simple societies look to their deities for technical help (for example, with weather, pests, and illness) while people in large, complex ones look to deities for personal relationships.

Horton's definition of religion as an extension of human social relationships seems to fit contemporary Western common sense and most of what we call religion. Moreover, it leaves open the question of whether the relationships are really *with* anything or anyone, or are illusory, and thus should suit both believers and nonbelievers. However, Horton's discussion seems a variant of the wish-fulfillment theory of religion (what people can't get in human society, they seek elsewhere[158]) and objections to that theory (for example, much in religion is frightening) apply here as well.

Horton later (1967) provides a different and more powerful approach consistent with his definition. In "African Traditional Thought and Western Science" he summarizes the religious thought of the Kalabari of the Niger River Delta and compares it to Western scientific thought. Both traditions, Horton says, are theoretical enterprises. They aim to reduce the chaos, complexity, and plurality of the world to order, simplicity, and unity by positing a limited number of theoretical entities underlying endlessly varied phenomena. Contemporary Western physicists, for example, have atoms, electrons, and electromagnetic waves, while the Kalabari have ancestors, heroes, water people, and creators. Both traditions create theory by analogy with more familiar phenomena. Physicists developed the early modern notion of the atom by analogy with the solar system, whereas the Kalabari developed their notion of ancestors and other spirits by analogy with lineage elders and other humans.

Horton argues that religious and scientific theories also are alike in placing experience in a causal context broader than that of daily life and common sense. Both science and religion explain particular observable events such as storms, shark bite, or the chemical behavior of table salt by more general statements such as those asserting relations between human beings and deities or between sodium and chlorine. Both traditions have several levels of theory, and both postulate theoretical entities that are different from (for instance, they are more abstract than) the entities of daily life. Electrons, for example, do not have color or temperature, and gods do not have birthplaces or grave sites. Religion and science alike aim to interpret the world coherently and plausibly, using analogy to posit a few principles underlying endless diversity.

Having shown how religion resembles science, Horton also suggests how it differs. Most distinctive is not its personalism (or anthropomorphism) but its conservatism and mixed motives. Traditional religion especially is conservative because the communities that sustain it are closed to other cultures and their novel ideas. Traditional cultures, unlike science, therefore lack alternatives and regard their own theories as given, as synonymous with order and stability, and hence as sacred. Any threat to the theories is a threat of chaos and provokes anxiety and protection of established beliefs.[159] In addition, religion, unlike science, is intertwined with culture as a whole, which gives it "mixed motives." Whereas science is intellectual and concerned only with consistent and parsimonious explanation, religion combines art, entertainment, morality, and politics with explanation. Its theory thus is constrained and colored by other concerns.

Notably, a difference Horton does *not* find important is that religious worldviews make humanlike beings central, while scientific worldviews do not. The personalism of religion, he says, is simply its "idiom." As explanatory principles, spirits and electrons are much alike; the choice seems almost arbitrary. Small, traditional societies produce personalistic models because the most predictable phenomena their members know are their own social relationships. Their rudimentary technology, in contrast, offers no machines to provide reliable or compelling models. Modern, complex societies, on the other hand, give mechanistic accounts of the world because their social relations are disorderly, while their machines are orderly and pervasive.

Horton's comparison of religion and science seems to need a minor and a major amendment. First, science really is not as open as Horton claims. Instead it, like religion, is a cultural (that is, shared, cumulative, and traditional) system that relies on an established community of opinion. Despite their progressive ideology, scientists, like other people, resist change and suspect novelty. Religious beliefs, on the other hand, may change.

Still, science at least nominally welcomes change, and religion does not. Scientific iconoclasts may be ignored, but they are not burned at the stake. Moreover, although the particulars of religious belief change, religion in general is tenacious, and the contents of its worldviews differ noticeably from those of scientific worldviews. Why do science and religion have opposing official attitudes toward changes in belief, and why does religious belief persist, while often conflicting with science and seemingly without intellectual means of support?

The answer to both questions lies in my second and more basic amendment to Horton: that the personalism of religion is no mere idiom. Rather, it is fundamental and characteristic. Horton, reconsidering his 1967 article, still says the "exchange of a personal for an impersonal idiom in theory seems to me a relatively superficial transformation."[160] I think the transformation is deeper. Science, in sharp contrast to religion, strives to eliminate anthropomorphism and to some degree succeeds. Religion, on the other hand, is built upon anthropomorphism. As Tylor observes, the difference between personalism and impersonalism (in his terms, animism and materialism) is the "deepest of all religious schisms"—that between religion and irreligion.

This divide helps account for religion's conservatism regarding beliefs. Religion is a social relationship, and this relationship is primarily with the object of belief rather than with other believers or a creed. Faith is not in a doctrine but in a person. To doubt a doctrine, as scientists are supposed to do, in religion is to doubt a social relationship—that with some god—and to doubt a relationship openly is to undermine it. Hence religions urge believers not to doubt, and certainly not in public.[161] Thus the content of belief shapes the treatment of belief, and the skepticism that is at least a nominal virtue for science is a vice for religion. Religious conservatism and scientific progressivism derive, then, not so much from characteristics of the differing communities in which they are found (the communities may be the same) as from the entailments of religious and nonreligious belief.

The difference between Horton's view of personalism and mine goes still deeper, to the reason for the tenacity, and the spontaneity, of religious belief.[162] The reason in question—and the nub of my theory—is that belief in gods organizes experience as significantly as possible by positing for nonhuman things and events the highest actual organization we know: that of human beings and their society. Because humans are highly organized, they are capable of generating a wide array of phenomena. Thus, much is explicable by appeal to humans or something modeled on them. As theoretical entities, gods are reducers of complexity and diversity because the entities on which they are modeled, real humans, are generators of complexity and diversity. Gods appear as powerful components of theory because they are modeled on powerful real organisms.

A religious interpretation of the world thus is a powerful one. It answers our quest for information and order, a quest intrinsic to sentient beings. In Horton's account, in contrast, religious models are merely opportune and can readily be supplanted by mechanistic models. His account also seems voluntaristic and overly rationalistic, and seems to give too much weight to conscious explanation and too little to unconscious perception and interpretation.[163]

Pivotally, Horton seems to underestimate the power and pervasiveness of humanlike models of the world generally and to overestimate their disappearance from modern culture. Here he draws a sharp line between modern and traditional thought: the "hidden world" of theoretical entities in traditional religious thought is personal, whereas the hidden world of modern thought is mechanical. Indeed, the two worlds are so distinct that "for a person who lives with one type of 'hidden world,' it is sometimes difficult even to imagine what it would be like to live with the other type."[164] This misses the continuing pervasiveness of anthropomorphism, which, though it has receded somewhat in science and other critical thought, has not at all disappeared. On the contrary, it flourishes, as we shall see, in every corner of the modern imagination.

Anthropomorphism as such, however, does not concern Horton. This may be because he contrasts both science and religion, as theoretical enterprises, with common sense as a practical enterprise.[165] Because he is not especially interested in common sense or in perception, he does not notice how broadly they share what he calls the personalistic idiom of religion. In my view, he rightly links science and religion but, by segregating common sense and ignoring perception, he wrongly ignores what they share with science and especially with religion. Science and religion do try to unify experience, and do interpret the world actively, but so does all cognition. Perception itself is thoroughly theoretical.[166] It faces just the same task of discovering form and order in an inchoate world as do science and religion, and addresses the task with the same principles. In doing so, it very often sees human form and order in nonhuman things and events.

The difference between Horton and myself suggests a need to rename and perhaps reformulate the approach called intellectualism or rationalism, since these terms connote conscious interpretive effort, logic, and articulation. Critics who charge Tylor with making philosophers of savages do so because they see interpretation and cognition as deliberate and articulate. But if perception is interpretive—if we never just "see," but always "see as"—then no line can be drawn between perception and cognition, and no world simply is given. Every world must be won by interpretation, of which common sense, science, and religion all are variants. Interpretation is not unique to humans; all animals that perceive, interpret. If the terms "intellectualism" and "rationalism" connote something cerebral—if they evoke symposia or the Thinker—we should use some name smacking less of the study and more of the animal sniffing out its world.[167]

Seeing that perception is interpretive also enables us to see anthropomorphism not merely as an idiom for conscious explanation, but as the result of a general, spontaneous, and unconscious interpretive tendency. This tendency, general among animals, is to find as much organization as possible in things and events. The tendency is powerful. Its mistakes may be idiosyncratic and fleeting, as in much secular anthropomorphism, or shared, elaborate, and enduring, as in much religious anthropomorphism.

Although my theory of religion is indebted most to Horton and intellectualism, it also draws on others. From Schleiermacher, James, Otto, and Eliade I take recognition that religious experience seems (but only that it *seems*) direct and unmediated. At the same time, I take Proudfoot's point that this experience, like being frightened by a bear, is a product of information and is situated in belief.

From Freud and later psychologists I take the notions that individuals depend on, and are attuned to, society; that our dependent relations are powerful and largely unconscious; and that our early childhood experience has lasting influence. These observations point to our experience of other people as a primary source (and to experience of nature, for example, as only a secondary source) of models for understanding the world. These notions show why, as Freud said, the "humanization of nature" is fundamental to religion.

From Durkheim comes further evidence that members of society, not lone individuals, create and share visions of the world, and that they see the world as a form of society because human society is their most important frame of reference. Durkheim also, unlike most of his followers, sees religion as an intellectual enterprise that is continuous with science. Both religion and science address the same topics—nature, people, and society—with the same logic, in order to classify and systematize them.

From Hume as from Tylor, among the intellectualists, my approach takes the argument that humans find themselves in an uncertain and ambiguous world and use themselves as a source of models with which to interpret it. Doing so, they see reflections of themselves everywhere.

Geertz points to the human search for meaning which, though it pervades culture, is most explicitly part of religion. In my view, meaning is an issue especially in religion because religion assumes, crucially, that the nonhuman world creates and transmits meaning as people do: by sending and receiving symbolic communication.

These theorists, though diverse, share some elements with each other and with me. They all note that humans need to deal with an inchoate universe and with each other, and all note a major response to these needs, namely, to assimilate the universe to human life. These theorists do not see, however, how general this assimilation is: how pervasively we find human features where they do not exist.

Nor do they see that the assimilation is based in a broad perceptual strategy. This strategy is to guess at as much order and meaning as we can. Uncertain of what we face, we bet on the most important possibility because if we are wrong we lose little and if we are right we gain much. Religion, asserting that the world is significantly humanlike, brings this strategy to its highest pitch.

2

Animism, Perception, and the Effort After Meaning

Now if we survey the universe . . . it bears a great resemblance to an animal or organized body, and seems actuated with a like principle of life and motion. . . . The world, therefore, I infer, is an animal.

David Hume, *Dialogues Concerning Natural Religion*

We often see nonliving things and events as alive, especially if they move, make noise, or otherwise stand out from the landscape. We credit our environment with more organization and more organisms than it has. Humans see boulders as bears, flying pieces of paper as birds, and stuck drawers as willful. Other animals also animate the world: cats see fluttering leaves as prey, horses see blowing bags as threats, and dogs hear sirens as howls. Our shared inclination to animate, moreover, is a strategy rather than an accident. To call this inclination a strategy, however, is not to say it is conscious. In fact, it almost never is.[1]

Animism as a term has several current uses. In studies of religion, it means belief in spirit beings while in psychology it means attributing life to the lifeless. The latter meaning is broader and encompasses the first. Although animism is not the same as anthropomorphism (the attribution of human characteristics to things or events that are not human), we often animate and anthropomorphize at the same time. We animate but do not anthropomorphize, for example, if we say an automobile purrs like a kit-

39

ten, and anthropomorphize but do not animate if we speak to our pet turtle. If we speak to the automobile, however, we both animate and anthropomorphize.

As we saw, belief in spirit beings is Tylor's definition both of animism and of religion. Tylor says this belief stems from an attempt to explain dreams and death. To account for these, people attribute spirits first to themselves and then to animals, plants, and inanimate objects. Thus Tylor's account, like mine, explains animism as an attempt at interpretation. Since Tylor, many anthropologists and other students of religion have adopted his term, animism, but most gloss over his account of the origin of animism and narrow his meaning to a second, related, sense: that form of religion that attributes a spirit to everything.

Jean Piaget and other developmental psychologists use the term animism in a third way: the "tendency among children to consider things as living and conscious."[2] Piaget attributes this tendency to "confusion or rather lack of differentiation between the psychic and the physical."[3] That is, children (and, according to some scholars, primitive peoples) confuse self with other. Children also confuse parents and other adults with events in the world at large. Piaget finds in children a related tendency, artificialism,[4] the belief that everything in the world is produced by humans or by a humanlike God, who they do not distinguish from humans. Artificialism and animism diminish with age. By early adolescence they are replaced by naturalism, in which most of the natural world (mountains, lakes, clouds) is inanimate and is made by natural process or at least by a God distinct from ordinary humans. Piaget regards naturalism as the adult and correct worldview.

Most developmental psychologists accept the essentials of Piaget's version.[5] They ask only such questions as whether child animism is complete, when it ceases, and whether it makes motion or sentience most prominent. Most assume animism rests on a childish failure to distinguish one's mind from events in nature and disappears in adults. Most also assume animism is a simple[6] and unambiguous phenomenon, and that it is clearly mistaken. At most, animism for modern adults is a matter of choice. For example, two contemporary psychologists of religion using animism in Piaget's sense write, "whereas primitive thinking instinctively sees the natural world as inhabited by spirits influencing man, animistic thinking in modern man is deliberate and conscious."[7]

Piaget's notion of animism is broader and somewhat better documented than Tylor's.[8] Still, two key aspects of Piaget's account are dubious: animism in Piaget's sense may diminish in adults, but it by no means disappears; and it seems to rest not so much on an inability of children (or of "primitives") to tell their own thoughts from natural processes[9] as on a persistent, real difficulty, for everyone, in distinguishing what is alive from what is not. Ambiguities in the notion of life, and practical difficulties in identifying animals and plants as such, make distinguishing the living from the nonliving perpetually problematic. The distinction is problematic both in ordinary perception and on further reflection. Typically it is made only in hindsight.[10] Animism, though by definition mistaken, is neither simple nor unambiguous.

A fourth and popular view defines animism as does Piaget (that is, seeing what is not alive as alive) but explains it as wishful thinking: people see what they want to see, and they want to see things as alive. We have encountered wishful thinking as a theory of religion and will meet it again as a theory of anthropomorphism. In all three cases, it has the same problem: there is no obvious correspondence between what people want and what they think they see. Instead, they often imagine they see what they fear. Perception and desire doubtless interact, but desire has no convincing priority.

Many animated and humanized things and events, for example, are more frightening than inanimate ones. Stephen Toulmin says, for instance, that animated celestial bodies are more menacing than inert ones. If astronomers were to see

> the heavenly bodies as living creatures once more, we should . . . have some reason for worrying. Not the least of the merits which Edmund Halley saw in Newton's theory was its power to banish anxieties of this sort:
>
> > "Now we know
> > The sharply veering ways of comets, once
> > A source of dread, nor longer do we quail
> > Beneath appearances of bearded stars."
> > The inertness of the stars . . . is surely
> > preferable to their possible malignancy.[11]

A writer on the origins of religion says that in our images of animals, "fear and anxiety [are] primordial."[12] Wish fulfillment, then, explains animism no better than it does religion.

Scholars of religion and psychologists find little in common[13] and seldom link their two usages of animism. However, intermediate usages do exist,[14] and psychological and religious versions of animism are so related that I shall offer a single account for both. This account holds that distinguishing what is alive from what is not is intrinsically difficult and that animism stems in part from this difficulty. The difficulty has two sources: animals in their natural environments typically are hard to see, and criteria for life are uncertain. Therefore we not infrequently are in doubt as to whether something is alive. When we are in doubt, the best strategy is to assume that it is.

My claim that animism results from a perceptual strategy (namely, when in doubt whether something is alive, assume that it is) draws on three linked observations: perception is interpretation, interpretation aims at significance, and significance generally corresponds to the degree of organization perceived.

Figure 2–1 **Rabbit or duck?** We never just "see" anything, but always "see *as.*" Thus, although we can see this figure as either rabbit or duck, we cannot see it as both at once.

Most perceptual psychologists now agree that perception is interpretive: it is a choice among ways of seeing something.[15] As Ludwig Wittgenstein remarks, we never merely see, but always "see as."[16] We may, he points out, see a given drawing (Fig. 2–1) either as the head of a duck or as that of a rabbit, but we cannot see it as both at once. We must choose one or the other. Thus there is no distinction between seeing and seeing as.

We always see "as" because the world arriving at our eyes and ears is, as James had it, a booming, buzzing confusion. We can give any sensation multiple interpretations. Put the other way around, any number of conditions may cause any sensation. The bright spot in the sky may be a flying saucer or a reflection in our windshield; the tickling on our ankle a spider or a loose thread. Perception is active inference, a mostly unconscious process of hypothesizing the causes of a given sensation or cluster of sensations. Stated this way, "interpretation" and "explanation" become closely related enterprises.[17] Since multiple interpretations are possible, our choice of interpretations constitutes a guess. As the art historian Ernst Gombrich puts it, perception is betting.[18]

Writing on cognition as pattern recognition, Margolis makes the same point with a different image: "the brain has a bias favoring seeing something rather than nothing, so that it tends to jump to a pattern that makes sense of a situation. Hence, even if there is no pattern objectively there, it tries to impute one." Cognition then uses "the basic building block of . . . 'jumping'—the cuing of a pattern on partial (nonrigorous) processing of cues. When we see a pattern in a situation, we are characteristically jumping, [since] we see 'beyond the information given.' "[19]

Rudolf Arnheim, the psychologist of art, similarly says that what we usually distinguish as cognition and perception really are the single activity of interpretation:

> the cognitive operations called thinking are not the privilege of mental processes above and beyond perception but the essential ingredients of perception itself. I am referring to such operations as active exploration, selection, grasping of essentials, simplification, abstraction, analysis and synthesis, completion, correction, comparison, problem solving, as well as combining, separating, putting in context. These operations are not the prerogative of any one mental function; they are the manner in which the minds of both man and animal treat cognitive material at any level.[20]

Among the results of this treatment, for example, is object constancy: we see familiar objects as having their typical shape and size, even viewed under widely differing circumstances. For instance, we see a wheel as circular even when we see it almost edge first, when the image we receive actually is a narrow ellipse.

Interpretation begins at an even lower level than object constancy. It extends down to shapes, colors, lines, and edges.[21] What we think of as "images" on our retinas, for example, our nerve endings receive only as collections of dots. Seeing these dots even as something as simple as a line means guessing the best configuration: that which is most coherent and most significant. Seeing a "line," the perceiver simultaneously guesses what structure gives rise to it: an edge, a pencil mark, a wire, or something else.[22] The same need to interpret applies in turn to each of these possibilities, and so on up to and including our most comprehensive ideas of the world.

All these interpretations are choices made by the criteria of coherence (fit with existing information) and significance (generation of new information). That which generates the most information is most significant or important to us, or, put yet another way, most meaningful. Hence we scan what registers at lower levels of complexity and integration (for example, dots and lines) with models from higher levels (for example, edges and objects) applying first the models we find most important. The higher the level of model we can apply, the more meaning we can generate.

What we see depends on what model we use. Looking at the starry night sky, the Greeks saw lines constituting particular constellations, because these configurations of stars fit particular stories of interest to them. Other peoples tell other stories and hence see other constellations and lines. Our perceptual world rests not upon the back of a giant turtle that rests on another, and so on, but on interested guesses all the way down.

Our ability to assemble meaning from fragments may be seen, for instance, in finding the right exit from a highway at night in the rain by peering at faint blurry images speeding across a streaked windshield.[23] A technique for imagining scenes and figures recommended to artists by Leonardo da Vinci (and independently by others, cross-culturally), shows the same power:

You should look at certain walls stained with damp, or at stones of uneven colour . . . you will see there battles and strange figures in violent action, expressions of faces and clothes and an infinity of things which you will be able to reduce to their complete and proper forms. In such walls the same thing happens as in the sound of bells, in whose stroke you may find every named word which you can imagine.[24]

Leonardo's exercise shows, as do inkblot tests, that very broad models can and do generate order and meaning from near chaos.

Such scanning for order and meaning is continuous, because the perceptual world always is underdetermined and always is coming into being. The scanning may be at low levels (for shape, color, depth, texture, position, and motion) or at high ones (for organisms, not merely objects).[25] At all levels, we keep trying models for fit. Perception consists in deciding on fit; but fit is relative and partial, and decisions are subject to change. Nietzsche aptly views the human world as an arduous, uncertain, and continuing project: "One may well admire man here as a mighty genius of construction, who succeeds in raising the superstructure of an infinitely complex conceptual cathedral on a moving foundation and, so to speak, on flowing water."[26]

Amidst this flux, our conjectures aim at information—for any "difference that makes a difference,"[27] a definition that applies also to "meaning"—about the world. The information we seek is not independent of needs and interests but is shaped by them, including a need for action. Explicating seeing "as," H. L. Piper writes, "the statement 'I can see B,' implies that I know how to go on. If I say 'I see a cave,' [not a black spot] it means I know how to go on in relation to it, e.g., I know what will happen if I fire a tracer bullet at it. If I say 'I see the drawing of the head of a rabbit,' I can . . . draw in the body."[28] The more successful an interpretation, the more it reveals and the more that information is integrated into our understandings and actions.

In making any interpretation we choose some context. Our choice depends on our purpose: "we choose between this and other ways of seeing the same object . . . by choosing between the uses we can make of each and between . . . systems into which each will fit."[29] For example, we attribute various hierarchies to the world, of varying interest. One is simply a hierarchy of scale among physical systems, with large ones containing smaller ones. Galaxies contain solar systems, which contain planets with moons, and so on down through molecules, atoms, and subatomic particles. We expect similar relations, such as inclusion, to obtain everywhere, between the structures of one scale and those above and below it.

A second hierarchy is internal to organisms, with nested systems related to each other and to the external world so as to perpetuate the organism: genes within chromosomes within cells within organs within organisms. Organisms thus are concentrations of structure. They are characterized, as Crick puts it, not only by their immense variety but also by their "highly organized complexity." Compared to inorganic matter, organisms are hot spots of order, humming with information, with process serving process. Erwin Schrödinger says they have the "astonishing gift of concentrating a 'stream of order' "[30] on themselves. In this they generally are sharply different from merely physical systems. A third and crucial hierarchy, then, comprises the organic and inorganic worlds: what is alive and what is not.

If perception requires choosing among interpretations and therefore requires betting, and if the payoff is discovering significance, then the first bets to cover—those with the biggest payoff—are bets as high on the scale of organization as possible. The discoveries of order they yield are those we most need.[31] Some such bets are built into perceptual systems genetically. Frogs and other animals are predisposed to see moving bugs, and herring gull chicks to see the red spots on their parents' beaks. Their visual fields are "hierarchic rather than homogeneous, in the sense that certain perceptual features stand out because of the needs to which they relate."[32] Built-in frog bets, for instance, are that a small moving image is food and that a large moving image is a predator.

Other bets are learned, especially in complex animals, but the principle of hierarchy and wager is the same. Consider guessing whether a large lump is a bear or a boulder. Facing uncertainty, most people bet on the bear. If they are right, the jackpot is whatever they know about bears (for example, whether this kind is aggressive, or climbs trees), applied to the context. If they are wrong the mistake usually is cheap. Conversely, mistaking a bear for a boulder may be costly. In the wild, the chance that a given lump is a bear never is even fifty/fifty, as boulders are more common. Bears are so important, however, that people bet against the odds. Jogging one evening outside Churchill, Manitoba, self-styled polar bear capital of the world, I saw in a few minutes three separate bears hunkered down in the brown tundra. All proved to be boulders.[33]

As bears remind us, such information about the world as the organization underlying large lumps is valuable. But organisms including ourselves are significant to each other not only as threats and resources—as concentrations of organized energy and thus potential prey, predators, or partners—but as information about their environments as well. Fishermen know that where gulls gather over the ocean, small fish likely are at the surface, chased by larger ones below. Patterns of organic form and behavior are revelatory in many ways.

The strategy for discovering these patterns is, again, that of Pascal's wager, namely, guessing high. Pascal's version is that in the face of unresolvable uncertainty as to whether God exists, one should bet He does, since the gain if one is right outweighs the loss if one is wrong. The principle is the same in betting something is alive. This strategy also resembles the one supposedly once recommended to an aspiring youth: When opportunity knocks, jump. "But how do you know when opportunity's knocking?" asks the young man. "Just keep jumping," is the reply. Similarly with seeing bears: we may often bet wrong, but we must keep jumping.

My point is not that the presence of life, or the distinction between what is alive and what is not, is uniquely important everywhere. Every context has its priorities. If we are working on a car and drop a nut in the grass, what we want is the nut. We scrutinize everything resembling it: pebbles, beetles, snails; all are subordinate to the object of our desire. The complex organism of a snail is nothing compared to the utility of the missing nut. Although what is important varies with the context, some distinctions and some kinds of things and events usually are more important than others. The hierarchy is fluid and shifting, but some things tend toward the top and others toward the bottom. Although the animate/inanimate distinction is important in most contexts, another distinction, that between human and nonhuman, usually is more important yet. Focused though we may be on finding a missing nut, unexpected footsteps approaching, or a throat being cleared, instantly distracts us.

Perceptual uncertainty may seem rare, since we seldom doubt for long what we are seeing. Bears and boulders quickly appear distinct. But perceptual uncertainty *is* the common state, for the reason given earlier: any sensation may be caused by an indefinite number of conditions. Normally, however, we are unaware of uncertainty because most perception is rapid and unconscious, and suppresses ambiguity.[34] Hence perception appears definite, even while interpretation fluctuates. This appearance of certainty evidently is useful: "The suppression of uncertainty and equivocation in perception suggests that we may be biologically programmed to act on the perceptual best bet, as if this bet involved no risk of error."[35] Lacking such suppression, we might all be Hamlets, marooned in chronic indecision.

The suppression of uncertainty is especially complete in familiar circumstances. Only in novel or baffling situations, as when we travel abroad, learn to ski or speak a new language, or confront the rabbit/duck, are we aware of ambiguity and the need to check our interpretations. Uncertainty and the interpretive quest, then, are mostly unconscious.

The number of models we use in interpretation and the patterns they generate are finite. Perception is categorical, not continuous: it segregates phenomena into categories or kinds within which differences seem smaller than they objectively are, and between which differences seem greater.[36] Hence the patterns for which we must at any moment scan can be limited. Perception turns endlessly diverse phenomena into kinds (tigers and tabbies into cats, wolves and chihuahuas into dogs, and dogs and cats into tame and wild) by emphasizing some analogies and patterns over others.

Which analogies and patterns we emphasize depends on our purposes and contexts. Employing analogy and discovering pattern involve the operations Arnheim attributes both to perception and to cognition: "combining, separating, putting in context,"[37] and so on. When these operations make shared patterns seem total, we see things or events as identical. The river we stepped in a moment ago seems the same river now. X is x, earlier or later. When the operations disclose no important shared patterns, we assign the things or events to different categories, for example, that of a "thing" such as a river and that of an "abstraction" such as time. X is x and y is y. When we find that things or events already assigned to different categories share some important pattern, and, for example, see time as a river, we see this as metaphor. X is, yet is not, a y.

Over the whole range of comparisons from metaphor to similarity to identity, however, perception is "seeing as." It is predication, an attribution of a pattern to an ambiguous instance. In that regard, "x is x" is the same as "x is a y." As Arnheim writes of vision, perception is not a "mechanical recording of elements but rather the apprehension of significant structural pattern."[38] To the extent we find shared patterns significant, we minimize differences. Since differences through time and space (for example, in the volume of a river) always exist, identity always is illusory, an artifact of extracting only the patterns that interest us. Hence any assertion of identity, examined closely enough, is metaphoric: it mentions only likeness in the face of known (or knowable) difference. All that distinguishes metaphor in the conventional sense from other assertions of identity, then, is that the gap of difference it leaps has been awarded categorical status.[39] Metaphor tacitly acknowledges difference while literal assertion of identity ignores it. Both rest on pattern recognition, however, and both claim to discover some key similarity.

Animism is primitive, and perception usually produces it whenever we meet a phenomenon we cannot clearly see as inanimate. Because much of the world is—we now believe—inanimate, we often do bet on inanimacy. Because part of the world also is animate and because the animate portions usually are more important, we more often bet on animacy.[40] If a thing or event seems even momentarily to fit that possibility, we see it as alive. Motion especially, as zoologists note for frogs and as Piaget notes for children, suggests life. So do unpredictability, intractability, and noise. A hat flying down a windy street seems to dodge our grasp, and storm gusts and thunder seem to assault us. Banging our eye on an unexpected door edge, we kick the door, because we see it in that moment, automatically and unconsciously, as a malefactor.[41] *It* appears to have struck *us*.

The human interest in moving and other lifelike things is, as noted, shared by other animals. The frog's eye transmits little to its brain except motion. Small moving things elicit flicks of the tongue and large moving things elicit leaps into water. Animism, then, results from a simple form of game theory employed by animals ranging at least from frogs to people: the best bets are the highest, because those have the highest payoffs and lowest risks.

Like frogs and other animals, we often misinterpret things and events. When we do, and later name our mistake, we may speak of an illusion. Illusions are inevitable. Two workers on artificial and natural intelligence write,

> No finite organism can completely model the infinite universe, [and] the senses can only provide a subset of the needed information; the organism must correct the measured values and guess at the needed missing ones. In most organisms these guesses are made automatically by algorithms embedded in their neural circuitry, and are the best bet the organism can make based on the past experience of its species. Even good bets occasionally fail, so it is likely that all organisms experience illusions.[42]

Animism in Piaget's sense is one of these illusions. Because we and other animals have a particular interest in perceiving life, this illusion is particularly common.

Animism in Tylor's sense, belief in spirit beings, differs mainly in that the forms of life it hypothesizes may be invisible and, in some cases, immaterial as well. Tylor saw spirit beings as an attempt to explain death and dreams. His view, though unsatisfactory as an explanation of religious belief, may help explain why some spirit beings are immaterial. However, the wager account of animism, taken together with the following accounts of invisibility, apparent immateriality, and the ambiguity of "life," explains more. Moreover, it has some evolutionary and ethological footing, and makes human perception, including some of its illusions, continuous with perception in other animals.

Invisibility, common in gods, ghosts, and other spirits, may seem an extraordinary attribute and peculiar to religious belief. Hume, for example, says the only point on which religions agree is that there is "invisible, intelligent power in the world."[43] Invisibility in people and other material entities—a recurrent theme in magic, folk tales, and science fiction—seems a fantasy.

Although absolute invisibility may elude people and animals, virtual invisibility does not. Small boys and professional soldiers know the magic of camouflage, and natural selection has produced highly camouflaged and practically invisible animals in every environment. A tawny, countershaded (darker above, lighter below) coyote walking on a tawny Colorado slope, for example, recently disappeared before my eyes merely by pausing and then reappeared simply by walking again. Rudyard Kipling's Ethiopian, hunting striped animals in the forest (in *How the Leopard Got His Spots*), complains, "I can smell Zebra and I can hear Zebra, but I can't *see* Zebra."

The idea of invisibility is based in broad experience. It is no peculiarity of the religious imagination, and we need invoke no irrationality to account for it. Real animals in their natural settings often are virtually

invisible, apparently immaterial, or deeply ambiguous. Deceptive coloration hides almost all animals from their enemies.[44] Colors, patterns, and
structures blend them visually with their backgrounds although they are
in full view or, what comes to the same thing, make them resemble specific parts of their environments.

Such deception often is complex and dynamic. Many animals turn
snow-white in winter and brown in summer. Lizards, flatfish, squids and
octopi, sea horses, and others quickly change color and pattern to match
new surroundings. Sargasso fish, some sea horses, and others mimic sea-
weed not only with colors and patterns but also with tendrils and fila-
ments. Insects and crabs disguise themselves by pasting on bits of debris.
Countershading along the bodies of mammals, birds, and fishes conceals
contour by hiding shadow. Fish, shrimp, jellyfish, and insects may be
largely transparent, and their opaque parts may be not only countershaded but also silvery and thus ambiguous. Various fishes of the dim
middle ocean depths eliminate shadow altogether with light-emitting cells
along their bellies, the brightness of which corresponds to ambient light
from above. Sensors along the backs of the fish cause these cells to match
changes in light from above, as by dimming when clouds pass between
the sun and sea.[45] Thus any animal looking up from below sees only the
even illumination of skylight.

Many organisms mimic specific parts of their environments. Insects
and spiders appear as twigs, grasses, leaves, droplets of water hanging
from leaves, or lichens on tree bark. Other insects mimic droppings (complete with splash marks) of birds, caterpillars, or lizards. Others look like
insects already bitten and discarded, or like larvae eaten by parasites. Some
look like thorns, lined up in a row along a branch. A few insects form
colonies mimicking local flowers.[46] Many vertebrates, especially frogs and
fishes, look like leaves (fresh or dried, flat or curled, often "insect-
chewed") and hold still or drift in a current, seemingly inert.

Other animals are visible but their locations are ambiguous. One
source of such ambiguity is the diffraction gratings of many beetles and
of some wasps and spiders.[47] These produce interference patterns in reflected light, making the insect's brightness and color change iridescently
with small changes in viewing angle, and making it difficult to judge the
insect's size, shape, and distance. Animals also produce spatial ambiguity
by flocking, swarming, or schooling. Birds, insects, and fish may move in
dense, rapidly changing formations, for example, in the complexly rolling
wave formed by some species of birds, with thousands of individuals flying and feeding in turn. Such groups confuse predators by making lo-
cating and tracking any individual difficult. They may seem immaterial,
as ephemeral as clouds—to which large flocks or swarms sometimes are
likened—as they scatter before a predator.

Another natural deception is false warning. Various harmless insects
and at least one snake wear bright colors very like those of poisonous
species. Caterpillars, moths, and butterflies may display "eye spot" pat-

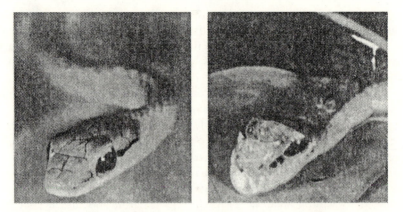

Figure 2–2 **Protective mimicry: Costa Rican snake and look-alike caterpillar.** Like other animals, we look for what is important to us and often think we see it when we really do not. For example, we readily see harmless things as dangerous ones that they resemble.

terns like the eyes of larger vertebrates, which frighten birds. A Costa Rican caterpillar (Fig. 2–2) has the color, shape, and "eyes" of the head and neck of a tree snake in its area. The European puss moth caterpillar inflates the skin around its head to make a gaping bright pink "mouth" topped by two "eyes." Such eye spots and mouth show again that significance (in this case, the danger), and animal estimates of that significance, generally correlate with degree of organization. In the cases above, insects are protected by looking like vertebrates. An opposite deception is false helplessness, as in the broken-wing display of some ground-nesting birds, given when a potential predator approaches eggs or nestlings. This lures the predator away and is compelling even to humans familiar with it.

Plants also deceive. Especially in deserts, many avoid herbivores by resembling stones or dead, or poisonous, plants. Some plants have flowers resembling female wasps, and thus are pollinated by males. Flytraps attract prey by smelling like flowers or carrion.

Just as some plants are protected by feigned death, so are various animals. The possum is best known but some snakes, insects, and fishes also play possum. Some snakes first display spasms, a deflected head, and jaws distortedly agape, deterring cats and mantids, which attack only live prey. Here the distinction between animate and inanimate, organized and disorganized, is bridged in yet another way.

Invisibility and ambiguity thus are not unique to gods, ghosts, or other spirits, nor merely products of the human imagination. Rather they, and deceit generally, pervade the relations of animals, including humans, with each other and with plants.[48] The reader may object that the invisibility of spirits is different: for example, it may be absolute, not relative.[49] But many deities are not absolutely invisible. Deities in varied cultures are visible much of the time. When they make themselves invisible, they may use means accessible to humans and other animals as well. The Homeric gods, for example, often wrap themselves or mortals in a cloud of smoke or mist, a trick also used by squids, octopi, and warships.

Natural deceit tricks animals into seeing other animals as inanimate or into simply not seeing them at all. In consequence, all must scan the apparently inanimate world for signs of life. A further result is that, like humans, other animals sometimes err by seeing something inanimate—a twig, a flying leaf—as an animal. This shows they have a "searching image,"[50] a model of what they are looking for, that somehow has been matched by another object. For example, H. E. Hinton reports a bird that, having found and eaten a twig-mimicking caterpillar, spent some time pecking at nearby twigs resembling it. Hinton himself mistook water droplets for droplet-mimicking bugs and, in order to tell some dropping-mimicking caterpillars from droppings, had to squeeze them.[51] Other ethologists report other illusions. Mark Bekoff says young coyotes pounce on twigs, apparently mistaking them for grasshoppers,[52] and Dorothy Cheney and Robert Seyfarth say infant vervet monkeys give eagle alarm calls not only on seeing eagles but also on seeing "herons, geese, bustards, and even a falling leaf."[53]

Particular illusions—searching images falsely satisfied—are fostered by particular contexts. A recent television broadcast on marsh wildlife showed a bobcat pursuing and cautiously sparring with a cottonmouth moccasin. When the snake escaped into shallow water, the bobcat followed. Encountering a partly submerged stick, it leaped back and struck several times at the stick, clearly having seen it as the snake. Similarly, a recreational runner in a New York suburb recently saw a pigeon sitting on the road in the distance, which on his approach proved to be a rounded gray cobblestone. Several days later he saw in the same neighborhood a gray stone which, as he came nearer, flew off. In another instance, fishermen on a pier saw a forty-foot whale in New York Harbor. The whale "seemed injured as it lolled and drifted"[54] offshore. A police launch investigating the report found a dark plastic bag of garbage, thirty feet long, rolling on the surface.

We mistake not only inanimate things for animate ones but also one animal for another. A journalist on safari, out for an evening jog, suddenly saw a

> movement snake-like across the width of the road only a few feet ahead in the dusky light that froze me in my tracks: a chilling perception that I had nearly stepped on the deadly puff adder. In the near dark I was able to distinguish the hideous configuration and slow movement. Carefully I moved closer. Then I saw not a serpent, but a column of black ants whose total body was a startling approximation of the dreaded snake, including its uniquely shaped head and rhythmic slow forward motion.[55]

Again the illusion consists in seeing a less significant phenomenon as a more significant one.

Particularly relevant to my account of religion are Jane Goodall's reports of chimpanzees responding to thunderstorms, which they dislike, with threat behavior.[56] The threats usually are from individual males but sometimes are from a group. They stamp, hoot, break branches (which they do at other times to threaten competitors and predators), and repeatedly charge down hillsides. Goodall sees the display as a threat against the storm and reports milder threats in the presence of rapid streams. She suggests that primitive man might similarly have "challenged the elements" and that although the chimpanzees cannot be called religious, early religious awe might have arisen in the same situation. My guess is that the display is indeed a threat against the storm and that the chimpanzees do perceive the storm as animate. Many humans have done so. In English, for example, storms "rage," thunder "growls," wind "howls,"[57] and hurricanes get personal names. Many people see storms as expressions of divine anger.

Perception of a storm as animate is not unreasonable. A thunderstorm has considerable coherence, visibility, and tangibility, with cloud, darkness, wind, rain, lighting, thunder and other noise, fresh cold air, and new smells. It can arrive and depart swiftly, often with a rush, and can leave behind "tracks" of moisture, broken branches, and lightning strikes. On the other hand, a thunderstorm is to some degree ambiguous and indeterminate. But plants and animals, individually or in groups, also may be ambiguous, invisible, apparently immaterial, and otherwise indeterminate. Given this ambiguity in organisms and given that both chimpanzees and storms engage in noisy displays including tree-shaking, it would not be surprising if chimpanzees, as Goodall suggests, regard a storm as something alive, that can be threatened.

Because even large and highly organized animals and plants may be hard to distinguish from their backgrounds, animals including ourselves sometimes perceive background as animate. The perceptual division between alive and not alive is blurred, in this case, by the vital invisibility conferred by natural selection. If a "rock" can prove to be a ptarmigan, a "leaf" a frog, and a "twig" a snake, why might not other rocks, leaves, or twigs also be more than they look? That lesson seems to have been learned by the bird and coyote pecking at or pouncing on what turns out to be only twigs. The naturalist and the runner learned it as well. Given the great range of appearance and behavior in organisms, why might not anything—trees, clouds, or the moon—also prove to have other behavior at its command?

Uncertainty about what is alive, then, is caused in part by natural deception. A broader and more complex cause of uncertainty contributes to this: some features typical of living things, such as motion, unpredictability, generation of heat, and growth, occur also in some nonliving ones, such as fire, wind, rivers, and crystals. Such features produce an apparent overlap with living things, independent of deception. Categorical perception often groups things and events having such features with the living.

In consequence, adults as well as children frequently see objects as animate or semianimate. Some simply equate motion with life. Thomas Hobbes, for example, writes that "life is but a motion of limbs"[58] and even that automata have a man-made life. L. B. Brown and R. H. Thouless find that college and university students equate "living" with "active" and "moving," and see objects as conscious.[59] Unlike most psychologists writing on animism, Brown and Thouless point out that educated adults often act as though inanimate objects were alive. Brown and Thouless suggest that biological measures of life such as reproduction and metabolism are not the only criteria possible and note that even students with biological training have animistic ideas. They also suggest that a key aspect of what Piaget and most others call animism in children is simply uncertainty about how the term "alive" is to be used.

Perception of wildfire supplies a striking example of adult animism. When National Public Radio interviewed workers fighting massive forest fires in the western United States in 1989, the firefighters said the fires were "devious," "cunning," or "lying in wait" and, when winds died during the night, were "resting up." Several years earlier, a national newspaper quoted firefighters on a major fire in Montana. Their field commander called the fire "one big dude."[60] Another spokesman said, "I swear these fires lay down at night or in a rain and they plan what to do." A firefighter extinguishing part of the fire concealed underground cried, "Gotcha!" The reporter himself credits the fire with metabolism and intention: it "developed its own feeding system, sucking air in from behind, heating it and blasting it out the front to preheat the woods ahead." None of these people probably would maintain that the fire truly is alive; yet all clearly at some level thought so.[61]

Even biologists have trouble deciding what is alive. "Life" is in important ways continuous with other phenomena rather than having clear boundaries and has many competing definitions.[62] The problem is old. Aristotle remarks, "nature proceeds little by little from inanimate things to living creatures in such a way that we are unable, in the continuous sequence, to determine the boundary line."[63] In the twentieth century, viruses have seemed a borderline case and, for some biologists, supernatural forces are another. James Lovelock thinks one common biological notion of life, as an open system that maintains itself by extracting energy from its environment, would apply equally to eddies in a stream, to hurricanes, and to flames.[64] Toulmin cites a biologist who says that "biologists no longer study life today. They no longer attempt to define it."[65] Thomas Sebeok writes that there "may not be an absolutely rigorous distinction between inanimate matter and matter in a living state."[66] Other writers have similar views.[67]

Small wonder, then, that children and laymen are not sure what is alive and what is not. In light of the natural deceit that disguises the animate as the inanimate and of the varied incidental continuities that blur their edges, an account of animism needs no special appeal to irrationality, projection, or childish confusion. We should expect to find animism not only among the "primitives" and children to whom it usually is attributed, nor only among birds, bobcats, coyotes, chimpanzees, runners, and university students, but throughout the sentient world. We should expect it not as an anomaly but as an inevitable result of normal perceptual uncertainty and of good perceptual strategy.

Only in hindsight does one see animism for what it is: a mistake of overinterpretation. Even good strategies sometimes fail, though, and risking overinterpretation by betting on the most significant possibility is no mistake.

As we cannot ask animals what they see (with the partial exception of signing with apes) and as ethologists and comparative psychologists have not investigated animism, evidence for animism in animals other than ourselves is patchy. For humans, however, a survey even of a few societies reveals animism among thinkers in many fields. These thinkers are neither childish nor especially confused. Since animism usually is attributed to simple societies, I shall concentrate on a few literate ones, primarily in the West.

Because many of my examples are from philosophers, writers, and painters, the reader may object that such examples are calculated metaphor or analogy and thus different from naive perception and representation. That is, these people may exploit something in their audience rather than express their own perceptions. Hence their animism would be inventive, not primitive. But this objection draws too great a distinction between perception and representation, and between the thought processes of creative people and those of others. If perception is interpretation and interpretation is the fitting of data to models, then representation, in the form of models, is intrinsic to perception. Perception and representation interact as a partially closed loop; the world for everyone rests on category, guess, and metaphor, most of which escapes criticism. Self-conscious animism still stems from an unconscious source. Artists may deliberately elaborate and use it, but first they experience it. They experience it in the same way as do the rest of us: a largely unconscious scanning with models for form. Thus although artistic animism may end in calculation, it begins in innocence.

Animism in Western culture appears long before writing and continues to the present in literature, philosophy, art, and science. The earliest suggestions are in the cave art of France and Spain, where animals often seem to emerge from preexisting stone contours that painters evidently saw as animals.[68] Gombrich suggests that "bulls and horses were first 'discovered' in these mysterious haunts before they were fixed and made visible to others by means of colored earth."[69] He, too, notes that real animals in their environments are hard to see: "Perhaps the conditions of their lives encouraged the early hunters to look for animal shapes . . . to scan the vague forms of patches and shadows for the revelation of a bison, much as the hunter must scan the dusky plains for the outline of the hoped-for prey."[70]

Much later, European myths clearly reflect an animated universe. In these myths the world originates, for example, either by organic growth (being born, as are animals, or germinating, as do seeds) or by being made, as by an artisan. These two alternatives, corresponding to Piaget's animism and artificialism, are perhaps root metaphors of creation everywhere.[71] Northrop Frye similarly sees artificialism and animism as the two possibilities for creation stories.[72] In any case, animism is ubiquitous in mythology; but it does not end there.

It continues, for example in Greek cosmology, even when that cosmology becomes more philosophic than religious. From the prephilosophic period, to the pre-Socratics, to Plato and Aristotle, Greek cosmologists regarded the primary substance of things as alive and the world as a living organism.[73] Surviving pre-Socratic writings are fragmentary, but according to Aristotle, Thales held that "all things are full of gods" and that magnets and amber have soul.[74] Anaximander and Anaximenes, like other pre-Socratics, evidently saw the entire world as an organism. Heraclitus saw fire as alive, as the stuff of human souls, and as interacting as an equal with earth, water, and other (for moderns) inanimate materials.[75] Early Pythagorean cosmogony pictured the original "one" as a seed and as beginning life by inhaling, as does an animal.[76] Many classical thinkers understood the joining of various substances as the result of sexual attraction.

Similar views continue in Plato, for whom both the cosmos as a whole and individual components, such as sun, stars, and planets, are living beings with souls and wills that are responsible for their motions. For Aristotle, similarly, the Unmoved Mover is alive and so are the heavenly bodies, the earth, and even the wind. Explaining changes in the relation of sea and land, he says, "the interior of the earth, like the bodies of plants and animals, has a prime and an old age."[77]

A few centuries later, Roman philosophers including Lucretius and Pliny attributed chance images of people and animals in rocks and clouds to the "generative powers of Nature."[78] Pliny also described artists deliberately creating chance images by flinging a paint-laden sponge at a panel. He attributed the result to *fortuna* as an animate and even personal force. To the mute animism of cave art, Pliny and Lucretius thus added an explicit claim that some concealed life produces spontaneous images of itself.

Though perhaps somewhat diminished by Christianity, animism has continued throughout Western culture. John Donne, for example, still could write, "Yea plants, yea stones, detest / And love."[79] Although animism in science has been weakened by mechanistic models since Isaac

Newton, even some scientists, philosophers of science, and mathematicians are animists.[80] The astronomer Johannes Kepler and the physicist Gustav Fechner[81] regarded planets and stars as animate. Sir Arthur Eddington said an electron "would not know how large it ought to be unless there existed independent lengths for it to measure itself against."[82] Teilhard de Chardin thought[83] consciousness is spread throughout the cosmos and cited J.B.S. Haldane, who said, "We do not find obvious evidence of life or mind in so-called inanimate matter . . . but if the scientific point of view is correct, we shall ultimately find them, at least in rudimentary forms, all through the universe."[84] Brown and Thouless comment that if these thinkers are animistic, animism must be "less irrational than commonly supposed."

Similar thinkers include Leonardo, who compared, for example, the circulation of water in the world to that of blood in animals:

> The waters return with constant motion from the lowest depths of the sea to the utmost height of the mountains, not obeying [gravity] . . . they resemble the blood of animated beings which always moves from the sea of the heart and flows toward the top of the head; and here it may burst a vein, as the blood rises from below to the level of the burst vein. When the water rushes out from the burst vein in the earth, it . . . always seeks low places.[85]

Similarly, Hegel regarded the entire cosmos as an organism; Eliade saw the "world as a living totality, periodically regenerating itself and, because of this regeneration, continually fruitful, rich and inexhaustible";[86] and Lovelock, author of the Gaia hypothesis,[87] sees the earth as an organism.

Animism appears in the social sciences as well, in the notion that states or societies have lives of their own. This notion arose in the West at least as early as Plato, in the *Timaeus*. Major proponents in modern times are Spencer, Durkheim, and Radcliffe-Brown, who with their followers have influenced social thought for most of the twentieth century. As functionalists, they see society as an organism whose features may be understood by the contribution they make to the life of the whole. They have counterparts further east. Lenin writes that society is not a "simple, mechanical aggregate [but] a social organism," and a Soviet sociologist, Viktor Afanasyev, writes that a society is a set of "organically interrelated processes and events [and a] dynamic and self-regulating system."[88]

The reader may object that whereas animism attributes life to the inanimate, the animism I see in functionalists attributes life only to a collection of living people. One might similarly call a Portugese man-of-war or a coral an organism. But biologists identify men-of-war and corals as colonies, not organisms. In contrast to these visible, coherent colonies, a society is an abstraction, though one always in danger of reification.[89] Whereas one can at least see a man-of-war, no one has seen a society. It is no more an organism than is a board of trustees.[90]

The link between functionalism and animism appears primitive. Piaget reports that the youngest children with whom he worked, for example, find life and function synonymous.[91] At least children between the ages of three and five think anything serving a human purpose is alive. Although functionalists are the most insistent of social scientists on being scientific, then, they also are the most animistic.

Animism also runs throughout Western literature. Although it exists in every period, its zenith occurs in English Romanticism, which makes the whole sensory world alive, sentient, and capable of communication. Motion again especially suggests life. Everything also participates in a larger sentient being which unites the universe as a single living entity. William Wordsworth, for example, imagines a "soul animating and informing all nature."[92]

As a movement, English Romanticism is only the most noted case of literary European animism, and it stands out largely as a reaction to Newtonian mechanism. Samuel Coleridge, for example, rejects "Newton and the other materialists," and Wordsworth rejects a "universe of death."[93] The Newtonian universe they attack is dualistic, divided between inanimate matter and an immaterial spirit shared only by men and a distant transcendent God. In this extreme dualism (first promulgated by Descartes), spirit alone is sentient, and not only sticks and stones but even nonhuman animals lack spirit and hence sensation and awareness. They are mere automata.

Newton makes the world a mechanism set in motion and left to run its course by an uninvolved God. In Newton's First Law of Motion, for example, "A body must continue in its state of rest or uniform motion in a straight line, unless acted upon by some external force." Here matter is inert, with "nothing in common with either life or mind. The material universe [is] a collection of bodies colliding like billiard balls."[94] As this mechanistic universe is the product of God, it still can be beautiful as an artifact—the common comparison is to a watch—and an object of respect. But it can hardly be an object of love. It is well ordered but largely uninhabited.

Newton's view spread rapidly in the eighteenth century, in part because the spread of industrialism showed the power of mechanical models and created a milieu to which they were central. Nonetheless, animism remained prominent in eighteenth-century literature, and by the turn of the century it was resurgent both in Britain and on the continent. The resurgence may have owed something to scientific advances for which Newtonian mechanics could not account, since "growth, reproduction, crystalline structure, chemical action, and electricity . . . seemed to contradict the assumption that matter was inert."[95] The Scottish philosopher Dugald Stewart wrote, for example, that whether we look to the "anatomy and physiology of animals, to the growth of vegetables, to the chemical attractions and repulsions, or to the motions of the heavenly bodies: we continually perceive the effect of powers that cannot belong to matter."[96] Scientists as well were animists, including the biologist Erasmus Darwin, the geologist James Hutton, and the chemist and Unitarian leader Joseph Priestley.

On the continent, the encyclopedist Denis Diderot imagined that "the world, like a huge animal, has a soul [which] may be an infinite system of perceptions" extending throughout matter: "From the elephant to the flea, from the flea to the living, sensitive molecule there is not a point in all nature which does not suffer and rejoice."[97] Matter was not only alive but also purposive; as Diderot's contemporary, J.B.R. Robinet, wrote, "All matter is organic, living and animal . . . This invisible world [upon which matter is based] is the aggregate of all the forces which continually strive to ameliorate their existence . . . "[98] Similar animism existed in Germany, again most clearly among the Romantics, and elsewhere in Europe. Despite Descartes and Newton, then, many Europeans continued to think "all matter was living, organic, and animal, that all natural objects, as organized forms of matter, had their own life and sensibility, and that the whole organization of the natural world was capable of intelligent purpose."[99]

The most striking animist is a Victorian, Charles Dickens. Both as narrator and through his leading characters, Dickens finds animal form, motion, and volition everywhere.[100] Among artifacts, he most animates houses, furniture, clothing, and portraits; but no object is too large or too small. Houses often are not only alive but also human. One "looked as if it were nodding in its sleep . . . The bricks of which it was built had originally been a deep dark red, but had grown yellow and discoloured like an old man's skin; the sturdy timbers had decayed like teeth."[101] Another "was leaning forward, trying to see who was passing on the narrow pavement below,"[102] and another "had it in its mind to slide down sideways; it had been propped up, however, and was leaning on some half-dozen gigantic crutches."[103]

All that moves—trains, pumps, door knockers, clocks—is especially alive. Locomotives stand "bubbling and trembling there, making the walls quake, as if they were dilating with the secret knowledge of great powers yet unsuspected in them, and strong purposes yet unachieved."[104] A locomotive about to run someone over has "red eyes, bleared and dim." The piston of a factory steam engine works "monstrously up and down, like the head of an elephant in a state of melancholy madness."[105] A handbag closes "like a bite"[106] and hats fall off pegs maliciously. Pens start to "become perversely animated, and to go wrong and crooked, and to stop and splash, and sidle into corners like a saddle-donkey."[107]

Motion is not necessary to animacy. Armchairs "looked uneasy in their minds, cocked their arms suspiciously and timidly, and kept on their guard. Others were fantastically grim and gaunt, as having drawn themselves up to their utmost height and put on their fiercest looks to stare all comers out of countenance."[108] Bottles have "necks like so many storks, and others [have] square Dutch-built bodies and short apoplectic throats."[109] Signboards grin and clothes converse.

The natural elements also are alive. The wind, rivers, sea, fire, and even fallen leaves have both movement and intention: "It was small tyranny for a respectable wind to go wreaking its vengeance on such poor creatures as the fallen leaves, but . . . [it] did so disperse and scatter them that they fled away, pell-mell . . . taking frantic flights into the air, and playing all manner of extraordinary gambols in the extremity of their distress."[110] Even the landscape has feelings, as when, seen through a cold window, "the colder landscape shudders in the wind."[111]

Dickens animates not only what can be seen or heard but also ideas and concepts: times of day, seasons of the year, time itself, hunger, poverty, and others. Time follows one character with "watching and attentive eyes"[112] and, "burrowing like a mole below the ground,"[113] kills another. Night has "black and dismal looks,"[114] and a winter day's "white face . . . came sluggishly on, veiled in a frosty mist."[115]

Like other sources considered so far, Dickens supports neither Tylor nor Piaget on the causes of animism. He is not especially concerned with spirit beings, although his work contains some. Nor is he confused and unable to distinguish the workings of his own mind from the workings of nature. Dickens also undercuts the wishful-thinking view of animism, as his objects often are ominous, malicious, or melancholy.

Although Dickens is the most diverse and persistent Western literary animist, he is in good company. Few writers, and few people, do not animate their environments. The Romantics and Dickens do it with special fervor, but animism is not tied to any period, genre, or style. It permeates writing just as it does perception. Three more recent examples complete our literary survey. The first is from a bicycling magazine: "Mountain bikes can't talk, but they can still let you know when something is going wrong. A dry chain squeaks for attention. Under-inflated tires roar with disapproval. Toed-out brake pads squeal with distress. And your bottom bracket clicks out its displeasure like a metronome."[116] The second, from *The New York Times,* says the wings of a B-52 bomber "flap slowly as the prehistoric creature bounds down the runway, struggling to fly."[117] The third is from T. S. Eliot:

> The yellow fog that rubs its back upon the window panes,
> The yellow smoke that rubs its muzzle on the window panes,
> Licked its tongue into the corners of the evening,
> Lingered upon the pools that stand in drains,
> Let fall upon its back the soot that falls from chimneys,
> Slipped by the terrace, made a sudden leap,
> And seeing that it was a soft October night
> Curled once about the house and fell asleep.[118]

From popular journalism to belles lettres and from the Greeks to the twentieth century, Western writers animate the world. Neither monotheism nor rationalism nor science—all thought antithetical to animism and all prominent in Western culture—have suppressed Western animism.

Turning briefly to a literate non-Western culture, that of China, we find a familiar view. The *Tao te Ching*, for example, describes the Tao or "Way" of the universe in animistic and sometimes anthropomorphic terms. The Tao "does not strive" yet is the "mother of all things" and has a "Breath," *ch'i*, that affects all things through inhalation and exhalation. Ch'i causes, among other effects, rain, wind, sunlight, heat, and cold, which are still known in modern China as the *wu ch'i* or "five breaths."[119] The *I Ching* similarly identifies wind as ch'i and as a "force of Heaven visibly stirring life."[120] *Yin* and *yang* categorize virtually everything as male, female, or some combination. A thousand years later, the classic of art theory, the *Mustard Seed Garden Manual of Painting*, represents rocks as living beings and finds social relations among mountains and trees. A modern commentator says the Chinese always have regarded rocks as the "bone structure of the earth, combining with water, which . . . represents the lifeblood [of the earth] as a living organism."[121]

Animism, then, is not peculiar to tribal or nonliterate culture, as often thought, but is common also in literate Europe and East Asia. And although literate expressions of animism may be self-conscious, they originate in the unconscious interpretive processes shared by all perception.

Last, a potpourri of idioms and practices from daily life in the contemporary United States suggests that animism is as diverse and pervasive as ever. Farmers and gardeners speak of what plants "like" and "do not like" among conditions of soil, water, and sunlight. Both plants and soil may be "thirsty" and too much fertilizer will "shock" a plant. Mechanics say an engine is "cranky" and not uncommonly claim machinery, tools, and materials are perverse and uncooperative. Drivers deny air to engines by means of a "choke." A pilot landing an airplane by feeling its responses to the controls may "play it like a fish," and Amelia Earhart once, asked about the reliability of her airplane, said, "even the finest engines can get indigestion." Ships, cars, and aircraft have gender. Wires carrying electrical current are "live."

More subtly, vehicles, including ships, cars, and aircraft, and to some degree houses, are bilaterally symmetrical, just as are animals. The practical requirements of mobility in two and three dimensions perhaps favor symmetry in vehicles, as in animals; but our unconscious animism probably is at least as important a cause. We name cars for mustangs, stingrays, impalas, rabbits, and jaguars, and the first form of Volkswagen imported into the United States became a "bug" or "beetle." Civilian airplanes have been cubs, pups, swifts, storks, and moths, while military planes have been mosquitoes, mustangs, wildcats, bear cats, cougars, and panthers. Cartoons of cars turn headlights into eyes and radiator grills into mouths. An airline company not long ago painted smiles on its airplanes. Fighter planes may get toothy jaws painted under their "noses." Elsewhere, fishermen paint eyes on the bows of their boats to help them avoid reefs. Thus our artifacts as well as our verbal expressions suggest our animism.

Animism, then, seems intrinsic to perception. It is grounded in a sound perceptual strategy: to discover as much significance as possible by interpreting things and events with the most significant model. Significance in turn depends upon organization, and an organism typically is more significant than is inorganic matter. An account of animism thus needs no speculation about death and dreams, no inability to tell self from other, no wish fulfillment, and no peculiar irrationality. Instead, animism is a thread of interpretation that necessarily runs throughout perception. The mistake embodied in animism—a mistake we can discover only after the fact—is the price of our need to discover living organisms. It is a cost occasionally incurred by any animal that perceives.

3

The Origin of Anthropomorphism

In order to explain a fact as general as [religion] by an illusion, it would be necessary that the illusion invoked . . . have causes of an equal generality.

Emile Durkheim, *The Elementary Forms of the Religious Life*

We find human faces in the moon, armies in the clouds.

David Hume, *The Natural History of Religion*

Faces and other human forms seem to pop out at us on all sides. Chance images in clouds, in landforms, and in ink blots present eyes, profiles, or whole figures. Voices murmur or whisper in wind and waves. We see the world not only as alive but also as humanlike. Anthropomorphism pervades our thought and action. No one, however, has adequately explained it.

Philosophers have mentioned anthropomorphism for over two thousand years. Theologians have done so almost as long, and scientists have done so since Francis Bacon, nearly five centuries ago. Most of these, and now even news commentators, caution against it. Still, not only has no good explanation been given for it but no sustained attempt at one has even been made.[1]

My explanation of anthropomorphism closely resembles that for animism. Both phenomena stem from the search for organization and significance, and both consist in overestimating them. Scanning the world for what most concerns us—living things and especially humans—we find many apparent cases. Some of these prove illusory. When they do, we are animating (attributing life to the nonliving) or anthropomorphizing (attributing human characteristics to the nonhuman). Central among human characteristics is symbolic interaction. Animism and anthropomorphism are on a continuum and may coexist: in verbally urging a balky computer, we both animate (give it life) and anthropomorphize (give it language).

My account of anthropomorphism supplies the "causes of an equal generality" that Durkheim, in the epigraph above, says would be necessary to explain religion as an illusion. These general causes are our quest for pattern and meaning and our strategy of looking for them at the highest level.

Philosophers agree that anthropomorphism is widespread in thought, but otherwise on this subject they differ. The first to mention it is the pre-Socratic Xenophanes, who says that if lions and horses could paint they would show their gods as lions and horses, just as humans show their gods as humans. Bacon notes that human understanding relies on causes that "have relation clearly to the nature of man rather than to the nature of the universe,"[2] and Spinoza says we comprehensively imagine the world as humanlike.[3] Hume writes of a "universal tendency among mankind to conceive all things like themselves,"[4] and Goethe says humans "*never* know how anthropomorphizing they are."[5] Nietzsche writes that even the scientist looks

> at bottom, only for metamorphoses of the world in man; he wrestles for an understanding of the world as a human-like thing and . . . regards the whole world as connected to man, as an infinitely broken echo of an original sound, that of man; as the manifold copy of an original picture, that of man.[6]

Feuerbach gives the most sustained treatment, but only of anthropomorphism in religion.[7] His view of religion as wish-fulfilling, illusory anthropomorphism is reversed by Frederick Ferré, who finds religious anthropomorphism appropriate and valid.[8]

Natural scientists, historians of science, psychologists, and ethnographers often warn against anthropomorphism but again offer no sustained theory. The psychologist Théodule Ribot thinks it pervasive and mysterious: "In consequence of a well-known though inexplicable instinctive tendency, man attributes purposes, will and causality similar to his own to all that acts and reacts around him."[9] Levi-Strauss, Horton, and other anthropologists write that it is cross-cultural, as do Lange and Freud. Other writers mention it in diverse areas.[10] Once more, however, no one gives an extended account.

Theologians take anthropomorphism most seriously, as it threatens their credibility most.[11] Almost all agree, together with philosophers of religion and comparative religionists, that it is universal and inevitable in religion. S.G.F. Brandon, for example, says anthropomorphism in religion "*inevitably* follows from the fact that man can conceive of deity only in terms of his own mental categories."[12] Thomas Aquinas admits Christian belief anthropomorphizes, though he thinks this reasonable, and Paul

Tillich complains that the popular God is a "heavenly, completely perfect person who resides above the world."[13] Tillich struggles to avoid anthropomorphism, but even other theologians find the result inscrutable. Although many religionists clearly see the anthropomorphism of religion, even they explain only why it is inevitable in religion and do not explain anthropomorphism in general.

Other scholars in varied disciplines[14] continue to comment on anthropomorphism, but neither at length nor cross-culturally. This raises the question of why a phenomenon of thought so widely noted should be so briefly treated. Three factors contribute to this disparity between acknowledgment and analysis. First, most writers see anthropomorphism as a trivial mistake with a pair of standard explanations: the easiest accounts of the world are those from the most familiar models, ourselves; and we find it comforting to humanize the world. Second, both secular rationalists and theologians find anthropomorphism embarrassing. Secular thinkers, especially scientists, see it as an unfortunate and persistent flaw in human thought. Theologians see it as a discomfiting sign that conceptions of God may be limited by, or even founded on, conceptions of ourselves. Third, many writers see anthropomorphism as an aberration with little relation to other perception and representation. If it is aberrant, understanding it might produce nothing broader and so would be of doubtful value. Anthropomorphism then is something simply to be detected and rooted out, ad hoc.

None of these reasons for the scant analysis of anthropomorphism, however, withstands scrutiny. First, the standard explanations of anthropomorphism as comforting and familiar are inadequate, because anthropomorphism often is far from comforting and because our self-understandings themselves are problematic, not self-evident.

Second, anthropomorphism is neither peculiar nor unreasonable. Rather, it is a plausible, though in hindsight mistaken, interpretation of things and events. It is inevitable in ordinary perception and cognition: at once spontaneous, reasonable, and deeply rooted. Far from irrational or nonempirical, using a humanlike model frequently is justified—that is, when a human in fact proves involved in the thing or event interpreted. Whether a human or something humanlike is involved, however, often becomes clear only after the fact. In this regard, anthropomorphic perceptions are like other perceptions. They are based in pattern discovery, in the effort after meaning, and in analogy and metaphor. When successful, humanlike models produce broad coherence and great significance. To say that a given perception or representation is anthropomorphic is to say that it claims more organization than actually is present, not that the underlying interpretive process is either aberrant or flawed.

Third and last, anthropomorphism is normal, not aberrant, because it results from a strategy universal in human perception. Hence it helps us understand perceptual and cognitive phenomena including religion. Most theologians say it is universal in religion and a few anthropologists and others say it is crucial there.[15] Nonetheless, prevailing theorists of religion pay it little attention. Their inattention reflects the lack both of an adequate theory of anthropomorphism and of an appreciation of its extent in our thought and action.

I shall call the standard explanations of anthropomorphism the "familiarity" and "comfort" accounts. The familiarity account holds that in order to explain the nonhuman world, we rely on our understandings of ourselves because these are easiest or most reliable. The comfort, or wish fulfillment, account holds that we feel better if we can see the nonhuman world as like ourselves. Each has several versions.

The familiarity account has two chief versions, which I shall call "confusion" and "analogy." These are on a continuum. They share the notion that anthropomorphism consists in extending models of what we know to what we do not know. They differ in that the confusion version assumes this extension is involuntary, unconscious, and indiscriminate, while the analogy version assumes it is voluntary, conscious, and discriminating.

We have already met the confusion version in Freud and Piaget as an explanation of animism. The confusion they posit mixes entities and processes that are internal, subjective, and mental with ones that are external, objective, and physical. Freud and Piaget think this confusion typical of children and of people in simple or primitive societies. Such people supposedly cannot distinguish their minds from events in the external world and therefore indiscriminately attribute their own thoughts and feelings to the world around them. They attribute to the world not only life but also such human capacities and activities as social relations and speech. Predecessors of Freud and Piaget in this view include Bacon and Spinoza,[16] Vico, Comte, and Feuerbach. Successors include a number of developmental psychologists and Leslie White, an anthropologist. Nietzsche also has a confusion view, but a more radical one.

Vico thinks religion originates in the involuntary and unselfconscious anthropomorphism of the first humans. These primitives had no language. They were imaginative, not rational, and communicated by signs. They attributed their own emotions, motives, and behavior, including making signs, to nature. Vico's primitives resemble Goodall's wild chimpanzees especially in their limited grasp of natural phenomena such as storms. They were robust giants, "destitute of any human custom and deprived of any human speech, and so in a state of wild animals." Dispersed through the forest, they were

> frightened and astonished by the great effect whose cause they did not know, and raised their eyes and became aware of the sky. And because in such a case the nature of the human mind leads it to attribute its own nature to the effect, and because in that state their nature was that of men all robust bodily strength, who expressed their very violent passions by shouting and grum-

bling, they pictured the sky to themselves as a great animated body . . . who meant to tell them something by the hiss of his bolts and the clap of his thunder.[17]

Vico says children see the world similarly: they typically "take inanimate things in their hands and talk to them in play as if they were living persons."[18] Thus both children and the earliest humans extend life and voice to the world.

Comte as well sees animism and anthropomorphism as innate, especially in children. As with Vico, they are the root of religion and stem from a confusion of one's self with the world. The earliest religion, fetishism, is "that tendency of our nature by which man conceives of all external bodies as animated by a life analogous to his own, with differences of mere intensity."[19] Early religion thus assumes "external bodies, even the most inert, to be animated by passion and will, more or less analogous to the personal impressions of the spectator."[20] For Comte as for Freud, people anthropomorphize because of their infantile experience of centrality and omnipotence.[21] Everyone imagines himself "in all respects, the center of the natural system, and consequently endowed with an indefinite control over phenomena. This . . . results from . . . the natural tendency which disposes men in general to form exaggerated ideas of their own importance and power."[22] Thus, anthropomorphism again stems from a failure to draw a line between inner and outer, self and not-self.

Feuerbach carries the idea further in the most sustained argument yet that religion is anthropomorphism. He counters Schleiermacher's attempt to found knowledge of God in immediate experience. Feuerbach agrees with Schleiermacher that God exists in human experience, but adds that he exists *only* there. God is nothing but man's experience of himself and represents the "inner nature of man as an objective external being." Religious thought is the "immediate, involuntary, unconscious contemplation of the human nature as another, distinct nature."[23] In a term popular in later psychology, God is a "projection." As for Vico and Comte, the projection is unconscious and merges the subjective and objective worlds.

Feuerbach's anthropomorphism, however, differs somewhat from those of Vico and Comte. For Feuerbach, it has three causes. As do his predecessors, he believes that one cause is cognitive confusion. Anthropomorphism and hence religion are simple, childish mistakes: "Religion is nothing else than man's primitive, and therefore childish, popular, but prejudiced, unemancipated consciousness of himself and of nature."[24] Second, anthropomorphism is wishful thinking, motivated by desire: "God springs out of the feeling of want; what man is in need of . . . that is God." Third, religious anthropomorphism is a means, albeit unwitting, of attaining self-consciousness. Humans were unable to conceive of themselves clearly until they had created their image outside themselves. This projection is the "original mode in which man becomes objective to himself."[25] It makes self-scrutiny possible. "Man, by means of the imagination, involuntarily contemplates his inner nature; he represents it as out of himself." Thus "religion is the first form of self-consciousness."[26] Paradoxically, that self-consciousness is disguised. It is a means to know ourselves, without our knowing the means.

In identifying religion as human self-consciousness, Feuerbach is a characteristically nineteenth-century introspectionist. Though he says people's attitudes toward other people are part of their religious awareness, his introspection still is individualistic. In this he accepts Schleiermacher's emphasis on inward experience. By saying that God is an externalized reification of individual consciousness, Feuerbach complements Durkheim, who says God is an externalized, collective reification of society.[27]

The fourth theorist of anthropomorphism as confusion is White, who, with Horton, is one of the few anthropologists to see anthropomorphism as central in religion. For White, as for Vico and Comte, animism and anthropomorphism both are confusions. White sees them even more definitely as mistakes:

> there have been, and logically can be, only two major types of philosophy: one in which the external world is interpreted in terms of the human ego; the other in which it is explained in terms of *itself*. In the first type, man unconsciously projects himself into the external world, describing and interpreting it in terms of his own psychic processes. The whole world is thus made alive and peopled with spirits who feel and behave as men do.[28]

Again as for Vico and Comte, these confusions are typical of primitive culture and stem from failure to distinguish self from other: "In the beginning of human history, man's philosophies were wholly animistic; he diffused his psyche throughout the cosmos; he confused the self with the not-self at almost every point."[29]

White thinks the confusion persists in varying degrees. For example, progress is greater in the natural sciences than in the social sciences because of the "varying ability of mankind to distinguish between the self and the not-self in various sectors of experience."[30] That is, we distinguish self and not-self better in physics than in psychology and therefore advance faster in physics.

Unlike Feuerbach, White finds no value in anthropomorphism or its relatives: "animistic, anthropomorphic and supernaturalistic philosophies were worse than worthless, for false knowledge is often worse than none at all." These philosophies answer our wishes, but at great cost: "they sustained man with illusions [but] as explanatory techniques, primitive philosophies were a total loss."[31] Though comforting, they have caused tragedies such as the countless deaths of alleged witches and heretics. White, then, refers to wish fulfillment but emphasizes confusion.

The most sophisticated and radical version of the confusion view of anthropomorphism is that of the philosopher F. A. Lange[32] and his better-known student, Nietzsche.[33] The term confusion may not even be appropriate, since Lange and Nietzsche see no possibility of *not* anthropomorphizing. In their view, it is not that we mix human perspectives with independent ones but that independent perspectives are inaccessible.[34] Much as Kant says that the categories of space and time are built into our perceptual apparatus, which then attributes them to the world, Lange and Nietzsche say the whole human world is the product of our sensory organization.[35] Our best efforts cannot extricate us: "We are like spiders in our own webs, and, whatever we may catch in them, it will only be something that our web is capable of catching."[36]

According to Nietzsche, our senses do not receive information passively, but shape, select, and simplify it according to our interests. Hence the only world we can apprehend or even imagine corresponds to our preoccupations. We must obtain food and shelter and establish and maintain social relationships. Our perceptions are geared to these goals. Neither science nor self-perception evades selectivity and bias. Even notions of force, causality, attraction, and repulsion are grounded in notions about ourselves, as agents with wills. We experience ourselves as acting for reasons and as feeling attracted and repelled. Scientific versions of force and causality are projections of these experiences.

Our ideas of ourselves, Nietzsche holds, are no more accurate, direct, or unbiased than our ideas of the nonhuman world. Instead, they are an inner phenomenology, equally constrained by unconscious selection: "everything of which we become conscious is arranged, simplified, schematized, interpreted through and through."[37] Hence our understandings of the nonhuman world, founded on our perceptions of ourselves and our social relations, are shaped and simplified by several layers of unconscious and inaccessible schemas, filters, and predispositions.[38] The very idea of truth is a human social construction, a "mobile army of metaphors, metonyms, anthropomorphisms; in short a collection of human relations that have been poetically and rhetorically elevated, transformed and decorated, and that after long usage appear to a people firm, canonical and binding."[39] Thus all human cognition anthropomorphizes.

In contrast, the analogy version of the familiarity theory makes using ourselves and other people as models a reasonable, limited extension of what is familiar to what is not. Whereas in the confusion view we mix self and not-self wholesale, in the analogy view we are selective. Chief advocates of this second view are Fontenelle, Hume, and Horton.

Fontenelle finds analogy in classical mythology, where explanations of unfamiliar phenomena always are copied from familiar ones.[40] A river, for example, may come from a god pouring water from a pitcher.[41] Storms, tides, and lightning make people imagine powerful humanlike agents behind these spectacular effects. Such ideas are not peculiar but are typical of all thought, including that of science: "we explain unknown natural things by those which we have before our eyes, and . . . carry over to natural science those things furnished us by experience."[42] Analogy is the basis of mythology and science alike.

Hume gives the classic version of anthropomorphism as analogy in his *Natural History of Religion*. He situates us in the indeterminacy of perception, with our resulting insecurity and our inability to predict or control our circumstances:

> We are placed in this world, as in a great theatre, where the true springs and causes of every event are entirely concealed from us; nor have we either sufficient wisdom to foresee, or power to prevent those ills, with which we are continually threatened. We hang in perpetual suspense between life and death, health and sickness, plenty and want, which are distributed amongst the human species by secret and unknown causes, whose operation is oft unexpected, and always unaccountable.[43]

The result of this perceptual uncertainty and physical insecurity is that we are always trying to understand our situation better, through our imagination: "These *unknown causes*, then, become the constant object of our hope and fear; and while the passions are kept in perpetual alarm by an anxious expectation of the events, the imagination is equally employed in forming ideas of those powers, on which we have so entire a dependence." If only we could look closely enough at our situation, we would find ourselves in a mechanistic, orderly universe in which "by a regular and constant machinery, all the events are produced, about which [we] are so much concerned." Most people, however, cannot look so closely. They can only think about the "*unknown causes* in a general and confused manner; though their imagination, perpetually employed on the same subject, must labour to form some particular and distinct idea of them."

In this situation, we would have to abandon our attempt to understand if we did not tend toward a system of interpretation that does satisfy us:

> There is an universal tendency among mankind to conceive all beings like themselves, and to transfer to every object, those qualities, with which they are familiarly acquainted, and of which they are intimately conscious. We find human faces in the moon, armies in the clouds; and by a natural propensity, if not corrected by experience and reflection, ascribe malice or good-will to every thing, that hurts or pleases us. Hence . . . trees, mountains and streams are personified, and the inanimate parts of nature acquire sentiment and passion.

We may not mean all our personifications literally, but even when we do not, they "prove a certain tendency in the imagination, without which they could neither be beautiful nor natural."

Moreover, religious anthropomorphism often *is* literal. People believe in invisible but otherwise humanlike gods in each grove and field. Even when we think of an all-powerful God, we transfer to him "human passions and infirmities [and] represent him as a jealous and revengeful, capricious and partial, and, in short, a wicked and foolish man, in every respect but his superior power and authority."

Anthropomorphism is not limited to religion or to unreflective people. Even "philosophers cannot exempt themselves from this natural frailty; but have oft ascribed . . . to inanimate matter the horror of a *vacuum,* sympathies, antipathies, and other affections of human nature." To the unknown causes in our lives, we ascribe "thought and reason and passion, and sometimes even the limbs and figures of men, in order to bring them nearer to a resemblance with ourselves."

Hume thus analyzes popular religion as anthropomorphism and describes anthropomorphism as permeating whatever evades exact understanding. The reason is not that we cannot tell self from other, but that we want *some* understanding of events around us and, failing a scientific one, fall back on one with which we are "familiarly acquainted" and "intimately conscious." Although anthropomorphism is mistaken it is not intrinsically absurd. If we look, for example, at ancient mythology with its humanlike beings we find no "monstrous" absurdity: "Where is the difficulty in conceiving, that the same powers or principles, whatever they were, which formed this visible world, men and animals, produced also a species of intelligent creatures, of more refined substance and greater authority than the rest?" No peculiarity of thought such as inability to tell self from not-self, then, marks anthropomorphism. Instead, like other analogies, it draws on what we know best.

Hume does not say why, if we know ourselves so well, we should so mistakenly use ourselves as a model. He does say we do it when we are most anxious. This observation suggests some wish fulfillment and irrationality, hinted at elsewhere. Nonetheless, Hume's dominant idea about anthropomorphism is that it is analogy and motivated by a cognitive purpose. It is not fundamentally different from other accounts and, despite being mistaken, is not clearly unreasonable. We "make ourselves the model of the whole universe"[44] and do so plausibly.

More recently, Joseph Agassi also writes that anthropomorphism is analogy but adds that it sometimes is mistaken and sometimes is not.[45] Agassi calls anthropomorphism a projection of human qualities but says that to reject it for that reason is to confuse the truth of an idea with its origin. He largely identifies anthropomorphism with animism: the "standard and most important variant of anthropomorphism is animism which sees a soul in everything in nature."

This identification implicitly makes two assumptions: that humans and only humans have souls and that animism is belief in these, rather than being the more general attribution of life to the lifeless. The first assumption contains two problems. First, it is ethnocentric, being merely one Western view. In other views, souls either do not exist or exist in loci other than humans alone. Second, if humans do not have souls, then anthropomorphism is not a projection, as Agassi admits, of actual human qualities but only of assumed human qualities. Thus this projection requires an assumption at each end of its trajectory. As to why such an uncertain projection should occur, Agassi only calls it an "inveterate tendency."

Agassi's second assumption, that animism consists in seeing a soul in everything, requires a notion of soul that is cross-cultural. As we saw with Tylor, however, no such conception seems to exist. Hence a broader notion of animism, as the attribution of life to things or events that do not have it, appears more useful. Even if life also is hard to define, at least such component notions as organization, energy, and significance explain it as a category based in strategy.

Still other versions of the analogy view of anthropomorphism focus not on the human organism as a whole, but only on the body. Leonard Barkan, for example, exploring the Western use of the body as an image of the world, writes that the "human body is both phylogenetically and ontogenetically one of the first and most basic entities the mind can grasp. In prehistory [it] is the only as well as the most obvious way of understanding a unity of diversity. Consequently, abstract unities of diversity are seen in the image of the body."[46] Barkan illustrates the pervasiveness of the body/world analogy with a broad range of examples.

The major modern writer on anthropomorphism as analogy, however, is Horton. As we saw, Horton details such similarities between science and religion, as the concerns to unify experience and to reduce apparent complexity to simplicity, apparent disorder to order, and apparent anomaly to regularity. Both science and religion do these by finding familiar principles in unfamiliar phenomena; that is, by positing analogies. Although religion has varied aims, the central aim of its analogies is the same as that of scientific analogies, namely, explanation.

The anthropomorphism Horton describes among the Kalabari draws not on subjective individual experience but on shared and codified social relationships. These are the relationships of lineages, villages, and waterways, which, when used as models of the world as a whole, yield the Kalabari ideas of ancestors, heroes, and water people. No question of any confusion of self and other arises since the source of the models already is outside the individual. Kalabari anthropomorphism thus is a rational extension of principles from known phenomena to phenomena less known.

Views of anthropomorphism as the use of the familiar to comprehend the unfamiliar, then, vary widely. They range from seeing anthropomorphism as a failure of cognition, based in an inability to distinguish self from other, to seeing it as a success at metaphoric and analogical model building, based in the pattern recognition that is a principle of science as well.

*   *   *

The idea that we anthropomorphize because it is comforting also is old
and widespread. This view is closely related to the wishful-thinking theory
of religion. Its standard form holds that discovering humanity around us
necessarily makes us feel better than not discovering humanity. It is compatible with the familiarity explanation and is present to a degree in the
writers mentioned above. Both Vico and Hume, for example, picture
anthropomorphism as arising under stress and as somehow reassuring.
For Vico, early humans were driven by terror to imagine more powerful
humans as the causes of thunder and lightning. Similarly for Hume, anxiety is the chief emotion under which we imagine hidden humanlike beings: "Apprehensions spring up with regard to futurity: And the mind,
sunk into diffidence, terror, and melancholy, has recourse to every
method of appeasing those secret intelligent powers, on whom our fortune is supposed entirely to depend."[47] In Feuerbach and in Horton's
early work, too, anthropomorphism has a wishful quality. For Feuerbach,
God is whatever humans lack. He embodies human hopes and aspirations. Similarly Horton, in an early essay,[48] sees what society provides and
what gods provide as complementary, whether this is technical help or
emotional community.

White is even more certain that "anthropomorphic philosophy" is
consoling: it is "wish and will projected from the human mind"[49] and
"sustained man with illusions [and] provided him with courage, comfort,
consolation, and confidence."[50] Confusion makes the illusion possible
but consolation motivates it. Similarly, Demetrious Loukatos thinks the
personal and animal names of coastal rocks and capes in Greece stem
from a fear of loneliness and a need for company:

> all personification imposed on any inanimate object is . . . due to man's need
> for a milieu of "human-like" beings, and to his fear of solitude. Always avoid-
> ing isolation in nature, man everywhere creates imaginary beings in the form
> of men or animals in order to populate his surroundings. It is much the same
> need that led him in ancient times to the conception of the many divinities
> who filled his solitude . . . in deserted places and on the seas, [travellers and
> navigators] personified the mountains and rocks, the islands and cliffs, putting
> themselves in relation to them.[51]

Eskimos sometimes give an explanation similar to Loukatos's, for *inuk-
shuk*, man-sized stone piles built along coastlines: these not only serve as
navigation markers but also keep travelers company. Alex Wayman,[52]
writing on the human body as microcosm, similarly suggests that people
see the macrocosm as a human body because, living in "times of hor-
rors," they want to be able to pray to it.

Freud, however, makes the comfort theory of anthropomorphism
clearest. "Humanization of nature" is the first step to religion and aims
primarily at reassurance. The common human condition is fear and suffering. Society constricts us, as do the "elements, which seem to mock

at all human control . . . and finally there is the painful riddle of death, against which no medicine has yet been found, nor probably will be. With these forces nature rises up against us, majestic, cruel and inexorable."[53] People console themselves by humanizing the world because social relations with something dangerous seem to offer control over it:

> Impersonal forces and destinies cannot be approached; they remain eternally remote. But if the elements have passions that rage as they do in our own souls, if death itself is not something spontaneous but the violent act of an evil Will, if everywhere in nature there are Beings around us of a kind that we know in our own society, then we can breathe freely, can feel at home in the uncanny. . . . Perhaps, indeed, we are not even defenceless. We can apply the same methods against these violent supermen that we employ in our own society; we can try to abjure them, to appease them, to bribe them, and, by so influencing them, we may rob them of a part of their power.[54]

The gods thus have a "threefold task: they must exorcise the terrors of nature, they must reconcile men to the cruelty of Fate, particularly as it is shown in death, and they must compensate them for the sufferings and privations"[55] of civilized life.

Are these two standard explanations of anthropomorphism, familiarity and comfort, adequate, or must a different account be given? At first they do seem plausible. On inspection, however, each encounters difficulties. Each has a little truth but neither is sufficient.

The comfort account draws its main appeal from evident human sociability. We are gregarious and mutually dependent throughout our lives. Our relationships with other people are by far our most meaningful ones, to the point that "relationship" in most contexts connotes society. Moreover, having a social relationship with some object, human or not, means being able to influence it. That is why Freud claimed that if the beings around us are like us then we can breathe freely. But beyond offering control, social relationships offer communion, as Loukatos notes in explaining anthropomorphism among ancient sailors.

Against the view that anthropomorphism is motivated by a need for company, however, I would point out that we engage in it not only when lonely but also when comfortably sociable, and further that many anthropomorphic conceptions are poor company. Against the view that it offers an apparent means to engage otherwise-uncontrollable natural phenomena, the most refractory beings we know are not inanimate or animal but human. That is why difficult materials or malfunctioning machinery often brings angry anthropomorphizing. Piaget similarly observed that children attribute humanlike life especially to difficult objects: "to explain the unforeseen resistance of some object he fails to make obey him, [the child] is compelled to regard it as living."[56] And a popular naturalist, describing a complex geological formation, draws on human contrariness:

> Klamath rocks [are] at times prankish. They like to stand on their heads and play practical jokes, pranks unappreciated by a hiker who finds a trail ending in a landslide or a roadbuilder who sees a steel culvert tipping into a gully. As with all pranksters, it is hard to get a straight story from Klamath rocks; they prefer to speak paradoxes, obscure codes, or apparent nonsense.[57]

Human uncooperativeness also underlies a distinction frequently made between magic and religion. That is, magic acts directly, without intervention by humanlike beings. Hence, if performed correctly, magic brings its result automatically and infallibly. In contrast, religion addresses a humanlike audience that may or may not respond as we desire. For an illusion of control, then, we would do better to use magic on the world than to anthropomorphize it.

The major objection to the wishful-thinking theory of religion also undermines the theory as applied to anthropomorphism: much anthropomorphism is far from comforting. That it is not comforting reflects actual human behavior, which often is threatening. Humans may be kind but they also may be cruel. Indeed, violence within our species seems more pronounced than within most others. *Homo lupus hominem:* man is a wolf to man.

Aggression also exists within other species, including those most like us. Wild chimpanzees sometimes kill other chimpanzees, and aggression occurs among other primates as well. Accordingly, their perceptions of each other are motivated not only by attraction but also by fear. Stares are threats to most monkeys and apes. Infant rhesus monkeys three weeks old already are frightened by the gaze of other monkeys.[58] Our anxieties about seeing and being seen by our fellow humans, then, parallel anxieties among our nonhuman relatives.

Instances of fright are plentiful and diverse. When the night wind slams a door in a house in which we had thought ourselves alone, or taps something against our window, we may hear it as a human but feel queasy, not comforted. Dimly sighting an overloaded garbage can in a twilit alley, we may see it as a crouching mugger and feel a jolt of fear, not a glow of sociability. A patrolling soldier hears every snapping twig, every bush rustled by the wind, as the enemy and is set on edge, not set at ease. One refugee writes of escape from Nazi Germany, "all at once the guides directed us to drop to the ground. Up on the hill an unexpected sentinel seemed to stand guard. The guides scouted around and discovered it was only a young sapling tree on the hillside."[59] A war reporter in Ethiopia writes, "At night the scrub trees assume vivid profiles, and the drivers laughingly recount how jittery Ethiopian soldiers used to waste ammunition firing at them."[60] Ancient Greek seafarers personified capes, rocks, and islands as "either friends or enemies . . . sometimes, veritable monsters to be avoided . . . any animated presence [was] acceptable, even . . . an agent of the devil"[61] Piaget says children also correlate uncertainty and humanity: "it is when some phenomenon appears doubtful, strange and above all frightening that the child credits it with a purpose."[62]

Anthropomorphism may be unfriendly in literature and art as well. An art historian, David Freedberg, says "anthropomorphization of an image makes its animate quality both more palpable and more terrifying."[63] We saw that Dickens's animism often is ominous. His anthropomorphism is equally so. Waves striking the shore produce voices foretelling the death of a character. Toys have malevolent human shapes, such as a "demoniacal Counsellor in a black gown, with an obnoxious head of hair, and a red cloth mouth, wide open, who was not to be endured."[64] Graphic artists, too, often show storms, winter, plague, death, and other phenomena as threatening persons.

Religious anthropomorphism also often is menacing. Some gods are friendly but others are not. Vishnu is balanced by Siva; Christ by Satan. Although Freud says we cannot deal with inanimate threats but *can* deal with humanlike ones, and hence imagine threats as having humanlike sources, dealing with the devil is notoriously dangerous. And although confronting something dangerous may be better than confronting nothing, as Freud claims, this leaves unclear why we should construct these particular interpretations.

The gods in general may be threatening and intractable. The God of the Old Testament is jealous and capricious. Even in recent Christian views, God may be wrathful and relations with Him uncertain.[65] Gods may be benevolent and dangerous by turns, or mostly dangerous. For modern Bolivian miners the gods are "always dangerous."[66] Minor as well as major figures are dangerous; a powerful Satan may be complemented by witches, goblins, trolls, Martians, or Sasquatch. Even writers who give a comfort account of anthropomorphic gods admit the solace they provide is mixed. Vico writes that Jove, source of lightning bolts, was not only popular and instructive but also disturbing.[67] Hume says a deity far superior to humans is apt to "sink the human mind into the lowest submission and abasement . . . mortification, penance, humility, and passive suffering."[68] Horton later gives up the comfort thesis for a cognitive one.

When not actively threatening, an anthropomorphic world still may be uncomfortable. In Donne, the "world's body becomes prey to the physical and spiritual ailments of man [and the] cosmos is saturated with feelings of man's mortality, disease, and unhappiness."[69] Anthropomorphizing the world, then, does not necessarily make it friendlier or more comfortable. Wishful thinking, at least in its usual sense—that of fantasizing, in the absence of any supporting evidence, that something is as one would have it—thus does not explain anthropomorphism.

Two variants of the comfort or wish-fulfillment theory, however, may advance the discussion. One of these pictures anthropomorphism as driven by various emotions, such as love, hatred, fear, lust, or anger, which require some object for their gratification. In this view, akin to

Freud's drive theory,[70] human action stems from a need to reduce psychological or physiological tensions. Anthropomorphism then consists in fantasizing some object, real or not, as an appropriate target on which to vent a feeling. It is a safety valve for excessive emotional pressure.

But this view of motivation credits emotions with a dubious simplicity and a dubious priority in the economy of thought and action. Emotions are not well understood. They are interpretive and complex, not primitive, and probably are learned.[71] They are not simply states of physiological arousal. Instead, as noted earlier, they involve interpretations, both of our internal conditions (for example, heart rate and blood pressure) and of external conditions (for example, something on one's path that might or might not be a bear). Moreover, they involve evaluating these conditions with regard to our purposes: "to produce an emotion out of sensory states [requires] an appraisal that those states are favorable or damaging to one's well-being. When we cognize an event as pleasant or unpleasant, we are not experiencing an emotion. However, when we [think we] may be personally benefited or harmed . . . the experience becomes an emotion."[72] Our emotions on seeing a bear depend on whether we are hunter or hunted, and our emotions on feeling pain in our jaw depend on whether we are in the hands of an inquisitor or a dentist.

Thus emotions are at least as much results of interpretations as they are causes. In Proudfoot's example, again, one is afraid because he sees a bear. One does not see a bear because he is afraid (unless he is afraid precisely because he already suspects a bear). Emotions have something to do with consciousness,[73] which in turn has something to do with reflection upon interpretation. The linguist Derek Bickerton thinks emotions are "bridges between representation and response that become essential as learning increasingly replaces fixed action patterns."[74] But they remain enigmatic and hence, though entailed in all human thought and action, do not make good prime movers. Levi-Strauss writes, "As affectivity is the most obscure side of man, there is the constant temptation to resort to it, forgetting that what is refractory to explanation is *ipso facto* unsuitable for use in explanation. A datum is not primary because it is incomprehensible."[75]

If anything is primary in our system of thought and action, it may be, instead, our search for information and meaning: for differences that make a difference. This search characterizes perception and cognition at every level, from seeing contrasts as edges to seeing the universe as an artifact. We do not search just consciously, at the surface of perception, but from the very bottom. All sentient organisms continually scan their environments for information, relate it to other information, and respond in some way to the news.

Emotions seem to inflect and reflect, interactively, this process of scanning and response. "Emotions appear to be powerful influences on how we think and interpret events. They are the *result* of cognition but in turn affect cognition."[76] Thus emotions do not seem elementary, but instead seem to be compound states of mind and body that include perceptions of situations. They are labels that classify and reify complex and continuous psychophysiological states. A contemporary psychologist suggests as much: an emotion is "an organic mix of action impulses and bodily expressions, diverse positive or dysphoric . . . cognitive-affective states, and physiological disturbances."[77] That the phrase "fight or flight" names a single physiological condition suggests that fear and anger, for example, may be distinguished by little more than whether one's chances look good or bad.

In any case, emotions are insufficient to explain anthropomorphism because they are at least as much its consequence as its cause. In a gripping science-fiction story,[78] a man alone in a house rocked by a fierce windstorm finds the wind swirling inside the rooms and suddenly realizes it is pursuing him. His realization is chilling. Does his fear of the wind cause him to think it is after him? No, the other way around: his fear is caused by his perception that the wind is alive and purposive.

Another variant of the wish-fulfillment theory might be derived from research on infant face perception and on mother/infant attachment, and from object-relations psychoanalysis. Many writers in these fields, reviewed in the next chapter, think humans are innately predisposed to perceive humans and to form social relations with them. Social contact with people, they say, is the deepest human need. The need stems from a long evolutionary history of gregariousness and early childhood dependency.

This research suggests sociability is inherent, somewhat as Noam Chomsky says language acquisition is inherent. Even this more ethological view of human interest in other people, however, would by itself not account for anthropomorphism. That we may be attracted to social relationships does not explain an interpretation of a shadow as a potential assailant, of a chipped stone as an ancient tool, or of the world as the handiwork of an absent God. In such cases no social relationship—pivotally, no symbolic interaction—is present. And, at least in the case of the threatening shadow, we do not *want* a relationship; instead our impulse is to avoid one. All three perceptions—of the potential assailant, the stone tool, and the crafted world—are significant, but none is the perception of a social partner. Rather, they are perceptions of danger and of two artifacts. Humans, humanlike beings, and human artifacts thus may interest us even when no relationship is desired or possible. We also may simply *avoid* humans as we would avoid tigers or avalanches. Any explanation of our predisposition to see humans, then, must posit more than a desire to engage them in social relationships.

Noticing that anthropomorphism can make the world either friendlier *or* unfriendlier does provide the germ of a view that incorporates both effects. That is, comforting or frightening, a humanlike model yields greater significance than does any other. Because humans habitually look

for meaning, interpretations with more meaning (that is, more information) are better than those with less, even if the meaning apalls us. This
is not wishful thinking either in ordinary language, where a "wish" is for
some desired substantive state, nor in the Freudian view, where wish
fulfillment is active self-deception. Seeing what frightens, angers, or repels
us simply is part of trying to understand the world. Thoreau writes, "Be
it life or death, we crave only reality."[79] So formulated, neither our search
for interpretations nor our discovery of misleading ones looks like wishful
thinking.

The other standard theory of anthropomorphism, that it relies on the
familiar to explain the unfamiliar, is stronger than the comfort theory but
again is insufficient. In some ways we are indeed familiar with ourselves,
and this familiarity does enable us to find analogies and continuities between humans and nonhuman things. However, the analogy version of
the familiarity theory requires self-knowledge that is both relatively significant and relatively reliable, while the confusion version requires that
we be unable to tell self from other. The two requirements contradict
each other and neither is clearly satisfied.

As for the analogy version, our knowledge of ourselves is no more
reliable than our knowledge of pots and pans or of cats and dogs. Instead,
it often is elusive and sometimes is illusory, as even a brief consideration
suggests. In assessing it we may distinguish two meanings of "ourselves."
One is our individual selves as distinct from other people and the other
is humans as distinct from nonhumans. In both cases, our knowledge is
less immediate and self-evident than we usually suppose.

With regard to ourselves as subjective individuals, for example, we
usually suppose we have direct, unmediated knowledge of our own
moods, emotions, motives, and intentions. Varied observers, however,
contradict this common assumption. One of Lear's loyalists, for instance,
ruefully says the king "hath ever but slenderly known himself." Freud
says we all know ourselves only slenderly and even systematically suppress
potential self-knowledge. Subsequent psychoanalytic clinical experience
shows at least that our motives and feelings often are unknown to us.
Nietzsche, as noted, more radically says all our ostensible knowledge both
of the external world and of ourselves is a constrained, filtered, and simplified interpretation. Schematization selects and shapes information to
suit our needs and interests and does so before the interpretations, even
of ourselves, become conscious. No knowledge is independent of needs
and interests. The same restrictions constrain knowledge of our bodies as
of our minds. Donne writes, "we are not sure we are ill; one hand asks
the other by the pulse, and our eye asks our urine how we do. O multiplied misery!"[80]

Recent psychologists, linguists, anthropologists, and even primatologists agree that our access to our own psyches is highly limited and
uncertain and uses much the same complex and uncertain inference as

judging those of others.[81] The evidence we use, moreover, varies with the assumptions to which we subscribe and the means we have for manipulating them. Emotions, for example, which we usually think unmediated and primitive, are interpretations of such information as pulse, perspiration, and respiration in particular contexts and probably are learned and culturally variable, not innate.[82]

Hence "self-analysis can be wrong, misinformed, and even self-deceptive."[83] The anthropologist James W. Fernandez[84] writes that the "prenomial subject" always is inchoate, and that a central mission of metaphor is to give that subject an identity. The scholar of religion Hans Penner says self-knowledge "presupposes knowledge of the world,"[85] and Piaget writes, "knowledge of one's self is the hardest of all knowledge."[86] Despite long and close association, our knowledge of ourselves is less like knowledge of a mastered instrument than like that of an unsuspected double agent.

Our knowledge of other people is even more indirect and complex. We have many of the same physical and behavioral clues about them that we have about ourselves, and also a few clues such as mannerisms, odors, facial color, and pupil dilation, which we typically do not have for ourselves. Interpretations of these, however, are even more inferential and uncertain than they are for ourselves because we have no access by introspection. As people are complex and subtle, our inferences often are partially or wholly mistaken and are always open to question.

That these judgments depend on assumption and belief becomes even clearer if we consider dealing with people of different cultures. A different language alone is enough to curtail our understanding drastically. When we encounter that difference coupled with an entirely different culture, our sense of what it means to be human may waver. People in many small-scale societies, such as those of gatherers and hunters, consequently regard only themselves as human. But familiarity even with people of the same culture does not bring complete reliability. We often have knowledge that is more reliable, if less complex, of familiar objects such as tools and common plants and animals.

Metaphor often construes humans in terms of natural phenomena: the king is a lion, a child blossoms, a heart is of stone. Such predication again suggests, as Fernandez[87] points out, that the boundaries of human nature are indeterminate and constantly negotiated using nonhuman points of reference. If our knowledge of people is "intimately familiar," as Hume writes, it nonetheless is deeply uncertain. Our self-knowledge, both individually and collectively, is more edifice than foundation. Our apparent familiarity with ourselves, seemingly plausible ground for analogies with nonhumans, offers unfirm footing. Hence we must have some reason for making these analogies other than close or reliable knowledge.

A possible reason is the other version of the familiarity theory, confusion: we cannot tell where we leave off and where the rest of the world begins. Thus we mix our notions of ourselves with notions of the world, willy-nilly. The confusion theory in turn has two major versions. In the first, Vico, Comte, Feuerbach, Piaget, Freud, and White point to a primitive but remediable failure to distinguish self and other. In the second, Lange and Nietzsche claim we cannot extricate observation from interest and therefore can only anthropomorphize. Both versions have elements of truth but again both have limitations.

The primitive confusion version seems true in the limited sense that we may find it hard to sort out the distinctive features of any class of entities. Given that the phenomenal world is endlessly complex, it is not surprising that we sometimes think two kinds of things or events, for example, humans and storms, share some feature, such as intention, which we later decide they do not. Similar uncertainties include whether computers are conscious and whether the nonhuman world, in whole or in part, has feelings.

However, the primitive confusion variant does not seem true in its more extreme versions, as when White says we may fail in some general way to tell self from other. Piaget says infants distinguish self and other by about one year, and the "feelings of participation which the child experiences [are] not so much between his self and things, but rather, between his parents or adults in general and the world of matter."[88] Other developmental psychologists agree that even young children distinguish self from other. Daniel Stern says infants *never* experience "total self-other undifferentiation. There is no confusion between self and other in the beginning or at any point in infancy."[89] The biologist Jenny Coy says many nonhuman animals also distinguish self and other, and suggests that successful interaction, such as cooperation, requires this.[90] Chimpanzees can recognize themselves individually in mirrors and monkeys can identify individual monkeys from photographs. All this means any global failure to distinguish self from other is unlikely in normal adults.

We are left with only the modest observation that we may mistakenly think nonhuman things and events share with us some features that they do not. But such a mistake can also happen regarding any pair of classes, such as whales and fishes, birds and bats, or insects and spiders, where both members are other than human. It requires no confusion of self and other.

Moreover, neither global nor partial confusion of self and other fits many typical cases of anthropomorphism. When a stroller in the park after dark mistakes a sack of garbage for a menacing man, or when a fugitive mistakes a sapling for a sentry, both have well-formed images of what they fear, based not so much on images of themselves as on images of others. The principle is the same as in the animism of mistaking a boulder for a bear: we have a schema of something of pressing interest and good reason to relax our standards for satisfying it. The reason, again, is that it usually is less costly to mistake boulder for bear than to mistake bear for boulder. Gombrich writes, "the greater the biological relevance an object has to us, the more will we be attuned to its recognition—and the more tolerant will therefore be our standards of formal correspondence."[91]

Sometimes, to be sure, a self/other confusion makes us think someone else is present. One can mistake echoes or imprints of his own footsteps for those of another's footsteps, and a jogger can hear the rustle of his own clothing or the jingle of his keys as sounds of another runner. Varied other traces of our own activities may appear as someone else's. But these situations are relatively few.

Nietzsche's account, that anthropomorphism is inevitable because we cannot step outside our own perceptual systems, is both more sweeping than the primitive confusion account and in some ways more convincing. It seems inescapable that the only world we perceive is the one we are equipped to perceive and that our equipment reflects our needs and interests. Indeed, a similar view guides much current work on perception. Michael Arbib and Allen Hanson contrast the classical view of perception with a view that is both more Nietzschean and more modern: earlier writers suggest that "the job of the visual system is to provide a veridical representation of the external world [but we think it] is not to provide the animal with a representation of the world *in abstracto* but to provide . . . the information it needs to interact with the world about it."[92]

Nietzsche goes further, however, to say that we inevitably perceive the world in terms of social relations and of ideas about ourselves.[93] Here I think he conflates two meanings of anthropomorphism, the conventional one and an idiosyncratic one. The conventional meaning is attributing human characteristics to nonhuman things or events, as in attributing language to dogs. The idiosyncratic meaning is attributing to things and events only those characteristics relevant to human needs and interests. This is better called anthropocentrism. For example, we see in wildflowers only those patterns reflecting light visible to humans, that is, that between infrared and ultraviolet, and we assume we see all there is to see about flowers. In contrast insects, whose view of flowers is privileged by highly evolved relations with them, see flower patterns visible by ultraviolet as well.

Anthropocentrism and anthropomorphism are easily confused if one assumes that "understanding" consists of some identity between that which understands (the mind) and that which is understood (the object). For example, the identity might be one of form, and understanding would require isomorphism between mind and object. If such isomorphism were necessary, humans could perceive only what is humanlike. We then would necessarily anthropomorphize; anthropomorphism and anthropocentrism would merge. If, for example, the human mind is rational, then isomorphism would require that any object to be understood must also be rational. But what it would mean for an object to be rational is hard to know.

In contrast, if to understand some object is to form an adequate model of it, isomorphism requires correspondence only between object and model. The model is both product and part of mind, but not equivalent to it. Instead the mind also has features related to its models, but different from them. Rationality, for example, may be defined as a capacity for apportioning means to ends. In modeling some thing or event, rationality then consists in assigning a limited number of features to the model, toward the end of understanding what is modeled. But this activity need not be shared by what is understood. We can form models of sandstorms and solar systems without their being able to do the same. Understanding implies some correspondence between the models we form and the phenomena we understand, but not between the phenomena and our minds as wholes. Thus we may be anthropocentric without anthropomorphizing, and although anthropocentrism may contribute to anthropomorphism, it does not explain it.

Nietzsche, in any case, aims more to show the pervasiveness of anthropomorphism than to explain it, so his account naturally has limitations for our purposes. Three limitations may be mentioned. First, emphasizing human anthropocentrism, he underemphasizes the similarity of human perception to perception in other animals.[94] The perceptual worlds of people and chimpanzees, for example, surely are more similar than those of chimpanzees and mosquitos. And if we are on a perceptual continuum with other animals, then our isolation is not complete. One interesting consequence is that not only humans but also other animals may anthropomorphize. Some apparently do occasionally mistake non-human things for humans.

Another limitation in Nietzsche's account is its lumping together of varied forms and degrees of anthropomorphism. Although he calls our entire sensory world anthropomorphic, some forms of anthropomorphism clearly are stronger or weaker than others. For example, human vision is similar in important ways to chimpanzee vision (both have color and good depth perception), so there likely is considerable overlap between what they and we see when we look, for example, at a bunch of bananas. Calling all our perceptions anthropomorphic diminishes both the fact that humans can easily imagine the charming Chiquita Banana and chimpanzees presumably cannot, and that seeing a banana as like us is more anthropomorphic than seeing chimps as like us.

Third, Nietzsche's claim that anthropomorphic perceptions, rather than just anthropocentric ones, serve our interests is dubious. Anthropomorphism, as he notes, is an illusion, even though like many illusions it is one result of a strategy that otherwise works well. But illusions often do not serve our interests, as when we are frightened by a dim shape that turns out to be a tree stump. Conflating anthropomorphism and anthropocentrism, Nietzsche's broad brush paints over a necessary distinction and avoids a necessary explanation.

Anthropomorphism may best be explained as the result of an attempt to see not what we want to see or what is easy to see, but what is *important* to see: what may affect us for better or worse. This invokes the same principle as does my explanation for animism. Because of the importance to us of the humans on which it is based, however, anthropomorphism takes the principle further than does animism. Humans are uniquely complex, highly organized, and powerful. We have uniquely dependent and intimate relations with each other. Accordingly our search for other humans and for transformations and analogues of other humans is highly motivated and complex. And, just as motivation to see animals despite animal camouflage necessarily results in mistaking twigs for grasshoppers and boulders for bears, so our motivation to see humans despite human camouflage results in our mistaking the nonhuman world for human.

Other humans are the most important factors in our environment. They are vital in everyone's experience, most obviously during our helpless infancy and long dependent childhood, when close support is crucial to survival.[95] Our dependency does not end with maturity, however, but continues throughout life. Nor is our mutual need only material; it is also emotional and intellectual. Indeed, our entire well-being is wrapped up in our relationships with our fellows. We are oriented to each other in manifold ways, conscious and unconscious, with an intensity and a preoccupation unrivaled by our relationships with any other entity.

Even the hermit flees company not because company is irrelevant but because it is all too relevant. Moreover he typically sees in his solitary environment some transformation of the humanity he left. In religious hermitage, this transformation is God. The anthropocentrism that Nietzsche saw everywhere does not evaporate when we leave other people physically. The duke in *As You Like It* says of his forest exile, "this our life, exempt from public haunt, finds tongues in trees, books in the running brooks, sermons in stones, and good in everything." People find heads, faces, and other parts of the body in landforms (Fig. 3–1) and social groupings in collections of artifacts (Fig. 3–2).

We have excellent reasons for anthropocentrism, which as Nietzsche says, serves our interests. These interests are no mere egotism, as some critics suggest. We are anthropocentric not only because we ourselves are humans and have special needs for humans, nor only because it gratifies us to be the paragon of animals. Rather, we attend to humans also because they are the most powerful organisms we know. Long before we had the potential to destroy all life, we were the dominant entities on earth. Long before we were dominant, we were significant, and not only to ourselves. Because of our power, we are important to other organisms as well.

Accordingly we keep a sharp eye out for our fellows, and other animals watch out for us too. Many nonhuman animals are to some degree anthropocentric in that they perceive humans as dangerous and avoid them. Even powerful predators may take pains to avoid people. Further, many animals even seem to anthropomorphize the environment, at least with a little help from us: many kinds of scarecrows, often with only a

Figure 3-1 **Old Man of the Mountains.** We scan every scene for humans and humanlike forms and discover them in all sorts of places and in all shapes and sizes.

sketchy likeness to humans, frighten various animals. What counts as a likeness varies with the environment, but likenesses need not seem close to be effective. In the flat, treeless Arctic landscape, for example, only humans have upright figures. Accordingly, Eskimos can frighten caribou into ambush simply by building upright piles of stones about the size of a man, capped with "hair" of dark moss. Avoiding these, the caribou encounter the real Eskimos. Evidently the caribou, whose eyesight is poor, mistake even these rough semblances for humans.

The dilemma of the caribou, as of all animals encountering deception, is a dilemma for us, too: how do we know when humans are present? How do we tell which phenomena are humans or signs of human presence and which are not? When soldiers carried branches from Birnam Wood as camouflage, a sentry told MacBeth the forest was moving. The dilemma is sharpened by the same situation that in general gives power to humans: that people, being complex and highly organized as individuals and as groups, produce highly complex and varied behavior. We

Love at first sip.

Figure 3-2 **Bacardi advertisement, 1977.** Artists and audiences alike see even inanimate things as humanlike. We may anthropomorphize objects simply by placing them together.

generate an endless array of artifacts and special effects, and appear in an endless array of guises. Even the unintended by-products of our activities are highly varied. Just a few of the possible marks of human passage across terrain include the tracks of bare feet, of boots, of automobile tires, and of skis. Since the advent of aircraft, we may leave no track at all. Further, the variety of behavior and artifacts within any one culture is multiplied by the differences between cultures.

Clothing and makeup greatly vary our appearance: not only our daily changes of clothing but also wigs and false moustaches, padding, stilts inside trousers, and costumes of stage horses and dragons change how we look. Over a few centuries, European military garb has ranged from threatening red uniforms with shakos to clothing of nearly invisible olive drab, gray, or (for ski troops) white. Its effects correspondingly range from making wearers appear larger than life to aiding them not to appear at all. Hunting camouflage also varies widely. Plains Indians approached bison on all fours under wolf skins, Eskimo hunted seals from behind white polar-bearskin shields, and contemporary American hunters often are dappled head to toe in browns and greens. One cannot confidently predict human appearance. As with animals, it may be hard to see camouflaged people even if they are in our line of sight.

Just as human appearance is varied and unpredictable, so is other human behavior. One variant of behavior has an effect similar to that of the iridescence that makes the distance of some insects indeterminate, or to that of the pheromones through which others communicate. This is action at a distance, by traps and snares, poisons, thrown stones, arrows, firearms, language and other symbolism, and, putatively, magic. All these enable us to have some desired effect without being immediately at the site. The actor may be behind the scenes, causing some effect while removed from the action. The effect is another kind of invisibility. The variability and unpredictability of human behavior and appearance increase when we cross cultural boundaries. Language, diet, housing, clothing, and economic activities are only the more apparent ways in which neighbors may differ from each other. Even body types, including size, skin and hair color, and physiognomy vary from group to group.

One corollary of the diversity and variability of human appearance and behavior is that there is no clear cross-cultural definition of a human. Within many cultures the boundaries differ from those of the contemporary West. There are what seem, to Westerners, various continua across our categories of animals, humans, and gods. People shade into gods in Japan, where all people and natural phenomena are *kami,* with differences only of magnitude; in China, where the official pantheon has included Confucius and other government officials; and in any culture where descent groups make ancestors important. In ancient Greece, humans might become demigods, and humans and gods might produce offspring. In Homer, the main difference between humans and gods is that humans are mortal. Euhemerus's theory that the gods originated as great men thus emerges naturally from his Greek milieu.

Similarly, in most "ancestor worship," as in East Asia, Africa, and elsewhere, only death separates what, in Western terms, are humanity and divinity.[96] And in ancestor worship the distinction made by death is not absolute; it is only a gradation within a community of kinspeople. Sir

James Frazer similarly says that man in primitive societies makes no clear distinction between a "god and a powerful sorcerer. His gods are often merely invisible magicians who behind the veil of nature work the same sort of charms and incantations which the human works in a visible and bodily form among his fellows."[97] Thus the category of human in many cultures is not closed at what, in Western terms, is the upper end but is continuous with that of gods.

At the other end of the category, humans in many cultures are continuous with animals in important ways. In shamanic cultures, the spirits of humans and animals are essentially the same, and the shaman often can change his or her shape, taking on that of varied animals. Moreover, special affinities connect people and some animals. In subarctic cultures the bear is particularly humanlike; for example, some Siberians call it the "old man of the forest." Another aspect of the continuity of humans and animals is that a people may classify only themselves as human and class foreigners as animals. Such classification is common among small, nonliterate societies, whose members may call themselves simply "the people." They may also subcategorize other peoples, as when Inuit think there are two kinds of Indians; one of which is human while the other is a kind of wolf.[98]

Europeans often think such classification of people into human and nonhuman is especially ethnocentric and peculiar to tribal societies, but some Europeans initially thought American Indians were nonhuman. The Spanish government and church, for example, debated the humanity of Central and South American Indians to decide whether they should be accorded souls and converted, or denied souls, expropriated, and exterminated.

At the same time Europeans were uncertain whether orangutans (the "old men of the forest" for Indonesians) and chimpanzees were human and whether tribes of people existed without language. No less a taxonomist than Linnaeus at first classed orangutans as human, as did Lord Monboddo. Contrasts and comparisons of the great apes and humans still fascinate us, though we wish mostly to see ourselves as different. A profound distinction between animals and people is ancient in the Judeo-Christian tradition, which arrays man with God. The distinction now is part of Western folk categories, ideology, and politics, as well as of religion.

Despite the Judeo-Christian separation of humans and animals, Western cultures have also seen strong continuities between them. Ostensible continuities have included abilities to plan, to speak, and to bear moral responsibility. From the thirteenth to the eighteenth century, for example, European courts held trials of animals accused of injuring or "murdering" humans, as courts in non-Western cultures also have done.[99] Animals found guilty often were executed.

At the same time, some humans were classed with animals. In thirteenth-century Burgundy, for example, Jews and animals (other than horses and oxen) guilty of homicide were "hung by their rear legs."[100] Not only Jews as a hybrid but other imaginary hybrids also populated medieval Europe: "the natural and the fabulous inhabited the world of twelfth-century zoology in perfect harmony. . . . Mermaids, women-serpents, werewolves, child-swans and semi-human savages populate the literature."[101] Thus in an earlier Europe, as elsewhere, the line between human and nonhuman was different from that now current, and evidently less distinct. Even in the twentieth century, the notion of the semihuman appears in Nazi propaganda about Jews and Poles, in the *exotiká* (mermaids and other partly human creatures) of Greek folklore, and in stories of abominable snowmen and wild children.[102]

Some contemporary writers question whether humans have any good claim to separation from other animals,[103] while most wish to maintain such a separation. One recent writer thinks injunctions against anthropomorphizing animals are prompted by a "heretic-baiting impulse,"[104] presumably reflecting a fear of destroying the human/nonhuman distinction. Additional, tacit reasons to maintain the distinction may be that it justifies exploiting other animals, that it protects us from injustice by humans, and that it offers a comforting superiority. In any case, our essential difference from apes has been variously asserted to be our possession of reason, of tools, of language, and of religion. We now know wild chimpanzees make and use tools, and captive ones appear to reason and to learn rudiments of symbolism, if not language itself. Religion still is sacrosanct but, if chimpanzees threaten rainstorms, it cannot be far behind.

Western folk and ideological commitments to the distinctiveness of humanity now are relatively firm, though not shared by most other cultures. Indeed, from our current vantage even the earlier uncertainty over whether apes are human seems strange. However, Darwin showed that the distinction between apes and humans is neither absolute nor timeless. Not only is the distinction merely one of degree but it also, if pursued backward through evolution, at some point disappears. Thus the unity of *Homo sapiens* as a natural category, seemingly clear to most twentieth-century Westerners, is undermined by this open-endedness. If we now find close kin neither among gods (though God still is "Father" for many) nor among natural phenomena at large, we at least find them among primates.

We see then that for humans generally, the category of human has no essence, no clear or distinct edges, and barely even a set of family resemblances. Man indeed is the "ultimate chameleon."[105] Accordingly, no characteristics of humans obviously can be ruled out, a priori, from other parts of the world. As tool making and rudimentary symbolism in apes remind us, ruling such characteristics out of the nonhuman world is work for empirical research, not for fiat. Our conceptions both of the human and of the nonhuman world are constantly subject to revision. They are conceptual cathedrals, in Nietzsche's image, on shifting foundations. Humans typically have language, laughter, music, breasts, and buttocks, but these are neither necessary nor sufficient criteria of humanity. Western conceptions of humans now exclude invisibility and the ability to fly unaided, but elsewhere shamans, witches, and magicians are thought to fly, become invisible, and change shape.

When we see there is no certain line between the human and the nonhuman, we can better see that it is not unreasonable to look for features we are acquainted with in humans elsewhere as well. In looking for them in the world at large, we continue to confront uncertainty. The invisibility and deceit we know in other animals and in ourselves, combined with the power of action at a distance we know especially in humans, mean virtually no phenomenon can be known with confidence *not* to be the result of human action. The complexity, diversity, and ingenuity of the humans of our experience and the ability of humans to produce effects without immediately revealing themselves make it prudent to suppose there may be similar hidden agents behind almost any effect.

One logical extreme of this supposition is that the entire world of our experience is merely a show staged by some master dramatist. The show may be entirely without substance and may even exist only in our minds, as in Bishop Berkeley's view that the world exists in the mind of the perceiver (though he found it parsimonious to make God's mind the final locus).[106] In some versions of experience as a product of mind, a deity or demon may direct that experience, as in variants of Buddhism and Hinduism. These often hold that we normally are under the influence of *maya,* cosmic illusion or divine creative magic.[107] A Western science-fiction version of the world as illusion pictures the perceiver as the victim of a master brain surgeon. The victim may, for example, be stretched on an operating table while the surgeon amuses himself by creating with electrodes the illusion of a world and a life in it.

Such visions of the world as the continuing, illusory creation of a hidden agent or agents are unusual, but the underlying principle that more significance and order is present than meets the eye is not. In Bacon's words, "The human understanding is of its own nature prone to suppose the existence of more order and regularity in the world than it finds."[108] The most order is supplied by the highest organization, and the highest organization we know is that of human beings. Interpretations of the world based on experience of ourselves and other humans offer not only the significance of a powerful agent but also that of an organizing agent. Models based on humans account for a uniquely wide range of phenomena because humans, whom the models reflect, generate a uniquely wide range of phenomena. Anthropomorphizing the world at large therefore produces a world that is significant both practically and intellectually.

Indeed, anthropomorphism offers the greatest intellectual coherence possible.[109] As humans are coherent yet uniquely diverse, so models based on them bring coherence to unique diversity. The point needs underscoring because the standard views of anthropomorphism, as we saw above, claim just the opposite: that anthropomorphism is oddly irrational and is based in confusion, in wishful thinking, or in both. Once we see that anthropomorphism results from our most powerful model, we can see that we are bound to engage in it everywhere, not only inevitably but also reasonably. We can see that human traits such as symbolism might be anywhere and that the universe *might* be linguistic. Once we decide a perception is anthropomorphic, reason requires that we correct it; but that decision can come only in hindsight, when we have a different interpretation of some phenomenon we had thought humanlike.

Anthropomorphism may appear somewhat disreputable. It may look like a shortcut to understanding, and one with a hidden agenda, at that. The search for comprehension that underlies it, however, comprises the same processes—economizing, generalizing, ordering, and system-building—as does the rest of thought. Norman Campbell writes of science that one of our "profoundest instincts [is] to regard the more general principle as the more . . . satisfactory."[110] Gilbert Harman finds thought largely a "matter of trying to increase the coherence of our total view."[111] Piaget says all organisms produce "structures of inclusion ordering correspondence everywhere."[112] Wittgenstein calls the desire for such organization "our craving for generality."[113] What they all mean is that we wish to bring as much experience as we can under as unified a scheme as we can.

Anthropomorphism, like other products of cognition, results not so much from a desire to find any particular pattern as from our more general need to find whatever pattern is most important. The most important pattern in most contexts is that with the highest organization. The highest organization we know is that of human thought and action. Therefore we typically scan the world with humanlike models. Scanning the world with humanlike models, we frequently suppose we find what we are looking for where in fact it does not exist. This is most apparent when we are most aware of ambiguities (a sound in the night, a shadow on our path, an unexpected death); but such cases are not aberrant. All perception is interpretive and all interpretation follows a pattern: we look first for what matters most.

4

Anthropomorphism as Perception

from the very beginning of its development . . . the child endows things with human activity.

Jean Piaget, *The Child's Conception of the World*

Whenever anything remotely facelike enters our field of vision, we are alerted and respond.

Ernst Gombrich, *Art and Illusion*

A couple of times I pulled up to a mail box thinking it was a rider. It's happened to all of us.

New York taxi driver

Nothing is so important to us as other humans. Because we are preoccupied with each other, we are sensitive to any possible human presence and have tolerant standards for detecting it. Mostly unconsciously, we fit the world first with diverse humanlike templates.[1] Our preoccupation with a human prototype guides perception in daily life. We attend to what fits the humanlike templates and temporarily ignore what does not. Sounds, shapes, and smells thus first evoke humans and we mistake mailboxes, signposts, and saplings for people. Evidence of anthropomorphism in perception, and reasons for it, come from artificial intelligence, from psychoanalysis, from experimental, clinical, and developmental psychology, and from ethnography.

The very frequency of warnings against anthropomorphism suggests its constancy in thought. People in many fields—literary critics, journalists, philosophers, scientists, and others—call attention to it. Some think scientific and technological advances are overcoming it. In science itself, this is to some degree true. However, as anthropomorphism is chased from one realm it springs up in another. If we no longer see the sun and moon as persons, we hear intelligent signals from space.[2] Unmasking instances of anthropomorphism, if we think this desirable (and most do), is like stamping out patches of a bigger fire because anthropomorphism stems from an effort broader than itself. Moreover, it is recognizable only in retrospect.

Anthropomorphism has as many forms as there are things and events to interpret. Its manifestations may seem too varied for one label,[3] but this diversity simply reflects the generative power of the model it employs. Because humans themselves appear in endless guises and produce endless effects, and because models of humans are infinitely multifaceted, an infinite number of things and events may be seen as like humans or as caused by them.

The myriad forms of anthropomorphism range continuously from literal to metaphoric. The most literal anthropomorphism in daily life is mistaking some nonhuman thing or event for a human. We may hear a door slammed by wind or a branch tapping at a window as human action, or hear water in a brook or gurgling in plumbing as a voice. We mistake many shapes, at a glance or in dim light, for those of people: tree stumps, sacks of garbage, car seats with headrests. We may recognize our mistake at a second glance, or only after acting on it, or not at all. A taxi driver says, "I always have clean windows because you have to keep looking for fares. . . . Always. Sometimes you get carried away. A couple of times I pulled up to a mail box thinking it was a rider. It's happened to all of us."[4] The response is automatic. A runner whose course takes him past a ground-level water tank topped by a man-sized pump frequently first sees the pump as a standing figure, despite its familiarity. Later, in twilight, the runner often first sees several bulky, cross-shaped mailboxes as people.

We may share such literal anthropomorphism with other animals. Konrad Lorenz tells of walking in a forest with his dog when they saw, in a distant clearing, an old man seated on a log. According to Lorenz, the dog clearly expected a social encounter; but when they came closer, the old man turned out to be a stump.

We may also alternate between seeing something as human and as another animal, specified or not. An ornithologist in a jungle became aware of a

> black shape somewhere behind me. I stopped, looked around, saw nothing, and walked on, slightly unnerved. Again I had a sense of a figure following me, quickly turned, and glimpsed a black creature vanishing behind a tree. I felt my heart pounding [and] began talking to myself in order to calm down: "Take it easy, Jared, there are no people here. Why would anyone follow

you? New Guinea doesn't have any known dangerous animals." [The next]
time I spun around quickly enough to see it. It was a black, insect-eating
bird called a Drongo, following me in order to capture insects.[5]

This writer sensed first a "shape," then a "figure," and then a "black
creature," (that is, first something alive, then a human, and then a nonhuman animal) before identifying a bird. Even after glimpsing it, he had
to tell himself explicitly that it was not human.

At a second level of anthropomorphism, people see things and events
as having important human attributes such as symbolism without mistaking them for humans. This includes both religious perception—as in seeing an earthquake or AIDS as messages or punishment, or a storm as
Thor—and secular perception, as in thinking plants, animals, or
machinery understand language.[6] Computers now are especially subject
to this second level of anthropomorphism. Karl Sheibe and Margaret Erwin[7] programmed computers for varying "intelligence" in games with
college students. The students personified the computers substantially,
the more so when the programs were more intelligent. Most called the
machines "you" and "he" and credited them with planning and
volition.[8]

We anthropomorphize animals at least as much as computers. We
involuntarily attribute personality traits, for example, to animals with postures or physiognomies resembling human gestures. Thus camels appear
arrogant or aloof because they carry their noses high and eagles appear
proud and decisive for the same reason, and because a bony ridge above
the eyes resembles gathered brows.[9] Dolphins appear friendly because the
corners of their mouths seem raised in a smile.

People often talk to dogs, cats, and horses and think—although language is specifically human—that the animals understand most of it (Fig.
4–1). Vicki Hearne, an animal trainer and professor of English, thinks
horses and dogs can have paranoid psychoses, take responsibility, exhibit
morality, engage in metaphysics, and understand stories. Hearne says of
one horse, "Stories about a sweet horsie who couldn't help herself and
needed only affection and gentleness were what made her crazy, but they
were the only stories she had—her only survival tools—and she quite
naturally didn't want to give them up."[10] But stories require symbolism,
which horses lack, so Hearne is anthropomorphizing.

Opinions that animals have language and other symbolic capacities
extend well back in European history. For at least half a millennium, as
we saw in the last chapter, Europeans held animals guilty of crimes and
subject to punishment including execution. Similar views persist. Around
the turn of the century, Ernest Seton Thompson wrote popular nature
books with wild-animal heroes and heroines with such human virtues as
loyalty, generosity, and kindness. Slightly later, Albert Payson Terhune's
collie stories gave extended foresight and other humanlike capacities to

Figure 4–1   **Gary Larson cartoon, 1983.** We anthropomorphize animals by talking to them and feeling that they understand more than they do.

dogs. One of his heroines, Lassie, stars in television shows and movies in which she understands language. Major film studios such as Disney continue to anthropomorphize animals, not merely in animation but also in ostensible natural-history films.

    Although the ability of computers and animals to interact complexly with us encourages anthropomorphism, it is not necessary. We anthropomorphize less-interactive objects as well. The "grilles of automobiles are the faces that we . . . present to the world. Indeed, the mouth-like grille and its adjacent headlights (eyes) seem to literally suggest a face."[11] We see other vehicles similarly. A restorer of old aircraft alternates between anthropomorphism and animism: "Airplanes almost seem to have personalities. . . . They have faces and forms that suggest more than mere function, and some of us grow very attached to them. When a species of

airplane, say . . . the DeHavilland Hornet, disappears . . . it is almost as if
a life form had become extinct."[12] Men give women's names to ships
and boats and paint women's names and figures on the noses of military
aircraft. We urge recalcitrant dishwashers and television sets to work and
may threaten or kick them if they do not.

We may also imagine that such machinery responds. An airline pilot
tells of a fellow captain who, in the days of propeller-driven airliners, once
had trouble starting his four engines. One engine would start but would
quit when a second or third started. This continued in varying combinations, ending with all engines stopped. The red-faced captain opened
his window, leaned out, shook his fist and yelled, "Run, you sons of
bitches, run!" On his next try, each engine started in turn and kept
running.

The writer John McPhee tells of more amicable connections between
ship captains and their ships. While working on a book about a captain,
he read the man an excerpt from an article, "Tips on Practical Shiphandling": "If . . . you feel, when laying your hand upon the rail, that you
are in contact with something alive, responsive to your slightest touch,
something that is part of you, something that you really love, then you
are in a good position to become truly expert at shiphandling." McPhee's
informant responded warmly:

> when I put my hand on a rail and think that I am associated with a living
> thing, and that I cannot only control it but that I have something going with
> it, we understand each other. It isn't all me taking and her giving. We work
> as a unit. I talk things over with her, and almost ask her, "Hey, can we do
> this?" I am not just demanding what this ship can do for me, I'm asking
> what I can do for her. "Look, old girl, you're in trouble. Let's see if we can
> help each other."[13]

The captain told McPhee he also felt that the ship could sense an approaching storm and could signal it by hesitating.

We do not need to interact with a mechanical process to anthropomorphize it. Fritz Heider and Marianne Simmel[14] showed viewers a short
animated film in which two triangles and a circle move on a surface. The
figures "bump into" each other, "follow" each other, and "enter" and
"leave" a rectangular enclosure through a swinging line "door." The
experimenters asked the viewers to write what happened. Virtually all saw
the figures as persons. One wrote, for example,

> A man has planned to meet a girl and the girl comes along with another
> man. The first man tells the second to go; the second tells the first, and he
> shakes his head. Then the two men have a fight, and the girl starts to go into
> the room to get out of the way and hesitates and finally goes in. She appar-
> ently does not want to be with the first man. The first man follows her into
> the room after having left the second in a rather weakened condition leaning
> on the wall outside the room.[15]

Here, flat geometrical figures on a flat surface suffice to evoke humans in sexual rivalry and conflict.

G. H. Mead also notes, as Scheibe and Erwin point out, that people think they have social relations with things:

> It is possible for inanimate objects, no less than for human organisms, to form parts of the generalized [social] other for any given human individual, in so far as he responds to such objects socially or in a social manner. . . . Anything—any object or set of objects, whether animate or inanimate, human or animal, or merely physical—towards which he acts . . . socially is an element in what for him is the generalized other.[16]

Thus no objectively humanlike traits at all are necessary for something to strike us as humanlike.

At a third level of anthropomorphism, we see or hear human form or action in things and events—faces in the moon and armies in clouds—as mere chance. Landforms in New Hampshire and Colorado offer the Old Man of the Mountain (Fig. 3–1) and the Devil's Thumb, respectively. In the contemporary West, people commonly see such human or animal images as accident plus imagination. The Rorschach inkblot test, for example, assumes that the blots are, apart from their bilateral symmetry, randomly shaped and that their significance is only that which a viewer gives them.

The various levels of anthropomorphism—the literal, partial, and accidental—may occur together in various combinations. In what to some people are chance images, for instance, in which they see only their minds working upon accidental configuration, others may find more meaning. For example, people may see an image as a signal from some agent. Through most of European history, philosophers and artists have debated whether chance images are accidents or providential.[17] In seventeenth-century Holland, a chance image in a sawn cross section of an apple tree trunk produced political turmoil when the sawyers saw it as a black-clad priest, and many people thought it presaged Spanish domination of Holland. Others denied it.[18]

Another veiled significance is asserted by the doctrine of signatures, held by many Renaissance Europeans: that certain natural objects have special relationships, such as curative powers, to parts of human anatomy. The signature, usually a likeness to anatomy, shows the presence of the power: "walnuts bear the whole signature of the head. The outward green cortex answers to the Pericranium, and a salt made of it is singularly good for wounds in that part, as the kernel is good for the brains, which it resembles."[19]

Interpretations of images and objects as humanlike may remain largely or completely unconscious. Modern advertising artists, for example, arrange objects in social groupings (commonly couples [Fig. 3–2] and sometimes families [Fig. 4–2]) whose sociality often is explicit.[20]

Figure 4–2 **Michelob advertisement, *Bring Our Family Home for the Holidays*, 1985.** Advertising artists frequently pose bottles as social groups and often clothe them as well.

Such groups are not peculiar to advertising, however, but reflect a much broader bent to see objects as having social relations.

Thus daily perception and representation anthropomorphize at varying levels of meaning, literalness, and consciousness. When the anthropomorphism is not literal we may call it metaphorical or analogical; but these terms do not distinguish anthropomorphic perception from other perception or indeed make any fundamental distinction among perceptions. The "cognitive processes implied by the words 'metaphor,' 'analogy,' 'model,' 'theory,' 'representation,' 'schema' "[21] strongly resemble each other. All these depend on classification and prototypes, which make "one thing in our experience stand for something else."[22] Regardless of level, humanlike models offer the dominant, though not exclusive or inevitable, model for our interpretation of the world.

Artificial intelligence; psychoanalysis; experimental, clinical, and developmental psychology; and ethnography offer further evidence that humanlike models dominate perception and suggest why this is so. Work in artificial intelligence reminds us both that perception is interpretation and that higher-level, more-encompassing interpretations take precedence over lower-level, less-encompassing ones. Psychologists using artificial intelligence to explore natural perception and representation find that programs for "seeing," for example, cannot simply analyze data and construct an image from the analysis. Rather, programs must possess equivalents of mental representations, to which they fit data. These representations correspond to what Richard Gregory calls "hypotheses," what Ernst Gombrich calls "guesses," what Ulrich Neisser calls "anticipatory schemas," and what Donald Griffin calls "searching images."[23] Using schemata, computer programs assign form and give meaning to data, which in turn may be images or other representations.

The data interpreted always are, for computers and for us, fragmentary and degenerate. In every scene, some objects partially obscure others. Shadows and reflections break up lines and surfaces. At any time, we see an object from only one point of view. The eye is optically imperfect, with chromatic and astigmatic aberrations in the lens and a network of blood vessels and other tissues between the lens and the light-sensitive layer of retina. Images on the retina are in two dimensions, not three. Plato's cave allegory, comparing our images of the world to shadows cast on a cave wall by unseen figures, is a classic statement of the fragmentation and degeneracy of the material with which perception begins.

Yet the world of experience is neither fragmentary nor degenerate nor flat. Instead, we experience a three-dimensional assemblage of complete objects with more or less clear outlines. Indeed, objects typically seem so complete and clear that our common sense is that we are perceptual blank slates, passively and directly receiving imprints from the world around us. We typically are unaware that, even in seeing simple forms, we actively construct.

The difficulty of producing vision in computers, however, has helped show how much rectification and judgment are required even for such apparently simple percepts as lines, edges, and surfaces. Both computers

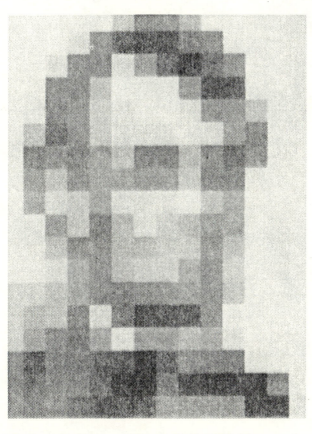

Figure 4–3 **Leon D. Harmon,** *Lincoln Grid,* **1973.** We grasp the world through schemas, applying to each scene the most significant schema we can imagine. The less information we have, the wider the range of schemas we can apply. This image looks like an arbitrary set of squares when seen clearly, but like a well-known face when blurred by squinting.

and humans are able to produce whole pictures from incomplete images. Computers, for instance, can turn blurry photographs into three-dimensional line drawings. Humans can turn a few squares in shades of gray into a portrait of a well-known person (Fig. 4–3). Squinting at this figure or viewing it at a distance, we see a familiar face. How do computers, and we, do it?

Evidently, they and we both scan data with schemata, or models. Hermann von Helmholtz calls perception "unconscious inference," but "unconscious attribution" would be more accurate. Michael Arbib and Allen Hanson write that expectations translate "fragmented surface cues into confident interpretations of the environment . . . fitting a set of very weak . . . hypotheses into a more reliable whole [by using] stored

Figure 4-4 Ronald C. James, *Dalmation*, 1966. The most significant
schema for a scene usually is that which makes the scene most coherent. A
schema that makes this image coherent features a dog sniffing a shadow-
dappled surface.

knowledge."[24] Computer programs and complex organisms alike, that
is, see the world by scanning fragmentary evidence with schemata and
thus "hallucinating" some whole upon sketchy data about parts.
A pioneering program for computer perception of photographs of
polyhedral bodies, for example, shows that the program, not the picture, must supply the lines.[25] Data do not so much give rise to perception as permit it, by allowing an acceptable fit with some schema
(Fig. 4-4).

At the lowest level of perception, our visual system seems preattentive, or keyed, to motion and to elements such as elongated blobs with
features of angular orientation, thickness, length, and color. Primitive
elements may also include line crossings and ends of lines. Detection of
all these is rapid and probably innate. At a higher and partially learned
level, we are keyed to objects, and need only the most fragmentary evidence. Seeing someone sitting at a desk with only a bit of chair showing
behind him, we already see a chair.[26]

We are even more keyed to our fellow humans. People viewing video-
tapes of bright spots attached to the joints of a moving person see a whole
person, even though the rest of the person is invisible, being dark against

a dark background.[27] We see, then, more than we are given. Arnheim says, "perception consists in fitting the stimulus material with templates."[28] Our templates, however, not only cut out material that does not fit but also supply material that is missing.

Schemata thus are central to perception. They are not arbitrary but serve purposes and needs. They represent aspects of the world that are important to us, and serve as guides to action in that world:

> models of the world are more or less good for a particular task. Thus our perceptual schemata of solid objects, spatial layout, support, occlusion . . . take the form they do because we might want to pick up objects, avoid bumping into them etc. Even if it were possible for our naive physical schemata to correspond to that of modern physics, i.e. with space being sparsely occupied by fundamental particles . . . such a schema would be useless for our everyday life.[29]

Recent ethologists have a similar view of schemata in animal perception. Griffin, for example, writes that foraging birds "look for a particular pattern that tells them where food can be found. Learned patterns may include the barely perceptible outline of a cryptically colored moth resting on the bark of a tree. . . . Somewhere in the animal's brain there must be a mechanism for recognizing what is called a searching image."[30] The searching image varies with the animal's needs. Foods, for example, may change with the seasons or time of day, as fishermen recognize in choosing lures. Even in perceiving a given object, the appropriate schema varies with one's purpose. We can see a dime either as small change or as an impromptu screwdriver.

Schemata range in complexity from those for lines and vertices; to those for surfaces, edges, and volumes; to those for inanimate objects, animate objects, and persons. In visual interpretation, computers and complex organisms may assign levels of structure to data in two ways.[31] One is "bottom up," starting with the elements of the lowest level, such as points, and working up to more complex interpretations such as lines, edges, and so on. This requires searching through a large number of interpretations and getting guidance from the patterns themselves. The opposite approach is "top down," starting with specific expectations of what is important to see. This requires that schemata be available for all important possibilities. Both approaches combine in ordinary perception, which thus is interactive.

The higher the level of hypothesis a cue can prompt, however, the more efficient the process, both in computers and in organisms.[32] Cognitive psychologists including Piaget, Neisser,[33] and Eleanor Rosch[34] note that structuring knowledge appropriately gives access to related knowledge. The higher the level of successful interpretation, the more information we gain. If we can guess, for example, that something near us in the bush is an elephant, we do not need to test whether it is herbivorous or has four columnar legs, a trunk, and floppy ears. Keith Oatley writes,

Figure 4–5 **Hallucinatory cube, after Max Clowes, 1973.** The most coherence is provided by the most highly organized schema. Schemas for three dimensions are more highly organized than those for two, so, although this photograph shows only two pieces of flat paper lying on a flat surface, we see a cube. Similarly, we see edges despite the absence of local evidence.

"it is advantageous to identify the most wide reaching, most meaningful hypotheses possible. After all, if you can see the cue of a nose, you not only know that there is a person in the scene but where to look for the eyes, and the body."[35] Rosch similarly says it is to an "organism's advantage to have as many properties as possible predictable from knowing any one property."[36]

High-level interpretations accordingly are more powerful than lower ones, and take precedence. Higher levels of interpretation can be used, for example, even in the face of contradictory evidence from lower levels. They thus may force changes in lower levels of interpretation, as when we see an apparent cube as having edges even where there is no local evidence of them (Fig. 4–5). This is part of what Harman, Piaget, and Wittgenstein mean in saying that thought is a matter of increasing the coherence of our total view, that we produce structures of inclusion ordering correspondence everywhere, and that we crave generality. That schemata serve needs, and that high-level interpretations take precedence over low-level ones, also are consistent with my view of anthropomorphism as powerful and pervasive because schemata of humans are especially useful and because they offer a high level of interpretation. One of our most pressing needs is to note the presence of other people; hence any schema for detecting humans has priority. People are uniquely highly organized; hence any schema of or for them is an interpretation at the highest level.

Other writers also observe that people are particularly well supplied with schemata for humans. Oatley, for example, says, "In human vision, we are clearly equipped with a rich repertoire of clues for invoking the schemata of people."[37] Arnheim remarks that a "few simple lines and dots are readily accepted as 'a face,' not only by civilized Westerners, who may be suspected of having agreed among one another on such 'sign language,' but also by babies, savages, and animals."[38] Gombrich explains our sensitivity to the human form by its "biological" significance to us.[39]

As do other schemata, our schemata for people both supply missing information and contradict some lower-level interpretations. Gregory shows that our schema for seeing a human face is so powerful that, at all but the closest distances, we see the concave inside of a mask as convex.[40] Even after seeing close up that the mask is concave, observers again involuntarily see it at a distance as convex, even though its shadows are wrong. Gombrich writes, "we respond with particular readiness to certain configurations of biological significance for our survival. The recognition of the human face, on this argument, is not wholly learned. It is based on some kind of inborn disposition. . . . Whenever anything remotely facelike enters our field of vision, we are alerted and respond."[41]

Is this disposition to see the human face inborn, as Gombrich suggests, or is it acquired? The evidence is uncertain. Young infants do attend to human faces and voices more than to other phenomena, which indicates at least that face and voice schemata become prominent early.[42] Researchers have investigated three aspects of face perception: individual features such as eyes and mouths, configurations constituting a face, and faces as communicating emotions. Infants perceive all these either shortly after birth or at least within a few months. Researchers disagree about the timing, however.[43]

On the innatist side is some evidence that infants can imitate facial gestures shortly after birth.[44] One author thinks this shows newborn infants "recognize certain human acts as like their own, and have a rich set of tools for building further bridges between themselves and others . . . neonates can apprehend the correspondence between [gestures] they see and [gestures] of their own whether they see them or not."[45] Another writes, "newborns come into the world already prepared to perceive and respond to people."[46] Other researchers think infants are born with an abstract awareness of what humans are, and with strategies such as imitation and interactional synchrony for signaling this awareness.[47]

Another claim that face perception is innate comes from investigators

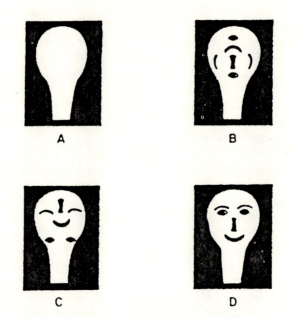

Figure 4-6 **Experimental face-like designs.** Humans are the most highly organized and significant things we know, so we are predisposed to look for them. Some researchers say infants respond to face-like images, such as these, at birth.

who showed head-shaped drawings to newborn infants (Fig. 4–6).[48] One drawing showed a face with eyes and mouth arranged normally, two showed them in unusual places, and one contained no eyes or mouth. The researchers measured how far the infants followed each picture with their gaze, found they followed the "normal" picture furthest, and concluded that newborns innately respond to faces and have a "general social orientation."[49] Others find no such preference in newborns, however, and say it appears only at between two and four months. Most researchers using live faces as stimuli find no discrimination among expressions until five or six months.[50]

Possible evidence for innate face perception also comes from work on other primates. As noted earlier, monkeys only three weeks old already are sensitive to faces looking at them. Young monkeys that have been raised alone and have never seen another monkey or even a mirror image show fear on seeing a picture of a threatening adult.[51] Further, monkey brains may have special areas for face perception: some cells in the macaque cortex respond to monkey faces seen from the front but not to partial or distorted faces.[52] If this is a special area for faces, it is possible that humans have it, too. That they do is suggested by human prosopagnosia, a disorder of face recognition caused by local brain damage.[53]

In sum, experimental and comparative evidence about innate predispositions to perceive humans is mixed. We still are "far from understanding when, or how, babies come to recognize . . . a human face."[54] Nonetheless, infants have this ability either at birth or at least by the first few months. From six months on, they closely attend anything suggesting other humans. By adulthood, people have an "extraordinary ability to recognize a face as that of a human being. They can accurately recognize objects as faces even in poorly focused photographs, in badly degraded computer images, and in rudimentary schematized drawings."[55]

However, since we also see faces in mountains, clouds, and automobiles, the ability to see faces in degraded or rudimentary images is not just a sensitivity to actual faces. Rather, it is a predisposition to see faces whether they are there or not. Our models of faces—whether acquired or innate—are powerful for good reason: "no other object in the visual world is quite so important to us."[56] Consequently, face and other human schemata emerge early. Throughout life, they cause us to find human features everywhere we look.

Another set of claims that humans are innately poised to perceive other humans and to interact with them comes from object-relations psychoanalysts.[57] These post-Freudians are interested in our relations with persons (the "objects") rather than in Freudian "drives." Where Freud saw motivation and behavior as propelled by individualistic, physiological urges, and social relationships merely as means to gratify these, the object-relations writers think our basic motivation is to establish social relationships. Drives, if there are any, are merely means to relationships. Whereas Freud saw bodily erogenous zones, for example, as sources of drives, object-relations analysts see them as channels for interactions, much as biologists see sexual urges as means to genetic exchange.

Thus these writers substitute an innate search for relationships for the innate effort to reduce physiological tension. The specificity of the search varies from writer to writer. Melanie Klein thinks children have inborn images of anatomy, such as breasts and wombs, and of persons, such as mothers and babies.[58] The infant has an "innate unconscious awareness of the existence of the mother."[59] Children's earliest relations are with these a priori persons and parts, which they know and seek prior to experience. These inherent images are the framework on which they build actual relationships.

For other writers, the search for humans is less specific and less anatomical but no less fundamental. Harry Stack Sullivan, for instance, thinks that loneliness is the most painful human experience, and that anxiety, an uncontrollable and disintegrating force, stems primarily from unsatisfactory social relations. To mitigate anxiety, we evoke fictitious others in illusory but familiar relationships: "in the fantasies of patients one comes across diagrammatic fragments . . . of a significant person from many years before [who] still acts in the fashion that was originally relevant."[60] Psychoanalysts Jay Greenberg and Stephen Mitchell write that passions and conflicts come not from drives but from "shifting and competing configurations composed of relations between the self and others, real and imagined."[61] The self, in turn, is a collection of "prominent me-you patterns loosely held together by a set of rationalizations and illusions."[62] Erich Fromm, like Sullivan, also sees isolation as a major human fear, and this fear as the source of our dominant passions and illusions, including beliefs in magic and in saviors.

W.R.D. Fairbairn, again abandoning Freud's notion of drive, sees the libido as seeking not pleasure but another human. Pleasure is merely a means to the libido's ends, a "signpost to the object," namely, a social relationship. Freud, he thinks, mistook means for ends; the "essential striving of the child is not for pleasure but for contact."[63] The attachment theorist John Bowlby, like Fairbairn, emphasizes the primacy of a child's relations with its mother. Bowlby draws on biology, especially ethology and natural selection, to account for a programmed pattern of attachment between mother and child. This "archaic heritage" includes five "instinctual responses: sucking, smiling, clinging, crying, and following," which bind mother and child together.[64] The mother is important to the child not so much as a source of food or other specific physiological needs, as Freud thought, but globally, as a social other.

D. W. Winnicott also depicts the infant as crucially needing a relationship with a mother and as having a general orientation toward, and an anticipation and expectancy of, her.[65] Its needs are complex, subtle, and interactive: for example, to be held, and to be mirrored, both responsively and nonintrusively. As Greenberg and Mitchell describe Winnicott's view, the infant is "dominated by a search for connection, attachment, engagement with other human beings. It is this search that subsumes and imparts meaning to all other dimensions of human life."[66] Stern writes similarly that from the earliest period, infant "social capacities are operating with vigorous goal-directedness to assure social interactions."[67] All these writers agree the infant

> brings to his experience [not] an array of loosely organized body-based tensions but . . . a complex, coherent set of interests, sensitivities, and expectations which draw the infant into human relationship . . . research findings have catalogued the exquisite synchrony between the infant's inborn visual, auditory, [and] tactile preferences and rhythms and physical attributes of human caretakers as well as their intuitive responsiveness to the baby.[68]

Hence, "initially the self does not seek tension reduction or instinctual expression but relatedness, attachment, connection to others."[69] It has a repertoire of means to achieve these. Thus the human imperative is, in E. M. Forster's words (in *Howards End*), "Only connect."

For a theory of anthropomorphism, and of religion, the object-relations school[70] provides a position midway between comfort and cognitivism. Its members point out the shortcomings of wish fulfillment as an explanation of perception and of action. The "hedonistic vision of drive theory is contradicted by the facts of human behavior. People are notoriously inept at finding pleasure; they repeatedly engineer situations which make them unhappy. Only a fundamental need for human contact at any cost accounts for the perpetuation of unpleasure in the lives of so many people."[71] The object-relations view, then, accounts for repetitive or prolonged attachments to unsatisfying partners, as Freud's pleasure principle does not. Contact itself, whether pleasurable or painful, comes first. One might still say, however, that having a relationship, satisfactory or not, constitutes the most important comfort of all.[72]

That models of humans do take priority in perception also gets support from the projective tests of clinical psychologists. People largely interpret Rorschach ink blots, for example, as images of persons or parts of persons. Such interpretations predominate by age three, increase steadily for eight years, and remain predominant throughout life.[73] Interpretations of blots as certain nonhuman animals such as bats and butterflies are next in frequency.[74] These are followed by other animals and distantly by plants and inanimate objects. A recent cross-cultural study suggests that this predominance of humans in inkblot interpretations is universal.[75]

Developmental psychology as well suggests anthropomorphism is central to human thought. Most salient is Piaget's research on children's conceptions of the world.[76] These conceptions, especially among the youngest children, are both anthropocentric and anthropomorphic.

Piaget generally uses two other terms: children are "animists," meaning that they attribute life, usually with consciousness and volition, to nonliving things. They also are "artificialists," meaning they assume that natural objects and events are produced by human activity. As Piaget uses these terms, they mean almost the same as anthropomorphism, since the behavior they label is based on children's experience of humans and consists in attributing human mental and moral traits, and human activities, to the nonhuman world.

In over 600 observations, Piaget asked children, most of them from Geneva and between four and twelve years old, whether various natural phenomena were conscious or alive and how they originated. Such questions, he points out, are by no means foreign to children but often are asked by children themselves. The questions were open-ended and concerned phenomena such as the sun, moon and stars, night and day, clouds, thunder and lightning, snow and ice, rivers, lakes, trees, mountains, and the earth.

Piaget found that the youngest children see virtually all phenomena simultaneously as alive, conscious, and made by humans for human purposes. The children thus are animists and artificialists at once. They find no conflict in objects being both alive and manufactured. Their world consists of a "society of living beings"[77] which humans have produced and in which humans hold first place. Everything exists to serve human needs and does so consciously. Everything is well ordered; nothing is random or accidental. Children assume human manufacture and purpose everywhere: Who made the sun? Why is there a moon? Who made my baby brother?

Piaget investigated ideas about consciousness separately from ideas about life, because children do not think consciousness and life must coincide. A stream, for example, may not be alive but still may feel its own motion, while on the other hand, a rolling stone may be alive but unable to feel a prick.

Piaget divides ideas about consciousness into four stages. Children in the first stage (typically up to six or seven years) think anything that is somehow active is conscious. Clouds and wind are conscious because they move and the sun and moon are conscious because they give light. Similarly, a wooden bench feels being burned, a wall feels being knocked down, and a string feels being twisted. Anything that is the seat of some action, feels it. In the second stage, from six or seven years to eight or nine, children limit consciousness to things that move: sun, moon, wind, fire, bicycles, and clocks, but not stones or chairs. In the third stage, from eight or nine years to eleven or twelve, children limit consciousness even further, to things which move of their own accord, including most moving natural phenomena but not such things as bicycles and boats. After eleven or twelve, children usually attribute consciousness only to animals, although sometimes to plants as well.

Ideas about the presence of life develop similarly. In the first stage, children regard as living everything with an activity, use, or function. Since they assume virtually everything has a function, virtually everything is alive. A child of three, watching a stone roll down a bank, says "Look at the stone. It's afraid of the grass." A child of two and a half brings his toy motor to the window and says, "Motor see the snow."[78]

Children in this stage implicitly assume a "fundamental final cause in nature and a *continuum* of forces"[79] serving human ends. Things serve humans with an immanent force that constitutes their life. Each object is guided by its use:[80]

> Is the sun alive?—*Yes.*—Why?—*It gives light.*—Is a candle alive?—*No.*—Why not?—*(Yes) because it gives light. It is alive when it is giving light, but it isn't alive when it is not giving light.*—Is a bicycle alive?—*No, when it doesn't go it isn't alive. When it goes it is alive.*—Is a mountain alive?—*No.*—Why not?—*Because it doesn't do anything (!)*—Is a tree alive?—*No; when it has fruit it's alive. When it hasn't any, it isn't alive.*[81]

These children also refer to objects as "who" rather than "what" and regard them morally, as potentially either good or bad. They also see the sun and moon as following them, a persistent perception.

In the second stage, children identify life primarily with movement: "Is a cat alive?—*Yes.*—A snail?—*Yes.*—A table?—*No.*—Why not?—*It can't move.*—Is a bicycle alive?—*Yes.*—Why?—*It can go.*"[82] Another child recalls Goodall's chimps, which threaten rapid streams: "Is a stream alive?—*Yes, it goes.*—Is the lake alive?—*Yes, it is always moving a bit.*—

Is a cloud alive?—*Yes, you can see it moving.*"[83] In the third stage, children distinguish spontaneous motion from motion imposed from outside: bicycles move because the rider pedals, boats because someone rows them, and clouds because the wind pushes them. The only difference from the prior stage is that younger children suppose motion is inherent in whatever moves. In the fourth stage, children restrict life to animals and plants, but still may attribute will to objects they see as neither conscious nor alive. They may, for example, struggle to remove the lid from a jar and remark that the lid does not want to come off. This leads Piaget to suggest (as does Nietzsche) that the animistic notion of will underlies the later physical notion of force.

Piaget divides artificialism, the belief that natural objects and events are produced by humans, into four stages as well. In the first, "diffuse artificialism," children imagine production not as manufacture but as spatial transfer; new babies, for example, "come from" somewhere. Processes of production and control are not detailed. The world is magical: self and not-self are indistinct and humans can control the world by will and at a distance. Animism and artificialism still are merged. The sun and moon, for example, are animate in that they follow us and artificial in that they were made by us, for light and warmth. The world again is a purposeful society of living beings.

Piaget calls the second stage of artificialism, from five or six years to seven or eight, mythological. Now children begin to imagine specific origins. Humans made the sun, for example, by striking a match or tossing a flaming ball into the sky. Although all is manufactured, however, all still is alive as well. Birth and manufacture still are not distinguished. Babies may be molded by hand. Other natural phenomena also issue from human bodies: wind originates in human breathing, clouds in condensation from breath, rain in perspiration or spit, and rivers and lakes in urine. At the same time, these products are alive and purposeful.

The third stage, from seven or eight years to nine or ten, is technical artificialism. Now children begin to look at details of human technique and production. They come to understand the mechanisms of such machines as bicycles and the limits of human ability to create and control. They begin to see some processes as intrinsic to nature while still attributing the general order to humans. The world becomes a mix of direct and indirect human production. For example, humans establish river courses but the water originates in rain falling naturally. Similarly, planets and clouds no longer are direct human products but still may be condensations of smoke from chimneys. As children begin to see properties as inherent in matter, and technique as limited, they see contradictions between artificialism and animism. Human manufactures no longer are alive and living things are not manufactured. A table, for example, cannot feel anything "because it has been made."[84]

The fourth and last stage, after nine or ten years, is immanent artificialism. Now children cease seeing nature as made by humans and attribute natural processes to nature itself. Natural objects such as the stars and planets are not made but born from other natural objects: stars from the sun or moon, and the moon from the sun. However, children do not abandon artificialism; they relocate it in nature, which "inherits the attributes of man and manufactures in the style of the craftsman or artist."[85] Design in the world persists; nature still is imbued with purpose. The sun and clouds may originate independently of humans and by natural rather than divine processes, yet be made for warmth, light, and rain. Both force and purpose are intrinsic to each object or process. At this point, Piaget says, children's artificialism is the same as that of Aristotle's physics.[86]

Animism and artificialism, which in Piaget's usage together amount to anthropomorphism, thus are both spontaneous and pervasive in early childhood. They slowly diminish through childhood and, by early adolescence, children's views approximate those of adults.

Why do animism and artificialism exist and why do they diminish? The causes Piaget gives are not entirely convincing. He first describes animism as a primitive assumption, not a construct: it is neither compounded from experience nor learned from adults, and indeed contradiction by adults has little influence. Although it is primitive, Piaget suggests four sources. Two are unique: an initial phase of innate, diffuse animism, the "general tendency to confuse the living and the inert," and a later, systematic animism, a set of explicit animistic beliefs.

Diffuse animism results from an "indissociation" of ideas in the primitive consciousness: the youngest children distinguish neither purposive and nonpurposive action nor self and other. They regard the world as a continuous whole, simultaneously physical and psychical. Their indissociation is not totally mistaken but reflects an actual continuity of organism and environment, a "continuity of exchanges." However, children *are* mistaken in attributing mental traits to the environment. This mistake is persistent because no direct experience can show that the environment is *not* animated. Only a growing awareness of the nature of language (that a name is not the thing named and that no direct link connects will and matter) and of the boundaries of one's own mind lead gradually to a withdrawal of mind from things.

Systematic animism results from egocentrism, which makes everything seem to revolve around the self. Thus the sun and moon seem to follow the child, and all objects, either by resistance or by compliance, appear oriented to it. That apparent orientation invites the child to "introject" its feelings and motives into objects[87] and to think objects come into existence, and leave it, depending upon whether the child sees them or not.

In addition to indissociation and egocentrism, Piaget says, two social causes of animism also exist. First, the child's earliest experience is an intense social relation with its parents, which makes the child seem the center of a highly social world. From this early experience it assumes the whole world is social. Second, the child soon is involved in a network of moral obligations. Parents seem omniscient, which means the child's deeds and misdeeds can be seen everywhere, and objects seem its parents' agents.

Artificialism arises for some of the same reasons as animism, including awareness of self as agent and awareness of parents. The child is aware of itself as an agent in two ways. One is physiological: it breathes and urinates, among other functions. These are the sources of wind and water. The other is manipulation. The child makes things with its hands, largely as a means of understanding. This is a central activity and mode of becoming. Most important, the child experiences its parents as omnipotent as well as omniscient[88] and itself as their central concern. Since they are benevolent, they use their limitless power for the child's well-being. Hence the world is their construction for the child's benefit.

As a description of children's anthropomorphism, Piaget's account is powerful and well documented.[89] As an explanation of that anthropomorphism, however, it is implausible in several ways. For instance, he describes very young children as experiencing themselves and the world as a continuum; but elsewhere he reports that children distinguish self from not-self by about one year. More recent researchers, such as Stern, say this distinction comes earlier, even at birth, and Coy says it occurs among animals as well.[90] Once the self/other distinction is made, it is not clear how the global confusion to which Piaget attributes anthropomorphism could occur. Similarly, egocentrism may indeed lead children to attribute their purposes and activities to inanimate objects; but, if so, Piaget's view of such attribution as a confusion to be outgrown raises the question of why it persists in adults. Piaget thinks the attribution largely disappears but, in fact, it does not.

Piaget also underestimates the persistence of artificialism and the depth of its source. He appears to be correct in saying that children's early experiences of their parents as a social world and of themselves as physical, manipulative agents, are principal sources of their humanlike models. However, he does not acknowledge, except in brief references to religion, that these models continue broadly into adult life. Their persistence suggests that something more sustains them than immature confusion.

What gives rise to them and sustains them, in my view, is the perceptual strategy described earlier, which has good reason to persist. An illusion—a failed or erroneous interpretation—does not necessarily mean that the perceptual guess leading to it is irrational.[91] Apart from finding adults similar to children and emphasizing strategy rather than confusion, however, my view does not conflict with Piaget's. Rather, it builds on his description of the child's world and on his location of the sources of anthropomorphic models in the experience of self and of others.

Anthropomorphism is prominent in perception not only in the West but also around the world. Because few cross-cultural studies of perception directly concern anthropomorphism,[92] much of the evidence is circumstantial. However, anthropomorphism in ethnography, journalism, folk literature, and other sources is so pervasive and so similar across cultures as to indicate a common perceptual basis. Moreover, recurring themes in these sources echo Piaget's animism and artificialism: things and events are willful and intelligent, natural processes are purposive, and objects such as celestial bodies are either born (for example, from other celestial bodies) or made by humans or humanlike deities. Little or nothing escapes being anthropomorphized at some time or place and at some level of thought. People see animals, plants, artifacts, inanimate phenomena such as wind and rain, and abstractions such as death and time as more or less humanlike. They humanize animals most comprehensively but humanize other phenomena almost as much.

Indeed, no boundaries exist cross-culturally between animate and inanimate or human and nonhuman. Consequently the very labels animism and anthropomorphism, since they assume distinctions between living and nonliving and human and nonhuman, are culture-bound. They constitute a judgment made in hindsight or in looking at other people's perceptions that we or they have attributed to particular phenomena more organization than the phenomena have. Similarly—to anticipate the final chapter—no clear border separates religious from nonreligious thought and action. Observers have long noted that religions contain, or are continuous with, magic. Religions also contain and are continuous with science, philosophy, art, common sense, and other categories, just as these intermingle with each other. All these classifications are somewhat arbitrary, though useful for certain purposes.

As we survey anthropomorphism cross-culturally, these continuities raise the question, Where does anthropomorphism that is secular end and that which is religious begin? Although I try to separate them, treating secular anthropomorphism mainly here and religious anthropomorphism in chapter 7, no clear line can be drawn. The boundaries are porous and the closer we look, the larger are the holes. Nonetheless, we can name representative characteristics for each side. Religious anthropomorphism typically is elaborate, shared, and enduring; secular anthropomorphism typically is ad hoc, idiosyncratic, and fleeting. The anthropomorphism we call religion also is relatively systematic, and addresses relatively powerful and important entities, such as gods, which have a key human capacity, that for symbolic interaction.

However, the continuity of religious and nonreligious spheres means there is no break either between our conceptions of gods and our conceptions of ordinary humans or between religious anthropomorphism and secular anthropomorphism. Demeter and Chiquita Banana, Thor and Jack Frost are of one piece. The rest of this chapter sketches the universal sea of anthropomorphism on which rise ripples of religiosit and waves of religion. Later I shall depict the waves as part of the sea.

*   *   *

Folk literature around the world[93] anthropomorphizes nature thoroughly and diversely. Europeans, we saw, for at least five hundred years regarded animals as both morally and legally responsible. Many other peoples do so as well. Stories from every continent explain, for example, physical and behavioral characteristics of animals as rewards or punishments, or as results of trade with, or theft from, other animals.[94] Kipling's "Just So" stories, such as *How the Rhinoceros Got His Skin,* are instances. Just as widespread are ascriptions of language to animals, including mammals, birds, reptiles, amphibians, fishes, and insects. All are said to speak, either in a human language or in one that a human may learn. They also commonly are said to feel jealousy, envy, love, and anger, and to sing, whistle, laugh, or cry.

Animals also widely live in kingdoms, with kings and parliaments, or in other political communities. They conduct warfare (usually between domesticated and wild animals or between two species, such as a predator and its prey), make peace treaties and alliances (often between species), and conduct legal relationships including lawsuits and criminal trials. They marry, again throughout the animal kingdom and often across species. They conduct humanlike relationships with humans; are farmers, laborers, merchants, tollkeepers, physicians, and musicians;[95] and observe human religions.

In short, animals of all sorts are conceived as having human social characteristics and relationships. The pervasiveness of this assimilation is reflected in a recent *New Yorker* cartoon (Fig. 4–7) in which a dog and cat standing at a bar make small talk about their shared anthropomorphism.

Other natural phenomena also are anthropomorphized widely. Some, such as plants and viruses, are alive by contemporary Western standards. Among plants, food crops especially are assimilated to people (Fig. 4–8)—for example, corn among the Pueblo peoples, yams among Dobuans, and rice in Southeast Asia. The Iban, for instance, identify the spirits of rice with those of humans. Rice "is 'just like one of us' [and] is accorded the utmost reverence and respect. . . . [It has] human moods and attitudes: it is 'unhappy,' 'feels unwanted'—Iban women 'take pity' on mall grains while harvesting, it 'catches cold,' 'needs company,' and 'likes attention.' "[96] In the United States, the giant saguaro cactus is a popular symbol of the Southwest largely because of its raised arms. Thieves now endanger the existence of this species because the cacti are "majestic and somewhat human in appearance," resembling "giant human stick figures that seem to wave, beckon, or pray."[97] A botanical-garden employee says other endangered cacti get little notice because they "aren't somehow human." Other Americans talk to their house plants, believing the plants then grow better. In Russian popular thought, women are equated with birches and men with oaks.[98]

Other things and events, though labeled inanimate in the contemporary West, still are humanized here and elsewhere. In the United States,

"So you're anthropomorphic too? It's a small world."

Figure 4–7   The search for humanlike form is pervasive. "Anthropomorphism" labels apparent discoveries of such form where it does not exist. Drawing by Handelsman; © 1989 The New Yorker Magazine, Inc.

we recall the firefighters who see forest fires as devious and as lying in wait. People worldwide anthropomorphize such inanimate phenomena as the sun, moon, stars, wind, rain, and earthquakes. In India, among the San of South Africa, on the Gold Coast, in New Guinea, in the Tua-motus, and among Indians of eastern Brazil and elsewhere in South America, the sun is a man who left the earth. Alternately the sun was born (from a first couple, a goddess, an ogre, or the moon) or was tossed into the sky by humans. Its daily course across the sky often is a journey. At night it may close its doors, hide, be kept in a pot or box, bathe in a stream to cool off, or worship God. Sometimes it is a king, as in India,

Figure 4–8 **American postcard, 1915.** Folk and commercial art widely attribute human features to living things, and especially to foodstuffs.

in Jewish myth, and in Africa. It may sit on a throne and keep cattle, sheep, or horses.[99]

The sun and moon everywhere have social relations, usually as man and woman. Often they are husband and wife, sometimes brother and sister, sometimes lovers. In the preconquest Andes they were a "primeval pair created by a supreme being [and might] appear in human form emitting rays that end in serpent heads. Their union is consummated in a holy place, usually depicted as high on the mountain slopes and surrounded with . . . symbols of fertility."[100] Elsewhere the sun and moon wed, are jealous, quarrel, hold contests, or pursue each other. Occasionally, as in North and South America and in India, they are brothers, and sometimes they are sisters or friends.

The moon sometimes originates by birth and sometimes, as in India, North and South America, and among the Norse, as a transformed human. The moon may be infatuated with a human and woo, abduct, cohabit with, marry, or have a child with him or her, as in Europe, North America, South America, and India. The moon's phases may be caused by its sickness and recovery, starving and eating, menstrual periods, or punishment for wrongdoing.[101]

Alternatively to *being* a human, the moon may have a human visible in it. The human often, as in Europe, China, and North, Central, and South America, is there for punishment. Sometimes the image is an animal, such as a rabbit, frog, or jaguar, as in, respectively, India, Japan, and Central and South America. Other human images in the moon are marks of her mother's hand on her shoulder (India), dung or ashes smeared on his or her face by the sun (India), children with a yoke and bucket (Iceland), a woman threshing grain (India and China), a woman in the moon's oven (Samoa), and a goddess beating tapa under a tree (Tonga).[102]

Such perceptions may be not only traditional but also spontaneous and idiosyncratic. Eldridge Cleaver, the former Black Panther leader, reportedly once looked out a window and "saw the faces of Karl Marx, Mao Tse-tung, and Fidel Castro appear and then disappear on the face of the moon." Cleaver then "saw the face of Jesus and [soon] became a born-again Christian."[103] During the recent Persian Gulf War, thousands of Jordanians are said to have seen Saddam Hussein's face in the moon.[104]

As have sun and moon, the stars almost everywhere have been conceived as transformed animals and people. They descend to earth as humans almost everywhere and may even marry humans. They may sing or speak. Sometimes they are the children of the moon, as in Jewish tradition and in India, Indonesia, the Philippines, and South America. They may be children of the sun but then be eaten by him and so not exist during the day, as in India, Africa, and ancient Rome. Constellations as well as individual stars may be persons or artifacts. The Milky Way, for instance, has been a hunting party, milk from a woman's breast, semen of the gods, a road, a seam stitched in the sky, smoke, and a racetrack.[105]

Weather similarly may be either humanlike or an artifact of humanlike activity. The rainbow has been a god's bow, a divine bridge, a transformed king (with the lesser rainbow as wife), the contents of a god's drinking cup, and the horse of the rain god. The wind is the breathing of a deity or spirit in China and parts of North and South America, is caused by the deity's movements among the San, is a person with a mosquito fan among the Iatmul, and comes through holes (the stars) in the sky-tent among the Eskimo. Rain widely stems from tears, urine, or a container in the sky. Rain also may be a person, as among the Bantu,[106] and the clouds may be its hair. Clouds also may be smoke from human fires, as they commonly are among Piaget's children. Lightning may be a flashing sword, the whip or messenger of a god, or the twinkling of a personified thunder's eyes. Thunder also may be a god's voice (in Jewish, Chinese, and other interpretations) or gun or other weapons (India and North America), a waterskin dragged along the sky floor (India), or drums of the dead (Africa).[107]

As does other anthropomorphism, that concerning weather may spring up to suit the occasion. A newspaper reports ice on Long Island Sound as

> such a real, living threat that local residents talk about it as though it were a person. "She forms around the spiles that hold up the docks and when the tide comes in she lifts the spiles up and heaves the dock. . . . When the ice is freed from the shore, she has a power all her own. She swings this way and that way and knocks down everything in her path."[108]

In another modern instance, a television weatherman calls high- and low-pressure systems good guys and bad guys, and his weather map represents them with happy and sad faces like Greek theater masks.[109]

Landscapes also suggest humanity, as we have seen in the coastal geography of ancient Greece and in the mountains of New Hampshire (Fig. 3–1). Other instances are plentiful. The Papago Indians know two peaks in Arizona as the Twin Sisters, and Colorado has another Twin Sisters and a Mummy Mountain. The Ute of Colorado see in Sleeping Ute Mountain the feet, knees, and folded arms of a reclining man who changes his blankets with the seasons, under cover of fog or cloud: to green in summer, yellow and red in autumn, and white in winter. Wyoming has the Grand Tetons or big breasts. For the Andeans of Mount Kaata,

> the mountain is a human body. Their fields are used and their different products are exchanged in accord with the different functional parts of that body. . . . The land is understood in terms of the human body . . . people feed the mountain body with gifts and sacrifice, and the mountain reciprocates with food for all the people.[110]

For other Andeans, mountains, "high hills [and] huge stones . . . were once people. . . . The first people to emerge were converted into stones, mountains, condors, falcons, and other animals and birds."[111] Here the anthropomorphism is systematized; it includes a full social relationship between land and people, and is in fact part of a religious system.

Mountains, caves, and other landscape features are alive and human-like elsewhere in the world. In China, Huang Shan, a highly eroded mountain in Anhui Province, displays animal and human shapes including two cats chasing a mouse and a mandarin watching a chess game. A cave at Guilin has stalactites and stalagmites seen as artifacts, as animals including camels, and, on opposite sides of a chamber, as a long-separated husband and wife. Steep peaks and valleys in the Gaolan area of Hubei include a sleeping Buddha, a barking dog, and two lovers in conversation.

An American news story on Lebanon begins, "A mountain peak here

[is] the eyes and ears of the Israeli military."[112] Mountains may compete: a news story titled "Everest, the Old Champion, Is Crowned Anew,"[113] is subtitled "It's Taller Than Rival, K-2, After All," and begins, "Everest is still king of the mountains." Another story, "In Haiti, the Land Is Worn Nearly to the Bone," reports a local as saying, "the rocks have children here."[114] One journalist anthropomorphizes an entire Arctic landscape: "Clouds swirl muscularly. . . . The frigid snow squeaks underfoot as if it were alive, the ice on the river rumbles, and in the 'drunken forest,' where trees struggle to root themselves in spite of the permafrost, wood snaps like a gunshot in a cold snap."[115]

Earthquakes and volcanos also are animated and personified. In the modern West, for example, volcanos either are "active" or "dormant." When Mount St. Helens erupted, a seismologist called the volcano a "baby in geologic terms" and a U.S. Forest Service spokesman said it might "start spitting . . . or just lay down and go back to sleep."[116] In ordinary language, cliffs have faces, rivers have mouths, mountains have feet, and hills have shoulders and brows. Coastal geography has headlands, capes, and arms of the sea.

The sea is notoriously moody: raging or calm, cruel or fickle. It is a demanding mistress. A sailor may be rocked in the cradle of the deep or be swallowed and end in Davy Jones's locker. A resident of the Outer Banks thinks construction on land that once was an inlet is dangerous because the "sea never forgets where it's been."[117] Humans "assault" the sea with toxins and it may be "dying." A news article on pollution begins, "SOTTOMARINA, Italy—All summer long this year the Adriatic was hot and languid and getting sicker by the day. Eventually one little part of the sea almost died. . . . When the seasons changed, the sea began healing itself."[118] The article reports the Italian Environment Minister as saying that both the sea and the Po River (an "artery" bearing the nearly fatal toxins) "cry out for vengeance." Some Iatmul clans say waves are a "person (Kontumali) independent of the wind."[119]

People also personify the entire Earth, frequently as a mother, in cultures including European, Semitic, Finno-Ugric, Siberian, Indian, African, and North American ones.[120] Lucretius, for example, pictured the first animals and humans as born from wombs in the ground. English speakers refer to the earth's bosom and bowels, and recently the rain forests have become its lungs. As in the Andes, human relations with the earth may be social and require reciprocity. North American Indians, for example, sometimes buried arrowheads in return for the raw materials from which they were made.

Nature as a whole may be a mother, a trope so common in the contemporary United States, for example, as to be almost invisible. Versions of nature as mother vary widely, even within a single culture. Frequently they reflect moral judgments, usually positive but sometimes negative. In the West these now may be self-conscious or flippant. Recent American variants include a letter to a newspaper, reporting atmospheric pollution by trees and volcanos, which the editor headed, "Mother Nature Exposed as Polluter."[121] An article on human effects on weather begins,

> SANTA MONICA, Calif.—Has Mother Nature lost her virginity? Apparently so, according [to scientists]. Our weather, they believe, is no longer conceived immaculately in the sky by an act of God; human adulterations . . . have sowed [*sic*] the seeds of the rains and storms we have reaped this winter. 'Tis a pity. When Mother Nature was pure, weather was uncontroversial.[122]

Another article suggests that wilderness may induce a "little wildness" and that if, "as Freud said, we all desire our mothers, shouldn't we feel something analogous for mother nature?"[123] In a similarly incestuous vein, an article on bicycling extols the "eroticism of rolling over the very skin of Mother Earth."[124]

Not only nature but also artifacts—machinery, clothing, pottery, glass bottles, mailboxes, and virtually everything else—are humanlike cross-culturally. Among anthropomorphic machinery we already have noted cars, ships, airplanes, and computers. Machine noises may also sound humanlike:

> The engine, the engine. Its thump and clatter, all mixed up with the smell of diesel oil and the continuous slight motion of the sea, is so regular and monotonous that you keep on hearing voices in it. Sometimes, when the revs are low, there's a man under the boards reciting poems that you vaguely remember in a resonant bass. Sometimes the noise rises to the bright nonsense of a cocktail party in the flat downstairs. At present, though, you're stuck with your usual cruising companion at sixteen hundred revs, an indignant old fool grumbling in the cellar.
>
> *Where'd I put it? Can't remember. Gerroff, you, blast and damn you. Where'd I put it? Can't remember. Sodding thingummy. Where'd I put it? Can't remember.*[125]

Clothing, doubtless aided by its shape and association with the body, often is animate and personal. A checkroom attendant says down coats "have a life of their own. They visit each other and I'm convinced that they mate. . . . I restrain them but they get away from me. They do have a certain personality, I feel, adolescent, hippie."[126] Another attendant feels "like I'm being mugged by down coats." Umbrellas also may be humanlike:

> gusting winds caused his umbrella to take on a life of its own. After repeatedly trying to get Mr. Sedacca's attention by tapping him on the head, the umbrella fended off a potential interloper with a swat in the face. Finally, tattered and torn from its wind-blown animation, it was laid low, feebly flapping about the feet of its owner in abject submission.[127]

A writer waiting for Samuel Beckett in the Paris Post Office Museum anthropomorphized postboxes: "They were generally the same height.

. . . When I stood in the room surrounded by them, the mail slots began to look like mouths and I felt that they might begin conversing with one another."[128] The writer reports feeling he was in a Beckett play. But no literary impulse is needed to see a mailbox as a person; witness the taxi driver who several times mistook one for a rider.

Pottery also is seen as humanlike and is formed and decorated accordingly. (See chapter 5, especially Fig. 5–17 through Fig. 5–24). Three archaeologists, Nicholas David, Judy Sterner, and Kodzo Gavua, recently have noted that African pottery may be anthropomorphized.[129] Pertinently for my theory of religion, their epigraph is from Paul Tillich: "he who can read the style of a culture can discover its ultimate concern, its religious substance." However, they think anthropomorphism is peculiar to pottery and that pots are seen as people because they are transformed by heat as humans are transformed by culture.

We have seen that pottery is not alone, though, and that nothing needs special transformation to be seen as humanlike. An African anthropologist, Simiyu Wandibba, responds to the archaeologists as I do: "Human nature is such that we tend to see many of the objects we create in our 'own image.' Thus, we apply body-part terms to such objects as gourds, wooden vessels, and even metal and plastic objects of modern craftsmanship."[130]

More evidence appears constantly. A recent news article subtitled "New Household Objects Show Warmth and Personality" says this "generation" of products has "sensuous lines, tactile surfaces and biomorphic shapes."[131] National Public Radio reports, "you don't burp square Tupperware; you only burp round Tupperware."[132] Animated and anthropomorphic artifacts, however, are just one more aspect of a very general phenomenon. We see not only artifacts but everything, at some time and to some degree, in our image.

Abstractions as well are personified or animated everywhere. Death, for example, often is a person, sometimes a human skeleton. He may be cheated, deceived, imprisoned, or fought, and may come on horseback or send messengers. Anthropomorphized abstractions are no prerogative of simpler societies. Michael Taussig even thinks modern societies more than others personify aspects of social relations, such as work, markets, and society, making them "animate entities with a life-force of their own akin to spirits or gods."[133] Other frequently personified abstractions include youth, old age, illness, truth, justice, the seasons, virtues and sins, war, poverty, crime, heat, and cold.

Even this brief ethnographic survey shows that people around the world see virtually everything, at one time or another, as significantly humanlike. One might object that concerns other than perception motivate some of the texts reported. One might argue, for instance, that anthropomorphism is not perceptual but conceptual, that it is a representation or secondary elaboration, and that it is motivated by aims other than simply seeing what is. To sustain this objection, however, one would have to draw a line between percepts and concepts. Such a line cannot be drawn because perception already is interpretation. It is a choice of one possibility from many, since sense data define nothing in particular. Perception draws data together with a template, a process already conceptual and representational. Hence the percept/concept distinction collapses. Even if such a distinction could be made, anthropomorphism would range across both sides of it.

The pervasive anthropomorphism indicated by ethnography and folk literature doubtless has the same perceptual roots as that indicated by psychology. The research reviewed suggests these roots run deep. Work in artificial intelligence shows once more that perception is interpretation and that the highest-level interpretations are the most powerful and guide perception. Object-relations psychoanalysts and attachment theorists say we search innately for persons and for social relationships. Developmental psychologists show that children and even infants interpret phenomena as humanlike, as caused by humans, or both. Clinical and experimental psychologists, and ethnographers, show that adults do so as well. In sum, the research shows that a generalized anthropomorphism is spontaneous and primitive in children and persists in adults.

Human perception thus anthropomorphizes throughout life, at many levels, and for strategic reasons. Although those reasons are sound and deeply rooted, they also are a source of recurring illusion. As with any persistent illusion, understanding the breadth and depth of that source alerts us to its affects far afield. And, as sailors find the fresh water of the Amazon flowing in a broad fan on the surface of the sea far out of sight of land, we find anthropomorphism in our thoughts and actions far from any apparent motive.

5

Anthropomorphism in the Arts

—The trees. "I think that I shall never see slash A poem lovely as a tree."
—"A tree whose hungry mouth is pressed slash Against the earth's sweet flowing breast."
—Why "mouth"?
—Why "breast"?
—The working of the creative mind.
—An unfathomable mystery.
—Never to be fathomed.

Donald Barthelme, "The Leap"

Anthropomorphism pervades not only the spontaneous perceptions and utterances of daily life but also the more self-conscious productions of writers, artists, and scientists. These groups have varying attitudes toward anthropomorphism, however. While scientists try to suppress it, creative writers and visual artists develop and use it. Anthropomorphism permeates the arts for the same reason it does other thought and action: we strive for meaning by scanning and shaping the world with meaningful forms, and of these the human form is preeminent.[1]

As with animism in art, one might object that anthropomorphism in art differs from naive anthropomorphism in that it is calculated to exploit some tendency in its audience. Thus it is intentional and contrived, not spontaneous. However, although artists certainly calculate and manipulate, their representations still originate in the same unconscious perceptual process as in other people. As with animism, artists often deliberately use anthropomorphism, but first they experience it.

Creative writers anthropomorphize inveterately. Brief images range from Homer's recurrent "rosy-fingered Dawn" through the Bible's "wine is a mocker" and the "battle-lusting" swords of Norse sagas to Thoreau's making the earth "express its summer thoughts in beans." Sustained images also are common. Writers who develop earth and sky as persons, for example, range from Aeschylus to Forster. In a fragment of a lost play, Aeschylus makes the earth and sky lovers: "The pure sky [Ouranos] desires to penetrate the earth, and the earth is filled with love so that she longs for blissful union with the sky. The rain falling from the beautiful sky [Ouranos] impregnates the earth, so that she gives birth to fodder and grain for flocks and men."[2]

Two millennia later Forster, in *A Passage to India,* follows Aeschylus (and many others) in making earth and sky, respectively, female and male. Unlike Aeschylus, Forster also gives the earth fists and fingers: "League after league the earth lies flat, heaves a little, is flat again. Only in the south, where a group of fists and fingers are thrust up through the soil, is the endless expanse interrupted. These fists and fingers are the Marabar Hills."[3] Thomas Hardy's Egdon Heath, as a fall evening approached, "embrowned itself[4] moment by moment." Hardy gives the heath a face, character, feelings, social relationships, and an explicit likeness to humanity:

> The face of the heath by its mere complexion added half an hour to the evening; it could in like manner retard the dawn, sadden noon, anticipate the frowning of storms [and] was, indeed, a near relation of night. . . . like man, slighted and enduring; and withal singularly colossal and mysterious in its swarthy monotony. As with some persons who have lived long apart, solitude seemed to look out of its countenance. It had a lonely face, suggesting tragic possibilities.[5]

Scholars find anthropomorphism—though most call it personification or the pathetic fallacy—throughout literature. Morton Bloomfield, for example, says personification, giving "general characteristics of an individual human being [to an] inanimate notion or object,"[6] has "universal power and long-lived popularity,"[7] and in the "whole range of Western literature from Homer down to today [is] one of the most popular of all literary modes."

Personification, in the broad sense of representing a thing or abstraction as a person, is popular in non-Western literature as well. In the last chapter we saw it in folk literature everywhere. It is equally common in the great literary traditions. In ancient Mesopotamian literature, for instance, personified abstractions engage each other in disputes.[8] Examples exist in Sumerian, Akkadian, Syriac, Arabic, and Persian. A Syriac poem begins,

> 1. The months of the year gather together
> to present the beauty of their produce;
> the Year sits there as mistress

to hear the case between them.
Come and listen . . . [9]

The Bible also personifies, as in the Nineteenth Psalm:

> The heavens declare the glory of God; and the firmament
> sheweth his handiwork.
> Day unto day uttereth speech, and night unto night
> sheweth knowledge.
> There is no speech nor language where their voice is not
> heard.

The Chinese classics personify as well. The *Tao te Ching*, for example, says the Tao, or Way, cannot be characterized yet it is the "mysterious female" and "mother of all things." The *Tao te Ching* also personifies specific natural phenomena: wind and rain, Arthur Waley notes, are "utterances of nature, parallel to speech in man."[10] Confucius's *Analects*, though emphasizing human social relations, also personifies nature. Stars, for example, "do homage" to the pole star (Book II:1) and a mountain "knows ritual" (Book III:6).

Most scholars see the pathetic fallacy, the imputation of human feelings to an inanimate object or to the natural world, as a corollary of personification.[11] More precisely, in my view, it is an aspect of personification, as personification is an aspect of anthropomorphism. Although the pathetic fallacy has been in critical disfavor since the midnineteenth century, some scholars call it "almost unavoidable."[12] Indeed, Frye says all of literature is an attempt to find a human face in nature and that civilization itself is the "process of making a total human form out of nature."[13]

Frye notwithstanding, most writers on literature see personification and the pathetic fallacy as peculiar to literature and especially to poetry. Moreover, most modern literary commentators think personification aberrant, peculiarly unrealistic, and even disreputable. Bloomfield writes, "personification allegory is considered the most unimportant part of . . . allegory and symbolism and has earned the epithets 'reality-drained' and 'paper-thin.' "[14] Two centuries earlier, Joseph Addison also found personification particularly removed from reality. Poetry, for example, is fantastic because it "shews us Persons who are not to be found in being, and represents even the Faculties of the Soul, with her several Virtues and Vices, in a sensible Shape and Character."[15]

Most scholars find personification artificial, as a deliberate figure of speech for a literary purpose. They call it variously a "technique," a "trope," a "metaphor," a "conceit," a "move," or a "literary mode," and treat it solely as a phenomenon of language and especially of rhetoric.[16] Few scholars[17] think personification either spontaneous or part of a broader worldview, and fewer still identify it as a form of anthropomorphism.

Beyond an agreement that personification and the pathetic fallacy are peculiar and preeminently literary, there is little consensus. Bloomfield remarks that despite its disrepute, personification has attracted a "good deal of speculation in modern literary theory."[18] If so, the speculation is unsystematic. Definitions vary widely, even within individual writers. Bloomfield, as noted, describes personification almost synonymously with anthropomorphism; yet elsewhere he contrasts not human and non-human but living and nonliving: personification consists in "animating inanimate objects or abstract notions."[19] This broader definition thus makes animism also a kind of personification.

Many writers think personification especially concretizes abstractions, such as truth, beauty, and justice. Bloomfield says personification normally applies to abstract nouns, and Jane Hedley says it is "the trope that is constituted as a yoking of the abstract with the concrete, the universal with the particular."[20] But Bloomfield admits personification is "obscured by conflicting theories and a wavering, and even contradictory, terminology."[21]

Other writers are equally tentative. Many are uncertain whether the crucial attribute is animation or personality.[22] Lavinia Griffiths, for example, first calls personification the "translation whereby things absent, abstract, inanimate, are made human and present" and a "grammatical transformation of a noun or other part of speech into a proper name," but warns, "a working definition of the figure . . . is not easy."[23] Later she changes the predicate from personality to animation: personification attributes "animateness to a substantive which is grammatically inanimate."[24] Still others focus on humanity but nonetheless present a portmanteau definition, as in the "attribution of human characteristics or feelings to nonhuman organisms, inanimate objects, or abstract ideas."[25] This definition, like Bloomfield's, would apply equally well to anthropomorphism.

Scholar's attitudes toward personification are as varied as their definitions. Classical and medieval rhetoricians commend its energy and life. Quintilian, for example, identifies personification with animation, the most "powerful" metaphor: "effects of extraordinary sublimity are produced when the theme is exalted by a bold and almost hazardous metaphor and inanimate objects are given life and action, as in the phrase 'Araxes' flood that scorns a bridge' (*Aeneid* 8.728)."[26] Classical practice corresponds to classical endorsement. Personification pervades Greek and Roman literature from beginning to end, from Homer, Hesiod, and Aeschylus to Cicero and Prudentius.[27]

Personification is prominent in European literature throughout the Middle Ages and, in allegory, dominates popular literature from the thirteenth to the eighteenth centuries. It is salient in poetry through the eighteenth century, when it was used to ornament repetitious language,[28] and is common in otherwise naturalistic descriptions of landscapes and natural events. Eighteenth-century theorists even make it the criterion for poetry.[29] Only in the early nineteenth century is personification criticized, first by Wordsworth and then by Ruskin, the author of the phrase, the pathetic fallacy. Wordsworth writes, for example, "personifications of abstract ideas rarely occur in these volumes; and, I hope, are utterly rejected, as an ordinary device to elevate the style."[30]

Ruskin is more severe. He explains the pathetic fallacy as perception distorted by emotion: "All violent feelings have the same effect. They produce in us a falseness in our impressions of external things, which I would generally characterize as the 'pathetic fallacy.' "[31] People commonly think this "eminently poetical, because passionate," but the "greatest poets do not often admit this kind of falseness."[32] Moreover, the fallacy reflects a "morbid state of mind" and a mind and body too "weak to deal fully with what is before them."[33]

Occasionally Ruskin is more sympathetic to the fallacy or at least to believers in the monotheistic, dualistic worldview he thinks conducive to it. Whereas immanentist Greek pantheism assumed life in all things, now,

> imagining our God upon a cloudy throne, far above the earth, and not in the flowers or waters, we approach those visible things with a theory that they are dead; governed by physical laws. . . . But coming to them, we find the theory fail; that they are not dead; . . . the instinctive sense of their being alive is too strong for us; and in scorn of all physical law, the wilful fountain sings, and the kindly flowers rejoice. And then, puzzled, and yet happy; pleased, and yet ashamed of being so; accepting sympathy from nature, which we do not believe it gives, and giving sympathy to nature, which we do not believe it receives,—mixing, besides . . . purposeful play and conceit with these involuntary fellowships,—we fall necessarily into the curious web of hesitant sentiment, pathetic fallacy, and wandering fancy, which form a great part of our modern view of nature.[34]

Thus modern Europeans spontaneously reencounter what their monotheism left behind but reenter this enchanted world with warring belief and disbelief.

Whether because of Ruskin's attack or because the milieu that produced it continues, the pathetic fallacy has been in critical disrepute ever since. Some scholars even think it defunct. They claim that "attribution of human feeling to the natural world" is absent in modern poetry,[35] that in the twentieth century it has "largely fallen out of literary use,"[36] that it is "not a common device in today's prose writing,"[37] and that "our mountains do not frown, our trees do not dance in the wind, our sunbeams do not smile. We struggle to avoid the pathetic fallacy."[38]

Despite reports of their demise, however, the pathetic fallacy and personification in fact have remained vigorous throughout the twentieth century. Imagist theory, for example, "precludes the pathetic fallacy implicitly and explicitly [but] Imagist practice provides for the device in loving abundance."[39] Allen Tate, in the early 1940s, wrote that the "standard poetics of our time [is] projection of feeling"[40]—that is, the pathetic fallacy. T. S. Eliot, supposedly modern in his disuse of personification, wrote, "Let us go then, you and I, / When the evening is spread out against the sky / Like a patient etherized upon a table."[41] Elsewhere in Eliot, a boat behaves "gaily," light is "sad," and a moon "smiles."[42] R. S. Sharma, one of the few who see personification as part of a more general anthropomorphism, finds both in modern poets. He cites Sylvia Plath's "Mushrooms": "We shall by morning / Inherit the earth / Our foot's in the door,"[43] and Stephen Spender's "The Express": "After the first powerful plain manifesto / The black statement of pistons, without more fuss / But gliding like a queen, she leaves the station."[44]

Again, H. L. Van Brunt's "Ossabaw Suite"[45] personifies (and more broadly, anthropomorphizes) ten items—horseshoe crabs, a creek, oysters, islands, a garden, palms, oaks, japonicas, tulip trees, and azaleas— in thirteen lines. In "Song of Salt and Pepper," Patricia Storace personifies these items as "Dinner twins, / who remind us that nothing / we know of remains uncoupled . . ."[46] She calls them married and hopes they "remain in nightly wedding." In James Wright's poetry and in the European poetry he translates, personification is central.[47] Other examples are legion.

Twentieth-century prose also continues to personify. James Joyce does so frequently. In *Ulysses,* for example, Dedalus looks at a math book and sees dancers: "Across the page the symbols moved in grave morrice, in the mummery of their letters, wearing the quaint caps of squares and cubes. Give hands, traverse, bow to partner: so: imps of fancy of the Moors."[48]

Instances elsewhere range from concrete to abstract and from comic to philosophic. Suckers, a kind of fish, have "chubby humanoid lips and appear to be begging for cigars. It's possible to envision them wearing suspenders and sitting on park benches, acting like heirs to the continent's watershed."[49] Computers now are special foci of personification.[50] Male computers are practical jokers, poets, and lovers, are suicidal, and struggle for power with each other and with humans. Female computers are "shy, sweet, gentle, respectful, and humble."[51] More abstractly, a literary column claims "Language is Smarter than We are." Moreover, language "is not sentimental about us. It is fond of quibbles and indifferent to truths."[52] Making language a person, this writer follows a long tradition: Socrates complained that written language "doesn't know how to address the right people, and not address the wrong. And when it is ill treated and unfairly abused it always needs its parent to come to its help, being unable to defend itself."[53] Personification itself may be personified, as in the pathetic fallacy's "century of prosperity."[54]

Other recent writers also find personification durable and reappraise Ruskin's attack. Antony Hecht[55] refutes Ruskin's claim that great poets do not commit the pathetic fallacy, pointing out that Homer repeatedly makes spears "hungry for flesh" and has the river Scamander argue and fight with Achilles. A classicist (unconcerned with Ruskin) writes, personifications make their appearance very early in Greek poetry. Already in the Iliad we meet with Terror and Panic and Discord. . . . Hera converses with Sleep, holding him by the hand . . . and Sleep and his twin brother Death carry away the dead body of Sarpedon to Lycia.[56]

Shakespeare abounds with pathetic fallacy. For instance, *2 Henry IV* personifies rumor extensively.[57] *1 Henry IV*, 1.3 personifies wounds and a river in describing Mortimer's courage, which

> Needs no more but one tongue for all those wounds,
> Those mouthed wounds, which valiantly he took
> When on the gentle Severn's sedgy bank,
> . . . .
> Three times [the opponents] breathed,
>   and three times they did drink,
> Upon agreement, of swift Severn's flood;
> Who then, affrighted with their bloody looks,
> Ran fearfully among the trembling reeds
> And hid his crisp head in the hollow bank . . .

Antony and Cleopatra personifies repeatedly and even notes that imagination animates perception:

> Sometimes we see a cloud that's dragonish;
> A vapour sometime like a bear or lion,
> A tower'd citadel, a pendent rock,
> A forked mountain, or blue promontory
> With trees upon't, that nod unto the world,
> And mock our eyes with air . . .

Major poets since Shakespeare also are rich and varied sources. Donne, for example, begins "The Sun Rising" with the lines, "Busy old foole, unruly sunne, / Why dost thou thus, / Through windowes and through curtaines call on us?" Milton's *Paradise Lost* personifies Sin and Death. Blake personifies constantly—for instance, in the first line of "Song": "When early morn walks forth in sober grey . . . " Keats's "To Autumn" begins, "Season of mists and mellow fruitfulness, / Close bosom-friend of the maturing sun; / Conspiring with him . . . " Shelley personifies wind, the season, leaves, and other natural phenomena in "Ode to the West Wind."

Although they criticize the pathetic fallacy, even Wordsworth and Ruskin personify extensively. Wordsworth, for example, personifies London, the sun, the Thames, and houses in just the few lines of "Composed Upon Westminster Bridge." In a brief description of mountain scenery, Ruskin personifies or animates paths, a curve, ferns, foam, crowns, and sunshine.[58] Elsewhere, Ruskin makes plants belong to "tribes" and "families," grasses "essentially a clothing for healthy and pure ground," and sedges a "clothing of waste and more or less poor or uncultivable soils."

He pictures other plants as "delighting in interrupted moisture."[59] As do many others, Ruskin also makes the sky and earth male and female.[60]

Literary anthropomorphism is not always so overt but may be subtle, implicit, or ambiguous. Some cases are "so unsustained that they are easily not noticed. Personification metaphors [may] lie half-hidden in the discourse."[61] The opening lines of Baudelaire's "Correspondances," for example, including "La Nature est un temple," are ambiguously anthropomorphic. "Vivants piliers," among later lines, suggests the "erect shape of human bodies naturally enough endowed with speech [but] 'piliers' as anthropomorphic columns and trees, is suggested only by 'des forêts de symboles.' " We "cannot be certain whether we have ever left the world of humans and whether it is therefore . . . anthropomorphism at all . . . the possibility of anthropomorphic (mis)reading is part of the text."[62] Thus the trope ranges from overt to covert, simple to complex, and clear to ambiguous.

Personification, then, pervades literature. It has an "extraordinary persistence [in] even the most original poets."[63] Yet its causes remain unclear for the same reason as do those of anthropomorphism in general: personification intuitively seems self-explanatory and somewhat distasteful to modern theorists. Hence they do not address it seriously. They offer, at most, one of the common explanations for anthropomorphism, namely, familiarity and its variants, confusion and analogy. Ruskin, for example, thinks we personify because we are confused by violent feelings.[64] Paul de Man also appears as a confusion theorist, if somewhat enigmatically: "anthropomorphism seems to be the illusionary resuscitation of the natural breath of language, frozen into stone by the semantic power of the trope."[65] Sharma is poised between confusion and analogy. He sees personification as anthropomorphism but has no clear theory of the latter. It may be innate: "Anthropomorphism [is] an original means of linguistic cognition, based, perhaps, on a natural tendency of the human mind." In our primitive forebears, it "stemmed from an unconscious drive."[66]

Bloomfield merely calls personification a "complex and fascinating phenomenon" whose "variety [helps explain] its universal power and long-lived popularity."[67] Mark Turner is an analogist: "We are people. We know a lot about ourselves. And we often make sense of other things by viewing them as people too."[68] The same objections apply to the confusion and analogy explanations here, however, as when those explanations address anthropomorphism in general: confusion between ourselves and others is not salient, and at the same time our knowledge of ourselves is not direct or reliable.

Griffiths, too, sees personification as analogy, but goes a useful step further. She calls the line between a personification and an ordinary mimetic character unclear, since a personification may quit its role as "rhetorical figure, escape from the discourse and take up habitation and shape

within the story."[69] Distinctions between human and nonhuman, living
and not-living, and real and imaginary, then, may be arbitrary. Just as
personifications merge with mimetic characters, literary characters merge
with living ones—for example, when we hear of, but have not met, a real
person.[70] As are perceptions of gods and humans, perceptions of personifications and of persons are continuous. Hence personification, like anthropomorphism in general, is more solidly cognitive than usually
thought; it is the interpretation of the nonhuman, or only fractionally
human, in terms of human characteristics.

Griffiths's suggestion is similarly cognitive. To her, personification
"allows for exploration of an abstraction—and of a person. It also allows
for exploration of the relationship between experience and the words used
to make sense of it, and of the relationship between words and the fictions
which they compose."[71] Personification is neither confusion nor simple
analogy, then, but an investigation of systems in terms of other systems.
As Griffiths writes, "nothing one comes across explains itself: things only
make sense in relation to other things or systems."

Personification thus is another form of interpreting the world at the
highest level. That personifications are continuous with mimetic characters, however, reminds us that metaphor works in two directions at once:
subject and predicate modify each other simultaneously. At some point
we do not know whether we are faced with an abstraction personified or
a person abstracted. The line between what is human and what is not is
as indistinct in literature as elsewhere in perception and representation.

Visual artists anthropomorphize as pervasively as writers, and for the same
reason: they pursue meaning, of which the human form provides the
most. As do writers, artists pursue meaning largely intuitively. Gombrich
notes that for artists "the question is not whether nature 'really looks'
like [their] pictorial devices"[72] but whether these devices suggest aspects
of nature important to humans. Art reflects "this tendency of ours to
look for meaning rather than to take in the real appearance of the world."

Portraying that real appearance, Gombrich points out, is neither possible nor necessary. No painting of eyes, for example, can include their
motion. Yet even rudimentary eyes trigger a response, in us as in other
animals such as birds, which avoid butterflies with eye markings on their
wings.[73] The illusion is "not one of visual reality, it is one of meaning:
the eyes appear to give the image sight." The artist simulates not reality,
but only those aspects of it that are important to us. "If it is really part
of our biological heritage that certain perceptual configurations can 'trigger' specific reactions, it is clear that these reactions are adjusted to our
survival in the real world, not to our contemplation of pictures . . . in
other words the response to meaning guides [perception]."[74]

Gombrich's account of illusion in art is much the same as my account
of animism and anthropomorphism: illusions are failed perceptual bets. Illusions are systematic, because perceptual bets represent systematic inter-

ests. Should we not "picture the organism as scanning the world for meaningful configurations—meaningful, that is, in relation to its chances of survival? Danger has to be avoided, food and mates have to be found."[75] Failures of particular bets in particular circumstances do not mean the bets stem from bad strategies—only that they are bets and not certainties.

The more meaningful a configuration and the more elaborate our interpretive apparatus, the more sensitive we are:

> When the organism is "keyed up," not only the goal itself elicits strong reactions, but anything that may . . . point to the presence of the goal. It should be clear that this widening of the waveband to which the organism can respond has both advantages and disadvantages for its survival chances. Being hyper-alerted, it is more likely to detect the goal, but it is also more prone to jump to false conclusions. Scanning the world for meaning, it is confronted with the necessity to interpret the evidence.[76]

Our ability to see the real world in art is given by our sensitivity to the world's most meaningful features and by our ability to isolate them from less meaningful features. We bet, first, that we see what is significant to see. Art records and elaborates that bet. As Arnheim writes, "vision is not a mechanical recording of elements but rather the apprehension of significant structural pattern."[77]

The cause of anthropomorphism—the effort after meaning—is the same in all art forms, whether commercial, folk, tribal, or fine. These forms vary in context and aim, however, and their anthropomorphism varies correspondingly. Commercial art aims foremost to catch the viewer's attention, even if only briefly. Hence subtlety, complexity, and ultimate persuasiveness yield to boldness. Fine art, in contrast, assumes an audience and justifies itself by some insight. The difference may be adequacy of representation:

> no student of the arts would deny that individual artists or cultures form the world after their own image [i.e., anthropomorphically. However,] more often than not the situations we face have their own characteristics, which demand that we perceive them appropriately. Looking at the world proved to require an interplay between properties supplied by the object and the nature of the observing subject. This objective element in experience justifies attempts to distinguish between adequate and inadequate conceptions of reality.[78]

In commercial art, the inadequacy of anthropomorphism as a conception of reality often is quickly apparent, but immaterial. In fine art, on the other hand, anthropomorphism usually is coherent with some larger scheme and is less readily dismissed.

Commercial artists anthropomorphize both to entertain and to sell, and both explicitly and implicitly. Mickey Mouse and Donald Duck, explicitly anthropomorphic, are known worldwide. Other anthropomorphic animals in contemporary American commercial art include company emblems such as the hat-wearing turtle of Turtle Wax, the bipedal tiger of

Exxon gasoline, and the jersey-clad bee of Bumble Bee tuna. Plant and fruit characters include Chiquita Banana, Mr. Peanut, and the California Raisins.

Commercial artists the world over give humanlike behavior and anatomy to all manner of nonhuman phenomena: animals, plants, mountains, seas, the whole Earth, the sun and moon, the weather, machinery, buildings, letters of the alphabet, and abstractions. Male and female skyscrapers eye each other discreetly at the rail of a pleasure liner (Fig. 5–1). Automatic coffee makers discuss better brews (Fig. 5–2), a cellular telephone competes with a Rhodes Scholar (Fig. 5–3), a sweating red pepper plays football (Fig. 5–4), and a hungry mailbox eats letters (Fig. 5–5). A character in a short story notices a dairy advertisement in which a "smiling chunk of Swiss cheese held hands with a cheerful stick-legged quart of buttermilk."[79] A summer squash wears a straw hat in a Japanese bank advertisement, and in a bar advertisement a squid pours sake for an octopus. A Chinese billboard for civic cleanliness gives a waste bin eyes, arms, legs, and a mouth.

Moods and motivations of such portrayals vary as much as the things portrayed. Because most commercial art aims to please, many representations look friendly, seeming to support the comfort theory. Others do not look friendly, however. An anthropomorphic missile streaks down from a night sky onto a city (Fig. 5–6), a gasoline pump hose strangles a driver (Fig. 5–7), an injured dollar leans on a crutch (Fig. 5–8), and a Hitlerian crematorium gives the Nazi salute (Fig. 5–9). Styles and subjects vary greatly and convey both reassurances and threats.

Commercial artists anthropomorphize with varying degrees of openness, as in portraying inanimate objects in social groups. Such groups may be arranged as though leaning against each other (Fig. 3–2), dreaming of one another (Fig. 5–10), caroling (Fig. 4–2), or marrying (Fig. 5–11), and range from overt to covert. Hidden anthropomorphism in commercial art parallels hidden anthropomorphism in painting, photography, architecture, and literature.[80] Even cinema contains hidden anthropomorphism. For example, in Ingmar Bergman's stage directions, a forest "sighs and stirs ponderously," a wind "presses out a pained sound," trees "stand quiet and waiting," an old house creaks "as if it were moving quite cautiously in its sleep," and a car "comes slowly shuffling along."[81]

Much anthropomorphic advertising seems to escape conscious perception, even that of writers on subliminal techniques.[82] Advertising researchers nonetheless have a working knowledge of implicit anthropomorphism. A researcher for a soap manufacturer, for example, asked respondents to describe roles shampoo might play in a dream. One respondent suggested "a genie, a savior, Tinkerbell sprinkling handfuls of gold dust."[83] The researcher recommended that the bottle be made more feminine. Other researchers ask people to finish sentences such as, "M & M's candies went to a party last night and———."[84] Still others

Figure 5–1 Hudson Talbott, *Cruising around Manhattan* (greeting card), 1980. We imagine social relationships even among buildings.

Figure 5–2 **Mr. Automatic Coffee Advertisement, 1977.** Appliances may relate by competing.

Figure 5–3 **Telecommunications Advertisement, 1984.** Objects need little external resemblance to humans in order to seem humanlike.

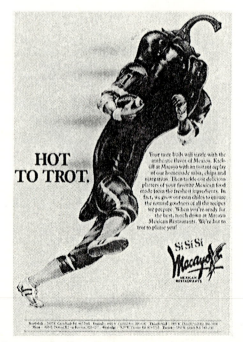

Figure 5–4 **Macayo Mexican Restaurants Advertisement, 1989.** We often imagine vegetables as people, and sometimes as active competitors.

Figure 5–5 **British Postcard, 1941.** Openings meant to receive objects are readily seen as mouths.

Figure 5–7 **Chrysler Advertisement, 1980.** This leering gasoline pump with its constricting, snakelike hose also undermines the comfort theory.

Figure 5–6 Time Magazine Cover, 1956. A common explanation of anthropomorphism is that it comforts us. However, much anthropomorphism is frightening, not comforting.

Figure 5–8 **Book Review Illustration, 1981.** A crippled American dollar again is not comforting.

Figure 5–9 **Illustration for a Review of a Book on Nazi Germany, 1978.** This Hitlerian crematorium casts further doubt on the explanation of anthropomorphism as a mechanism for providing comfort.

Figure 5–10   Vodka Advertisement, 1984. Anthropomorphism in advertising often is subtle, implicit, or unconscious. A paired bottle and glass generally represent a man and a woman.

Figure 5–11   Liqueur Advertisement, *Love is Grande,* **1987.** Bottles not only dream about other objects; they may also marry them.

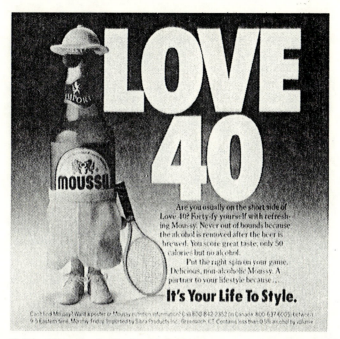

Figure 5–12 **Nonalcoholic Beer Advertisement, Late 1980s.** Beverages without alcohol do better in sports.

Figure 5–13 **Rum Advertisement, 1989.** Objects may engage in complex emotional relationships with no more encouragement than appropriate placement and an allusive caption.

Figure 5–14 **Vodka Advertisement, 1986.** Glasses/women often adjust their posture to bottles/men.

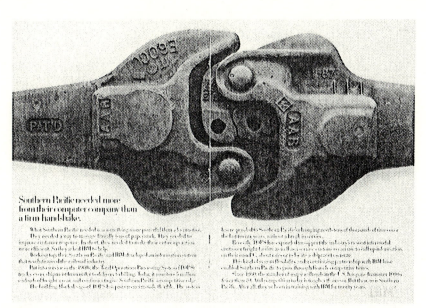

Figure 5–15 IBM Advertisement, 1987. Models of humans generate endless applications. Here a handshake provides an interpretation of train couplings.

Figure 5–16 Liqueur Advertisement, 1989. Transformations of things into people and vice versa reflect their equivalence.

Figure 5-17 **Double Pottery Vase from the Congo, Circa 1910.** People universally see pottery as humanlike.

Figure 5-18 **Mangbetu Pottery Vase, Circa 1910.** Pottery in human form ranges from statuary, through explicitly humanlike vessels such as this, to containers that are only vaguely humanlike.

Figure 5–19 **Pottery Figurines from the Western Mexican State of Colima (Late Preclassic, 400 B.C.–A.D. 200).** Juxtaposing pottery figurines makes us feel they are interacting.

Figure 5–20 **Spouted Pottery Jar from Colima.** Pottery may be functional and highly humanlike at the same time.

Figure 5–21 **Effigy Pot from the Congo, Circa 1910.** The human shape easily lends itself to a vessel form.

Figure 5–22 **Pot from a Cave in Guerrero, Mexico.** Some pottery subordinates sculpture to containment, while still retaining elements of humanity.

Figure 5-23 **Effigy Bowl from Chihuahua, Mexico.** A vessel may be midway between container and person, as here.

Figure 5-24 **Clay Covered Jar from Teotihuacan (Classic, A.D. 250–750).** An obvious jar may still be compellingly personal.

Figure 5–25 **German New Year's Card, 1908.** Letters and numbers often are anthropomorphized.

Figure 5–26 **Seymour Chwast,** *Bestial Bold,* **1980.** Diverse shapes can be turned into faces simply by adding one or two circles and a row of squares.

Figure 5–27 **Giuseppe Arcimboldo,** *Winter,* **1563.** Kunsthistoriches Museum, Vienna. Explicit anthropomorphism in Western fine art has diminished since Greek and Roman times. This example again undercuts the comfort theory.

Figure 5–28 **Foliage Mask from the Temple of Bacchus at Baalbek, Second Century C.E. (after Janson).** Artists find faces in natural foliage, as this mask suggests.

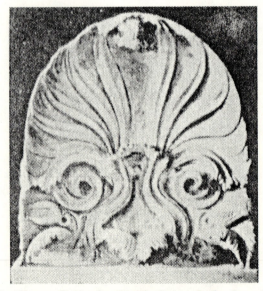

Figure 5–29 **Upper End of a Greek Grave Stele, Late Fourth Century B.C.E. (Epigraphic Museum, Athens; after Janson).** The Greeks thought steles could think and even speak.

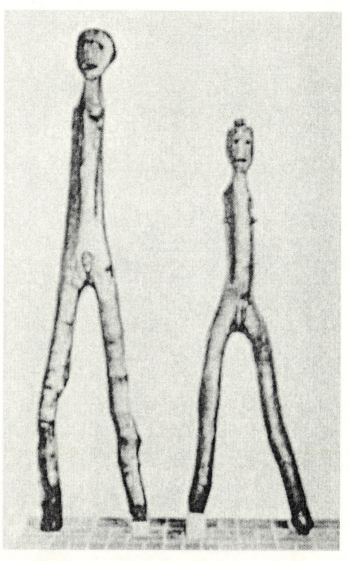

Figure 5-30 Figurines Carved from Forked Branches, Germany, 500 B.C.E.–500 C.E. (Landesmuseum, Schleswig; after Janson). People often accentuate humanlike forms found in nature. These may represent deities.

Figure 5–31 **Foliage Mask on the Base of the *Rider*, Bamberg Ca-thedral, Circa 1230 C.E.** Foliage masks have recurred in architecture for at least 2000 years.

Figure 5–32 **De Gheyn, *Rocks Overrun by Plants Forming Grotesque Heads*, Early Seventeenth Century.** Institute Néerlandais, Paris. Rocks and plants combine readily as heads and hair.

Figure 5–33 **Albrecht Dürer,** *Ruined Alpine Hut* **(detail), Circa 1514.** Biblioteca Ambrosiana, Milan. Dürer frequently found faces and other anatomy in cliffs, buildings, and furniture.

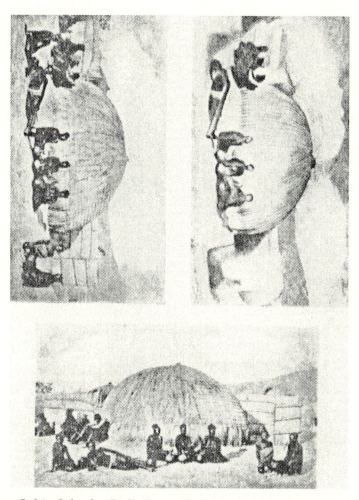

Figure 5–34 **Salvador Dali,** *Paranoic Visage,* **1931.** Musée Nationale d'Art Moderne, Paris. Leafing through a stack of photographs, Dali found what he thought was an unknown Picasso (upper right). Then he saw it actually was an African village.

Figure 5–35 **Anonymous,** *Enigmatic Landscape,* **1830–1840.** Dr. Gunter Bohmer Collection, Munich. Viewed upright, the picture contains two figures in the upper left part of the ridge. Rotated ninety degrees to the right, it contains a face.

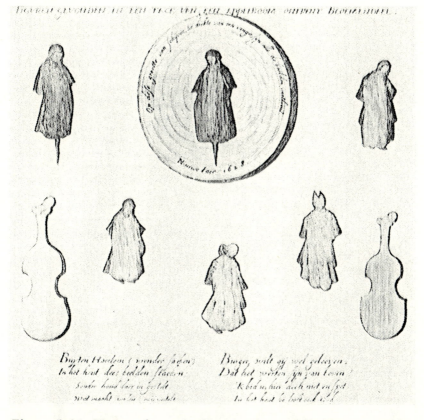

Figure 5–36 **Figures from the Trunk of an Apple Tree in Seventeenth-Century Holland.** Municipal Archives, Haarlem. An image found in a cross section of an apple trunk was widely seen as a priest and as an omen of Spanish conquest.

Figure 5–37 Spaghetti Christ, 1991. Many people have seen Jesus' face in the spaghetti in this billboard in Atlanta, Georgia.

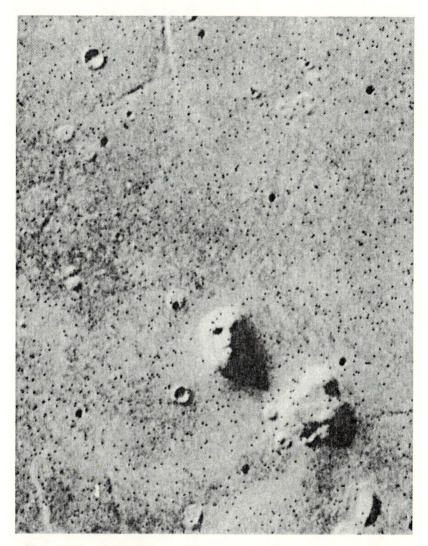

Figure 5–38 **Martian Apparition, 1991.** People see a face in this photograph of the surface of Mars taken by a National Aeronautics and Space Administration spacecraft. Some see it as a signal to Earth from an extraterrestrial civilization or from a deity.

Figure 5–39 Nicholas Roerich, *Warrior of Light*, 1933. Though relatively uncommon in twentieth-century fine art, anthropomorphic chance images still occur there.

Figure 5–40 **Flower Ballet, 1983.** Photographers also find humanlike forms throughout nature.

Figure 5–41 **Hawser Coupling, 1992.** Photographers find humanlike forms in artifacts as well.

Figure 5–42 **Anthropomorphic Animals, Late Eighteenth Century.**
Grandville made a career of joining animal heads with human figures
representing various classes and occupations.

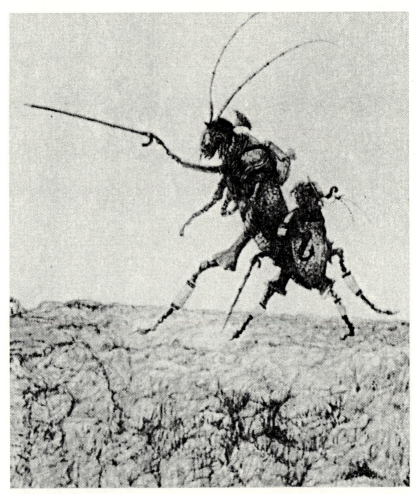

Figure 5–43 **Ernst von Maydell,** *A-Climbing We Will Go,* **Circa 1941.** Humanlike insects are relatively rare in Western art. This was inspired by a fable by La Fontaine.

Figure 5–44 **Kawanabe Kyôsai (1831–1889),** *Mice Transcribing a Book* **(detail), Edo period.** Japanese and other non-Western artists frequently liken both animate and inanimate things to humans.

Figure 5-45 **Palazzetto Zuccari, Rome.** Architects, like others, often see openings as mouths.

ask people to say whether a brand is a man or woman, how old it is, what car it drives, and what music it likes. Another researcher asked half a group of women to

> playact coffee; the other half, Borden's Cremora. "None wanted to act out coffee, which they saw as dark, tough, rugged, and manly," says [the researcher] so he took the part and found himself embraced. The women told him they were softening him and making him milder. [He] told Cremora executives to feminize its package and to describe the interaction of coffee and Cremora in terms of a male-female relationship.[85]

Other researchers also find coffee perceived as male. The marketing firm that designed the current jar and label for Taster's Choice coffee found that a label with a woman's picture caused tasters to find the coffee weak, so they put a man's face on a jar "not unlike a man's torso." This "vaguely masculine contour" was a success.[86]

Appliance design also subtly anthropomorphizes and animates. One designer says products must "deliver emotion," and another says they must "speak to emotional values and fulfillment."[87] The "subliminal message of [his] cooktop [is] 'take life a little easier.'" A Black & Decker vacuum cleaner has air vents resembling fish gills. The company's design director calls the gills "design animism" and says, "This friendly little animal *looks* like it wants to lean down and suck up dirt and water."[88]

One writer who sees implicit figures, including human anatomical parts, in subliminal advertising is Wilson Bryan Key. He finds significant forms mainly in small details of advertising images, however, rather than in images as wholes. Often the details are so small or indistinct that Key must hypothesize a special sensory system to detect them. Nonetheless, Key finds moods and motivations similar to those one can infer among the explicit subjects of the images. While much of his analysis[89] is unconvincing, he does point out that advertisements present significant images, including those of people, of which we are unconscious.

Anthropomorphism in such images, however, usually is not in small details but in whole objects and in relations among them. A beer bottle (Fig. 5–12), for example, may have tennis togs and a racquet. Bottles may also be sociable, whether openly (Figs. 4–2, 5–11) or somewhat less so (Figs. 3–2, 5–10). They frequently are couples, often are families, and even are love triangles (Fig. 5–13). Implicit couples often have a larger, angular male and a smaller, curvaceous female (Fig. 3–2). Sometimes sex coding includes color, with a blue male and pink or warm-toned female. In liquor advertisements, the male usually is a bottle and the female is a glass. Bottles/men usually stand erect and face outward, while glasses/women face them rather than the viewer, bend toward them, or otherwise accommodate their posture to them (Fig. 5–14).[90]

Bottles are anthropomorphized more than are other objects, doubtless because they are upright cylinders. The tendency to see them as people is widespread. Joyce writes, for example, "A porter-bottle stood up, stogged to its waist, in the cakey sand dough. A sentinel . . . "[91] Criticizing pagan images, Augustine writes, "it is as if vessels were set up to denote the gods . . . the image that has a human form signifies the rational soul, since it is in that sort of vessel, so to speak, that the substance is contained."[92] Transformations of humanity in commercial art, as elsewhere, are endless. Bananas get faces, clothes, and extremities; detergents romp with children; train couplings shake hands (Fig. 5–15). Occasionally the transformation is acted out for us, as when a television advertisement for cars turns a man into an automobile.[93] The crouching figure of an actor becomes, through frame-by-frame substitutions, a Renault hatchback: "His torso is transformed into the body of the car. His eyeglasses become headlights. His jacket, which flaps in the wind, slams shut. And his fingers meet to form the grill."[94] In another public transformation, in a print advertisement, an ice skater turns into a liqueur bottle (Fig. 5–16).

The equivalence and transformation of people and nonhuman objects doubtless is ancient; it is basic, for example, to shamanism, and appears cross-culturally. Commercial art, among other evidence, shows that this equivalence is not, as the philosopher-anthropologist Levy-Bruhl[95] supposed, limited to "primitive" thought. As with shamanism, with literature, and with perception and representation generally, metaphor in visual art works in two directions at once. Looking at Mickey Mouse, we do not know whether we see a mouse in man's clothing or a man in a mouse's body. We probably see both.

Folk and tribal artists around the world also anthropomorphize, and again evidently for the same reasons. As in literature and in commercial art, no clear line can be drawn between humans with nonhuman features and nonhuman phenomena with human features.

This indeterminacy, in fact, complicates the oldest tribal art known, that of the Paleolithic period. Most figures in Paleolithic art clearly are those of animals, while a few clearly are human. However, many have some human traits, such as bipedalism, upright posture, or flat faces, but still are only ambiguously human.[96] Consequently, writers on Paleolithic art often call them not humans but "anthropomorphs." Many anthropomorphs that previously had been interpreted as humans recently have been seen as anthropomorphized animals.

One scholar who endorses this reinterpretation says it makes the "somewhat human-like features selected by the artists . . . problematical."[97] He suggests people see animals as humanlike more than they see humans as animallike, and therefore anthropomorphs are "animals in vaguely human guise [rather] than the converse." His suggestion supports my view that anthropomorphism stems from our tendency to interpret things and events with the highest models possible. We tend to interpret upward, not downward. We see nonhuman phenomena as humans more than the reverse, and correct our overestimation afterward if we must. Our modern first interpretation of Paleolithic anthropomorphs as human, later changed to seeing them as animal, may be one more example of this overestimation and correction.

Post-Paleolithic tribal and folk art also anthropomorphize, sometimes explicitly and sometimes not, and in many media. As noted earlier, three archaeologists point out similarities between decorations of pots and of people among the Mafa and Bulahay of Cameroon. They suggest that these peoples see pots as people, but also suggest that pots are special in being so regarded. They ask whether members of other cultures see pots as people, too.[98]

In fact, members of other cultures do see pots as people. Many African peoples anthropomorphize pots (Figs. 5–17, 5–18). For Karanga-speakers in Zimbabwe, "most pots symbolize women and, more specifically, the womb."[99] These people compare pots before and during firing to girls before and during puberty. The Shona say clay cones used to support food bowls, and a large bowl used to cook the daily porridge, represent breasts. Shona also equate the neck of the pot with the neck of the cervix[100] and incise pots with equivalents of the tattoos on women's abdomens and of beaded belts worn to protect fertility. They also apply both breasts and depressions representing eyes to some pots.

Anthropomorphic pottery ranges continuously from realistic human statues and figurines (Fig. 5–19), through explicitly humanlike containers (Figs. 5–20, 5–21), to vessels with only a suggestion of humanity (Fig. 5–22). The earliest known ceramic, for example, is not a vessel at all but a Paleolithic European figurine. Other realistic pottery figures include Japanese grave goods (*haniwa*) of the third to sixth centuries, the soldiers of the Chinese emperor Ch'in Shih Huang-ti's tomb from the third century B.C.E., a Mesopotamian vessel from the early first millennium B.C.E., early Hebrew ancestor images,[101] and pre-Columbian figurines from the Americas over a number of centuries. Anthropomorphic pots may appear pensive or fearful, as in an effigy bowl from Chihuahua (Fig. 5–23); intensely interactive, as in a double pottery vase from the Congo (Fig. 5–17); or imploring with arms extended, as in a covered jar from Teotihuacan (Fig. 5–24).

We might also see the special connection between pottery and anthropomorphism suggested by the archaeologists in ancient Near and Middle Eastern and Greek creation myths, where gods often are potters who make men from clay. The Bible contains many instances, including "But now, O Lord, thou *art* our father; we are the clay, and thou our potter . . . " (Isaiah 64:8). The Gilgamesh epic has a major character created from clay; and a Babylonian creation myth has humanity made from clay mixed with a god's blood.[102] Greek myths include similar themes, as in Prometheus's creation of men, and Haephestus's creation of the first woman, from clay.

Although the malleability of clay and its widespread use in figurines make it apt stuff for mythic creation, myths also use other materials for human origins, such as stone, wood, and flour or dough. And although people anthropomorphize pots widely, they do so with other artifacts as well. The Zulu, for example, put humanlike decorations not only on pottery but also on "milk pails, headrests, spoons, mats, beadwork, meat plates."[103]

Anthropomorphism seems endless in other folk and tribal visual media. Two diverse instances will suffice. One is the creation of faces and figures from numerals (Fig. 5–25) and from letters of the alphabet. Folk artists, commercial artists, and grafittists commonly add eyes and a mouth to the letter *o*, using its round or oval shape as the outline of a face. They similarly make eyes of contiguous *o*s, as in the word "look," by putting pupils into the *o*s, often adding a mouth below. The Jewish artists of the fifteenth-century Kennicott Bible made letters into animals and naked humans, and Arab calligraphers also turn letters into animals and vice versa.[104] Modern secular lettering may use anthropomorphism, animism, or a mixture of both (Fig. 5–26).

The second instance is baked goods such as cookies and cakes, anthropomorphized either explicitly or implicitly. Commercial art offers such explicit figures as the Pillsbury Doughboy and Mr. Pretzel, and folk art has the gingerbread man. A New York specialty shop, the Erotic Bakery, bakes cakes shaped like breasts and other sexual parts. Other baked anthropomorphisms may be implicit. An anthropologist studying weddings, for example, suggests that the wedding cake represents the bride.[105] His suggestion is indirectly supported by a prominent Swiss-born pastry chef, Albert Kumin. When a journalist asked Kumin what his favorite creations were, he answered, "I have no favorites. I love all my girls." The journalist asked whether any of his cakes were boys and the chef said, "Maybe other bakers' are. Mine are all girls."[106] Although male baked goods exist as well, Kumin's choice of gender fits more frequent English-language equations of women and baked goods: honey bun, tart, cookie, cupcake, dish.[107]

As in commercial and tribal art, anthropomorphism in fine art takes many forms, some explicit and some implicit. The form most noted in fine art, as in literature, is personification. As do literary critics, most scholars of art mean by personification the self-conscious portrayal of abstractions or invisible entities as concrete humans: Liberty with a torch, Justice with blindfold and scales. Personification thus is a deliberate device for concretizing what otherwise is intangible. Most scholars of art think it peculiar to the arts, not a general feature of perception and representation. And, again as in other kinds of representation, the distinction between nonhuman phenomena seen as human, and humans seen as nonhuman phenomena, may be unclear.

A few scholars do see personification in art as at least implicitly part of a broader anthropomorphism. The classicist Roger Hinks, for example, describes the change from myth to allegory in Greek and Roman art as an evolution from a spontaneous, popular anthropomorphism to a self-

conscious, philosophical, and sceptical one. Myth for Hinks is the religious account of the world and is involuntary anthropomorphism, while
allegory is premeditated literary anthropomorphism. Both humanize the
world, however, for the same reason: the Greek and Roman "instinct for
reducing all experience to anthropomorphic terms."[108]

In early Greece, this instinct was purely religious, not allegorical.
Later, in Hellenistic Greece, the credibility of myth faded among intel-
lectuals and their anthropomorphism became a consciously figurative
means to a rhetorical end. It was only then that the "personification
of an abstract concept was deliberately invented, and that its creator
had a clear distinction in his mind between the philosophic notion
and the human shape in which he chose to attire it."[109] All Greek art,
however, comprehensively represents the world, including the natural,
social, and mental orders, as persons. Indeed, these three orders themselves are divinities, respectively, Dike, Themis, and Mnemosyne, all
represented as women. Within each order, everything becomes human:
"Every notion . . . is converted into a chain of human metaphors."[110]
The winds, for example, variously are "bearded winged figures . .
.youthful beardless figures . . . heads with puffed-out cheeks . . . young
girls with fluttering draperies, [or] young men mounted on spirited
steeds."[111]

Abstractions also are personified. Time is the deity Kronos, shown
sometimes as a mature and perhaps ageless man and sometimes as an old
one. Time's subdivisions also are persons. The four seasons may be static
figures with seasonal fruits, dancing figures, processions of decorated
women, small boys, or busts of young women. Months, night and day,
sunrise and sunset, the heavenly bodies, the sky, the sea, and other elements are personified as well. In short, the "ancient mind [by] its invar-
iable instinct . . . gave a human shape to each and every experience of the
natural order."[112]

As with the natural order, so also with the social order. Greek and
Roman artists personified cities, peoples, and continents. Cities were not
mere collections of buildings and people but "divine beings with an immortal conscious personality, capable of assuming a corporeal shape."[113]
Correspondingly, they were shown as persons, alone or consorting with
gods, heroes, and historical figures. At first this personification was a god,
the city's patron deity, but later it became a secular figure. Occasionally
artists also directly personified the population of a city in the form of
Demos.

On the largest scale, Greek artists personified the entire inhabited
earth, the *oikumene*. In a relief of the apotheosis of Homer, for example,
the *oikumene* is a woman bearing a standard measuring vessel on her
head, representing the civilized world. A later Roman version, Orbis Ter-
rarum, is a "real being: the Genius of the Roman Empire. She is no
longer the shadowy rhetorical abstraction of the [apotheosis] relief, but
a power to be worshipped and commemorated on public monuments."[114]

The mental order likewise is personified in whole and in part. One common representation embodies thought or mind as a silent dialogue, a conversation with the self. In reliefs on sarcophagi and elsewhere, this metaphor often takes the form of the Poet conversing with his Muse. Here the poet, a portrait of the deceased, represents the mortal self including the body, while the muse is the immortal soul. The image is allegorical, mixing the particular person and the immortal principle.

Other aspects of mind also become persons, again often juxtaposed with real persons. A late classical picture, for example, shows the princess Juliana Anicia flanked by Magnanimity and Intelligence, with Gratitude prostrate before her.[115] Other paintings, sculptures, and reliefs personify virtually every named mental experience.

Similar personification continues in Western art through the Middle Ages and Renaissance to the present. Gothic stonecutters, for example, often portray moral qualities in human form at column-heads. Botticelli's *Allegory of Spring* is a young woman walking with female attendants through a vernal wood. Arcimboldo, the outstanding Renaissance personifier, composes human faces representing the seasons and other topics, variously of fruits, vegetables, fishes, mammals, and other items associated with his subject. Spring, for example, is a woman's bust composed of flowers. Summer is a bust of fruits; Fire is one of burning sticks, logs and candles, flints, and allied items; and Water is one of fishes and crustaceans. Winter, again a bust, is a grotesquely gnarled stump (Fig. 5–27).

In the early nineteenth century, Prud'hon shows *Justice and Divine Vengeance Pursuing Crime* as two aerial figures chasing a fugitive on foot, and in the twentieth century, Käthe Kollwitz personifies war as woman with a scythe. A recent cover of *The New Yorker*[116] personifies fall as fashion models on a runway, each clothed in a single red, yellow, or orange leaf. Artists in all periods commonly personify death as a skeleton, often carrying a scythe or wearing a hood.

Non-Western artists also personify. Inuit artists often represent animal spirits as humans, sometimes peeking from the open mouth of an animal. American Indian, African, Australian, Melanesian, and other artists similarly show animal spirits or deities either as human figures or as anthropomorphic animal figures. In China, the classic *Mustard Seed Garden Manual of Painting* recommends painting natural phenomena as engaged in social relations with each other.[117]

Western classicists often distinguish representations of gods from representations of abstract ideas and natural phenomena. They call the former anthropomorphism and the latter personification. Some, such as Hinks, find a transition in classical art from anthropomorphism (spontaneous, naive, and literal) to personification (deliberate and figurative). Although describing this shift as evolutionary, such scholars nonetheless usually regard anthropomorphism and personification as distinct.

Relations between classical art, religion, and worldview, however, belie both this traditional divide between anthropomorphism and personification and the one-way evolution from former to latter. First, no clear break exists between representations of abstractions on the one hand and of concrete phenomena on the other. Rather, there is a continuum from one to the other, all points of which classical artists anthropomorphize equally. Time, for example, highly abstract, may be an aged man. Months and days, a little more concrete, also may be humans. Still more concrete phenomena, such as crops and the sea, also are personified.

Second, anthropomorphism ranges continuously from religious to secular. The Greek city, for example, was personified first as a guardian divinity, then as a secular allegorical person (similar to Uncle Sam and John Bull in the United States and Britain), and then as another divinity, the city's *tyche* or Fortune. Abstractions that to moderns seem candidates only for personification were worshiped. These were not "mere philosophical concepts which poetic license found convenient to clothe in human form," but gods. Athens, for example, had "altars and sanctuaries of Victory, Fortune, Friendship, Forgetfulness, Modesty, Mercy, Peace, and many more."[118]

Most classicists set off personification from anthropomorphism as especially reflective or as especially concretizing. Hinks tries to maintain this distinction but seems to find it tenuous, in terms both of what modern viewers can see and of classical intention: "the iconography of these personages does not always indicate clearly whether . . . the figure represented [is] a genuine mythical being or [is] a conscious personified abstraction. *Probably this ambiguity reflects the inner indifference of the artist toward such distinctions.*"[119] If, as Hinks admits here, the distinction is unintended by the artist, it may be a distinction without a difference. In that case personification, in Greek and Roman art as elsewhere, is better viewed as just another aspect of our broader humanization of the world: as anthropomorphism of which the artist has become aware.

The self-consciousness and concretization usually thought to separate personification from other anthropomorphism do not seem linked sufficiently to do so. In literature, for example, Milton's Death is a self-conscious personification, but not concrete. Homeric gods, in contrast, are highly concrete; yet Homeric religion is not evidently self-conscious. Similarly, fortune, victory, friendship, and other abstractions become Greek gods, with altars and sanctuaries, but without evident self-consciousness. On the other hand, Jewish and Christian theologians are, almost by definition, self-conscious, including a consciousness of their own anthropomorphism. Yet, although most wish to avoid anthropomorphism, they do not speak of avoiding personification, because they assume God *is* a person.

A further survey of art history confirms that personification in the traditional sense is only the most evident aspect of anthropomorphism in fine art. Because little work on anthropomorphism exists in art history,[120] the survey must be brief. Its results, however, are consistent both with theory of art and with my account so far.

The traditional explanations of anthropomorphism are the same in art as elsewhere: it is comforting or it accounts for what we do not know by what we do. Here as elsewhere, however, these views are largely mistaken. Again, a better explanation is that perception is interpretation, interpretation is the provision of meaning, and the form with the greatest meaning is that of humans. Because human manifestations vary widely, and because a human presence is so important, we superimpose widely different human forms on widely different phenomena.

Discussing perception in art and life, Arnheim explains the attention people and other animals give any sudden change in their environments. Change "may be inconsequential; but it may also be vitally important. Whether an event matters or not can be found out only by paying attention to it . . . [this is] a highly appropriate reaction, whose great generality is required by the large variety of stimuli relevant to the purpose."[121] That is, any event may matter, so watch out. The more events one can scan, the better.

We appropriately react to *all* changes in deciding which matter and which do not, Arnheim says, because this decision is "so generic and comprehensive that every happening at all belongs in its purview. The broad reaction is not a failure to discriminate but an asset."[122] With this reaction, we intensify our usual testing of models against whatever change has occurred, emphasizing the model most important to us. Thus "direct observation, far from being a mere rag-picker, is an exploration by the form-seeking and form-imposing mind."[123] The form imposed may be "inappropriate objectively and yet sensible in terms of the situation as the person or animal experiences it . . . the pressure of any need tends to broaden the range of stimuli to which the individual responds."[124]

Hence in producing or looking at pictures as in looking at the world directly, we impose models, prototypes, schemata, templates, or, as Arnheim calls them here, norm images. Varying figures can be seen as a single norm image:

> For example, there is a norm image of the human figure, symmetrical, upright, frontal, as reflected in the drawings of children and other early stages of pictorial conception. Whether or not a particular figure, encountered in daily life or in a picture, is recognized and accepted as human depends on whether the beholder can see it as a derivate of his norm figure. . . . A figure can also be bent and twisted in many of the postures to which the joints of the body lend themselves and yet be recognized as a declension of the familiar form.[125]

Arnheim's account of the flexibility of norm images, and the pressure to see them, applies, of course, also to anthropomorphism. It does so not only in art but also in our seeing gods in natural things and events.

Gombrich says explicitly that anthropomorphism in art results from our biological interests: we "respond with particular readiness to certain configurations of biological significance for our survival. The recognition of the human face, on this argument, is not wholly learned. It is based on some kind of inborn disposition."[126] Inborn or not, this disposition is universal. Artists appeal to it:

> Whenever anything remotely facelike enters our field of vision, we are alerted and respond. We all know the feeling when fever or fatigue has loosened the triggers of our reactions and a pattern on the wallpaper suddenly appears to look or leer at us with a threatening grin. . . . given this disposition of ours to meet the design halfway, the artist may find that he has accidentally made a face.[127]

Thus in art as elsewhere, interests shape interpretations.

Indeed, the art critic Adrian Stokes thinks our interests cause a "pre-eminence in aesthetic form [of] an underlying image of the body" and there is a "sense in which all art is of the body."[128] J. D. Harding, a friend and drawing teacher of Ruskin's, anticipates both Gombrich's observation that the human form commands attention and Stokes's claim that it is the principal basis of esthetics. Harding makes from the body a general theory of beauty. The esthetic sense begins in contemplating it: "By the perpetual contemplation of the human form, and the study of its perfections, the artist . . . beautifies his own conceptions of the forms of all things. From this model he derives the power for his imagination imperceptibly to raise and refine whatever else he does."[129] Harding's claim might be reformulated to say that studying the human form helps the artist find that form elsewhere. In any case, his claim is at least compatible with my own—that our interest in the human form shapes our interpretations of the world generally.

Such shaping appears also in chance images—apparent images found in nature or otherwise created unintentionally. Mention of chance images of people and animals begins at least with Aristotle, Lucretius, and Philostratus, who mention images seen in clouds.[130] Pliny mentions images seen in blots and rocks as well. Leone Battista Alberti, in the fifteenth century, attributed the origin of sculpture to the discovery of chance images in solid objects.[131] Recently Heinz Ladendorf suggested that the foliage masks in Greek and Roman decorative carvings (Fig. 5–28) began as chance images in Attic grave stele ornaments which, intentionally or not, sometimes are facelike (Fig. 5–29). Such a stone, H. W. Janson writes, "evokes the image of a standing figure, and its upper terminus thus may be viewed as its 'head.' Perhaps this notion was unconsciously present in the carver's mind. In any event he must have become aware at some point of the face hidden among the foliage, and from then on the effect was exploited quite explicitly."[132]

Similar transformations occur in other times and places. People often see plants as having human form and modify them to emphasize it. In northern Germany, a carver of about Pliny's time turned forked tree

branches, suggesting armless figures, into figurines (Fig. 5–30) now interpreted as deities. In the American Southwest, as noted, saguaro cacti,
and in East Asia the ginseng root, suggest figures. Again, these objects
often are changed to resemble figures even more. Such visual images are
as widespread as their analogues in folklore.

European interest in chance images and in art derived from them
continued unabated after the classical period (Fig. 5–31). Janson says
Michael Psellus, for example, held that "demons can change their appearance as easily as the ever-changing configurations of clouds, which
may resemble the shape of men, bears, dragons."[133] Albertus Magnus
recorded images in clouds and in blocks of marble. Images in agates,
popular during the Middle Ages, appear in medieval mineralogy and in
reliquaries.[134]

Medieval and later art, like classical art, reflects discoveries of such
images, for example, in the tiny faces in striped marble columns in a
gospel book of Charlemagne's time, in faces in the ground in a Gothic
nativity scene, in a face in a butterfly's wing in a fifteenth-century manuscript, and in continued foliage masks.[135] In the late fifteenth century
Andrea Mantegna painted faces, horses, and riders in the clouds,[136] and
the early seventeenth century includes Josse de Momper's *Anthropomorphic Landscape,* a massive head and shoulders comprising an abrupt stony
outcrop with buildings and bushy trees as eyes, nose, and hair and Jacques
de Gheyn II's *Rocks Overrun by Plants Forming Grotesque Heads* (Fig.
5–32).

Anthropomorphism in fine art, as in commercial art, may be hidden.
Albrecht Dürer, for example, frequently gives subtle human form to natural formations and sometimes to artifacts such as buildings and water
cocks.[137] Dürer experimented with pillows in order to discover faces in
the creases, and gave his landscapes, mountains, cliffs, and wall fragments
covert craggy faces and bushy hair (Fig. 5–33). These echo more explicit
human figures in the picture. Breughel similarly anthropomorphizes a
building in *Mad Meg.* Here, as in Dürer, the hidden figures require special
attentiveness.

Other anthropomorphism is more explicit, even if still ambiguous.
The ambiguity sometimes depends on picture orientation, as in Salvador
Dali's discovery of the *Paranoiac Visage* in a photo of an African village
(Fig. 5–34). He saw the village as a face because he had been studying
Picasso and because the photo was rotated ninety degrees from normal:
"I had been obsessed by a long reflexion on Picasso's faces [and] was
looking for an address in a pile of papers when suddenly I was struck by
the reproduction of a face I thought was by Picasso, an absolutely unknown one. Suddenly the face disappeared and I realized my illusion."[138]
Another picture whose anthropomorphism depends on orientation is the
anonymous nineteenth-century lithograph, *Enigmatic Landscape* (Fig. 5–
35). This picture is doubly ambiguous, with human images at two levels

at once. Viewed upright it shows mountain peaks which, scrutinized for a moment, reveal two oversized human figures. Rotated ninety degrees to the right, its figures become part of the nose, brow, and upper lip of an immense face. Nonhuman prominences become its lower lip and chin.

On at least one occasion, on the other hand, an artist specifically denies the validity of a chance human image. People in early seventeenth-century Holland, as mentioned earlier, widely saw an image found in a cross section of an old apple tree as a Catholic priest (Fig. 5–36).[139] Many supposed it presaged the appearance of priests, and hence Spanish domination. In rebuttal, an engraver, Pieter Saenredam, made other views of cross sections of the tree to show how variously they could be seen. He pointed out the influence of context and urged viewers to see things as they are. Saenredam was unusual, however; few artists before or since seem explicitly to reject such discoveries.

Chance images of humans still attract wide audiences today. The context of these images (to which popular responses range from the skeptical to the religious) may be mundane or celestial. In Progresso, Texas, for instance, people recently have streamed into an auto-parts store to see an image of the Virgin Mary in the floor of a shower stall. In Atlanta, many say they see Jesus' face in a forkful of spaghetti pictured on billboards advertising the Pizza Hut chain of fast-food restaurants (Fig. 5–37). In a recent photograph of Mars taken from an American spacecraft, many see a Sphinx-like face (Fig. 5–38). Each of these images has been widely interpreted as the work of some superhuman agency.

Artists continue to find the human form everywhere. The Russian painter Nicholas Roerich, for example, finds a horse and rider in the clouds in *Warrior of Light* (Fig. 5–39). The American landscape painter and lithographer Russell Chatham has compared his landscapes of Montana, which he calls "gentle," to nudes, and a critic calls them "intimate."[140] Another American artist, James Turrell, does large environmental works. He calls the earth's shadow at dusk an "eyelid," and a volcano chosen for a site, a "female form."[141] Painters find apparent human images in artifacts as well. The visionary folk artist Howard Finster says he began his painting career when told to do so by a face in a daub of paint on his finger. Photographers similarly discover human form in both nature and artifacts (Figs. 5–40, 5–41).

A few critics find implicit anthropomorphism in contemporary art, as Gombrich and Arnheim find it in earlier art. Roland Barthes thinks the ideal landscape photograph suggests a maternal body, the only place, in Anatole Broyard's paraphrase, "of which one can say with so much certainty that one has already been there."[142] Another critic finds two quite different levels of humanity in Donald Sultan's print series, *Black Lemons:* "Obviously, one lemon alone, two lemons with a distance between them, or three lemons touching allude to a single person, a couple, a classical triangular relationship . . . the Lemons [also] look like full and generous bosoms."[143] Another critic personifies painting itself: "Painting is the most astounding sorceress. She can persuade us through the most evident falsehoods that she is pure Truth."[144]

Still another critic, Parker Tyler, finds anthropomorphism in abstract as well as in representational art. He writes that representational perspective, for example, implicitly makes man the measure of the world, which it presents from the level of a human eye. Perspective came into being "as the world seen as background of the resurrected Greek statue."[145] Even abstract, geometric painting, as in Mondrian, is implicitly anthropomorphic since it represents psychological tensions. Indeed, Tyler continues, any "painting is an anthropomorphic product, being strictly personal, unique, and immediate, in the way a razor, for instance, is not."[146] Here we have something like Nietzsche's radical conception of anthropomorphism as intrinsic in human perception, and something like his equation of anthropomorphism and anthropocentrism.

In addition to personification and chance images, other manifestations appear frequently. Francois-Nicolas Martinet in the eighteenth century, for example, portrayed musical instruments as people, and Grandville in the nineteenth century made a career of anthropomorphic animals and zoomorphic humans (Fig. 5–42). Courbet also depicts faces and figures in rocks and trees. In the early twentieth century, Ernst von Maydell painted insects in human clothing and activities (Fig. 5–43). In addition to such explicit forms, implicit anthropomorphism also is widespread. A Russian émigré painter now in New York, for example, sees the still lifes of other painters as implicitly social gatherings of objects, much like the sociable objects in commercial art.[147]

Non-Western fine art also gives human attributes to nature, often more systematically than does Western art. Chinese artists, for example, often give features of the landscape covert but distinct social relations with each other. The seventeenth-century classic of art theory, the *Mustard Seed Garden Manual of Painting*, mentions a wealth of human characteristics in nature and recommends that landscapes embody customary social relationships.

In this tradition, for example, plants exemplify human virtues. The orchid, bamboo, plum tree, and chrysanthemum are known as "the Four Gentlemen." The bamboo plant has

> all the ideal qualities of a scholar and gentleman. . . . It is gentle and graceful in fair weather, strong and resilient under adverse conditions. Its suppleness, adaptability, uprightness, firmness, vigor, freshness, and even the sweet melancholy of the rustle of its leaves have been translated into qualities of mind, spirit, and character. Su tung-p'o referred to bamboos as "those dear princely joints (*pao chieh chün*)."[148]

Paintings of plants should suggest human relationships. Bamboo leaves, for example, should include some "withdrawing" or "conceding" to others. Two trees together may be painted in two ways:

Draw a large tree and add a small one; this is called *fu lao* (carrying the old on the back). Draw a small tree and add a large one; this is called *hsieh yu* (leading the young by the hand).

Old trees should show a grave dignity and an air of compassion. Young trees should appear modest and retiring. They should stand together gazing at each other.[149]

Rocks are alive and have "always been interpreted as the bone structure of the earth, combining with water, which in its many forms represents the lifeblood, to compose a picture as a living organism."[150] In painting rocks, capturing their *ch'i*, spirit, matters most: "One should certainly never paint rocks without *ch'i* . . . rocks must be alive."[151] Rocks also may be familial: "Small rocks near water are like children gathered around with arms outstretched toward the mother rock. On a mountain it is the large rock, the elder, that seems to reach out and gather the children about him. There is kinship among rocks."[152]

Mountains are people too. They have humanlike bodies, social relationships, and characters:

In estimating the body of the mountain and placing its head, the brushstroke over the top . . . is the top of the skull. . . . Other features of the picture, whether tree or rock, pay homage to the summit. The relationship is like that between an emperor and his ministers. For this reason, when Kuo Hsi painted mountains, he made the main one lofty, vibrant, expansive, sturdy, heroic, and also with an air of spiritual purity.[153]

Mountains may also be host and guest. One painting groups "guest peaks" as a range. Elsewhere a main peak "raises its head and spreads its arms, [and] all the forms are included and united within it." Elsewhere again, a mountain is like a "great emperor presiding in his audience hall, the ministers prone around him. In this picture, the mountain is like an emperor deep in silent thought at a moment when he is alone in his palace."[154]

Japanese artists also anthropomorphize. Painters of the seventeenth and eighteenth centuries, for example, show mice in kimonos transcribing a book (Fig. 5–44), rabbit warriors, and frogs carrying parasols. The late eighteenth-century painter Jakuju's *Vegetable Parinirvana* gives the roles of the Buddha and his disciples to cucumbers, radishes, and eggplants.

People everywhere animate or anthropomorphize not only the natural world but also art itself, as David Freedberg shows in a recent history. Freedberg notes "traces of animism in our own perception of and response to images: not animism in the nineteenth-century ethnographic sense of the transference of spirits to inanimate objects, but rather in the sense of the degree of life or liveliness believed to inhere in an image."[155] He finds these traces surprising in Westerners, who want to think only primitive cultures attribute life to images.

In fact, Freedberg shows more than traces of animism, in both Western and other responses to art. Partly anticipated by Richard Wollheim, who says a painting is "like a body" and has a "conspicuous equivalence" with it,[156] Freedberg shows people often act toward images as toward living things: they become sexually aroused by them, drape them, talk to them, attack them, and dismember them. Western and non-Western cultures alike have countless Pygmalion tales: statues and pictures move, crucifixes bleed, and portraits weep. In Southeast Asia, a widespread Buddhist ritual is the addition of eyes to a sculpture, which brings it to life. Chinese and other folk literatures tell of many painters whose creations come to life with the addition of eyes. Our tendency to see an image as a real object also gives manikins their power and makes us feel followed by the eyes of a portrait.

Freedberg finds the tendency to animate and anthropomorphize images universal: "Even in cultures (such as Islam and Judaism) with prevailing interdicts against anthropomorphic representation . . . the will to image [anthropomorphically] cannot be suppressed."[157] Perception does not "turn every image into something that we perceive as lifelike or lively or living, but it does so very often." Moreover, "Response to all images . . . is predicated on the progressive reconstitution of material object [*sic*] as living." That is, we always animate. We "search for the figure, for parts of the body, even the *membra disjecta,* for signs of biological form."[158]

Freedberg does not make clear, however, why we do this, except that we "conflate the appearance of visual forms with reality." Freedberg's central interest is this conflation, but in pursuing it he shows that we animate and anthropomorphize, not only in producing art but also in viewing it.

Further, he shows also that our representations of the world are interwoven with our perceptions of it. Hence we experience a break neither between reality and imagination nor between the human beings we attribute to reality and the humanlike beings we often attribute to imagination. That is—and this is my point—we experience no break in the continuum between humans and other beings, such as deities, that are humanlike.

Architecture, like the graphic arts, often makes the human form a model. Frequently this modeling is conscious. It may be simple and direct. The cross-shaped plan of churches, for example, represents a body with outstretched arms. Imitation of the body may also be more complex. Stokes, for example, thinks buildings are "not only the most common but the most general symbol of our living and breathing: the house besides, is the . . . symbol of the Mother: it is our upright bodies built cell by cell: a ledge is the foot, the knee and the brow. While we project our own being onto all things, the works of man, particularly houses . . . reflect ourselves more directly."[159]

This reflection has a long history. Barkan notes that in medieval and Renaissance Europe, architects "unify their buildings either by literally copying the body . . . or by abstractly emulating its harmonic laws."[160]

In doing so, they continue a tradition going back at least to the first century B.C.E. Vitruvius, in *De Architectura*, repeatedly compared architectural form to the human body.[161] Vitruvius thought symmetry necessary to architecture, proportion necessary to symmetry, and the body necessary to proportion: "For without symmetry and proportion no temple can have a regular plan; that is, it must have an exact proportion worked out after the fashion of the members of a finely shaped human body."[162] The human body is central to architecture because it is simple and unified on the outside and complex and diverse on the inside.

Vitruvius attributes the shape of Greek columns directly to the body. The earliest columns, the Doric, were "derived on the simple proportional basis of man's feet being one-sixth of his height."[163] Later columns have a convex molding "as if a shoe" under the bases, and are dressed "in two manners; one manlike in appearance, bare, unadorned; the other feminine."[164] Ionic, feminine capitals have "volutes, like graceful curling hair, hanging over right and left. And arranging cymatia and festoons in place of hair, they ornamented the front, and, over all the trunk, they let fluting fall, like the folds of matronly robes."[165] Later yet, Corinthian columns are more specifically feminine: Vitruvius says their slender grace commemorates a particular Corinthian girl. Columns with an even more literal human shape are the caryatids, explicitly women.

Vitruvius's successors, especially in the Renaissance, made the body not only the model but the measure as well, both of the man-made world and of nature. Medieval observers point out that the foot, the pace (the length of a stride), the cubit (the length from elbow to forefinger tip), and other aspects of the body are widely used standards of measurement, which they think shows an intrinsic relationship of humans to the world. The stationary and moving body also provide various geometric figures that the rotating extremities describe: triangles, circles, squares, and others.

Containing both proportions and measures, the body, which especially for the Middle Ages is a microcosm, contains everything. William Austin writes that the body has

> all the *Geometricall* proportions that are, or can be imagined: For as all *numbers* and *proportions*, for measure (both of *inches, spannes, digits, cubits,* feet, &c.) are derived from the members, and dimensions of the humane body: so is also the body answerable to *all proportions, buildings,* and *figures,* that are. Not onely answerable (I *say*) to the *whole world* (of which it is an epitome) but for the most part, to every particular *figure, character, building,* and fabrick in the world.[166]

Man is both the measure and the shape of the universe. Accordingly, medieval and Renaissance architects wishing to represent the macrocosm looked to the body as its model. This is clearest in their greatest building, the Gothic church. The church often is viewed as a body. A contemporary account gives it a "chancel which together with the sanctuary stands as head and neck; a choir with stalls as the chest; a cross on both sides of this same choir like two sleeves or two wings extended toward the north and south, and these are like the hips and legs."[167]

A Renaissance writer, Lomazzo, says not only churches but also the "Measures of ships, temples, and other things were first drawn from the imitation of mans [*sic*] bodie."[168] He says the ark, for example, was built in the proportions of a human body, "for as a man's bodie consisteth of three hundred minutes in length, fiftie in breadth, and thirtie in thickness: So was the Arke 300 Cubits long, 50 broad, and thirtie thick or high."[169] Another writer credits the ark with human personality and anatomy, including apertures.[170]

Parallels between edifice and body may be intricate. For Lomazzo, Barkan notes, "each building imitates a whole series of structurally discontinuous parts of the human body. Theaters, for instance, are derived from the oval of the head, the oval formed by the 'bendings of his hands,' and various other oval contortions of the body." Often, however, imitation of the body is more literal, giving "both external unity and internal coherence." A fifteenth-century Italian plan, for instance, inscribes a body in the "familiar pattern of a centralized church in order to demonstrate the form's essential unity inside and out."[171]

Churches, which especially benefited from man as model, did so in part because that model gave entry to the cosmos. Barkan writes, "Since the perfectly proportioned church is an *aemulatio* of the human body, which in turn is a miniature of the cosmos, the individual human being beholding that church experiences an internal, almost involuntary sense of the rightness of God's whole creation."[172] Gianozzo Manetti, a biographer of Pope Nicholas V, shows the anthropomorphism of a church the pope built and writes that since the "form of this temple was a likeness for the human body, [then doubtless] that body would be chosen as the noblest form since we know that the form of man is greatly preferred to all other forms, both of animate and of inanimate objects. Indeed many most learned men have thought it was in fact made as a likeness of the whole world."[173] Varied levels of anthropomorphism in the Gothic church and other structures, then, were well known to both medieval and Renaissance writers.

A modern historian of art, Peter Fingesten, extends the view. Citing scripture comparing Christ to a temple, and medieval views of the church as a body, he says since the "interior of the cathedral is anthropomorphic, then the stained glass windows are its 'skin.' . . . Apse windows . . . represent 'eyes,' for the apse is the 'head' of the cathedral."[174] Fingesten finds a skeleton as well, in the "ribbed vaulting, or the bone structure of the cathedral." He thinks this structure's later evolution was stimulated by medieval medical schools, whose "anatomical studies, particularly of the rib cage, helped the builders to clarify the allegory of the interior of Gothic cathedrals."[175] Hence the interior organization is "not so much a ribbed vault . . . as a rib-cage. . . . The nave vaulting overhead seems to breathe and move; the succession of vaults gives the impression of a flexible rather than rigid system." Fingesten also notes that architectural members have anthropomorphic names.

Later anatomy becomes still more detailed. Looking west from the narthex, the crowns of vaults are "a continuous band of vertebrae."[176] The French web is an incipient spinal cord, which English builders complete with a horizontal rib ridge. Slightly later, "small liernes connecting tiercerons may represent intercostal muscles running obliquely between the ribs."[177]

In addition to skin, eyes, skeleton, and muscles, Fingesten finds female genitalia. He says a medieval increase in devotions to Mary, including literature comparing her to architectural structures,[178] led "to a reinterpretation of important elements of the cathedral. The door, a favorite symbol of Christ . . . became the virginal door of Mary, or the 'Gate, through which has passed the King!' . . . The deeply splayed porches with their pointed arches certainly have anatomical connotations."[179] Stokes sees houses similarly: a house is a "womb substitute in whose passages we move with freedom . . . the exterior comes to symbolize the post-natal world, the mother's divorced original aspects or parts smoothed into the momentous whole . . . a good building is the monument to physique."[180]

People elsewhere in the world also find sexual anatomy and other human qualities in buildings. The Christian-influenced Bwiti cult of the Fang people in West Africa similarly conceives the chapel as body.[181] As are Christian churches, the Bwiti chapel is a crucified figure. The body here, however, is not cruciform but folds its hands across its chest as in a Fang reliquary figure. From the ceiling hang cords and raffia strips "variously conceived of as [its] tendons, veins, nerves, or arteries."[182] As is Fingesten's church, the chapel is androgynous, though more female than male. A cult member says, "The chapel is a person crucified. . . . She lies on her back. . . . In the center of the chapel is the fire which is the heart. . . . The *akôn aba* is [the] sex organ. It is of the man and the woman."[183]

Ritual amplifies the Bwiti chapel as body. In an entrance dance, for example, women place at the altar a small sacred "stone of birth," the essence of creation, which makes fertility possible. This stone corresponds to the homunculus from which women form a child. Chapel and body are further assimilated by the entrance dances of the men, who

> arrive at the birth entrance of the chapel and halt there. The leaders place their hands on the thatch or lintel piece above them. Then the entire group in close-packed formation backs up and comes forward again. At each successive surge forward they penetrate more deeply into the chapel. This continues until the male group is entirely within and ready to begin the circle dances. These ritual actions at the birth entrance are explained [predominantly] as (1) the difficult birth of men out of this life into the spiritual world of the ancestors, and (2) the entrance of the male organ into the female

body. The first explanation confirms the assimilation of the chapel space to the spiritual world and the second explanation confirms the assimilation of the chapel to the female body.[184]

As in Fingesten's church as Mary, this chapel has not only a general human anatomy but also a specifically sexual one.

The houses of the horticultural Atoni of Indonesian Timor embody, as do church and Bwiti chapel, a model both humanlike and cosmic.[185] The roof peak has two horizontal beams, the "fire cranium" and the "sun cranium." Four "mother posts," including one "head mother post," support rafters and ceiling. Peripheral wall posts are "feet" or "child posts." Major doorjambs are called " 'to support,' usually in the moral sense 'to be responsible for.' "[186] Major areas of the house also are divided into male and female. The Winnnebago of Wisconsin see the teepee as a mother. The tent poles are her ribs, the hearth is her heart, and the sound of the ceremonial drum is her heartbeat.

Westerners posit still other likenesses of buildings and people. The architect Charles Le Corbusier writes of New York's George Washington Bridge, "The structure is so pure, so resolute, so regular that here, finally, steel architecture seems to laugh." Less happily, an editorialist writes, "An abandoned New York tenement with broken windows is like a corpse with open eyes. The city government ultimately comes and closes the lids by nailing gray sheets of galvanized steel to the exterior frames. . . . The city has no vaccines to keep ill buildings alive [but officials have] hit upon a placebo. They close the dead building's eyes, but decorate the lids so that even a nearby observer would think them alive and moist."[187]

Some buildings are too lively: the villain of a movie, *The Amityville Horror,* is a three-story house with a "sadistic persona" and attic windows "glaring like crazed and bloodshot eyes."[188] Others are more benign: On Long Island, an architect's home has a two-story, shingled human face, in which den windows are almond eyes and the bedroom window is a mouth. A newspaper description begins, "Why is this house smiling?"[189] Doorways also may be mouths, as in a mansion (Fig. 5–46) in Rome.

Buildings often have names as well. A report on naming commercial buildings says T'ing C. Pei, son of architect I. M. Pei, thinks there "must be a psychological need to humanize something that otherwise would be just brick and mortar."[190] That need extends to more than brick and mortar.

The structures, images, and events in which writers and visual artists find human form and behavior seem limitless. Writers, from the earliest to the most recent, show human characteristics not only in personification and the pathetic fallacy, but also in anthropomorphism more broadly. Visual artists as well, from Paleolithic times to the present, anthropomorphize the world endlessly. Often they do so explicitly, but their conscious activity stems from the unconscious strategy informing all perception and representation: to apply the most important schema first.

Still, one might ask, if our impulse to interpret the world with a humanlike schema is so strong and so general, why is it not even more manifest in fine art? Why do contemporary painting and sculpture, for example, not constantly and openly attribute human features to nature, as do commercial, folk, and tribal art? I suggest three answers.

First, the relative scarcity of overt anthropomorphism in fine art is largely Western and modern. Fine art, in fact, can and does anthropomorphize, as in classical Greece, Rome, and China. Judaism and Christianity diminish classical anthropomorphism, however, by limiting humanity to ordinary humans, on the one hand, and to a transcendent God who must not be pictured, on the other. In separating man and God from the rest of the world, Judaism, Christianity, and Islam empty nature of human features.

Second, Western art still is preoccupied with the human prototype, and is constrained only against using it on nature. The human prototype still dominates, through depictions of ordinary human beings. Moreover, even landscapes and seascapes, whose topics nominally are nonhuman, usually contain at least diminutive figures or structures that define the scale and show what people do in it. Man still is the measure. Humans, with their humanlike though usually invisible God, still are at the center of the postclassical Western world. The impulse to employ the prototype directly on nature also occasionally breaks through, as in Dürer, Breughel, Arcimboldo, Courbet, and others.

Last, contemporary fine art does not anthropomorphize heavily and overtly because contemporary science rejects anthropomorphism, and the industrial landscape, manufactured by humans, militates against it. Within the mechanistic worldview that science and industrialism foster in modern culture, open anthropomorphism is suspect. Contemporary artists in the industrialized world now anthropomorphize relatively little, or covertly, partly because they consciously conceive nature as nonhuman.

Nonetheless, artists, like other people, match the world first against a single prototype. Though single, that human prototype has myriad aspects. Whatever we can fit to the human model, we do, until we have reason not to; and we can fit almost everything to it.

6

Anthropomorphism in Philosophy and Science

Oh! Oh! Oh! you eight colourful guys,
You won't let quarks materialize
You're tricky, but now we realize
You hold together our nucleis.

Anonymous, in F. Wilczek and B. Devine, Longing for the Harmonies

Philosophers and scientists have criticized anthropomorphism since the time of Bacon, yet they are not immune to it themselves. Despite philosophical and scientific scepticism and scrutiny,[1] no satisfactory analysis of anthropomorphism exists, and warnings against it are not entirely effective.

Bacon and Spinoza give the earliest substantive accounts. They are followed by Hume, Feuerbach, Lange, and Nietzsche, reviewed earlier. Explanations and evaluations remain diverse. While most modern writers are critical of anthropomorphism, a few find it not only inevitable but also unproblematic.[2] Few philosophers since Nietzsche give it much attention, however.

Yet the impulse to find human form in the world persists in science and philosophy, as elsewhere. And, as elsewhere, it takes many forms. The diversity of these forms and their persistence despite longstanding criticism indicate once more that the source of anthropomorphism runs deep.

* * *

Classical Western philosophy, including cosmology, arose in the same
period in which anthropomorphism in classical art became self-conscious.
The rise of philosophy brought increased debate about the nature of gods
and shifts in emphasis from performance to criticism and from manipulation to reflection. As did artists of the time, however, classical philosophers refined and rationalized animistic and humanlike models of the
world but did not abandon them. Plato and Aristotle, for example, saw
the celestial bodies as alive and divine, continuing a view that had been
common in Middle Eastern religion for centuries.[3]

Greek philosophical images of the world thus resemble those of prephilosophical religion, most obviously in Zeus as supreme ruler: Heraclitus calls war King and Father, and Plato uses these terms for the
Craftsman and cosmic Reason.[4] Greek cosmology differs from its parent
religion largely in making animism and anthropomorphism more general
and abstract. Prephilosophical religion offers a universe of very human
persons and social relationships. In contrast, Greek philosophy offers a
larger scale and broader principles (making the universe, for example, a
political entity, an organism, or both) and no active relationships.

The philosophers also criticize their own images and distinguish categories, such as animate and inanimate, society and nature.[5] But they do not
stop anthropomorphizing. Two types, which may be called immediate anthropomorphism and artificialism, stand out. The former images the cosmos
as a humanlike being, usually containing other humanlike beings, who usually constitute a society. The latter images the cosmos as an artifact of a humanlike being.[6] The first view of cosmos as society is in the earliest fragment
of philosophical text, Anaximander's Fr. 1. It apparently describes "opposed
substances which make up the differentiated world."[7] It shows those substances as involved in a legal relationship, with mutual injustices, assess-
ments, penalties, and damages: "they pay the penalty and recompense to
one another for their injustice, according to the assessment of time."[8]

Later Greek cosmology personifies three political relationships among
substances: Strife or War; Justice, or a contract between equals; and Monarchy, or the supreme rule of a single principle. The first relationship has
the cosmos in constant aggression, even anarchy; the second makes it an
oligarchy or limited democracy; and the third makes it a monarchy.[9] Heraclitus, for example, depicts Justice and Law as broad principles affecting
even the sun, which "will not overstep his limits; otherwise the Erinyes,
the servants of Justice, will find him out."[10] War and Strife rule, however.
Empedocles describes Strife and Love (together with earth, air, fire, and
water) as the fundamental forces. Strife and Love are equals, are of the
same age, and take turns ruling, as determined by an oath.

Monarchy, the third controlling principle, takes varied forms. Anaxagoras and Diogenes respectively identify it as Mind and Air. Plato (despite his attack on Homer's anthropomorphism)[11] pictures a monarchic
cosmos in the *Timaeus,* where the Craftsman issues ordinances to be

administered by other gods. Plato also has Socrates say that reason, "king of heaven and earth,"[12] decrees the preservation and well-being of the cosmos. Aristotle says there can be only one first principle, because "things should not be badly governed."[13] He thus links the very notion of cosmos, "good order," to a single ruler. Community as well as monarchy has some role in the cosmos, as in Socrates's remark, "a sense of community and friendship and orderliness and temperance and justice hold together the heaven and the earth and gods and men, and for this reason they call the whole a world-order."[14]

The cosmos is not only social and political but also alive, in whole and in part. Often it is physically anthropomorphic as well. Sometimes it is a macrocosmic human form: "Zeus is first and last, one royal body, containing fire water earth and air, night and day, Metis and Eros. The sky is his head, the stars his hair, the sun and moon his eyes, the air his intelligence."[15] Anaximenes seems to see such a microcosm/macrocosm: "just as our soul . . . being air, holds us together, so does wind or air enclose the whole world."[16] Part of the Hippocratic Corpus, *On Regimen,* also compares the universe to the human body; the sea, for example, corresponds to the belly. Another Hippocratic work, *On Sevens,* again compares the earth with the body, as the classicist G.E.R. Lloyd notes: "the stony core of the earth corresponds to the bones, its surface to flesh, the 'hot and wet' that exist in the earth to marrow and the brain, the water of rivers to blood in the veins, air to breath."[17]

For Plato, the cosmos is a composite living creature "of which all other living creatures [are parts]. . . . For the god, wishing to make this world most nearly like that intelligible thing which is best and in every way complete, fashioned it as a single visible living creature, containing within itself all living things."[18] Any correspondence between this generalized, composite creature and humans may seem slight. Indeed, Plato lists human features that are absent, not ones that are present. As had Parmenides, he pictures the cosmos as a sphere: the god "turned its shape rounded and spherical, equidistant every way from centre to extremity . . . for he judged uniformity to be immeasurably better than its opposite."[19]

Yet the human form implicitly is the standard from which Plato starts. The cosmos

> had no need of eyes, for nothing visible was left outside; nor of hearing, for there was nothing outside to be heard. There was no surrounding air to require breathing, nor yet was it in need of any organ to receive food into itself. . . . It had no need of hands to grasp with or to defend itself, nor yet of feet or anything that would serve to stand upon.[20]

That the human body is part of the model for this limbless ball becomes clear when we learn that the essence of the human body is its spherical head. The head is designed to contain the immortal, rational part of humans, the soul. The rest of the body is appended as a support system:

> Copying the round shape of the universe, they confined the two divine rev-
> olutions in a spherical body—the head, as we now call it—which is the di-
> vinest part of us and lord over all the rest. . . . Accordingly, that the head
> might not roll upon the ground with its heights and hollows of all sorts, and
> have no means to surmount the one or to climb out of the other, they gave
> it the body as a vehicle for ease of travel [and] . . . set the face on the globe
> of the head on [the front] and fixed in it organs for all the forethought of
> the soul.[21]

Like the head, the bodies of the universe and the created gods are
spheres, whose motions are the rational ones of rotation and orbital revolution. Engaging only in these perfect motions, neither the cosmos nor
its celestial components need limbs or other organs. Their perfect bodies
consist only of the essential element, the head. Thus the essential human
shape and the shape of the cosmos are one.

Similarly in Aristotle, the Whole has no obvious physical likeness to
humans, yet its organization is at least that of a complex animal. Like
Plato's cosmos, it has a top and a bottom, a right and left. It moves in
one direction rather than another because it is "better to move forward."
Its front "is that toward which sensations are directed, i.e., toward which
the animal looks."[22]

Humans and the cosmos are as similar spiritually and mentally as they
are physically. Plato says the cosmos is "in truth a living creature endowed
with soul and with reason." Like people, it is sociable, but unlike them,
it can keep itself company. It not only is made by a god but, having both
soul and self-sufficiency, it *is* a god:

> All this, then, was the plan of the god who is for ever [that is, who is im-
> mortal] for the god who was sometime to be [that is, the cosmos] . . . he
> made it smooth and uniform, everywhere equidistant from its centre, a body
> whole and complete, with complete bodies for its parts. And in the centre
> he set a soul and caused it to extend throughout the whole and further
> wrapped its body round with soul on the outside; and so he established one
> world alone, round and revolving in a circle, solitary but able by reason of
> its excellence to bear itself company, needing no other acquaintance or friend
> but sufficient to itself. On all accounts the world which he brought into being
> was a blessed god.[23]

Within this cosmos-god, the planets, sun, moon, and stars also are alive,
intelligent, and divine. Each has a soul[24] that causes its motion, and varying degrees of intelligence, volition, and power. The Sun is a leader because he has superior intelligence.[25] The planets display varying power by
following their own courses. Sometimes they race. Venus and Mercury
show their power "intermittently, sometimes dropping behind the Sun,
but then quickening their pace to overtake and pass him."[26]

Like other living creatures, planets come into being and learn their
appointed tasks. The eldest is the Earth, made by the Craftsman to care
for humans: "Earth he designed to be at once our nurse [and] guardian."[27] The Earth not only lives but breathes, causing the tides: it "re-

spires and causes certain refluxes by its inhalations and exhalations . . . [when it inhales] all the rivers flow together into the chasm, and then flow back again out of it."[28] Celestial bodies also think. Stars, for example, rotate steadily on their axes because "each always thinks the same thoughts about the same things."[29]

Aristotle, too, sees the heavenly bodies as alive. Their life accounts for their motion. Book Lambda of his *Metaphysics*, in fact, conceives all nature as moved by desire. Even where his world scheme is most mechanical or impersonal, it still is goal-directed. The Unmoved Mover itself is intellection or reason: "*nous* nousing itself."[30] Since reason is, for Aristotle, the characteristic of man, man and final principle again are the same.

Plato personifies body and soul as well. The soul is senior to, and mistress of, the body: "Now this soul [was not] younger than the body; for when [the god] joined them together, he would not have suffered the elder to be ruled by the younger [but] made soul prior to body and more venerable in birth and excellence, to be the body's mistress and governor." Plato compares his trinity of Becoming, Receptacle, and eternal Form to child, mother, and father: "we must conceive three things: that which becomes; that in which it becomes; and the model in whose likeness that which becomes is born. Indeed we may fittingly compare the Recipient to a mother, the model to a father, and the nature that arises between them to their offspring."[31]

Another anthropomorphic conception of the universe is that it is an artifact.[32] Plato and Aristotle both say all natural phenomena are designed and executed by gods (or Nature) using various skills and crafts. Plato's cosmos, in whole and in part, is made by a divine artificer, the Craftsman. In the *Timaeus*, the first Greek account of the cosmos as the product of craft rather than of organic evolution, gods bake, turn lathes, bore holes, model in wax, and fasten with glue, rivets, and bolts.[33] At times they join several crafts, as in producing bone by techniques from metallurgy, ceramics, and perhaps from baking.

Plato's Craftsman has diverse relations to the universe: he is its king and pilot, artisan and genitor. Plato admits that "to discover the maker and father of the universe is hard indeed, and . . . to declare him to all men is impossible."[34] All his images, however, show an intelligent, purposeful, and benevolent being, sometimes obscure, but always humanlike. The world this Craftsman made is not only anthropomorphic but also anthropocentric. Nothing is accidental and most features have purpose for human life. The Craftsman even set the planets in their courses so that humans would learn counting and mathematics by reckoning time.

Aristotle's Nature, like Plato's Craftsman, is rational and humanlike. Aristotle compares her to a painter who sketches an outline and fills in the colors, to a good housekeeper, and to an intelligent human being.[35] She creates, devises, and adorns. She is economic of means, doing nothing superfluous. If we are to grasp the cause of the stars, for example, "we must start from this, that everything which has a function exists for the sake of that function."[36] Although Nature, like the Craftsman, is "sometimes unable to achieve her ends because of the material with which she has to work,"[37] everything she does is for the sake of something. In general, that something is perfection.

The drive to perfection is manifest in motion, whose purpose is the self-realization of the moving object. Self-realization is a constant process, not a final state. An Aristotle scholar, J. H. Randall, says Aristotle's "nature is like an army forever marking time, but never marching anywhere."[38] Randall finds Aristotle's thought largely naturalistic but also "theistic," in Book Lambda at least, in that Aristotle accounts for natural processes by their feelings and emotions. This theism is rational, however:

> Not the blind forces of nature, not Newtonian inertia, the sheer continuance in motion—to Aristotle this would have seemed unintelligible. . . . [For him] there must be a force like "love"—desire, aspiration, the striving toward perfection. That is what makes men go round; and if men are a fair sampling of nature, that may be what makes nature go round too. For Aristotle, such a force, such a drive or *horme,* is "implanted" in every natural process: the urge to perfect one's own being.[39]

Whether or not Aristotle's attribution of love or aspiration to cosmic processes is theistic, it *is* anthropomorphic: it assumes "men are a fair sampling of nature." It makes intellect and love features of the cosmos as a whole. Even the attractive power of the Unmoved Mover, by which things and events move toward perfection, is more like a human emotion than like a physical force.[40]

Thus Greek philosophy, though growing away from Greek religion, keeps the latter's fundamental anthropomorphism. Although the philosophers are not primarily concerned with gods, they see the cosmos as socially organized, as driven by humanlike desires and enterprises, and as the result of humanlike activities. It has been made intentionally by an agent and contains various humanlike beings. Moreover, it is such a being itself.

Aristotle's anthropomorphic cosmos persists in European thought through the Middle Ages and into the Renaissance. The human body and the body of the universe remain microcosm and macrocosm, and the body politic occupies a middle ground. Often the parallels are elaborate. Medieval writers on church and state "specified and physicalized the anthropomorphic analogy with worlds of detail not dreamed of by Plato, Aristotle, or St. Paul."[41] Their comparisons take many forms. A codex of the twelfth century, for example, says that the

> sovereign [means] the first head. For judges are the heads of other men, who are ruled by them just as limbs are ruled by their heads. But the sovereign is the head of judges, and they are ruled by him. After the sovereign there are the princes, who are like the eyes of the emperor. After the princes are the

high lords who are like the hands. After the high lords are the nobles, like the chest. After the nobles are the petty judges, like the feet of the emperor.[42]

This anatomizing continues unbroken into the late Middle Ages and beyond. In the fifteenth century, for example, Nicholas of Cusa compared lawmaking with "eating, including biting, tasting, chewing, and digesting."[43] Moreover, the world as a whole remains animate. Nicholas's near-contemporary, the astrologer and philosopher Marsilio Ficino, writes, "inasmuch as the world is not an aggregate of dead elements but rather an animate being, there can be in it no . . . 'parts' that possess an independent existence next to and outside the whole. [Each 'part' is] an *organ* possessing its definite place and necessary function in the whole complex life of the cosmos."[44] This "animate being" also is humanlike in most ways. The popular Renaissance symbol of the *melothesia,* for instance, inscribes a man's body, with outstretched arms and legs, in the circle of the cosmos.[45] The doctrine of signatures prevalent in Renaissance Europe holds that "the natural world contains creations that are sympathetic to particular features of our internal anatomy, and further, that these natural creations are somehow signed so that they bear a veiled similarity to the part of our anatomy which they can be made to treat."[46] Thus walnuts correspond to the head, orchids to the pubis, and eyebright to the eyes.

Another correspondence is that both body and world are in constant, systematic flux. Leonardo, as noted earlier, writes that the hydraulics of water in the world parallels that of blood in the body. The entire world is alive for Leonardo, with a willing spirit.

> Now you see that the hope and the desire of returning to the first state of chaos, is like the moth to the light. . . . But this desire is the very quintessence, the spirit of the elements, which finding itself imprisoned with the soul is ever longing to return from the human body to its giver. And you must know that this same longing is that quintessence, inseparable from nature, and that man is the image of the world.[47]

Renaissance writers in England further elaborate the anthropomorphic commonwealth. They include even scientists like the anatomist William Harvey, who shows orderliness in human affairs by showing orderliness in the circulatory system. Harvey writes, in dedicating *The Motion of the Heart* to King Charles, "The heart of animals is the foundation of their life, the sovereign of everything within them, the sun of their microcosm. . . . The King, in like manner, is the foundation of his kingdom, the sun of the world around him, the heart of the republic."[48]

Although Harvey extends his science to the social world, he seems more self-consciously metaphoric than his predecessors. His era also brings the first unambiguous criticism of anthropomorphism in science, that of Francis Bacon.

Bacon   No clear beginning can be found for science in the modern sense, but most historians of science regard Bacon as the prophet of empiricism and hence of the separation of science from philosophy. Bacon also sounds the first clear warning against anthropomorphism. He rejects Aristotle, for example, largely for the latter's anthropomorphism.[49] Bacon's warning has become a hallmark of subsequent science.

Bacon says Aristotle "corrupted natural [science] by his logic,"[50] fashioning the world out of categories, a priori, rather than looking to experience. Anthropomorphism is one result. For example, a central Aristotelian principle, the urge of all things to perfect themselves, is really only a human urge. "Final causes," or ends at which processes aim, Bacon says, "have relation clearly to the nature of man rather than to the nature of the universe."[51] Aristotle's mistake, Bacon notes, is not unique to him. Instead, we all tend to suppose that nature, like ourselves, has ends in mind. We suppose so because we look continually for explanations. Failing to find explanations in nature, we try to understand nature as we do ourselves.

This impulse to understand nature as ourselves is intrinsic, even compulsive. "Although the most general principles in nature [cannot] be referred to a cause, nevertheless the human understanding being unable to rest still seeks something prior in the order of nature. And . . . struggling toward that which is further off it falls back upon that which is nearer at hand, namely, on final causes."[52] But final causes really belong only to humans; that is, only humans set and work toward goals. Bacon thus rejects teleology, and seems the first to do so.[53]

Bacon finds the source of teleology and other anthropomorphism in four sets of "idols and false notions."[54] These are the idols of the tribe, cave, marketplace, and theater. The first set comprises a general anthropomorphism:

> The Idols of the Tribe have their foundations in human nature itself, and in the tribe or race of men. For it is a false assumption that the sense of man is the measure of things. On the contrary, all perceptions as well of the sense as of the mind are according to the measure of the individual and not according to the measure of the universe. And the human understanding is like a false mirror, which, receiving rays irregularly, distorts and discolors the nature of things by mingling its own nature with it.[55]

Because of our inevitable anthropocentrism, Bacon says, all perceptions, sensory and mental, mingle human nature with the nature of things. This mingling is inevitable: its "foundation [is] in human nature itself."

The second set of idols, those of the cave, is individual. "For everyone (besides the errors common to human nature in general) has a cave or den of his own, which refracts and discolors the light of nature, owing either to his own proper and peculiar nature; or to his education and conversation with others." This set, then, is variable, idiosyncratic, and "governed as it were by chance."

A third set, the idols of the marketplace, corresponds roughly to popular culture. Here "words are imposed according to the apprehension of the vulgar. And therefore the ill and unfit choice of words wonderfully obstructs the understanding."[56] The last set, fallacies created by philosophers, Bacon calls idols of the theater, "because in my judgment all the received systems are but so many stage plays, representing worlds of their own creation."

Much of what passes for knowledge, then, compounds four kinds of errors: those intrinsic to human perception, those bred by idiosyncratic experience, those caused by the inadequacies of ordinary language, and those created by philosophic speculation. These four constitute an anthropocentric, self-perpetuating system of beliefs that obstruct, skew, and color our world.

We normally do not notice the inadequacies of this system, however, for three reasons. First, our perception is categorical, simplified by sets and kinds. We assimilate everything to these, emphasizing differences between them and minimizing differences within them and expecting symmetries: "human understanding is of its own nature prone to suppose the existence of more order and regularity in the world than it finds. . . . Hence the fiction that all celestial bodies move in perfect circles."

Second, we prefer confirming evidence to disconfirming evidence: "human understanding when it has once adopted an opinion . . . draws all things else to support and agree with it . . . it is the peculiar and perpetual error of the human intellect to be more moved and excited by affirmatives than by negatives."

Third (anticipating Nietzsche and Freud), our perceptions are not objective, neutral, or independent of our feelings but are motivated by them: "The human understanding is no dry light, but receives an infusion from the will and affections." We are impatient at difficult research. We reject "sober things, because they narrow hope." We are swayed by popular opinion, by hopes and fears, and by arrogance and pride, but we do not realize that this is so. "Numberless, in short, are the ways, and sometimes imperceptible, in which the affections color and infect the understanding."

Our most generic mistake, however, is our anthropocentrism—our tacit sense that we are the center and hence the measure of things. Since our knowledge is shot through with the four idols, with simplified perceptions, and with confirmed beliefs, the trap of measuring the universe by ourselves is hard to escape. Bacon recommends, among other means of escape, that we scrutinize sensory experience, weigh confirming and disconfirming evidence equally, and sustain a spirit of skepticism.

Bacon himself, nonetheless, does not entirely escape the trap. He accounts for the behavior of matter, for example, by "desires" such as that for mutual contact. His matter also has a sense of its own dimensions and is clannish:

there is in bodies a desire of mutual contact, so as not to suffer the unity of nature to be quite separated or broken and a vacuum thus made . . . there is in bodies a desire of resuming their natural dimensions or tension, so that if compressed within or extended beyond them, they immediately strive to recover themselves, and fall back to their old volume and extent . . . [and] there is in bodies a desire of congregating toward masses of kindred nature—of dense bodies, for instance, toward the globe of the earth, of thin and rare bodies toward the compass of the sky.[57]

Thus, though Bacon observes that we always see things and events as like ourselves and that this has foundations in our nature, he fails to root out the tendency in himself. Nonetheless, he marks a turning point.

Galileo, Bacon's contemporary, similarly says human knowledge cannot be the measure of the universe. A character in *Dialogue on the Great World Systems,* evidently speaking for Galileo, finds "extraordinary foolish those who would make human comprehension the measure of what Nature has a power or knowledge to effect, whereas on the contrary there is not any least effect in Nature which can be fully understood."[58] Yet this stricture itself anthropomorphizes, making Nature an artificer with "power" and "knowledge." The same speaker contrasts the limited human knowledge of agriculture with Nature's infinite knowledge and ability:

> What has the [human] knowledge of planting a vine in a trench to do with the knowledge that it takes to make it sprout forth, to attract nourishment, select this good part from that other to make of it leaves, another part to make sprouts, another part to make grapes . . . for such are the works of most wise Nature? This is only one particular operation of the innumerable ones which Nature carries out, and it alone is enough to reveal an infinite wisdom.[59]

Another character in the *Dialogue* shows that the moon and earth are similar in "their reciprocal response as well to injuries as to favours." The moon suffers injuries and bravely takes revenge: "The Moon is often deprived of light and eclipsed, at the height of its illumination, by the Earth between it and the Sun, and by way of revenge interposes itself in like manner between the Earth and the Sun." Although this revenge "does not measure to the injury," still, "bearing in mind the smallness of the Moon's body, in comparison to the magnitude of the Earth's, it cannot be denied that its will and, as it were, valour are very great."[60] Thus, while human understanding is incommensurable with nature, the moon still is vulnerable, vengeful, and valorous, the earth is trespassing, and nature is purposive.[61]

The seventeenth-century philosopher Benedict de Spinoza offers a critique of anthropocentrism and anthropomorphism similar to Bacon's.[62] Our view of the world, Spinoza says, is scarcely more than an extension of our view of ourselves. We evaluate and understand the world solely in terms of its utility for, and effects upon, us. What we call good or bad in nature, for example, is simply that which is agreeable or disagreeable to us. We take the world in general to be equivalent to its impact on us: "if the motion which objects we see communicate to our nerves be conducive to health, the objects causing it are styled *beautiful;* if a contrary motion be excited, they are styled *ugly.*"[63] Similarly, we suppose that nature is purposive because we are, and because aspects of nature are relevant to our purposes.

The human worldview according to Spinoza is like the child's worldview according to Piaget. People think nature acts "as men themselves act, namely, with an end in view," because people are ignorant of natural causes and because they themselves do all things "for an end, namely, for that which is useful to them." Thus "they only look for a knowledge of the final causes [that is, purposes] of events, and when these are learned, they are content." But when "they cannot learn such causes from external causes, they are compelled to turn to considering themselves, and reflecting what end would have induced them personally to bring about the given event, and thus they necessarily judge other natures by their own." Finding much about themselves and the world that is useful, they look

> on the whole of nature as a means for obtaining such conveniences. Now as they are aware, that they found these conveniences and did not make them, they think they have cause for believing, that some other being has made them for their use. As they look upon things as means, they cannot believe them to be self-created; but, judging from the means which they are accustomed to prepare for themselves, they are bound to believe in some ruler or rulers of the universe . . . who have arranged and adapted everything for human use. . . . [People thus] endeavour to show that nature does nothing in vain, i.e., nothing which is useless to man.

Actually, however, "nature has no particular goal in view, and . . . final causes are mere human figments." Consequently, "explanations commonly given of nature are mere modes of imagining, and do not indicate the true nature of anything, but only the constitution of the imagination."

In short, the world we see combines three images: of ourselves, of those aspects of the world our senses take in, and of how those aspects conform to our purposes. We are caught in anthropocentrism and anthropomorphism almost as completely as Lange and Nietzsche will say two centuries later. For Spinoza, both familiarity and confusion are at work. For Spinoza as for Bacon, however, it still seems possible to see the real nature of the world by applying enough skepticism, reason, and observation.

Several subsequent philosophers also warn against anthropomorphism. Hume, as we saw, explains it by familiarity: we are in the world as in a vast, mysterious theater, in which we are vulnerable and ignorant. Desperate to understand events, we use ourselves as models. Again, however, we can largely extricate ourselves from anthropomorphism by skepticism and reason. Kant extends Hume's analysis, saying one can never know an object of perception in itself, a *Ding an sich.* One can only know the world as rendered by forms of perception and categories of the human understanding. Even space and time are intuitions imposed by mental organization. Feuerbach, as noted, adds that religious anthropomorphism is a projection of our own nature, especially our aspirations and desires. It is at once a wish fulfillment and a self-exploration.

Building on Kant, on such scientists as Hermann von Helmholtz, Emil Du Bois-Reymond, and Georg Lichtenberg,[64] and on Lange, Nietzsche brings the critique of anthropomorphism to its logical extreme, finding human knowledge comprehensively and inevitably human-centered and hence inevitably anthropomorphic. In this conclusion, he seems to conflate anthropocentrism and anthropomorphism. I agree that humans are inevitably anthropocentric. Anthropomorphism, however, is a mistake by definition. The very fact that in many cases we can see our anthropomorphizing implies that in other cases we do not make the same mistake. As a philosopher, Mary Midgley, says, "mistakes can only count as mistakes if we take the correcting insight to be less mistaken."[65]

Without following Nietzsche to his radical conclusion, we may benefit from his observation that scientists, though warned by Bacon and Spinoza, continue to anthropomorphize. In Nietzsche's view, science does so fundamentally. The concept of causation, for example, is simply our application to the nonhuman world of our experience of ourselves. We see ourselves as voluntary agents bringing about effects we desire, and physical things and events as doing the same. This experience is illusory, even regarding ourselves. Similarly, force (like cause, irreducible in Newtonian physics) is an extension of our sensations of muscular effort. The notions of attraction and repulsion similarly stem from our subjective experience of ourselves.

Other ideas in physics, according to Nietzsche, stem from our predilections for perceiving the world in certain modes. One predilection is for sensuous intuition. We like atomism because atoms are picturable and pictures seem based immediately on sensation. We think our sensations trustworthy because they appear direct and unmediated. But sensations and intuitions already involve primitive interpretation. George Stack, a modern Nietzsche scholar, says cognition and synthesis "percolate down into unconscious sensory processes. The senses have a tendency towards form-giving activity just as reason does; and they engage in a pre-judgmental process of making alike, similar or equal what they encounter."[66]

Nietzsche thus notes unconscious interpretation and categorical perception. Doing so, he amplifies Bacon's observation that human understanding is prone to suppose "more order and regularity in the world than it finds." Nietzsche, elaborating both Bacon and Spinoza, says physical concepts are useful fictions: "the inventive power that creates categories is working in the service of our needs, namely of security and rapid intelligibility on the basis of conventions and signs."[67] Notions of matter and force reflect not only interpretations of our experience as agents but also the structure of language: they correspond to subject and predicate.

We suppose that properties must have things to which they belong, because predicates must have subjects.[68]

We suppose entities exist as discrete units because we suppose we exist as discrete units. But this also is a mistake. As Stack puts it, the notion "thing" is simply a "resting place for our thoughts, an assumption that is more a figment of our mind than a real object."[69] For Nietzsche, neither isolated things nor identical things exist; their putative isolation and identity consist only in our extraction of properties and relationships that interest us. Thus science is pervaded by "hypothetical entities or 'substances,' by hypostatizations, by reifications."[70] Scientists do not really explain phenomena but only describe them, since the very concepts they use are "things which do not exist, with lines, surfaces, bodies, atoms, divisible times, divisible spaces—how can explanation ever be possible when we first make everything a *conception*, our conception! It is sufficient to regard science as the exactest humanizing of things that is possible."[71]

Nonetheless Nietzsche, having persistently criticized anthropomorphism in science and elsewhere, finally yields to it himself. Perhaps reverting to an early fascination with the power of nature and certainly deciding anthropomorphism cannot be transcended,[72] he comes to speak even of inorganic matter as analogous to the human world of feelings. Matter, he thinks, may constitute a "more primitive world of affect" and all of nature is pervaded by the will to power.[73]

Since Nietzsche, no philosopher has so avidly pursued the topic. Indeed, few seem to take it seriously. Agassi, for example, in "Anthropomorphism in Science," calls anthropomorphism "inveterate" but does not try to account for it.[74] Agassi also says anthropomorphism may be either mistaken or correct. This contradicts his own definition of anthropomorphism as projecting "human qualities into natural phenomena." For anthropomorphism to be correct, humans and natural phenomena must share the quality in question. If they do, that quality is not uniquely human.[75] Furthermore, the very notion of projection implies that some perceptions are *not* projected—that they are independent of the observer and not anthropocentric.[76] But as Nietzsche and others point out, anthropocentrism is inescapable since we can avoid neither human interests nor human senses. The real distinction, then, is between analogies of the human and nonhuman world that are valid and those that are anthropomorphic.

Surprisingly, Agassi questions whether anthropomorphism is "still alive." He thinks it is "possible that we still hold . . . versions of anthropomorphism" but that increasing generality and abstraction in science insulate us from it, and that it is not a problem in the human sciences.

Scientists and historians of science, in contrast, continue to warn of anthropomorphism. The geologist and biologist Stephen Jay Gould remarks that the impediments to scientific understanding "most difficult to dislodge are those biases that escape our scrutiny because they seem so obviously, even ineluctably, just. We know ourselves best and tend to view other creatures as mirrors of our own constitution and social arrangements."[77]

Whether or not its cause really is that we know ourselves best, the difficulty Gould points out is perennial. Lloyd remarks, for example, that animism hindered Greek dynamics. They understood gravity, for instance, as "like attracts like," a principle they applied to inanimate objects as well as to humans and other animals. In the fifth century B.C.E. Democritus thought, according to Sextus Empiricus, that just as "animals flock together by their kinds, doves with doves and cranes with cranes [so] the same happens with inanimate objects, too, as we can see with seeds in a sieve and pebbles on the sea-shore."[78] The development of dynamics therefore required its isolation from biology and psychology. Gravity, vortices, and other inanimate phenomena had to be seen as different from animal behavior. Aristotle recognized this difference, but his view that all natural motions are progressions of elements toward their forms, each actualizing its potentiality, may have made measurement of specific factors seem unnecessary.[79]

Two millennia later, writers in various sciences still see anthropomorphism as constantly recurring and as constantly needing to be rooted out. A few scientists say, as do a few philosophers, that anthropomorphism sometimes is valid and sometimes not. However, most, like Bacon, identify science largely with eliminating human features from representations of nature, and see this as a continual process. A sociologist of science, Barry Barnes, thinks science is the "most elaborated and systematized of all forms of knowledge, and the least anthropomorphic,"[80] and that its effort to avoid anthropomorphism is central. A primatologist, Linda Fedigan, writes that a key achievement of science is the "realization that we are not the center of, nor the prototype for, all else in the universe, [but] while anthropomorphism is to be avoided or minimized, it will not be eliminated."[81]

No scientific discipline is immune. Observers charge physicists, for instance, with anthropomorphism as early as Aristotle and as late as charmed particles. In the early twentieth century, the sociologist and economist Thorstein Veblen, much like Nietzsche, found the notions of causality and force in physics metaphysical and dramaturgical. Action at a distance, he said, is a problem for physicists only because of their "irrepressible anthropomorphism."[82] Since interaction in the human sphere requires contact or at least some tangible medium, they think interaction in the nonhuman world also requires contact. Shortly after Veblen, the physicist Max Planck wrote that progress in theoretical physics depends on "elimination of the anthropomorphous elements, particularly the specific sense-perceptions."[83] Such a freeing of physics from sense perception helps unify the physical sciences through ever more general concepts.

Percy Nunn, a philosopher contemporary to Planck, suggests that the very notion of matter in physics is anthropomorphic. Nunn says every kind of matter historically conceived by physicists, such as phlogiston, caloric, ether, and most recently electricity, eventually is superceded and discarded as anthropomorphic. The Newtonian "vocabulary of mechanics—vis [force] inertiae, vis impressa, vis viva; centripetal and centrifugal force; work, energy, least action—shows clearly . . . experiences of effort and resistance, of compulsion and yielding."[84] Anthropomorphism is "too deeply rooted in human nature to be easily suppressed. The average student of physics to-day is probably still at heart an anthropomorphist. He takes his science to be a hunt after causes [that] convey into the transactions between material bodies features of the traffic between man's mind and his environment."[85]

Nunn shows that Albert Einstein's work entails, as does Planck's, abandoning both ordinary sensory information and ordinary (that is, anthropomorphic) physical conceptions. However, Nunn himself finally yields to an anthropomorphic impulse, though only for didactic reasons. Critiquing physical conceptions of matter, he suggests the electron is another anthropomorphic fiction. His account is ironic:

> Lastly we come to the electron, which is the reigning monarch in physical theory. Is it to be its fate also to be devoured by its children, or is its kingdom secure for ever? When we consider the men who have given their allegiance to it and the magnitude of the conquests they have achieved in its name, it seems impertinent to question the permanence of its rule—until one remembers how great were the votaries of ether, and what triumphs they won under its banner.[86]

Later, Nunn again uses anthropomorphism to suggest the problems inherent in extending any understanding based on familiar phenomena. In this case the model is Ernest Rutherford's planetary scheme of the atom, as developed by Niels Bohr. Nunn again is tongue in cheek, yet apt: "the Bohr atom, though it masquerades as [a planetary] system, refuses to behave like one. It owns no firm allegiance to the fundamental principles that govern the behavior of matter . . . but picks and chooses those it will follow. Thus it is obedient as regards the orbits of its electrons, but flatly contumacious as regards the radiation they ought to emit."[87]

More recent commentators on physics remain conscious of the problem. A philosopher of science, Adolf Grünbaum, for example, continues a debate among physicists over whether the concept of entropy is anthropomorphic.[88] Nonetheless, physicists and related scientists continue to produce a welter of anthropomorphisms at various levels and with varying subtlety and self-consciousness. Examples range from the brief, consciously metaphoric, and inconsequential, such as the left- and right-handedness of molecules, to the large scale and systematic, such as the notions that the universe is a computer or in some other way shows design and that human life is somehow central or necessary to the universe.

In physics, as elsewhere, anthropomorphism often is divisible into the artificialism and the immediate anthropomorphism found in Aristotle and in young children. Sometimes they coexist, as when physicists look both for atomic and subatomic "building blocks" (as though someone were doing the building) and for "families" of particles. Among the families, some members are "children," such as the particles Murray Gell-Mann named quarks, after Mr. Finn's children ("Three quarks for Muster Mark") in Joyce's *Finnegan's Wake*.[89] Others are "daughters," as in radioactive isotopes of uranium 235.

On a larger, molecular scale, a hypothesis known as Maxwell's demon flourishes. James Clerk Maxwell, author of the kinetic theory of gases, invented this demon to show the virtual impossibility of violating the second law of thermodynamics, entropy.[90] The demon is of atomic scale and able to distinguish gas molecules moving fast from those moving slowly. It stands at a tiny doorway between two containers of gas of equal energy. By allowing molecules of high velocity to pass through in one direction while blocking those of low velocity, the demon raises the temperature of one container and lowers that of the other, producing disequilibrium and apparently reversing entropy.

Maxwell meant the demon as an instrument of negative physics, to show that only by the efforts of an impossible creature could the second law be voided. However, his hypothesis has proved attractive enough to come alive in the literature of theoretical physics. Meant as an impossibility, the demon has produced enduring scientific interest in its hypothetical effects.

Both immediate anthropomorphism and artificialism also occur in astrophysics, as when physicists speak of stars as sentient, willful, or alive, or as being made. A scientist at the National Oceanic and Atmospheric Administration, for example, told reporters that "most solar astronomers would say the sun barely notices the planets are out there."[91] An astrophysicist describes the final stages of star formation as an act of will: "the star seeks simultaneously to accrete more material and to shed excess angular momentum."[92] Others speak of the "birth," "death," and "maternity wards" of stars. The astronomer Sir William Herschel, in contrast to these organismic images, shows artificialism: clusters of stars with frequent collisions and star destruction "may be the laboratories of the universe [wherein] remedies for the decay of the whole are prepared."[93]

Another artificialist view of the universe is that of Edward Fredkin, a computer scientist. Fredkin thinks the universe is a vast computer that ultimately consists of bits of information in process and was built to answer some cosmic question.[94] Another astrophysicist, Alan Guth, addresses the origin and end of the universe, like the Greeks, with animism and artificialism at once: successive universes are "parent" and "child" and, at the same time, humans might possibly create universes; in fact, ours may have been so created.[95]

Stars and other extraterrestrial entities also may speak to us. John

Bolton, an Australian astronomer, says that since quasar radio emissions are short-wave, quasar "voices are higher pitched" than those of other sources.[96] While neither Bolton nor many others think quasars send their signals deliberately, many astronomers do think sentient sources of interstellar messages possible and even likely. Some actively look for them and have agreed internationally on how to verify and announce their discovery. A few, such as Carl Sagan, think of themselves as pursuing a new discipline, exobiology, in search of message-senders. The pursuit has been called "almost a religion."[97]

A search for messages is, in itself, not necessarily anthropomorphic. So far, however, the search has been made entirely in terms of signals that contemporary humans themselves might send,[98] and apparent messages from space have proved illusory. In 1967, several days of excitement followed a discovery by Jocelyn Bell, a graduate student in England, who "detected unfamiliar radio signals from space that repeated with clock-like regularity."[99] Her small research group went "feverishly to work amidst wild speculations that they were hearing messages from space." What they had discovered, however, was not an intentional signal but a new kind of star, a pulsar. A decade earlier, a Harvard graduate student, Frank Drake, similarly discovered an apparent message among radio signals from the constellation Pleiades. When he encountered a sharp, strong, and unfamiliar signal, "It hit me that this looked like an intelligent signal from the Pleiades. You feel a very special emotion—enlightenment, rapture, eye-opening."[100] This signal also proved illusory, however, as it was a radio transmission from earth.

Another phenomenon recently seen as a message is an image in a photograph (Fig. 5–39) of the Cydonia region of Mars, taken in 1976 by the National Aeronautics and Space Administration's Viking Mission. Many people see the image as a face. Some regard it as a signal to Earth, either from an alien civilization or from a supernatural being. At least one commercial company has been formed to urge that a projected NASA unmanned space mission in 1993 look closely at it.

The step from a general anthropomorphism, and especially from this sensitivity to messages, to religion can be short. Many physicists and other scientists have taken such a step on the basis of apparent design, or at least order, in the universe. Newton, like many others, saw design in organisms: "the first contrivance of those very artificial parts of animals, the eyes, ears [etc.] . . . can be the effects of nothing else than the wisdom and skill of a powerful and ever living Agent." Newton also saw design in the general order of the universe: "This most beautiful system of the sun, planets and comets could only proceed from the counsel and domination of an intelligent and powerful being."[101] Einstein wrote that the scientist's "religious feeling takes the form of a rapturous amazement at the harmony of natural law, which reveals an intelligence of such superiority that, compared with it, all the systematic thinking and acting of human beings is an utterly insignificant reflection."[102] Such extrapolations from apparent design or order may be spontaneous, not necessarily shaped by prior religious belief.

Another extrapolation from apparent natural order, parallel to the religious one, is the "anthropic principle." Despite its unitary sound, this phrase labels a mixed and open-ended collection of claims, methods, and attitudes[103] centering on the observation that human life is made possible by a particular series of properties of matter and on the assertion that this series is unlikely to have come about by chance. A number of prominent scientists,[104] especially physicists, have joined this observation and this assertion to conclude that the human place in the universe is somehow peculiarly privileged.

One of the first proponents of the anthropic principle, Brandon Carter, writes, "we must be prepared to take account of the fact that our location in the universe is *necessarily* privileged to the extent of being compatible with our existence as observers."[105] This much is unsurprising and indeed tautologous. But Carter later asserts more boldly that the universe must include intelligent life: the "Universe . . . must be such as to admit the creation of observers within it." Another physicist, Frank Tipler, writes similarly, "intelligent life *must* evolve somewhere in any physically realistic universe."[106] Others have allied opinions, holding human life central and even necessary to the universe.[107]

Just as the form and significance of the anthropic principle vary from writer to writer, so do the arguments given for it. Most hinge on the notion that the series of universal properties, especially the "large number coincidences" of cosmology,[108] which make life possible, must be more than accidental. The paths from this notion to others, such as the claim that humans are central to the universe, however, are diverse and tangled. Some resemble the argument from design, yet do not postulate a God. Tipler and John Barrow think the anthropic principle *is* the design argument, but admit there are "few attempts to frame a precise statement of the Principle."[109] Advocates of other versions grant that the anthropic principle resembles religion (in hypothesizing, for instance, a universal mind) but still distinguish it as scientific.[110]

Still other scientists and philosophers of science reject anthropism as muddled and groundless. John Earman, for example, suggests that its attraction is largely the "seductive idea that there must be an overarching Principle. . . . The current widespread interest in anthropic reasoning is no doubt due largely to intimations that (in Dyson's words) the mind plays an essential role in the functioning of the universe. And yet when these intimations are followed up, all that one finds are empty teases or else unbridled and muddled speculation."[111] Another critic, Heinz Pagels, says the anthropic principle "confronts us with a new mystery: How can such a sterile idea reproduce itself so prolifically?"[112]

The explanation of this mystery is, once more, the explanation of the anthropocentrism and anthropomorphism noted in science from Bacon to Nietzsche and beyond: our perpetual and involuntary search for the

most significant patterns. Immersed in this search, we see, as Bacon
pointed out, more pattern than exists. Anthropists see the universe as
designed and humans as central to it. The medley of arguments for anthropism, and the medley of anthropisms, seem impelled by the same
unconscious, strategic, perceptual practice we have seen at work elsewhere.[113] At best, anthropism appears an uneasy union of anthropocentrism and anthropomorphism, elevated to a principle.

Biologists are as susceptible to anthropomorphism as are physicists. An
entomologist criticizes the

> tendency to interpret activities as if bees have human characteristics and val-
> ues. This contributes as little to understanding bee behvavior as the converse
> interpretation that humans have the values and characteristics of bees. A clear
> distinction must be made between two very different creatures. It is only
> natural that we as humans tend to ascribe certain human characteristics to
> anything we observe, particularly animals. Thus, bees [are considered] *angry*
> when they sting or *clever* when they build comb[s].[114]

Textbooks usually refer to a "division of labor" among bees. This mis-
leadingly implies that bees "consciously and actively divide 'responsibil-
ities' or 'duties' and also 'perform labor.' . . . If one accepts these terms
literally, it is logical to think that there [is an] administrative hierarchy
within the colony. The implication usually is that the queen bee is somehow active in organizing the activities."[115] However, the queen in fact
plays no such active role, and all activities in the hive can proceed without her.

Beekeeping literature also reflects the attitudes this entomologist indicates. A beekeeper writes that her bees, "in their fussy dislike of foreign
material in their hives, would . . . set themselves the task of chewing [it]
away."[116] Queenless bees drift "tentatively, without the aggressive assur-
ance" of others, and some are "so meek that the guard bees grudgingly
accept them." Earlier writers show the same tendency. Virgil sees in bees
"Great-hearted leaders in such tiny states, / Orderly custom, yes! and
national aims, / Tribes and their tribal conflicts . . . "[117] Until 1609 the
largest bee in the hive, the center of much activity, was known widely as
the king bee. In that year Charles Butler pointed out that this bee is not
male but female and should be called the queen. Despite being such a
close observer, Butler continues anthropomorphically:

> The drone is a grosse, stingless bee, that spendeth his time in gluttony and
> idleness. . . . For however hee brave it with his round velvet cap, his fine
> gown, his full paunch and his loud voice; yet is hee but an idle companion,
> living by the sweat of others' brows. Hee worketh not at all, either at home
> or abroad; and yet spendeth as much as two labourers: you shall never find
> his maw without a good drop of the purest nectar. In the heat of the day he
> flieth abroad, aloft, and about, and that with no small noise, as though hee
> would do some great act: but it is only for his pleasure, and to get him a
> stomach; and then returns hee presently to his cheer.[118]

Linnaeus, father of taxonomy, showed a more subtle and undoubtedly unconscious anthropomorphism in naming stages of insect development. He called the newly hatched stage a "larva," or mask, and the adult an "imago," or essential form—in which, in Aristotelian fashion, the insect ultimately fulfills itself. Linnaeus thus transposes the Western view of children as incomplete adults upon insects, in a "dubious comparison of human and insect life cycles."[119] A modern entomologist says his colleagues still understand social insects in terms of their own preoccupations. Their image of insect colonies "has evolved from that of a quaint class-structured society (as the established terminology will forever remind us), to that of a remorselessly efficient super-organism, to that of an endlessly squabbling nuclear family."[120]

The entomologist whose anthropomorphism is most widely known and criticized is E. O. Wilson.[121] In an attempt to found a new discipline, sociobiology, Wilson uses a number of terms from human society to describe animal societies. These include both metaphors now traditional in entomology, such as "slavery," "caste," "specialists," and "generalists," and new ones such as "xenophobia," "altruism," and "aggression."[122] As a critic notes, Wilson applies "xenophobia" to "aggression against newcomer animals, whatever form that aggression may take;" he uses "altruistic behavior" for "such distinct 'behaviors' as forgoing reproduction in sterile castes of insects and the feeding of the adults of certain wasps by their larvae;" and he describes as "aggression" an "incredible variety of 'competitive' behaviors including fighting, ritualized posturings, marking items with chemicals, and so on."[123] Another critic thinks anthropomorphism is intrinsic to sociobiology, especially in its attempt to "biologicize" ethics.[124]

Microbiologists, neuroscientists, and other laboratory biologists also anthropomorphize, often applying social and linguistic terms to communications within and among cells. A biochemist says eicosanoids, derived from fatty acids, are "how the cells chatter back and forth with each other. We have to understand the significance of all these voices when they whisper or shout, why or what it all means."[125] A neuroscientist says nerve cells in vertebrate spinal cords may vary in "who talks to whom."[126] The medical researcher and writer Lewis Thomas says the kind of tissue cells become depends on "messages exchanged among populations of cells and on the environment cells find themselves in . . . the brain [probably] works in somewhat the same way. There are vast populations of cells in close communication with one another, rather than a single cell, a chairman of the board, who sits and does the thinking."[127] Richard Dawkins, a sociobiologist, attributes "selfishness" and other societal traits to genes.[128]

Similarly, a writer on DNA describes Linus Pauling as learning how atoms are "allowed in nature to behave in one another's intimate company. Pauling was the anthropologist confronted with an imperfectly known language that turns out to belong to a rich, strange culture whose every interchange is governed by precise rules of hierarchy, status, and payment."[129] A physicist writing on biology describes "messenger RNA," in what he admits is "somewhat anthropomorphic language," as a molecule "manufactured at the site of the DNA and sent out to be read by the so-called ribosomes, which follow its instructions to manufacture the amino acids."[130] A geneticist refers to the "wisdom" of genes and calls those left after a mass extinction a "superbly fit set of survivors."[131] And an immunologist who thinks such metaphors hinder understanding says his colleagues "imbue immune system components with the ability to think, recognize and act."[132] Crick similarly warns biologists, especially those trained as physicists, against unconsciously supposing that the organisms they study are the results of design.

On a larger biological scale, the biochemist James Lovelock claims the entire Earth is an organism, which he calls Gaia. Lovelock's descriptions of Gaia vary, but a recent one is the "biosphere as an adaptive control system that can maintain the Earth in homeostasis."[133] However, more than the biosphere seems involved, since Lovelock says Gaia's waste products include "rock subducting to merge with the mantle." Thus her "physiology" includes both biosphere and geology. Nonetheless, Lovelock says physiology is the proper science for studying this organism.

Although concerned to avoid the "twin blights of anthropomorphism and teleology," Lovelock avoids neither. He finds it hard to "avoid talking of Gaia as though she were known to be sentient," and he regards all life as a "single living entity, capable of manipulating the Earth's atmosphere to suit its overall needs and endowed with faculties and powers far beyond those of its constituent parts."[134] Here Gaia combines intention, manipulation, faculties, and powers. Lovelock also anthropomorphizes organisms, crediting them with setting goals: "One of the most characteristic properties of all living organisms . . . is their capacity to . . . set a goal and then strive to achieve it."[135] But Bacon and Spinoza, three centuries earlier, pointed out that setting goals is specifically human.

Lovelock's anthropomorphism extends to portraying the Earth as a rebel and the Earth's fellow planets as a family. If Gaia's "intelligence network" were destroyed, he says, "our lifeless Earth, no longer a colourful misfit, a planet that broke all the rules, would fall soberly into line, in barren steady state, between its dead brother and sister, Mars and Venus."

Although Lovelock has few followers among other scientists, his lay audience is broad and his notion is of ancient lineage. Lovelock, his adherents, and even his critics, however, seem hardly aware of the antiquity of his idea. Lovelock subtitles his book *A New Look at Life on Earth* and usually traces Gaia's history only to the mid-1960s. He does credit the eighteenth-century geologist James Hutton with the idea of the earth as a superorganism, to be studied physiologically. He also mentions Mother Earth as an old religious belief. However, he does not mention that Plato, Aristotle, and their many followers in the West for some two millennia also regarded the Earth and other planets as organisms with physiologies and minds, and indeed often souls. In this context, Lovelock is more original in calling the other planets dead than in calling the Earth alive.

Though the idea that the Earth is alive, sentient, and purposeful is old and widespread, it has little currency among contemporary biologists. Another idea with anthropomorphic content, however, has immense currency. This is Charles Darwin's principle of evolution by natural selection. Natural selection, Darwin says, is nature's equivalent of artificial selection, or selection by human breeders of domestic plants and animals. Like artificial selection, it chooses or rejects given traits in a population and so progressively suits the population to an environment. Thus Darwin openly models his two central ideas—active choice and progress toward a goal—on human experience. As Robert Young, a historian and philosopher of science, notes, in "moving from artificial to natural, Darwin retains the anthropomorphic conception of *selection,* with all its voluntarist overtones."[136]

In an 1842 sketch, Darwin wonders what results might follow "if every part of a plant or animal was to vary . . . and if a being infinitely more sagacious than man (not an omniscient creator) during thousands and thousands of years were to select all the variations which tended towards certain ends,"[137] Here Darwin imagines an agent choosing variations with some end in mind. He then introduces the "selecting power of nature, infinitely wise" as well as "rigid and scrutinizing." The sketch imputes mechanism, use, contrivance, and (by comparison) art to nature: "We must look at every complicated mechanism and instinct, as the summary of a long history of useful contrivances, much like a work of art." Darwin continues in a paper written in 1858 with his codiscoverer, A. R. Wallace, that there is "an unerring power at work in [natural selection] which selects exclusively for the good of each organic being."[138]

Young finds the anthropomorphism and voluntarism throughout *On the Origin of Species* remarkable. Seventeenth-century science already had "banished purposes, intentions, and anthropomorphic expressions [and so] it is surprising to find such rank anthropomorphism at the heart of the most celebrated unifying theory in biology."[139] The chapter on "Natural Selection," for example, makes natural selection a strict, tireless, benevolent person: "natural selection is daily and hourly scrutinizing, throughout the world, every variation, even the slightest; rejecting that which is bad, preserving and adding up all that is good; silently and insensibly working, whenever and wherever opportunity offers, at the improvement of each organic being."[140] Elsewhere Darwin repeatedly refers to nature's "unerring skill" and calls nature a "powerful agent always ready to act and select."

Darwin's contemporaries also were aware of his anthropomorphism. Wallace called it to his attention in a letter of 1866, noting that one critic charged that Darwin's natural selection "requires the constant watching of an intelligent 'chooser,' like man's selection to which you so often compare it." Wallace reports that another critic says "you do not see that 'thought and direction are essential to the action of Natural Selection.' The same objection has been made a score of times by your chief opponents." Wallace thinks the criticism "arises almost entirely from your choice of the term 'Natural Selection' and . . . so frequently personifying nature as 'selecting,' as 'preferring,' as 'seeking only the good of the species,' etc."[141] Darwin defended his anthropomorphism with a standard response: it was a shorthand, not meant literally.

The defense ultimately is unnecessary, for Darwin really depends on chance operating on a large scale, not on nature's "scrutiny." Darwin was so well received, however, precisely because inconsistencies and ambiguities in his language allowed theists still to see design and intent at work in the universe, albeit with God at greater remove. Wallace himself, for example, objected to the anthropomorphism but later came to think guidance by a "superior intelligence" necessary for human evolution.

Young's essay on Darwin's metaphor ends in an almost Nietzschean skepticism. He joins other critical theorists in asking whether any fundamental scientific theory can be a pure, positivist discovery and concludes it cannot. Instead, theory always exists in a nexus of interests and assumptions that are both human and historic: "At the heart of its science we find a culture's values. Both are irreducibly anthropomorphic and social."[142]

The same issues of bias and human interests affect the social sciences as well. Anthropologists (and ethologists) studying primates, for example, debate whether monkey and ape behavior is best described in minimal, ostensibly nonanthropomorphic units of sound and gesture such as "open-mouth gape," or in larger units of action that express such intentions and emotions as threat, deception, and affection.[143] Some say that minimal units of description avoid anthropomorphism, but others, some of whom think anthropomorphism both inevitable and useful,[144] say such minimalism also avoids meaning.[145]

Differences in culture affect opinions about how strictly anthropomorphism in primatology must be avoided. In the West until quite recently, it has been virtually taboo. In contrast, Japanese primatologists, whom Western researchers often see as anthropomorphizing, seem unconcerned with the issue and may even pray at shrines for the souls of deceased monkeys.[146] The Western taboo may reflect, in addition to Bacon's injunction, the Judeo-Christian alliance of man with God against nature, strengthened by Descartes's view that nonhuman animals are soulless machines. However, the taboo sometimes influences the form of anthropomorphism without eliminating it. Primatologists may "reject some terms and embrace others, which, while no less anthropomorphic, are selected from a more acceptable lexicon. Currently, labels which imply sentimentality . . . are rejected, while . . . little criticism is leveled at equally anthropomorphic labels [such as] 'murder,' 'rape,' 'slavery,' [and] 'selfish.' "[147]

Social scientists also anthropomorphize, usually while reifying some abstraction. Psychologists, especially Freudians, give life and volition to varied mental entities such as the id, ego, and superego.[148] Freud writes, for example, "the ego is in the habit of transforming the id's will into action as if it were its own,"[149] and Harry Stack Sullivan aptly charges him with "anthropomorphic reifications."[150] Sociologists and anthropologists including Spencer, Durkheim, Radcliffe-Brown, and A. L. Kroeber, in a tradition going back at least to the Greeks, credit society or culture with a life, purpose, and will of its own. These functionalist scholars suppose that society or culture is an organism (usually humanlike) and see virtually all aspects of society or culture as having some purpose in sustaining the whole. They think culture, like Aristotle's Nature, does nothing in vain. This assumption, however, attributes purposes and goals to culture that, as Bacon, Spinoza, and others point out, belong to individual humans.

Anthropomorphism is even more common in popular science and in writing by scientists outside their disciplines. A recent news article on protein structure, for example, begins, "An animal cell is a tiny, tumultuous factory, where tens of thousands of proteins . . . labor to keep their shop alive."[151] And the geologist John Wesley Powell writes in his diary of the first trip down the Grand Canyon, "Clouds are playing in the canyon today . . . baby clouds creep out of side canyons, glide around points, and creep back again. . . . The clouds are children of the heavens, and when they play among the rocks, they lift them to the region above."[152]

Somewhere between the anthropomorphism of professional scientists and that of popular science writers and off-duty scientists is that of highly trained technicians such as astronauts and cosmonauts. Flights into space evoke humanizing perceptions and representations as diverse as those on earth. The best-known concern the Earth itself. Because some are familiar, such as the Earth as a mother, they may seem unsurprising. A Soviet cosmonaut, Aleksandr Aleksandrov, writes, "And then it struck me that we are all children of our Earth. It does not matter what country you look at. We are all Earth's children and we should treat her as our Mother."[153] Another cosmonaut, Yuri Glazkov, similarly feels both nurtured and indebted: "Nature has been limitlessly kind to us, having helped humankind appear, stand up, and grow stronger. She has generously given us everything she has amassed over the billions of years of inanimate development. We have grown strong and powerful, yet how have we answered this goodness?"[154]

Other perceptions from space find specific anatomical features on the Earth, such as eyes. Oleg Makarov saw "the mirror of the Amazon basin, with its swamps and backwaters, like the bewitching eye of the continent, flashing up a friendly wink: Earth's greeting to space."[155] The entire

Earth may be an eye. The astronaut Alan Bean writes that from his vantage on the moon, "I felt pretty sure that in ancient cultures they would have worshipped the Earth and thought it was an eye, because it would change from blue to white and you would see something moving up there that did look like a colored eye."[156]

Others find evidence of sickness, once more undercutting the comfort theory: Robert Overmyer writes, "Africa looked ill with its sandstorms and the dried-out areas."[157] Other pathology afflicts not the Earth but natural phenomena aboard the spacecraft. Vitali Sevastyanov says, "I once saw ice crystals on the porthole glass. They were alien and asymmetrical, one might say like invalids from the miraculous world of terrestrial crystals."[158]

Like terrestrial perceptions, those from space show spontaneous artificialism, the sense that the world is designed. Igor Volk reports, "Several days after looking at the Earth a childish thought occurred to me—that we the cosmonauts are being deceived. If we are the first ones in space, then who was it who made the globe correctly?" On the other hand, real artifacts such as the spaceship itself may appear as persons. Aleksandr Volkov recalls a polyandrous wedding: "The rocket was breathing, a cloud of white vapor flowing from her slender shape, which was covered in a bridal gown of frosting. She was awaiting us and we walked toward her."[159] These two scenes reflect once more the two major illusory results of our search for human form and action: artificialism, or the sense of design, and immediate anthropomorphism.

This survey of philosophy and science, with a brief excursion into space, shows that anthropomorphism occurs even in the most systematically self-critical domains of thought and in the most technical undertakings. The survey may seem to support Nietzsche's claim that it does so fundamentally, intrinsically, and inevitably. However, most philosophers and scientists, and I, agree instead with Bacon that at least egregious anthropomorphism can in principle largely be eliminated and that doing so improves our understanding of the world. It is in this regard that science and philosophy differ most sharply from religion, which, almost all observers agree, is inseparable from anthropomorphism.

Although philosophers and scientists are the people wariest of anthropomorphism, and although most now regard it as unalloyed error, they are as prone to it as the rest of us. And while modern reflection tends to diminish it, some forms, generally judged inoffensive, survive. Anthropomorphism, then, though fundamental neither to philosophy nor to science, criticized by both and evidently antithetical at least to science, continues to appear in them. If we find it in the margins even of these enterprises, in religion, from which it appears inextricable, we should not be surprised to find it at the center.

7

Religion as Anthropomorphism

And God said, Let us make man in our image, after our likeness ...

Genesis 1:26

Religions are never about a God of cosmic force, but rather about the God of human personality.

Rabindranath Tagore, *The Religion of Man*

Or how do you Mystics, who maintain the absolute incomprehensibility of the Deity, differ from skeptics or atheists who assert that the first cause of All is unknown and unintelligible?

David Hume, *Dialogues Concerning Natural Religion*

People who say religion anthropomorphizes usually mean one of two different things: either that it attributes human characteristics to gods or that, in claiming gods exist, it attributes human characteristics to nature. In the former meaning, religion makes gods humanlike at least in crediting them with the capacity for symbolic action. In the latter, which is what I mean, religion makes nature humanlike by seeing gods there.

Gods may have animal or other nonhuman forms, or no visible form at all, but all interact symbolically with humans: they communicate with humans through language or an allied system of symbols, or both. Some theologians try to understand God nonanthropomorphically, but their God either interacts symbolically with humans or cannot be understood. Some religions have cognate philosophical, psychological, or ethical traditions without gods, but all religions have gods or a god.[1]

Religious thought spans polar positions concerning the likeness of gods and humans. One position, held by most believers, is that gods and humans are much alike, even continuous. The other, held by some theologians, is that they differ radically. But people who find gods radically different from humans tend to find them incomprehensible as well. Hence such people seem closer, as Hume suggests, to atheists and skeptics than to religious adherents.[2] For most people, gods and humans are similar. Sometimes they defy distinction. No single attribute separates them everywhere. In various cultures gods eat, drink, make war and love, have offspring, fall sick, grow old, and die, very much as humans do. They communicate with humans through phenomena such as thunder, rainbows, and traffic accidents, and sometimes directly in speech. Humans respond with, or initiate, messages of their own.

Just as gods resemble and are continuous with people, religion resembles and is continuous with other systems of thought and action, such as science, art, and common sense. Even when set apart, as in the modern West, religion interacts and intermingles with them. Religion, like other systems, is a means of interpreting and influencing the world. In so doing, all religious and much nonreligious thought posits beings that are humanlike but not human. Religion differs from other systems mainly in making humanlike beings central.[3]

For many people, religious anthropomorphism consists of seeing God or gods as humanlike. In contrast, my claim is that God or gods consist in seeing the world as humanlike. Most theologians and philosophers admit they cannot separate religion from anthropomorphism but attribute this principally to human anthropocentrism. That explanation confuses anthropomorphism and anthropocentrism. A simpler explanation is that religion *is* anthropomorphism.

People in many disciplines have said religion anthropomorphizes. Many say it does so characteristically and intrinsically. A classicist, Martin Nilsson, writes that the Homeric gods are "neither more nor less than man-like."[4] Another classicist, Gilbert Murray, says that except for the opinions of "some few philosophers [all gods are] as a matter of course anthropomorphic."[5]

A number of scholars in other fields, some of them mentioned in earlier chapters, agree. Among anthropologists, Tylor, for example, sees gods as humanlike spirit beings. More explicitly, Franz Boas sees most religion as a "dogmatized development" of anthropomorphism,[6] and White's view is similar. Horton also makes anthropomorphism central to religion. Levi-Strauss says "religion consists in a *humanization of natural laws*" and in "anthropomorphization of nature."[7] Several other anthropologists say much the same.[8]

Social philosophers including Fontenelle, Vico, Comte, and Spencer, as noted, also say gods are modeled on humans. Spencer writes, "We cannot take a step towards constructing an idea of God without the ascription of human attributes."[9] Writers in related fields share this view. Freud calls anthropomorphism the first step toward religion, and Feuerbach says if God's "predicates are anthropomorphisms, the subject of them is an anthropomorphism too."[10]

Even more telling than secular writers are theologians and assenting philosophers of religion (especially those of the Abrahamic religions), since these are the people who find anthropomorphism most problematic. These expert witnesses, whose reluctance enhances their credibility, almost all agree that religion inevitably anthropomorphizes. R. J. Z. Werblowsky calls anthropomorphism a "central problem" in theology, history of religions, and religious philosophy.[11] E. Bolaji Idowu says it has "always been a concomitant of religion, all religions, every faith. In the purest religion . . . there can be no way of avoiding anthropomorphism."[12] The admitted inability of religious writers, despite their apparent desire, to extricate religion from anthropomorphism suggests there is nothing much to extricate.

Why theologians find anthropomorphism so problematic is not entirely clear, but two causes probably contribute. One is the historic transcendence and otherness of the Abrahamic God. Supreme and absolute, with neither origin myth nor pedigree,[13] He created the world, not from preexisting stuff as do most creators, but from nothing at all. Hence there is "no natural bond between God and nature, for nature did not share in any of God's substance."[14] A great chasm also separates God from humans, His mere creatures. Such a transcendent God could share no important properties with the created world.[15] Moreover, if theologians did admit any shared property they would not know where to stop.

A second reason theologians dislike anthropomorphism may be that the possibility that God consists *only* in anthropomorphizing occurs to them, too. Despite the chasm between God and humans, the Hebrew and Christian Bibles, the Koran, and other religious texts attribute diverse human behavior and anatomy to Him. It is easy to see these features as reflections of ourselves, and difficult to conceive of nonhuman attributes that are meaningful. The step to thinking anthropomorphic reflections are *all* that is there may be larger, but it is in the same direction.

In any case, there is a broad consensus among theologians in both acknowledging anthropomorphism and in thinking it a difficulty. The earliest-known comment is in Xenophanes's often-quoted, seemingly sardonic fragments: "But if oxen (and horses) and lions . . . could draw with hands and create works of art like those made by men, horses would draw pictures of gods like horses, and oxen of gods like oxen. . . . Aethiopians have gods with snub noses and black hair, Thracians have gods with grey eyes and red hair."[16] Like many later critics of anthropomorphism, Xenophanes evidently did not question the gods themselves but only their human attributes. Later Western writers think the Greek gods especially anthropomorphic, but gods in many other religions are equally so.

Jewish, Christian, and Muslim theologians, among other religious thinkers, wish to eliminate anthropomorphism but admit they cannot. One reason they cannot is that it is so embedded in their scriptures. The Bible shows God as humanlike both mentally and physically, as befits his proposal to make "man in our image." In the second version of the creation, for example, God makes man from earth (Genesis 2:7), as a potter would. Later, Adam and Eve hear his voice as he walks in the garden in the cool of the day. Since they are hidden, he must call out to ask where they are. He is not omnipresent, omnipotent, or omniscient: He is in a particular place, gets about by walking, likes shade, cannot see people hiding in bushes, and speaks with Adam and Eve directly.

He has humanlike emotions as well: jealousy, anger, love, vengefulness. He can also be boastful and capricious, as when, to win a bet, He lets Satan torment Job. He has other human traits thoughout the Bible, and the New Testament gives Him a completely human form, in Jesus. God's biblical physicality and caprice now are problematic for some people, but are actually more typical of gods than the ineffability which mystics and a few theologians assert.

Jewish commentators frequently mention anthropomorphism in the Bible and elsewhere. Arthur Marmorstein finds it fundamental to all religion.[17] Gedaliahu Stroumsa says rabbinic thinkers recognize it widely and that in antiquity, God had not only "human feelings, but also a body of gigantic or cosmic dimensions."[18] Martin Buber calls encounter with God "sublime anthropomorphism" and what is met "compellingly anthropomorphic, something demanding reciprocity, a primary Thou."[19] Ismar Schorsch calls the medieval *Hymn of Glory* a "cascade of concrete, physical descriptions of God," in one of which, for example, God's head has the "curly locks of youth, black as a raven."[20] Jacob Neusner shows that the dual Torah (the written Torah and oral commentary of the first six centuries of the Common Era) gives God diverse images, all "in the model of human beings."[21]

These images continue a long Jewish tradition in which God "wants, cares, demands, regrets, says, and does—just like human beings. God is not merely a collection of abstract theological attributes [but a] specific, highly particular personality, whom people can know, envision, engage, persuade, impress."[22] Indeed the dual Torah, especially in a series of biographical stories, makes God incarnate.[23] He sits, banters with humans, loses debates, is discovered by Moses tying crowns onto the letters of the Torah, and sometimes is hardly more than a sage. Some commentators find such depictions of God demeaning and incompatible with the mystery and grandeur of creation. The twelfth-century philosopher Rabbi Moses ben Maimonides, among others, tries to mitigate them by the negative path, the *via negativa,* of giving God no positive attributes at all. But this path ends in obscurity and never has been the mainstream of Jewish belief.[24]

Christian writers, beginning at least in the second century with Clement of Alexandria, also worry about anthropomorphism. Most find it inevitable. Thomas Aquinas says that if we take the *via negativa,* there is no reason "why some names more than others should be applied to God."[25] Among modern writers, W. J. Duggan calls anthropomorphism "indispensable,"[26] Frederick Ferré calls it "essential,"[27] and F. B. Jevons says it "has characterized religion from the beginning [and] characterizes it to the end."[28] Yet most Christian writers, like most Jewish ones, think human qualities contradict God's infinite majesty and power.

The problem has always existed. The early church fathers struggled to reconcile biblical anthropomorphism with a Platonic conception of spirit as immaterial, ideal, and absolute.[29] Like Maimonides, they found human attributes incompatible with mystery and majesty, and saw no place to stop once they admitted any such attributes. Hence many wished to admit none. Clement, for example, allows neither human form nor human passions in God. He says biblical ascriptions are metaphors adapted to the limitations of human understanding. "Therefore when the Hebrews mention hands and feet and mouth and eyes and entrances and exits and exhibitions of wrath and threatening, let no one suppose . . . that these terms express passions of God." He continues, "Reverence rather requires . . . an allegorical meaning . . . you must not entertain the notion at all of figure and motion, or standing or seating, or place, or right or left, as appertaining to the Father of the universe, although these terms are in Scripture."[30]

Other church fathers agree, claiming, for example, that biblical references to God's face are metaphorical. Basil says turning His face away means God is leaving us alone amongst difficulties. Gregory of Nazianzus says God's face means His oversight, Theodoret says it means His benevolence and restoration of freedom, and John of Damascus says it means His display and self-revelation through works.[31]

Nonetheless, even physical anthropomorphism in the church proved tenacious. Two centuries after Clement, Augustine still wrestled with it. He suggests physical anthropomorphism was widespread: lay Christians "think of God in a human form and suppose that he is such."[32] Many, as noted, saw Him as a "very large man." Augustine himself resisted this, but long saw God as a material object.[33]

Despite official disfavor, a physically humanlike God has persisted. In the late nineteenth century, for example, F. W. Newman, a classicist, religious rationalist, and brother of Cardinal Newman, reprinted a poem sent him. The poet writes of death, the solitary voyage of the soul, and evidence in nature of God's dominion. He finds evidence in nature unconsoling, however. He wants to see a face:

> No! let me gaze, not on some sea far reaching
>   nor star-sprent sky,
> But on a *Face* in which mine own, beseeching,
>   May read reply.[34]

Newman approvingly notes that the poet calls God "Father" and attributes to him "*a mind that understands us,* and *a soul that loves us.* To believe this firmly . . . is the core of religion." However, Newman continues, the poet also wants to see a face. Here "he drops out of rational and spiritual religion into a credulity which has everywhere induced baneful idolatry, assimilating God to man. A face? and why not a hand? why not a foot? Does God need eyes and nose? To suppose it, is to abandon the first principles of manly religion, and go back into ancient puerilities."[35] Newman further suggests that the poet is not alone: many people's notion, he says, still is that God can be seen in Heaven and looks like us.[36] Mormons, as noted, continue to think so today.

Most Muslims, like most Jews and Christians, try to avoid anthropomorphism but the struggle is chronic in Islam as elsewhere. H.A.R. Gibb and J. H. Kramers summarize it:

> TASHBIH, assimilating, comparing (God to man), and TA'TIL, emptying, divesting (God of all attributes), are the names of two opposite views within the Islamic doctrine of the nature of God; both are regarded as heresies and grave sins in dogma. The fierce dispute over these conceptions, by which even the dogma of the Kur'an is influenced, is explained by the central position of the doctrine of the nature of God in Islam. The formal cause is to be found in the Kur'an, which strongly emphasizes the absolute uniqueness of God and yet at the same time plainly describes him in the language of anthropomorphism, giving him a face, eyes and hands and talking of his speaking and sitting.[37]

Muslim theologians respond to this contradiction with much the same range of positions as do Jewish and Christian ones: from a nearly literal anthropomorphism, to a claim that qualities attributed to God have a special, metaphorical meaning, to the *via negativa.*

Recent theologians and philosophers of religion continue to struggle with anthropomorphism. Humphrey Palmer says it is "anathema" yet ubiquitous in theology, causing the "difficulty theologians have in meaning what they say."[38] S.G.F. Brandon says it "inevitably follows from the fact that man can conceive of deity only in terms of his own mental categories . . . but theologians have been aware of this fact and guarded against its grosser forms."[39] Virtually all writers, however, agree theologians can guard *only* against its grosser forms, because eliminating all forms eliminates religion. Kai Nielsen writes, "we seem at least to be at a loss to understand what it is we are asserting or denying when we use . . . nonanthropomorphic god-talk."[40] Hugo Meynell admits he sees God anthropomorphically but says the "intelligence and will of the human subject provide the best model for . . . God," and asks, "if we can find no such analogy had we not better abandon all talk about God?"[41] Alexander Gallus agrees with Karl Jaspers that "if religion is demythologized, it is no longer religion."[42]

Other writers say much the same.[43] Feuerbach puts it most sharply:

"To the truly religious man, God is not being without qualities. . . . The denial of determinate, positive predicates . . . is nothing else than a denial of religion, with, however, an appearance of religion in its favour, so that it is not recognized as a denial; it is simply a subtle, disguised atheism."[44] It seems, then, we can say neither that God is like us nor that He is unlike us. If we say He is like us, His stature as absolute and as the ground of being is diminished and there is no clear point at which we can draw *any* distinction between Him and us. If we say He is totally unlike us, He becomes incomprehensible and hence meaningless.

Meynell and others hope to resolve this paradox and save religion through analogy, faith, or other means. Most recently Ferré wishes, in "In Praise of Anthropomorphism," to reconsider this "deep seated antagonism to anthropomorphism in discourse about God, and to offer reasons to praise rather than bury such speech."[45] Ferré's praise, however, amounts to admitting once more that if we cannot say anything anthropomorphic about God, we cannot say anything at all. The reason people do not want to say anything anthropomorphic, he writes, is that it might demean the sacred. But their response has "self-destructive consequences. It is only by affirming anthropomorphic discourse" that we can affirm God. Ferré concludes that anthropomorphism not only is "*not necessarily demeaning* religiously to the Most High [that is, we need not think Him mean or petty, for example] but also is *necessarily not avoidable* logically if the language of either the believer or the philosopher is not to be emptied of all content."[46] This, however, merely makes a virtue of necessity.

Ferré is one of the few philosophers of religion to acknowledge that anthropomorphism is not restricted to religion but is more general. "Helpful suggestions," he says, "sometimes come from unexpected directions, and in this case we might profit from contemplating the issue of anthropomorphic language as it relates not to . . . God, but rather to . . . animals." He says anthropomorphism in both cases may be justified because, just as supposing animals are like us may turn out to be right, supposing God is like us also may be right. I agree that either or both may prove to be like us. However, to the extent that either does turn out to be like us, the term anthropomorphism does not apply. Anthropomorphism (toward animals or anything else) by definition is an overestimate of likeness. It is not simply an assumption of likeness since, in fact, many things *are* like us in various ways. It is a mistake about likeness. We can label it anthropomorphism only after seeing it as an error. Anthropomorphizing animals, then, only shows once more that we tend to see human features where they do not exist.

The most determined modern attempt to rid religion of anthropomorphism belongs to Paul Tillich. Trying to eliminate the disease, however, he kills the patient. He says the word "religion" is derogatory[47] and the traditional names of the Christian deity must be abandoned. The name God, he says, makes the deity an object among other objects. The terms Lord and Father are anthropomorphic. Ordinary religion, using these names, makes divinity a heavenly, perfect person residing above the world.[48]

Tillich therefore creates new names for God: "being-itself," "Ground of Being," "the Unconditional," and others. Religion is "directedness of the spirit toward the unconditioned meaning."[49] But these terms and phrases elude most believers and even other theologians. Trying to explain them, Tillich remains vague: "The name of this infinite and inexhaustible depth and ground of all being is God. That depth is what the word God means. And if that word has not much meaning for you, translate it, and speak of the depths of your life, of the source of your being, of your ultimate concern, of what you take seriously without any reservation."[50] This is equally obscure. Like birdshot fired at a flock in general, it hits nothing at all. The less anthropomorphic Tillich makes God, the more God becomes incomprehensible.

Accordingly, relatively few theologians and philosophers, and fewer lay believers, adopt Tillich's God. Most want something more substantial. René Williamson, for example, says the "Christian God is a person, a living person," whereas Tillich's is "devoid of color and power . . . abstruse and spectral . . . bloodless" and fails to reach ordinary people.[51] Donald Crosby says Tillich's phrase, "ultimate concern," has an "unsettling ambiguity,"[52] and David Pailin finds him "tortuous."[53] Gaskin thinks theologians like Tillich suffer a "modern loss of nerve."[54] While avoiding concrete anthropomorphism, most theologians and philosophers try to avoid the "radical 'purging' that leads either to mystical silence or to atheism."[55] Richard Swinburne, for instance, begins an influential book, "By a theist I understand a man who believes that there is a God. By a 'God' he understands something like a person."[56] Not only most theologians but also most children see gods as humanlike, usually quite concretely. Robert Coles writes, "the phrase 'I pictured His face' is one I have heard in schools and in homes all over the world."[57]

Some modern philosophers such as R. B. Braithwaite and D. Z. Phillips[58] try to avoid the problem of anthropomorphism by subtracting from religion any claim about what really exists, including gods, and reducing religion to advice about how to live. In their view, religion consists not of picturing gods and asserting some relationship with them but only of recommending behaviors, attitudes, or values. The advantage of this suggestion is that if religion is merely a recommendation of values, it is no longer subject to tests of truth. However, this view is less than what most people mean by religion. Most believers, in particular, mean more by God or gods, and by praying to them, than making or getting recommendations.[59]

Philosophers who turn religion into advice, then, underrepresent the religions they try to justify. Gaskin refers dryly to their "radical inventiveness."[60] Freud is more astringent yet. He accuses religious philosophers of dishonesty and "intellectual misdemeanour," and continues,

"Philosophers stretch the meaning of words until they retain scarcely anything of their original sense. They give the name of 'God' to some vague abstraction which they have created themselves [and] boast that they have recognized a higher, purer concept of God, notwithstanding that their God is now nothing more than an insubstantial shadow."[61]

The search for a solution to the problem of anthropomorphism is ongoing. However, it appears self-contradictory. As Moshe Greenberg puts it, "contemplative thinkers among Jews, Christians, and Moslems have always recognized the predominance of anthropomorphism as the mode of religious perception and discourse and have declared it an obstacle to true knowledge of God."[62] Most theologians admit that to eliminate anthropomorphism is to eliminate religion. That religion cannot be extricated from anthropomorphism suggests that anthropomorphism is more even than its matrix. Rather, religion looks like anthropomorphism, part and parcel.

Among people who say religion *is* anthropomorphism, two philosophers and an anthropologist—Hume, Feuerbach, and Horton—carry the point farthest. Although discussed earlier, these three bear revisiting since in some ways, I take up where they leave off.

Hume, called both "terminally destructive" of religion and "pivotal" in its study,[63] says the only agreement among religions is that there is invisible, intelligent power in the world. Hume thinks even this rather abstract notion is anthropomorphism, caused by our being familiar with ourselves but not with the world in general.

I differ with Hume in two ways. The first, and minor, difference is that Hume's apparent suggestion that gods necessarily and peculiarly are invisible seems mistaken. On the one hand, the gods of many religions, including Christianity and Judaism, are invisible only contingently. They may be seen if they wish. Others, such as Homer's, frequently or normally are visible. When they are invisible, it is by such concrete means as cloud, mist, haze, or darkness, which are not distinctively divine. On the other hand, humans and many other animals also may be invisible by virtue of camouflage. Hence invisibility is neither universal in gods nor unique to them.

The second difference is that whereas Hume thinks we anthropomorphize because we are more familiar with ourselves than with anything else, I think we are as mysterious to ourselves as is the world in general. We have only limited access to the workings of our own minds and bodies, but these are vastly more complex than are most natural systems. The familiarity account would require that we know correspondingly much more about ourselves than about the nonhuman world; but we do not. Moreover, what we do know, we misuse when we anthropomorphize. Hence familiarity cannot provide the primary account. Instead, I believe we anthropomorphize because we perceive the world in terms of our interests, which usually involve humans.

My explanation of anthropomorphism as the result of a process that is mostly unconscious appears to resolve a problem for Hume: people seem to have an innate sense that nature shows design. If design exists, a designer must as well. Accordingly, apparent design in nature has long been an argument for the existence of a god. The seeming innateness of our feeling that such design exists strengthens the argument, backing logic with intuition.

Xenophon first records the argument from design around 390 B.C.E.[64] He finds the organs of animals strikingly well suited to sustain them, and quotes Socrates: "With such signs of forethought in these arrangements, can you doubt whether they are the work of chance or design?" Xenophon also remarks of reproductive organs, "Undoubtedly these, too, look like the contrivances of one who deliberately willed the existence of living creatures."[65] Aquinas, much later, makes the argument formal: "We see that things which lack knowledge, such as natural bodies, act for an end. . . . Now whatever lacks knowledge cannot move towards an end, unless it be directed by some being endowed with knowledge and intelligence. . . . Therefore some intelligent being exists by whom all natural things are directed to their end; and this being we call God."[66] Newton, William Paley, Einstein, and many others also see the workings of a superior intelligence in the order of the universe.[67] Recently Swinburne urged, "The universe might so naturally have been chaotic, but it is not—it is very orderly."[68]

However, Hume undermines the argument from order to a god. If we use only the evidence of order and do not multiply hypotheses, all the argument supports is some remote likelihood that something in the universe bears remote analogy to our own intelligence.[69] This something need have neither agency, purpose, morality, nor any other intelligible likeness to, or concern for, humans. It might simply be a set of general natural laws (and in fact, with regard to organic order, Hume anticipates Darwin on natural selection[70]). The notion of "god" here is so attenuated that both theists and atheists could agree on it. It does not amount to a god anyone would worship.

Nonetheless, Hume admits that the rational argument from design is not the only apparent reason to believe in a god. The argument is accompanied, as Gaskin writes, by an evidently universal "propensity of the mind to 'see' design in natural order" and an "insistent *feeling* in most of us that natural order springs from a designer."[71] Hume acknowledges this feeling in a dialogue between Philo and Cleanthes, who argues that God exists. Cleanthes says, "tell me, from your own feeling, if the idea of a contriver does not immediately flow in upon you with a force like that of sensation."[72] Philo cannot reply.

Hume concedes this feeling is a problem. He says it stems partly from similarities between the workings of nature and of our minds. There are also differences, however. The question is, why do the differences "not weaken [our seeing design in nature] so much as we might naturally expect. A Theory to solve this would be very acceptable."[73]

My account may be the theory Hume desires. It holds that all anthropomorphism stems from a practice that is largely unconscious. We search everywhere, involuntarily and unknowingly, for human form and results of human action, and often seem to find them where they do not exist. What we find is highly diverse, including a wide range both of human anatomy and of human artifacts. Some of these perceptions prove well founded, while many others do not. Finding mistakes does not discourage the search, however, nor prevent the systematic illusions occasionally encountered in the pursuit of any systematic interest. The feeling of design in nature is one of these illusions.

The same account applies to certain cosmic questions and answers about the origin and destiny of the universe: where does the stuff of the universe come from, why does the universe exist, and what is the human place in it?[74] Against the background of our pervasive anthropomorphism, such queries resemble the anthropomorphizing questions of Piaget's children. The very asking implies human experience and purpose. The anthropocentrism of these cosmic questions is apparent, for example, even in our reluctance to accept infinite regress as an answer. We usually posit instead some beginning cause, often a quite human one such as Plato's Craftsman, or the God of the Abrahamic religions, or the gods of many tribal origin myths. Even where the cosmos does continue without beginning or end, as in Hinduism and Buddhism, actions of humanlike beings usually punctuate its cycles.

Feuerbach also sees religion as anthropomorphism, but his account differs from Hume's. Whereas for Hume religious thought concerns the external world, for Feuerbach it concerns the human self. Ordinary perception contrasts with religious perception: "In the perception of the senses consciousness of the object is distinguishable from consciousness of self; but in religion, consciousness of the object and self-consciousness coincide."[75]

My own account has elements of both Hume and Feuerbach, plus a bit of Nietzsche. With Hume, I think religious thought concerns the world in general. Like Feuerbach, I think the strong privilege of humanlike models is given not so much by familiarity as by preoccupation. Like Nietzsche, I think that preoccupations and hence perception are controlled by interests. Recent psychologists and anthropologists show our interest in humans is broadly based, on needs not only for food and shelter but also for social interaction itself. We thus are interested in humans for a wide range of reasons beyond wanting to improve, explore, or perfect ourselves, which for Feuerbach is the root of religion.

Contrasting sense perception with religious perception, Feuerbach thinks sense perception is objective and direct while religious perception is subjective and, as a reflection of the self, indirect: "The object of the senses is in itself indifferent—independent of the disposition or of the judgment; but the object of religion is [not]."[76] Here, too, Feuerbach errs. All perception is interpretation and depends on our choice of schemata, or models, which in turn is ordered by our concerns.

Once we acknowledge that interests shape perception, we can see anthropomorphism not as a peculiar projection of self, as Feuerbach does, but as the necessary occasional failure of a particular perceptual strategy. Hence anthropomorphism is not unique but is simply one interpretation among others, though by definition mistaken. Such a view lets us see all anthropomorphism, religious or not, as fitting nonhuman things or events to a humanlike template and as doing so for the same reasons.

Thus, unlike Feuerbach's approach, mine makes no claim that we see what we wish to see, or that the religious schema is especially lofty, refined, or moral. Rather, our motivation simply is to see what is important to see. Feuerbach, in contrast, thinks (perhaps because he emphasizes Christianity) that the object of religious anthropomorphism is to discover our best selves and to represent our highest aspirations: "the object of religion is . . . the most excellent, the first, the supreme being."[77] Accordingly, Feuerbach sees no connection between anthropomorphism in religion and that elsewhere.[78] For him, religion is unique as a mode of thought.

Moreover, it is unique to humans. His first major work on religion, *The Essence of Christianity,* begins, "Religion has its basis in the essential difference between man and the brute—the brutes have no religion." Although this claim is common and seems true in a narrow sense, it is undercut by animism in animals, most dramatically by the threats that chimpanzees direct against thunderstorms. Feuerbach, then, needlessly isolates religion from other human—and from other animal—perception and cognition.

Horton's view, that religious anthropomorphism constitutes a reasonable interpretation of the world, is closest to mine. However, Horton resembles Feuerbach and Hume in remaining silent on anthropomorphism outside religion. Even in religion, personalism, as he usually calls it, is only an opportune idiom and derives its power mainly from an absence of competing models. Personalism withers away in industrial societies, overshadowed by the idiom of machinery. In contrast, my account incorporates religion in a larger—and still quite lively—anthropomorphism. Doing so, it may partly answer a friendly critic of Horton, the scholar of religion Hans Penner.[79]

Penner likes Horton's linking of religious and scientific thought as explanatory and rational. However, he says Horton does not prove his claim that gods "serve to introduce unity into diversity, simplicity into complexity and order into disorder, regularity into anomaly."[80] Such proof, Penner says, would require showing that gods are significant and intelligible theoretical terms. Penner's request recalls Hume's question, "If an intelligent being is required to explain the order in nature then the intelligent agent will in turn need to be explained. . . . But if we stop at the agent explanation, and go no farther; why go so far?"[81]

We go so far because gods *are* significant and intelligible as theoretical terms. They are significant because they are modeled on highly organized, versatile, and hence powerful originals, and generate correspondingly diverse phenomena. Because real humans vary their behavior infinitely, humanlike beings, such as gods, similarly vary infinitely. Gods are uniquely intelligible if we define intelligibility as the ratio of information yielded to assumptions required. They give much explanatory return for little investment. Hypothesizing a humanlike being at work behind appearances accounts for effects of unparalleled diversity. This principle, that efficiency in explanations is the ratio of effects predicted to hypotheses made, underlies Occam's razor: do not multiply hypotheses unnecessarily.

The same principle applies to all models, whether based on humans, animals, plants, machines, or something else. Swinburne explains the power of molecules as theoretical entities similarly: the "postulation of molecules gave a neat and simple explanation of a whole host of chemical and physical phenomena and that was the justification for postulating their existence."[82] In general, the more highly organized the model, the greater the range of effects it can unify. Animism is widespread in part because an organismic model accounts for diverse phenomena, and anthropomorphism is even more widespread in part because a humanlike model accounts for still more.

As theories, then, humanlike models are parsimonious by virtue of the organization, diversity, and power of their originals. Diverse phenomena—a door slamming, a tapping at the window, a missing object, a light in the forest, and much more—can be explained by postulating a human behind them. Humanlike models thus account for a vast array of things and events. They explain much with little.[83]

Human beings offer great diversity, as do gods, and the characteristics attributed to these two classes greatly overlap. No attribute—neither mortality, power, knowledge, visibility, nor any other—separates gods and humans everywhere. The Western chasm between humans and gods is atypical.[84] Gods may be conceived as mortal, local, unethical, visible, plausible, ignorant, foolish, and weak, and humans may be conceived as immortal, omnipresent, ethical, invisible, implausible, knowledgable, wise, and powerful. The Homeric gods, for example, far from being perfectly good, or all-powerful or all-knowing, are, Nilsson says, "equipped with every human frailty . . . every human need and weakness." They are "fickle, even treacherous." They live as if in "some royal house in which there is constant entertaining," where Zeus rules "like Agamemnon over a troop of wilful and refractory vassals, each of whom is pursuing his own designs."[85] Another classicist, W.K.C. Guthrie, specifically says the Greeks saw gods and humans as continuous: "In the eyes of the warlike aristocracy gods and men together formed one society, organized on a basis of strongly marked class-distinctions as was the human society itself. The highest class of aristocrats were the gods."[86]

This likeness of gods and humans is reflected in euhemerism, an early and recurrent theory of religion as anthropomorphism. Euhemeros, in the late fourth century B.C.E, claimed gods originated as famous persons whose deeds and personalities had survived their historic identities. Euhemerus is not alone in the claim. Two near-contemporaries, Prodicus of Ceos and Persaeus, suggest that some gods began as humans who had discovered new crops.[87] The nub of euhemerism, then, is that gods are memories of specific real persons. Spencer, Tylor, and Freud offer modern versions, namely, gods as memories of deceased kin. These gods arise anew in every generation, for every person. Spencer and Tylor say they originate as various ancestors, especially parents, and originally are worshipped as such. Freud says they arise as one kind of ancestor, the father, worshiped unconsciously.

Ancestors certainly are one kind of god, and are continuous with living people, in a number of cultures. Wherever social groups based on descent, such as lineages and clans, are prominent, ancestors are central in religion.[88] Often they are its major figures. At the same time they often are much the same persons they were in life, though now disembodied. In Japan, for example, ancestors remain members of the household, which consists of all residents, living and dead. They are primary recipients of prayer. As seniors, they also receive the first food in the morning as well as greetings, gifts, news, and requests for help.[89] Similarly in Africa and elsewhere, the dead remain in a single community with the living and may be fed, talked to, and asked for help.[90] The very terms ancestor and worship here mislead by suggesting a greater break between living and dead than such cultures acknowledge.

Not only kin become gods. In Japan all prominent phenomena may be gods (*kami*), and national heroes and other prominent people (the emperor is only the most salient) may be enshrined. Similarly in China, Confucius and other historic figures have been deities and the popular pantheon mirrors the governmental hierarchy, with policemen, jailors, magistrates, governors, and an emperor.

Gods and humans again are both similar and continuous in India, where the "man-god continuum [is] central and crucial."[91] According to Vedic ritual texts, for example, the gods have their own priests, whom they ask what sacrifice might bring victory over the demons.[92] Relations of gods and humans vary; they may, for example, swap places. Hindu myths include a time when gods and humans lived together[93] and humans who aspire through austerities to the position of Indra, chief of gods.[94] Indra, on the other hand, is neither austere nor far removed from people.

He is a drinking champion and, in the *Ramayana*, takes the shape of Ahalya's husband in order to seduce her.[95]

Reflecting such shifting forms and relationships, some Hindus emphasize distinctions and others emphasize continuity. In Kerala State, "whether the gods and human spirits are a continuum or two distinct though interacting categories [is] discussed by rural philosophers. . . . Is the god X a man who became a god or was he a real god? Was Rama a good king elevated to the rank of a god or was he an incarnation of Vishnu?"[96] The Nayars, Izhavas, and Kurichiyas, honoring the dead, find "little difference between the gods and shades,"[97] and expert Kurichiyas agree that seven gods are deified humans.

Indeed, gods and humans are both similar and continuous in most parts of the world. Gods may be jealous of humans or infatuated with them, may make love or war with them, or may be forced by them to take refuge underground.[98] In many cultures gods are not eternal but are born, often of nonhuman parents such as trees, animals, or sea-foam, but sometimes of humans.[99] They may die of old age or be killed. (Even in the West, where gods generally are immortal, Hume suggests the Creator may perhaps age and die.) They may be the ancestors of humans. They may be physically imperfect: one-legged, or with a hand bitten or cut off, or otherwise mutilated. They eat and drink, sometimes ambrosia or other unearthly delicacies, but also milk (from their dairy herds) and other human foods.[100]

Many human traits may be present at once. A.F.C. Wallace notes that the Great Gods of Dahomey are "humanlike beings" with an "active social life" including sex, war, and economic enterprises.[101] Erland Ehnmark says a "richly developed anthropomorphism is by no means peculiar to Homer." Hittite gods, for instance, "eat and drink [and] feel hunger. They work as craftsmen. They are liable to afflictions and employ magic to ward off sickness. They have horses and chariots. They keep harems. They assemble in a council to deliberate. They have human passions. They wage war against the gods of other peoples."[102] In Siberia, "countless tales relate how God has a magnificent home in the sky . . . a wife and children, servants, cattle, and other property."[103] The Koryak Supreme Being is an "old man living in a settlement in heaven and having a wife and children."[104] The Copper Eskimo great spirit, Kannakapfaluk, "lives in a snow hut just like the Eskimos, with a lamp and sleeping-platform and all the usual household paraphernalia."[105] In Polynesia, Ehnmark finds little difference between gods and powerful chiefs.[106] Similar examples of humanlike gods are legion. Although we know the Greek gods for their anthropomorphism, they are by no means exceptional.

Durkheim and many others hold that although some religions anthropomorphize, others do not. Buddhism in particular, they say, has no gods. But, as we saw, that is not true. Buddhism in fact has many gods, from local bodhisattvas to the Buddha himself. While some religions, such as Christianity, Judaism, and Buddhism, have cognate systems without deities, these are philosophical, psychological, or ethical, not religious. As religions, all these traditions have one or more gods.

Hindu and other mythologies contain countless visitations of gods in human form, blurring the line between gods and humans in yet another way. One result is that apparent humans may turn out to be gods and vice versa. The Hawaiians evidently saw Captain Cook as a god, possibly as a departed god who had predicted his return in a winged vessel.[107] The Aztecs seem to have thought Cortez a god. The dual Torah and New Testament, as noted, similarly portray God as incarnate. In Shinto all people, indeed all notable phenomena, are gods (*kami*), although relatively few merit worship.

Gods that are too insignificant to merit worship, like many *kami*, also are continuous with other human and humanlike figures. Varied writers, especially psychoanalysts, have noted this continuity in children's thought. Pierre Bovet, drawing on Piaget, shows that children's notions of God closely resemble their notions of their parents.[108] More recently Ana-Maria Rizzuto, rejecting Freud's focus on fathers alone, finds models of deity in many members of the family.[109] More generally, Coles remarks, "In the lives of children God joins company with kings, superheroes, witches, monsters, friends, brothers and sisters, parents, teachers, police, firefighters, and on and on."[110] Evidently God's otherness is not a spontaneous, primitive, or universal idea, even in the West.

Similar continuities of deities and secular figures occur throughout adult thought, both traditional and modern. Ehnmark notes that gods cannot be clearly separated from "household spirits and trolls, hobgoblins, fairies, and the like in traditional beliefs. [These] are almost wholly human; yet they are supernatural, and it is difficult to find any essential feature which distinguishes them from the proper gods."[111] Presently anthropomorphized computers and similar complex machinery may constitute, or house, such minor gods. American airmen of the Second World War sometimes attributed mysterious difficulties with their aircraft to gremlins, small gnomes that recently have returned, half-human, half-reptile, to star in several movies. They join a throng of humanlike creatures (the modern versions of trolls, hobgoblins, and fairies) especially in science-fiction and horror genres.

Occasionally gods in human form may be glimpsed coming into being. M. Singleton describes the first visit of smallpox to a WaBungu village in Southwest Tanzania in the late nineteenth century.[112] According to documents and a now-elderly witness, a dirty old man asked a group of small boys the direction to their village. After being directed, he suddenly disappeared. Within days smallpox made its first appearance among the villagers, who then saw the old man as having been Smallpox himself. A person everyone had taken for an ordinary and quite unimposing old man proved a deity, and henceforth was worshipped as such.

We can see the continuity of gods and humans from the other side as well: from ways in which our notions of humans may resemble our notions of gods. Benson Saler[113] notes, for example, that people attribute to some humans certain traits conventionally given to gods, such as superhuman strength, speed, beauty, appetite, altruism, and others.

Similarly, our relations with humans may be like those with gods. For example, relationships with both may be imaginary. Many observers such as Freud and Malinowski suppose relationships with gods are peculiar in that they are products of fantasy. However, an anthropologist, John Caughey, shows that if they are fantasy, they are by no means unique.[114] Rather, people commonly also imagine extensive relationships with other people. Fantasy relationships, especially those with famous persons, are an "important, powerful, and pervasive aspect of contemporary . . . life."[115]

Caughey emphasizes, as I do, the similarity of religious and secular thought regarding persons and relationships with them. He notes that non-Western societies generally include ostensible persons, such as ancestors, not recognized by secular Westerners and that any account of those societies omitting these persons is incomplete and ethnocentric. The most important of these persons usually are termed, in Western translation, gods. Similarly in secular society, imaginary relationships with famous persons may apotheosize them. Media figures, Caughey observes, are "better than ordinary people"; they are "godlike."[116] For the Greeks, immortality was the chief manner in which gods differed from humans; but heroes such as Hercules and Achilles, enjoying either a heroic death or the special favor of gods, also were called immortal.[117] Recently a South African said on hearing of Nelson Mandela's release from prison, "He is our god."[118] Other persons sometimes seen as godlike include Confucius and Shakespeare, Mao Tse-Tung and Joseph Stalin.

Some people think deities with animal forms (usually called theriomorphic or zoomorphic) prove anthropomorphism is not universal in religion. Durkheim writes, "anthropomorphism, far from being primitive, is rather the mark of a relatively advanced civilization."[119] He cites gods with plant and animal forms in several tribal cultures and concludes, "It is not at all true that man has had . . . an inclination to impose his own form upon things." But Durkheim is mistaken. The evidence is massive that we have just this inclination. More important, physical form is not the unifying element of humans, or of gods. Symbolic action—communication through conventional systems of signifiers and conceptions—is, a point to which we shall return. What matters is not so much the physical appearance of gods as their behavior.[120]

Humans resemble, and are continuous with, not only gods but also other things and events, animate and inanimate. Descent relates us anatomically and behaviorally to primates and other animals. Various analogies and other relationships link us to the inorganic world. Although modern Western culture, shaped by Judeo-Christian tradition, draws a sharp line between the human and nonhuman worlds, neither evolutionary biology nor many other cultures do so. At the same time, people in some cultures see other peoples as very different, often so much so that only their own tribe or family is truly human.

Given our perceived continuities with the nonhuman world and differences from other humans and our interest in discovering any humans where they exist, it is no wonder we often see nonhuman phenomena as humanlike. Because no clear line separates models of humans and models of other things and events, we are able to find, with no sense of incongruity, all manner of humanity in the nonhuman world.

Just as gods resemble and are continuous with humans, so religion resembles and is continuous with other systems of thought and action such as science, art, and common sense. Religion can be set apart only with difficulty, and continues to intermingle and interact with other systems. If it did not, and were in fact a separate domain, it would not have had its historic conflicts with science, such as those with Galileo and Darwin. It has such conflicts because religious accounts of the world, and religious activities, constantly overlap, resemble, and compete with those of secular life.[121]

This is not now the standard view, however. Since Schleiermacher, most Westerners have come to believe that religious thought is different from other thought. They think it irrational, nonrational, expressive, emotive, valuative, metaphoric, nonempirical, or all of these.[122] They may even think its claims meaningless because they are neither verifiable nor falsifiable.

One reason many people think religion is a separate mode of thought may be that they find it contradicted by science and wish to protect it by saying the two are incommensurable.[123] They say the goals and methods of science—to understand and manipulate the observable world by offering and testing hypotheses—are entirely different from those of religion. Two claims are made to support this view: that religious experience is uniquely direct and unmediated and that the major religious premise is the existence of spirit or superhuman beings, in a supernatural or nonempirical realm.[124] In both cases, religion seems nonempirical and thus different from other thought and action.

The notion that religion is direct and unmediated experience is, as we saw, unconvincing. Those who make this claim say such experience consists of having certain feelings, such as dependency, awe, or love. But dependency is on, and awe and love are toward, something. Hence this something also is implicit in the experience; it already is assumed.

The notion that religion differs from secular thought and action in that it deals with a nonempirical realm is supported by the fact that priests, shamans, and scriptures do tell us that God does this, other gods do that, and the souls of believers do something else. Such claims certainly are hard to prove or disprove.

But secular life is not so different. Newspapers, radio, and television tell us the president does this, Congress does that, and consumer confidence does something else. In both religious and secular cases, we may or may not believe these reports but have no good way to check them. In daily life we see images, or hear, of a figure purported to be the president, striding to a helicopter or answering reporters' questions. But some images turn out to be fictional or misleading, as when the president or a representative proves to have been misinformed or dissembling. Knowing this, we rein in our credulity. Reports of starvation, massacre, or other frightening, shocking, or unfamiliar experiences strike us as true, but somehow we still cannot or will not picture them clearly. We often do not know how to discover the truth about governments, markets, or influential persons and groups. Just as the inner workings of our bodies and minds are important but obscure, so are those of our societies.

Similarly, the figures and events of religion (souls in hell, or God rolling back the sea) are hardly more remarkable than those in the news (cities obliterated by atomic explosions, or men on the moon). As Hume remarks, the figures of classical mythology are not so implausible as to make their existence somewhere in the universe seem unlikely. All these figures and events, religious and secular alike, are subject to change and doubt. We may hear either secular or religious images corrected or abandoned, or find ourselves unable to imagine them, or find we can imagine them but doubt or reject them nonetheless.

Nor are these understandings and corrections in daily life and religion stranger, less certain, or more variable than those of science. In science we learn first that the sun circles the Earth and then the opposite; that the Earth, sun, and stars are alive and then that they are not; that species are immutable and then that they are mutable; or that mass and energy are conserved, then that they are relative and interchangeable. Similarly, we hear first that light is matter moving through a medium, then that it is waves through empty space, and then that it is both wave and particle. The atom is unitary; then it is made of electrons and a unitary nucleus; then the nucleus consists of particles, which in turn grow smaller and more numerous. Most of us have trouble imagining any of these phenomena clearly, just as we do with distant secular or religious events.

Durkheim, Horton, Barbour, and some others also find the topics and principles of religious and other thought, including scientific thought, more alike than different.[125] They say religion, like other systems, is an attempt to interpret and influence the world in general. Like other systems, it draws on a framework—largely shared with the other systems—of observation, logic, analogy, metaphor, and unspoken assumption in an attempt to make the world coherent. There is no unmediated experience. Religious experience "like scientific data, comes not in a raw form, but already interpreted in the light of theoretical or doctrinal concepts."[126]

Again, religion as a whole may be hard to falsify; but so may science. Both rest on assumption and analogy, model and metaphor, whose relationship to "reality" is indeterminate.[127] Scientists see their models neither as literally true nor just as useful fictions. In this regard, scientific models are like, for instance, understandings of God in Christian theology that make fatherhood the model of God's relation to humans.[128] Two recent psychologists of religion, Frazer Watts and Mark Williams, also say religious and secular thought are both similar and continuous. They, too, write that all perception is interpretation, that we entertain only one interpretation at a time, and that, given a context and a hypothesis, we need little confirming evidence. They reject the "common assumption that religious beliefs are arrived at by a process of 'faith' . . . distinct from the cognitive processes by which other human knowledge is acquired."[129] For example, the supposedly mystical sense of "something beyond knowledge" is not unique to religion, but common in our thoughts and feelings about other obscure or inchoate subjects, including ourselves. The mystical sense of unknowability should be understood not as "showing that it is impossible to know God, but as describing a common aspect of . . . subjective experiences."[130]

In a longstanding and still popular view, science, in contrast, is more certain. It is supposed to rest on observable facts and aim at definite laws. More recent accounts, however, make science less definite and more like other knowledge, including religious knowledge. A philosopher of science, Patrick Suppes, for example, denies any "rockbed of perceptual certainty." Instead, "when it comes to matters of knowledge, real houses are always built on sand and never on rock."[131] Other recent philosophers of science also emphasize uncertainty, probabilism, and metaphor in all knowledge.

Thus no clear criteria of evidence, logic, or certainty separate religion even from its supposed antithesis, science. Instead, they are separated most sharply by their attitude toward anthropomorphism: science tries to avoid it, while religion takes it as foundation. As the philosopher of science E. Thomas Lawson and the scholar of religion Robert McCauley write, religion "increases the number and influence of intentional agents while science . . . tries to minimize" them.[132]

Religious knowledge otherwise does not seem very different from secular knowledge.[133] Indeed, most peoples, including those of Europe until the sixteenth century, have not distinguished them.[134] Western Christendom before the Reformation, for example, shared a

> common religion of immanence. Heaven was never too far from earth. The sacred was diffused in the profane, the spiritual in the material. Divine power, embodied in the Church and its sacraments, reached down through innumerable points of contact to make itself felt: to forgive or punish, to protect against the ravages of nature, to heal, to soothe, and to work all sorts of wonders.[135]

Westerners may now find religion distinct but in most societies it simply is part of the fabric of the world.

As do other systems, religion aims to interpret and influence the world. Neither its patterns of thought nor the evidence about the world that it takes into account appear sharply different from those of other spheres. Both religious and nonreligious thought and action anthropomorphize. Religion differs from other systems mainly in making humanlike beings central. It makes them more complex and more humanlike, takes them more seriously, and does all this more systematically. Its power, however, derives from the same search for human form that underlies all anthropomorphism.

This raises the question, If we anthropomorphize comprehensively, what sets religion off from other anthropomorphism? The first answer is, nothing sets it off clearly or distinctly. As do other categories, the term religion somewhat arbitrarily labels one segment of a continuum. At best, the label serves certain purposes and interests. Saler[136] points out that, like other terms, "religion" is the product of a particular culture at a particular time, and any attempt to apply it cross-culturally therefore reifies and universalizes a culturally specific concept. Some scholars even suggest dropping the term. Others think it labels phenomena that have at least family resemblances, but debate what these resemblances are. Preus writes, "finding universal elements remains one of the key problems for defining religion."[137]

The concept of family resemblances, as given currency by Wittgenstein, means a set of features widely enough shared within some group to make the group identifiable, although none of those resemblances are shared by all members of the group. The phrase is animistic except when applied to a biological family, because it attributes relations of descent to phenomena which do not have them. Its basis in biology usually remains unrecognized, however.[138] If resemblances do exist in any domain, the key question is, what engenders them? If they belong to a family, what is their genealogy?

My answer, by now familiar, is that the progenitors of religions are our perceptual uncertainty and our need to see any people who are present. Religions are a family in that all are born from the search for human form and behavior, and all constitute claims to have found such form and behavior in the nonhuman world. However, their ancestry results in a more positive unity than mere family resemblance. All religions do share a feature: ostensible communication with humanlike, yet nonhuman, beings through some form of symbolic action.

Since humans are products of evolution, no absolute line separates them from other animals. Nonetheless, one major attribute distinguishes all present humans from other animals: our capacity for language and related symbolism. This capacity is central to us as organisms. It is no mere opportune use of anatomy and neurology, no fortuitous exploitation of tongue and larynx and brain. Rather, it is biologically broadly based and deeply integrated. It rests on a complex of anatomical, physiological, and neurological features coevolved over millions of years. The most distinctive features include speech centers[139] in the cerebral cortex specialized to produce concepts, associate concepts with words and phrases, and associate words and phrases with motor commands. The neurology of which these centers are part enables all normal infants to learn the speech of their community merely by exposure and informal interaction, without explicit training. No such ability exists among even our nearest relatives, the apes, although they can with effort be taught rudimentary symbolism.

Language is fundamental to our ability to interpret and influence the world and fundamentally shapes our attitudes toward it. It makes possible culture as the basis of human thought and action, and culture makes viable our modern biological form, *Homo sapiens.* Lacking specific thought and action genetically, we are viable because we acquire them semiotically. Oriented by nature and nurture to interpret and influence the world through language, we search for signs, symbols, and meanings everywhere. As is speech perception itself, this search is largely unconscious and involuntary.[140] We seem unable to stop it. Indeed, as Merleau-Ponty emphasizes, we are *"condemned to meaning."*[141]

Our search for signs and symbols is so characteristic, so central to our being, that *Homo sapiens* would be better called *Homo semioticus.*[142] Paul Ricoeur agrees with Wilhelm von Humboldt, "man *is* language."[143] Our capacity for symbolism, in turn, though evolved together with language, is not limited to it. Rather, we engage in symbolism "both consciously and unconsciously, while awake or asleep, neurotically or creatively in speech and writing, in the arts and sciences, with or without insight into its possibilities and implications."[144] We search for such things as the meaning of life, as though the context of life were semiotic. Richard Rorty mentions a "community feeling which unites us with anything humanoid. To be humanoid is to have a human face, and the most important part of that face is a mouth which we can imagine uttering sentences."[145] It is no coincidence that gods also are capable of symbolism. What we look for when we look for humanity is, most importantly, linguistic.

Thus a second answer to how religion differs from other anthropomorphism is that it attributes the most distinctive feature of humans, a capacity for language and related symbolism, to the world. Gods are persons in large part because they have this capacity. Gods may have other important features, such as emotions, forethought, or a moral sense, but these are made possible, and made known to humans, by symbolic action.[146]

Some philosophers and theologians also note a centrality of language to deity. Swinburne, for example, identifies God as a person and language as a key feature of persons. He begins a brief characterization of persons with language: there are "attributes which distinguish persons from animals. Persons use language to communicate and for private thought. They use language to argue."[147] Buber similarly describes God as linguistic, as one who speaks. He is "a God whom men trust because he addresses them by word and calls them."[148] Krasner also emphasizes communication: "ongoing, living communication between Being and being is . . . supported by the testimony of Jews since the beginning."[149] Similar testimony comes from other corners of the world. The shaiva tantras of Kashmir, for example, make the Word the major aspect of divine energy.[150]

Although language among humans typically is spoken, its potential media are unlimited because it depends on a code, not a medium. Hence we can and do look for messages everywhere and anywhere. We do not limit our scrutiny to events plainly stemming from known human beings. Indeed, we look at all things and events, from the flight of birds to the fall of meteors, as possible communications.

The anthropomorphism of assuming language in gods appears ineluctable: there is no religion without relationship, no relationship without significant communication, no significant communication without language, and no language without likeness. For the most rudimentary communication, humans may gesture; but even gesture depends on human likenesses such as smiling, frowning, eating, and breathing. In any case, communication requires some commonality in context, in communicative system, and in content. Fully human relationships require language in some form. Any god worth talking about—that is, any god we can talk with—must be at least so like us as to share our language and its context. A shared language already is more than all humans have in common.

Many writers, secular as well as religious, see language and symbolism as central to religion. Geertz and Bellah, for example, both define religion as systems of symbols and hence chiefly as systems of communication. Their view is widely shared.[151] In fact, religion sometimes is called, following Wittgenstein, a language-game. If it is, so is ordinary language among humans. The question is, between whom is the religious language-game played?

Answers diverge sharply. Humanists think the communication is just between humans. Functionalists and symbolists, for example, think it is a disguised way of saying things difficult to say directly. In contrast, religious believers think they are interacting with someone else. As believers see it, those with whom they communicate are gods: humanlike, yet different from ordinary humans.

According to James, believers are conscious of an "intercourse between themselves and higher powers with which they feel themselves to be related. This intercourse is . . . active and mutual."[152] They think that in prayer, "something is transacting."[153] Believers everywhere seem to suppose they speak or otherwise interact symbolically with gods.[154] Both for nonbelievers and for believers, symbolic communication is central to religion.

Religion thus credits gods with the most fundamental human characteristic. Some theologians, as noted, try to understand God nonanthropomorphically, but their God either interacts symbolically with humans or cannot be understood. To be understood, he must communicate. Werblowsky concludes a careful article on anthropomorphism in religion with the "simple question: can one pray to a nonanthropomorphic deity?"[155]

Another way religion differs from other anthropomorphism is in being more generalized, systematized, and integrated. By comparison, other sorts of anthropomorphism are ad hoc and idiosyncratic. What we recognize as religion already is to some degree institutionalized and rationalized. Religious experience has, for example, a cultural context with which it must be significantly congruent even if there also are incongruities. A "religion" usually has undergone many revisions. It therefore appears relatively coherent and credible to a spectrum of people and may even have an "aura of factuality" or a "uniquely realistic"[156] mood. It usually covers a broad range of experience: not just immediate things and events but also those distant in time and space. A cosmology, for example, usually is at least implicit in what we call religion.

If religion is generalized and systematized anthropomorphism, can it be said simply to be a mistake? If it is only a mistake, why does it persist?[157] These questions may seem presumptuous but they do not seem unanswerable. Nor are they irrelevant to humanistic, or even to social-scientific, concerns. On the contrary, they bear directly on our understanding of human thought and action. My answer is brief. The central religious assertion, that the nonhuman world is, in whole or in part, significantly humanlike, seems mistaken. That much, of course, is implicit when I claim, with Hume, Feuerbach, Horton, and a few others, that religion not only anthropomorphizes (as everyone admits) but *is* anthropomorphism.

As always when we assess the nature of the world, no proof is possible; proof is a matter of logic, not of fact. All one can do is provide evidence to persuade. My evidence has been the breadth and depth of anthropomorphism elsewhere in human thought, together with an explanation of anthropomorphism as the result of an unconscious perceptual strategy. If this evidence and this explanation are sound, we can link ad hoc and spontaneous instances (talking to the cat or seeing a sack of garbage as a mugger) with developed and systematic instances (finding messages in plagues and a designer in natural order) as a single phenomenon.

Other content in religion, such as philosophical, psychological, and ethical teachings, doubtless often is valid. We need not appeal to the truth of these teachings, however, to determine why religion persists. It persists because it is driven by models that are powerful, successful, and indeed vital for dealing with the most important phenomena in our lives: real humans.

Religion, as many theologians say, analogizes, though largely unawares. Even spontaneous, unsystematic analogies—voices in the wind and faces in clouds—are plausible and compelling enough to recur end-lessly. Their religious form, ordered and often abstracted, economizes thought and action by system-building. It exemplifies our "craving for generality," our "regard [of] the more general principle as the more . . . satisfactory," and our "trying to increase the coherence of our total view."[158] In these aims and in the ways it pursues them, religion is con-tinuous with other thought and action. Contrary to Geertz's "frank rec-ognition that religious belief involves not . . . induction from everyday experience—for then we would all be agnostics," religion does draw from everyday experience. For many people it *is* everyday experience. In dis-covering human form and action in and behind appearance, religion is indistinguishable from daily life. In its topics and aims, religious thought also resembles scientific thought, as Durkheim saw; both are concerned with "nature, man, society" and both try to "connect things with each other, to establish internal relations between them, to classify them and to systematize them . . . both pursue the same end; scientific thought is only a more perfect form of religious thought."[159]

Once we see religion as anthropomorphism, the question—Why does religion persist?—changes to, Why do humanlike models persist? This question is easier to answer. Humanlike models persist because they iden-tify and account for the crucial components of our world: humans and their activities and effects. Because such models are vital, employing them is our first, our automatic, and our most powerful approach to the world. In sum, religion arises and persists because the strategy from which it stems often succeeds in identifying phenomena—real humans and their actions—that are uniquely important.

A theory should correspond to observation, should be simple, and should be general. The theory offered meets these criteria. It corresponds to existing—although heretofore seemingly unrelated—observations: per-ception is interpretation, interpretation follows interests, we often anthropomorphize, and religion always anthropomorphizes. The theory lends itself to observation because its principal terms (such as anthropo-morphism, humanlike, model, things and events, and ambiguity) are themselves definable. These terms therefore are easily applied; they are "operational." I avoid the difficulty of defining and observing such elu-sive terms as "the sacred," "ultimate conditions of existence," and "grounds of being."

The theory is simple as well. It depends on a few general cognitive principles. It claims no universal functions for religion other than inter-pretation and influence, shared by all thought and action. Since it does not claim such specific functions as producing certain moods and moti-vations, articulating ultimate values, providing reassurance and emotional expression, or promoting social solidarity (though religion *may* do these things), it is not undermined by contrary instances. Although indicating what is central to religion, it requires no sharp line between religion and other thought and action; indeed it points to continuities. Nor is it subject to the ongoing controversy on the rationality of religion.[160] If religion is an attempt to interpret and influence the world, it may, like other such attempts, sometimes be rational and sometimes not.

The theory is general in several ways. It identifies religion, itself broad and diverse, as part of an even broader, more diverse, and more pervasive phenomenon, anthropomorphism. The approach accounts for anthropomorphism, in turn, as resulting from a universal perceptual process. In so doing, my account again asserts and depends on unity in the principles of religious and secular thought.

This generality has several results. One is an answer to the question of whether nonhuman animals have anything comparable to religion. The usual answer is No. This answer, when given by humanists, usually is based on the observations that religion is largely symbolic and that symbolism is virtually absent among animals. However, Goodall's work suggests that animals may have something comparable to religion. She cautions against "talk about 'religion' in relation to the chimpanzee" but continues that the "awe and wonder, that underlie most religions" may have started in "such primeval, uncomprehending surges of emotion"[161] as chimpanzee threat displays against thunderstorms and waterfalls.

My own suggestion about Goodall's chimps is that the displays are not mere "surges of emotion" but are, as they seem, directed threats. As threats, they stem from a chimpanzee interpretation of storms as living things that, like baboons, leopards, and other chimpanzees, can be frightened away. If religion is an interpretation of the nonhuman world as humanlike, then the animal analogue is an interpretation of the nonanimal world as animallike. That is, if religion is anthropomorphism, then the animal analogue is zoomorphism: the attribution of animal traits to what is not animal. Like Goodall, I hesitate to call chimpanzees religious, but since they seem to attribute to phenomena more organization than these have, their situation resembles that of religious people. Unlike Goodall, I think emotions are secondary in the situation she describes, as in Proudfoot's case of the bear that proves to be a log. Emotions, like behavior, are as much results as they are causes. They are results of understandings of situations as well as causes of action. What is important is the models used and the relation of those models to the world.

Another consequence of my approach is an explanation of several characteristics often attributed to religious thought or action. These features, which include faith, ritual, the supernatural, and the sacred, stem from the centrality of humanlike beings to religion. For example, faith, often thought the opposite of the scientific attitude, is an attitude primarily toward persons, not toward nature or even culture. It is an aspect of a social relation. Because religion is an ostensible social relationship, it tends to be nonempirical, since openly testing a social relationship (unlike a relation to a car or a computer) undermines it. Testing therefore may be explicitly prohibited. Judeo-Christian tradition, for example, forbids experimentation on the relationship between God and humans. However, if gods are tested and do fail, they may, like people, be abandoned. The importance of faith to religion does not mean testing is irrelevant, as often is supposed, but the opposite: it is too relevant to permit.

The same reasoning applies to the notion of the sacred. Though often thought peculiar to religion, the sacred also, as Durkheim suggests, is at base an aspect of human social relations. Social relations submit us to "inconvenience, privation, and sacrifice, without which social life would be impossible."[162] It is these requirements—that we be loyal, share resources, and go off to war—that are sacred, because vital, and hence protected by interdictions. Religion posits the same requirements in relations between humans and gods, and for the same reasons. Sacredness protects these relationships with the same prohibitions against testing as does faith.

Ritual also, which in one standard definition is any "ceremonial act or action [or] any formal and customarily repeated act or series of acts,"[163] is not unique to religion but occurs in other spheres of social life as well. Descriptions of ritual vary widely. Horton[164] thinks ritual characterizes relations among people who are socially distant, especially among those of different status, such as when an enlisted soldier addresses a general officer or a commoner addresses royalty. Correspondingly, it also characterizes relations in public between humans and gods, since gods typically are of higher status. But ritual has a wider role in social relations than this; formal and customarily repeated acts also occur in intimate relations, such as marital ones.[165] Ritual, then, typifies human social life whether religious or secular.

My approach further suggests that the current Western association of religion with the "supernatural" stems ultimately from the Western opposition of humans and nature, starting at least with Genesis. In this opposition (often linked, as by Kant, to the issue of free will), humans are above nature, not part of it. What is supernatural in religion similarly is what is above nature. Gods, like humans, are unpredictable and irreducible to natural law because they are above it. Thus when religion is seen as supernaturalism, it is because it applies models of humans who are supernatural.

My approach also explains views of religion as felt, not thought. Because our perceptual process is largely unconscious and because what we scan may be an inchoate assemblage of clues, we may experience such feelings as awe and fascination without any conscious object. When we do, it is as though the feelings were a direct, unmediated experience of something. Hence they strike Otto, Schleiermacher, and others as peculiarly revelatory.[166] Such feelings, however, stem from our unconscious suspicion that we are in the presence of something alive or humanlike, which in turn stems from a strategic practice. That practice is to scan—

once more, mostly unconsciously—with the most important models. When the models are as diverse and as general as those of humans, we can suspect human presence virtually anywhere and at any time.

Finally, my approach suggests why notions such as "ultimate conditions" are more typically the domain of religion than of science or even philosophy. Any ultimate condition of human existence consists of some relation between humans and the sum of all known things and events, human and nonhuman. Its ultimacy, at any given time, means the point at which analysis breaks down. Analysis may have banished anthropomorphism up to this point, but when analysis fails, perception defaults to a humanlike template. When the things and events we interpret are simple and close to hand—saplings, wind sounds, or household pets—we can compare alternative interpretations and weed out anthropomorphism relatively easily. When the things and events encompass "ultimate conditions," the weeding becomes Herculean. Lacking a Hercules, we inhabit a world whose periphery is rankly overgrown.

Approaching that periphery, whose "ultimacy" means its very resistance to analysis, we find our critical tools, such as science and philosophy, do not penetrate. When we press on nonetheless, we are thrown upon intuition: that is, upon hypotheses lacking alternatives. Such hypotheses typically posit human attributes. The resulting world is, in Nietzsche's words, an "infinitely broken echo of an original sound, that of man . . . the manifold copy of an original picture, that of man."

Durkheim thinks religion can be no illusion because it is so pervasive in human life. He says any attempt to explain it as an illusion must find causes as general as religion itself. The causes I have suggested—that perception is interpretation, that interpretation attends to the most important possibilities, and that the most important possibilities are humanlike—are more general yet. They are embedded in the conditions of our knowledge of the world, and they lead us to find humans, and signs of humans, and humanlike features, wherever we can.

We do find apparent humans, and echoes and copies of humans, both in our immediate environments and in our ultimate conditions. Mailboxes appear as persons, plagues appear as messages, and order appears as design. Anthropomorphism by definition is mistaken, but it also is reasonable and inevitable. Choosing among interpretations of the world, we remain condemned to meaning, and the greatest meaning has a human face. Occasionally our interpretations assign too little meaning and we fail to see some real face confronting us. More often our interpretations assign too much and we see a face where none is. Pursuing an uncertain course between too little meaning and too much, we chronically veer, mistaken but safe, toward too much.

Notes

Chapter 1

1. Smith (1962:21) calls religion "notoriously difficult to define. [There is] a bewildering variety of definitions; and no one of them has commanded wide acceptance." Saliba (1976:184) says this diversity has provoked dissatisfaction and "malaise," and Bowker (1976:361) writes, "nobody seems to know what [religion] is." Dresser (1929), Nadel (1954), Eister (1974), Machalek (1977), and Spilka et al. (1985) among others doubt a definition is possible. Poole (1986: 423) says anthropologists have "expended enormous, but largely unproductive, effort in an attempt to define religion," and Bloch (1985:698) thinks the "only solution seems to be to abandon the notion of religion as an analytical category."

2. Tillich (1973:40) similarly views such theories as exclusivist and calls theology the "attempt to derive the concept of religion from one's own revealed, and therefore true, religion."

3. Schleiermacher (1988), Otto (1950), and Eliade (1961). Proudfoot (1985) reviews their claim. He finds it incoherent and suggests that Schleiermacher and his successors make it largely in order to make religion immune to criticism from science. Horton (1982:209) similarly writes that both Schleiermacher's fideism, and sociological and anthropological symbolic approaches, survive because they "place traditional religious thought beyond the range of invidious comparison with Western scientific thought." Gaskin (1984:31) makes the same suggestion: "A weakness of theism in grounding its basic belief upon evidence and reason is that it may be shown to be incoherent or false . . . [This fear] has motivated the more eccentric and unhistorical theologies of the twentieth century."

4. Proudfoot 1985:75.

5. A modern philosopher of religion, David Pailin (1990:35), similarly says theologians who declare God ineffable "sabotage their own work. What is properly ineffable cannot be talked about." Hans Penner (1989:27, 15) agrees that such views have "ended in failure." Nonetheless, many other theologians, philosophers

of religion, and secular writers are influenced by this notion. For example, an anthropologist, Brian Morris (1987:4), declares himself an atheist but still says religion means whatever is sacred and "supraempirical." Another contemporary anthropologist, S. J. Tambiah (1990:6), thinks the "distinctive feature of religion [is] a special awareness of the transcendent. . . . " (Curiously, he says pagan gods are *not* transcendent.)

However, adherents of many religions fail to see that they constitute a community—as alleged by the theorists—made up of themselves and adherents of other religions; witness a long history of religious persecution and war. Moreover, psychologists of religion, from William James (1902:29) to Gordon Allport (1950: 4–6), deny there is any unique religious emotion or other standard religious experience.

6. See Flew 1951, Nielsen 1973, 1982, and Proudfoot 1985.

7. A psychologist, Richard Lazarus (1984), says all affect is at least partly dependent on cognition.

8. Psychologists find emotion hard to define, but most find it highly interpretive. Lazarus (op. cit., p. 125), for example, says psychologists see emotions as an "organic mix of action impulses and bodily expressions, diverse positive or dysphoric (subjective) cognitive-affective states, and physiological disturbances . . . an emotion is not definable solely by behavior, subjective reports, *or* physiological changes." Lazarus and other psychologists agree that understanding the relations between emotion, cognition, and action will require a better understanding of consciousness.

9. Writers in several fields besides psychology (Lazarus, op. cit.) make allied observations. A linguist, Derek Bickerton (1990:89), calls emotions "bridges between representation and response," and an anthropologist, Catherine Lutz (1988), says emotions are both learned and culturally variable.

10. Proudfoot, op. cit.

11. Two psychologists writing on religion, Fraser Watts and Mark Williams (1988), similarly write, "religious experience, like scientific data, comes not in a raw form, but already interpreted in the light of theoretical or doctrinal concepts."

12. Nielsen (1982), among many other publications. Here Nielsen especially addresses Peter Winch (1958, 1964). See also Nielsen 1973, 1974, 1984.

13. Idowu (1973:43), for example, challenges Freud with the question, why religion persists if mistaken:

> If the root of religion is a disease of the mind, how comes it that the disease virus is so universally potent and so utterly invincible? For religion is persistent as the most stubborn of human activities . . . Suppressed or repudiated or rejected in one form, it presents itself in another and yet another, and goes on with its organic life.

Tambiah (1990:50) similarly charges Sir E. B. Tylor with failing to explain "why higher religion . . . should persist in the face of science."

14. Evans-Pritchard 1965:120–121.

15. Geertz 1966:1, 4.

16. Wax 1984:5. He continues, if "Geertz is correct . . . there has been no progress during the last thirty years of study of religion; if Evans-Pritchard is correct, then there never was much . . . conceptual capital." Sociologists Stark and Bainbridge (1987:11) echo the theme: "there has been little theorizing about religion since the turn of the century . . . available 'theories' of religion remain largely the

product of 19th century social thought [but] nothing like Adam Smith's economic theory or Karl Marx's theory of revolution exists" for religion. James Boon (1987:312), another anthropologist, writes that contradictions prohibit "any possible synthesis."

17. Preus (1987: xvii), Penner (1989), and Wiebe (1984) find little interest in theory among students of religion, at least in the phenomenology and history of religion.

18. Other recent general reviewers include Lawson and McCauley (1990), Penner (1989), Preus (1987), and Crosby (1981). Reviewers of anthropological theories of religion include Morris (1987), Skorupski (1976), Saliba (1976), Banton (1966), and Evans-Pritchard (1965).

19. Diodorus Siculus lib.iii.47, cited in Hume 1957:31.

20. *Hecuba*, 956, in Hume 1957:31.

21. Spinoza 1951:3–4, in Morris 1987.

22. Hume 1957:30–31.

23. Ibid., p. 65.

24. Freud 1964:24.

25. Malinowski 1979:71.

26. Cohn 1961.

27. Worsley 1957.

28. Suffering and religious response may affect part, or all, of a society. Max Weber remarks that "the oppressed [need] a redeemer and prophet: the fortunate, the propertied, the ruling strata, [do] not" (in Gerth and Mills 1948:274).

29. Hegel 1942:162, in Morris 1987.

30. La Barre 1972 and Wallace 1956.

31. Gaskin 1988:185.

32. Freud 1964:25 and 47.

33. Freud 1961:30–31.

34. Malinowski 1979:45 [1931]. Malinowski (1931) does have another view of religion as well, in which its truth or falsity is not at issue. In this second view, religious myth functions as a social charter.

35. Ibid., p. 43.

36. Malinowski 1948:87.

37. Malcolm 1977:148.

38. Feuerbach 1957 [1841]:73.

39. Marx and Engels 1957:37–38, in Morris 1987.

40. La Barre (1972:45) writes, for example, "Religion is the feeling of what is desirable and comforting in crisis situations. 'There are no atheists in foxholes.' " Most recently two sociologists, Rodney Stark and William Bainbridge (1987:23), devote a book to the proposition that "the gods . . . exist as hopes in the human consciousness. . . . Humans have a persistent desire for rewards only the gods can grant."

41. Freud 1964:52–53.

42. Landow 1971:244.

43. Wollheim 1964:14.

44. Radcliffe-Brown 1979:55.

45. Geertz 1966:18.

46. Bateson and Bateson 1988.

47. Freud 1964:50. Popper calls psychoanalytic theory "compatible with everything that could happen." Miller 1985:128.

48. Freud 1964:30.
49. Robert Orsi (personal communication) has called my attention to these analysts, who include Melanie Klein, Harry Stack Sullivan, W.R.D. Fairbairn, D. W. Winnicott, and Heinz Kohut, among others. Where Freud describes humans as motivated primarily by drives (individualistic, physiological urges such as sexual or gastric tensions) that take any opportune object, the object-relations writers describe humans as motivated by a search for social relationships. Chapter 4 discusses both the object-relations writers and research on infant face perception.
50. Stern 1985:28.
51. Bruner 1977.
52. Geertz 1966.
53. de Unamuno 1972:49.
54. Functionalism in social science parallels functionalism in biology, which assumes that the first step to understanding such features of organisms as anatomy, physiology, and behavior is to understand what contribution they make to the survival of the organism. Social functionalists similarly think features of society and culture should be understood first by their contribution to a society's survival.

Functionalism in the social sciences, however, is increasingly criticized as tautologous. Hans Penner (op. cit., p. 106) reviews its place in the study of religion and asks how we can "explain the persistence of such a . . . seriously defective" theory. My answer is that functionalism is one form of anthropomorphism, in that it assumes design. It persists for the same reasons, set out in chapters 2–4, as does other anthropomorphism. Penner (op. cit., p. 106) notes that functionalism includes not just social functionalism, but most twentieth-century theory; it is "*the* theory for explaining things in the social sciences." I agree that it underlies much modern thought about religion (Wilson [1982:7], for example, says it has a "special appeal for sociologists of religion") but think that by itself it is only an approach, not a theory.
55. For a detailed analysis of symbolism in this sense, and of "intellectualism" as an opposing theory, see Skorupski (1976). Sperber (1975) gives another thorough critique of symbolism. Penner (1989:69–72) and Lawson and McCauley (1990: 37–41) also give recent brief views of symbolism, as well as of contrasting theories.
56. We need not ask whether Confucianism really is a religion, an ideology, or a social philosophy, as the very question arises from an essentialist view of categories that are better seen as on a continuum. In practice, Confucianism has spanned all these, as have Buddhism and other religions. Confucius evidently would have disavowed anything like divinity, but successive governments and other organizations made him, with other leaders and officials, the object of an official cult.
57. Morioka 1977:190.
58. Cited in Preus (1987:15); originally in *The Six Bookes of a Commonweal,* ed. Kenneth D. McRae (reprint, 1606, translation by Richard Knolles), IV.7; 536 I, K.
59. Preus 1987:15.
60. Cited in Preus (1987:16), from *The Six Bookes of a Commonweale,* ed. Kenneth D. McRae, IV.7; 539 E.
61. Vico, in Preus 1987:80.
62. In Preus (1987:126) from Comte, *The System of Positive Polity: Treatise on Sociology, Instituting the Religion of Humanity,* Volume II, translated by Frederic Harrison (1875). Preus notes that Comte also has a more individualistic theory of religion as anthropomorphism.

63. Freud 1962, 1964, Malinowski 1948, Radcliffe-Brown 1922, 1939, 1945.

64. Durkheim derives his notion of totems from Australian aboriginal societies, which employ natural phenomena as nominal ancestors, and hence as emblems, of clans. Durkheim says this is the earliest form of religion. In more complex societies, the totem may take the form of a deity such as the Judeo-Christian God.

Durkheim may well get the idea of the totem as symbol of an otherwise abstract and elusive society from Feuerbach. Some seventy years earlier, Feuerbach (1957 [1841]:153) had said that God represents the whole human species, rolled into one being. This unity is His appeal: "Because of this immediate unity of the species with individuality, this concentration of all that is universal and real in one personal being, God is a deeply moving object, enrapturing to the imagination; whereas, the idea of humanity has little power over the feelings, because humanity is only an abstraction; and the reality which presents itself to us in distinction from this abstraction is the multitude of separate, limited individuals."

65. Durkheim, op. cit., p. 467.

66. Nilsson 1949:152.

67. Swanson 1960. Swanson's world survey, correlating religious variation with social variation, associates religious ethical systems with social stratification and suggests that elites engender such systems to protect their privilege.

68. Hume 1957:72–73; emphasis his.

69. Ninian Smart (1976:30) thinks there is "no division between the sacred and the secular" in tribal society generally.

70. Durkheim, op. cit., p. 493.

71. Crick 1988.

72. Young 1985.

73. It is shared, for example, by Renford Bambrough (1977) and Peter Winch (1977), among many others.

74. As Leach (1968:1) notes.

75. Some of their variants thus are philosophical and psychological rather than religious. This open-endedness, though it contradicts an essentialist view of religion, would not surprise most historians, who see religions, like other institutions, not as timeless entities but as shifting accretions.

76. See, for example, Tambiah (1970) on Thai Buddhism. Moreover, Buddhist gods and other supernaturals are not limited to "popular" religion or to cosmology, but also exist in canon. Tambiah (op. cit., p. 33) notes that two of the *Tripitaka* (the Vinaya and Sutta Pitaka) of the Pali Theravada canon refer to "supernatural beings and occurrences" as well as the "skeleton of the pantheon and the framework of the cosmology . . . (e.g. Atanatiya Suttanta (Rhys Davids, Part III, 1957, Ch. 32))." Over time, the cosmology and mythical history have become "fantastically ornate."

77. Hardy (cited in Tambiah), for example, describes worship of the Buddha by Theravada Buddhists, and Tambiah (1970:44) says the description still is valid and applies "equally well to Ceylon, Burma, or Thailand."

78. Eliot cited in Tambiah, op. cit., p. 43.

79. Spiro 1966:92.

80. In the Samanna-Phala Sutta, the Buddha tells of some powers of an *arahat:*

being one he becomes many, or having become many becomes one again; he becomes visible or invisible; he goes, feeling no obstruction, to the further side of a wall or rampart or hill, as if through air . . . he walks on water without breaking through, as if on solid ground; he travels cross-legged in the sky . . . even the moon and the sun, so potent . . . does he touch with his hand. (Rhys Davids cited in Tambiah, op. cit., p. 49)

81. Spiro, op. cit., p. 93. Evans-Pritchard (1965:119) also notes that claims that Buddhism and Jainism are atheistic religions are "serious distortions," for the same reason.

82. William James (1902) and Sigmund Freud (1962), for example, point out the continuity of religion with other psychic phenomena. Keith Thomas (1971:50), among others, notes the continuity and interpenetration of religion with magic in particular: "The line between magic and religion is . . . impossible to draw in many primitive societies; it is equally difficult to draw in medieval England."

83. Skorupski (1976) carefully adduces further reasons, many of them logical, to doubt Durkheim's and subsequent symbolist views.

84. Durkheim 1965:477. Durkheim admits science elaborates the ideas it inherits from religion and "purges them of all accidental elements; in a general way, it brings a spirit of criticism into all its doings, which religion ignores." However, he continues, scientific method is not enough to distinguish science from religion.

85. Durkheim here anticipates Thomas Kuhn (1970).

86. Durkheim, op. cit., pp. 486–487.

87. Guthrie 1980.

88. Fontenelle, in Preus, op. cit., p. 43; original, *De l'origine des fable,* editor J.-R Carre, 40.

89. Fontenelle, in Preus, op. cit., p. 43.

90. Ibid., p. 44. Fontenelle here anticipates Jane Goodall's view of wild chimpanzee responses to thunderstorms (chapter 2).

91. In the first of two complementary essays, *Dialogues Concerning Natural Religion* and *The Natural History of Religion,* he finds insufficient basis in reason for religious belief. In the second essay he says belief springs not from reflection on the strongest evidence of God, apparent design in nature, but from the world's ambiguity and unpredictability and from our resulting "incessant hopes and fears." Nonetheless, religious belief in its elementary form is not offensive to reason.

92. Hume 1957:53.

93. Tylor 1979:11.

94. Bergson (1935:176) wrote, for example, "before man can philosophize man must live. . . . To connect religion with a system of ideas, with logic or pre-logic, is to turn our remote ancestors into philosophers."

95. Durkheim 1965:75.

96. For example, Levi-Strauss 1966, Griaule 1980, Conklin 1969, Lee 1979. Lee now thinks he first overestimated leisure among foragers; but even so, they clearly are more leisured than are people in industrial societies.

97. Geertz 1966.

98. Guthrie 1988.

99. Chapter 2 elaborates this claim.

100. Lowie 1970 [1924].

101. As Lowie (1970:109) puts it, "the charge of intellectualism is pointless because Tylor is concerned with tracing the origin of a concept, that is, of a cognitive element."

102. Horton 1960:206–207

103. James 1902:29
104. Allport 1950:4–6.
105. Tylor 1873:II, 359.
106. Evans-Pritchard (1965:25, 29), for example, calls it a "just-so story" and says there is "no evidence about how religious beliefs originated."
107. Evans-Pritchard 1965:26, Snaith 1944.
108. Teske 1986.
109. *Confessions* IV, 16. In Teske 1986, pp. 253–268.
110. Augustine, in Teske, op. cit., p. 256. I owe the point that Mormons view God as a very large man (who has preceded us to heaven) to Robert Orsi.
111. Lowie, op. cit., pp. 123, 130.
112. Ibid., pp. 133–134.
113. Ibid., p. 134.
114. Tylor 1979:12. Psychology also has invisible entities. Two psychoanalysts, Jay Greenberg and Stephen Mitchell (1983:104), for example, say "All psychoanalytic theory presumes invisible, hypothetical processes and events which are not susceptible to observation or experience."
115. Ian Barbour (1971:288) points out, in criticizing the term "immaterial" as ambiguous, that "there were those in Newton's day who argued that gravity is a spiritual power because it is invisible and acts at a distance." Theodor Raschke (1986:133) calls the strong and weak forces "today's 'angels.' "
116. Evans-Pritchard (op. cit., p. 15), for example, thinks religion is "absurd" to most anthropologists.
117. Tambiah 1990:6.
118. Evans-Pritchard 1950, 1965.
119. Evans-Pritchard 1965:29.
120. For example, Levi-Strauss 1966. Levi-Strauss analyzes mythology and basic structures of thought rather than religion as such, and offers no general view of religion except in brief asides. Nonetheless, he seems to view religious thought, as I do, as both rational and anthropomorphizing.
121. Barbour 1971:1.
122. The claim that the business of religion is to recommend certain attitudes and values is made, for example, by philosophers R. B. Braithwaite (1955) and D. Z. Phillips (1976) and by the anthropologist Clifford Geertz (1966), who says religion's function is to promote certain "moods and motivations."
123. Barbour 1976:5.
124. Geertz 1966.
125. Geertz 1966:14.
126. James 1902:53.
127. Geertz 1966:12.
128. For example, in *The Religion of Java* (1960) and *Islam Observed: Religious Development in Morocco and Indonesia* (1968). Munson (1986) similarly notes Geertz's lack of attention to the content of religious worldviews and his great attention instead to cultural style. Munson writes (p. 29) that Geertz reduces the "semantic substance of religion to the personality traits and behavior of the believer." Munson (p. 29) also quotes Sherry Ortner to the same effect: " 'Geertz's heart has always been more with the "ethos" side of culture than with the "worldview," more with the affective and stylistic dimensions than with the cognitive.' " In emphasizing affect, Geertz is closer to such religious writers as Schleiermacher, Otto, and Eliade than to most anthropologists.

129. Geertz 1973:130.
130. That formula would deny an idea of the "ultimate" to nonreligious people. But people do not have to be religious to have this idea.
131. Geertz 1966:26.
132. Ibid., pp. 27–28.
133. Ibid., p. 28.
134. Geertz 1973:129–30.
135. Barbour 1971:220–221.
136. Richardson 1951:76.
137. Detachment from worldly objects and relationships is urged by some religions including varieties of Christianity, Jainism, Hinduism, and Buddhism, but detachment from God or gods is not. Some forms of Buddhism advocate detachment rather generally, but these forms are more philosophical than religious.
138. Smart 1976:12. As psychologists Fraser Watts and Mark Williams (op. cit., p. 113) put it, people who pray "believe that they are not merely talking to themselves."
139. Geertz 1966:28.
140. Watts and Williams (op. cit., p. 4), for example, say they can write on the psychology of religion without "making any assumption about whether or not that presumed knowledge is justified or correct." Similarly, Spilka et al. (1985:2) write, "it is *not* the place of psychologists to challenge . . . theologies. God is not our domain. . . . We will not enter into debates of faith versus reason or religion versus science, nor will we question revelation or scripture."

Others think, as I do, that such neutrality subverts understanding. Skorupski (1976:203) rejects the "often-made claim that the truth-value of beliefs under study by the sociologist is irrelevant." Proudfoot (1985:177) also rejects it. Describing a religious conversion, he notes that the convert "believes that his experience has been produced by something outside of him. That belief is itself constitutive of the experience. An assessment of the event as experienced by the subject must therefore include an assessment of the truth or falsity of the belief." Another philosopher, Gaskin (1984:177), writes, "the practice of [a] religion makes no sense without the truth of its underlying beliefs about what is real." Tillich (1973:70) agrees: "It has become customary to subdivide the philosophy of religion into the double question concerning the *nature* and *truth* of religion. Where this division occurs . . . philosophy of religion has not yet been perfected."
141. Hans Penner (1989) thinks most twentieth-century theorists of religion, including Geertz, do share a theory, albeit a "bankrupt" one: functionalism. That most twentieth-century writers are functionalists (they think religion fulfills some need) seems true but, as noted earlier, I think functionalism by itself constitutes only a general approach, not a theory.
142. Proudfoot 1985:192.
143. Geertz tries to avoid the confusion inherent in the idea of "secular religion" by noting that a man can indeed be religious about golf, but not merely by playing passionately and regularly; he must also see it as symbolic of some transcendent truths. I would reply that, on one hand, some people think that they do see such truths in Marxism or football or golf, and that on the other many people, especially in immanentist religions, take religious truths to be concrete, particular, and close to hand, not transcendent.
144. As chapter 7 shows, most scholars of religion agree that religion inevitably anthropomorphizes. Ferré (1984:208–209), for example, says anthropomorphism

in religion is "not avoidable." Most recently, Penner (1989) says religion is characterized by "superhuman beings," and Lawson and McCauley (1990:5, 124) write, "what is unique to *religious* ritual systems is . . . superhuman *agents* . . . all religious rituals . . . presuppose the participation of the gods."

145. He writes later (1973:131) that religion constructs a "reality in which, to quote Max Weber, 'events are not just there and happen, but they have a meaning and happen because of that meaning.' " But Weber is not the first to note the compulsion toward meaning, nor does Geertz's reference sufficiently clarify the issues. Nietzsche earlier notes that the "death of God" entails a loss of meaning and threatens the subsequent world with chaos; and Tylor and other intellectualists also are concerned with meaning. The question remains, what is distinctive about a religious system of meanings?

146. Geertz 1973:140–41.

147. Bellah 1970:21.

148. Bellah 1967.

149. Penner (1989:7) similarly remarks that the notion of ultimacy is too broad and results in a good example of a bad definition, and Spiro (op. cit., p. 95) writes, "while religious beliefs are not always of ultimate concern, non-religious beliefs sometimes are." Chapter 7 further discusses Tillich.

150. Margolis 1987:31. Spiro (op. cit., p. 90) similarly writes, concerning functionalist definitions of religion, "Social solidarity, anxiety reduction, confidence in unpredictable situations, and the like, are functions which may be served by any or all cultural phenomena."

151. Douglas and Perry 1985:416–417.

152. Crick 1988.

153. The publications most relevant here are Horton 1960, 1967, 1973, and 1982.

154. Skorupski (1976:178) and Penner (1986:645), respectively. Skorupski gives the most thorough critique, generally a friendly one, of Horton and of intellectualism, in a book reviewing the intellectualist-symbolist debate in the anthropological theory of religion. Penner offers a more recent and briefer critique, devoted almost entirely to Horton.

155. Evidently Horton is more appreciated in British than in American anthropology. In the United States, Tambiah (1990:90–91), for example, dismisses him as "not sufficiently sensitive to the issue of commensurability between different mentalities" and as "tendentious" and "misguided."

156. Horton 1960:206.

157. Ibid., p. 211.

158. Horton is careful to say that he does not claim causal priority for the human side in this balance of human and divine relationships. He wishes to say only that some balance does exist between the two sides, in meeting human needs. Despite his disclaimer, however, the argument as a whole seems of the wish-fulfillment sort, and close to Feuerbach.

159. Horton later (1982) retracts the notion that traditional societies are more anxious about their theories than are modern societies, as well as the notions of closed versus open societies and of a lack of alternatives. This retraction, together with Horton's earlier work, obviates Tambiah's (1990:91) complaint that Horton makes African theoretical thought "inferior to Western scientific thought [because of such features]."

160. Horton 1982:256.

161. As Augustine explains (Teske 1986:260–261), even the fool says only in his heart that there is no God, because he dares not say it aloud.

162. This reason may be what Hans Penner wants when, in his careful critique, he charges (1986:663) that Horton does not say "what the *theory* [emphasis mine] is from which we can make the deduction that 'gods serve to introduce unity into diversity, simplicity into complexity.' " Chapter 7 develops this point further.

163. In this regard, Horton seems a rationalist in the strong sense of believing that people have good reasons, of which they are aware, for what they think and do. Such a belief—if indeed he holds it—however, undervalues the sense of immediacy, and the apparent independence of intellect, that many people have of their religious experience. It is unconscious processes, independent of conscious reason, that diverse writers including Schleiermacher, James, Otto, and Eliade note in insisting that religious experience is primary, affective, immediate, and unmediated by belief. In my view, Horton is sounder than these writers but is himself, perhaps in reaction to them, too rationalistic.

164. Horton 1982:237.

165. His more recent work softens this opposition, recognizing that all aspects of our worldview are in a sense theoretical. But he still segregates common sense as "primary theory," which he finds similar around the world, from religion and science as "secondary theory," which he finds culturally variable (Horton 1982: 216, 228).

166. Chapter 2. Churchland (1979, 1988) shows that common sense also is theoretical. As Lawson and McCauley (1990:29) remark, "failure to acknowledge the theoretical character of common sense invests it with an undeserved epistemological preeminence."

167. Tambiah (1990:3) criticizes intellectualism and rationalism more severely. He thinks, for example, that "Wilfred Cantwell Smith in *The Meaning and End of Religion* has made suspect the general application of a narrow rationalist definition of religion, born of the European Enlightenment, which has construed it primarily as a doctrine of beliefs and a system of intellectualistic constructs."

Chapter 2

1. Rather, "strategy" here is meant as Darwinian shorthand for a behavioral/neural practice that results from natural selection and that operates almost entirely without our awareness.

2. Piaget 1933:537. Chapter 4 discusses Piaget on animism and artificialism at more length.

3. Piaget probably is influenced here by Levy-Bruhl, whose stages of "primitive mentality" he cites, and perhaps by Freud on primitive societies. Freud similarly addresses animism evolutionarily: "Animism came to primitive man naturally and as a matter of course. He knew what things were like in the world, namely just as he felt himself to be . . . primitive man transposed the structural conditions of his own mind into the external world." (1955 [1913]:91]).

4. See Chapter 5. Piaget attributes the term, artificialism, to a study by L. Brunschvicg of the physics of Aristotle, *L'Experience Humaine et La Causalité Physique*, Livres V–VII, which asserts that Aristotle is by turns artificialist and animist.

5. Keil (1979:132), for example, notes criticism of Piaget (Huang 1943, Kling-

berg 1957, Margand 1977) but does not doubt "children agree that things such as the sun, the moon, and the wind are 'alive.' " Laurendeau and Pinard (1962) provide other evidence confirming child animism.

6. An exception is Keil (op. cit., p. 133), who writes, "childhood animism turns out to be extremely complex and not simply artifactual."

7. Watts and Williams 1988:141.

8. See Chapter 4. Piaget also may be understood as including much of Tylor's notion. Tylor's animism differs mainly in that his spirit beings may be invisible and immaterial, while for Piaget, animistic life is embodied. However, this difference is not crucial. A second difference is that Tylor's animism is more an adult phenomenon than a childish one, whereas for Piaget the reverse is true.

9. At least the stronger sense of this inability, namely, an inability to tell self from other, is implausible. Piaget elsewhere says that infants can tell self from other by around the end of their first year, and Stern (1985) says they do so from birth. Many nonhuman animals seem to do so as well. Coy (1988:80) writes, "many species show some ability to distinguish 'self' from 'non-self' . . . in that they can use complex methods of communication and receive feedback on the identity of other individuals, or even on their 'states of mind.' " Inagaki and Hatano (1987:1020) write that children's animism is a reasonable use of analogy, not a "sign of intellectual immaturity because constrained personification is a means for children to generate an educated guess about less familiar, nonhuman objects."

10. Piaget (1929:380) remarks similarly of the child's view of its parents as infallible that "it is only when the conviction decays that it is seen to have existed."

11. Toulmin 1982:78.

12. Mundkur 1988:174.

13. Theory of religion as an enterprise, for example, scarcely exists in contemporary psychology. For instance, Gorsuch's (1988) review of the psychology of religion reports little interest in psychology even in a definition of religion and asks whether a psychology of religion is possible. Similarly Spilka et al. (1985:4) recommend avoiding "unproductive, general, theoretical definitions" of religion. S.G.F. Brandon (1970:515) thinks "little has happened" in the psychology of religion since Freud and Jung, and W. H. Clark (1958:5) says the "psychology of religion has never enjoyed a wholly respectable academic status."

14. La Barre (1964) gives a good brief review of the range of notions of animism and animatism and offers his own psychoanalytic view.

15. The major opposing view, that perception is direct apprehension, is older and now associated primarily with J. J. Gibson (1966, 1979).

16. Wittgenstein's point here is made also by Friedrich Nietzsche (1966), Alfred Schutz (1962), and William James (1890).

17. A philosopher of science, E. Thomas Lawson (1990:12–31), and a scholar of religion, Robert McCauley, give a recent review of opinion on the relation of interpretation and explanation in understanding. Whereas many scholars make one process or the other primary, Lawson and McCauley think the two complement, inform, and interpenetrate each other: "Novel interpretations employ . . . theories already in place, whereas novel explanations [discover] new theories which, in turn, depend upon the sort of reorganization of knowledge that interpretive pursuits involve" (ibid., p. 15). They note, however, that such postmodernist philosophers as Richard Rorty (1982:199) think "*all* inquiry is ultimately interpretive," including the natural sciences. They also grant (p. 21) that "expla-

nation is riddled with interpretation." I tend to side with the postmodernists, since interpretation seems to choose, at the lowest level, among categories that are innate.

18. Gombrich 1973.

19. Margolis 1987:38–39.

20. Arnheim 1969:13.

21. Oatley 1978, Arbib and Hanson 1987.

22. The examples are from Oatley 1978.

23. The example is Richard Gregory's, in Miller (1983).

24. Gombrich 1969:188.

25. Arbib and Hanson 1987.

26. Nietzsche 1966:57.

27. The phrase is Gregory Bateson's (1972:381) definition of information.

28. Piper 1962:212.

29. Ibid., p. 220.

30. Schrödinger 1945:77.

31. Cognitive psychologists Eleanor Rosch (1976:384), Carolyn Mervis, Wayne Gray, David Johnson, and Penny Boyes-Braem say the "basic category cuts in the world [are] those which yield the most information for the least cognitive load." Among the most basic of these cuts, in my view, are those between animate and inanimate and between human and nonhuman.

32. Arnheim, op. cit., p. 23.

33. Runners subsequently mentioned in the text, unless otherwise identified, also are the author.

34. Kahneman and Tversky 1982a, Jackendoff 1987.

35. Kahneman and Tversky, op. cit., p. 513.

36. Harnad 1987, Neisser 1987.

37. Arnheim, op. cit., p. 13.

38. Arnheim 1974:6.

39. Goodman (1976:69) metaphorizes metaphor as an "affair between a predicate with a past and an object that yields while protesting." He continues, "metaphorical application of a label to an object defies an explicit or tacit prior denial of that label to that object."

40. People overwhelmingly see Rorschach ink blots, for example, as images of life forms. Chapter 4 elaborates this and other examples.

41. Franz Boas (1948:94) also assimilates animism, and anthropomorphism as well, to this kind of automatic response. Anthropomorphism in general, he says, "is not to be conceived as a rationalization but as an automatic reaction, like the unrepressed action of a person in our civilization, child or adult, who vents his spleen on an inanimate object that has been the cause of some accident."

42. Fischler and Firschein 1987:233.

43. Hume 1957:32.

44. H. B. Cott 1940; H. E. Hinton 1973.

45. Hinton, op. cit. Powerful lights along the leading edges of the wings of Second World War antisubmarine aircraft similarly made aircraft silhouettes invisible to surfaced submarines by matching the background skylight (Walter Guthrie, personal communication).

46. Hinton, op. cit.

47. Ibid.

48. One of the discoverers of diffraction gratings in insects, H. E. Hinton (op. cit., p. 134), finds natural deception disturbing because "not only does imagination . . . run riot but . . . one finds that nature has outstripped the most fevered imagination."

49. One might also object that the invisibility of gods is different in that it is supernatural. But this would be somewhat circular, and in any case the term "supernatural" is itself obscure and rarely applicable outside Western culture. It usually is used to indicate some break in the natural order. Often it implies a break caused by some power outside and superior to the natural order, as in miracles and marvels; but the nature of that power may be unspecified. Hallowell (1960), Evans-Pritchard (1965), and Saler (1977) all say the notion of the supernatural is largely Western and not applicable cross-culturally. Chapter 7 suggests that the concept of the supernatural itself probably is a form of anthropomorphism, consisting of applying to the world in general the Judeo-Christian model of humans as above nature.

50. Griffin 1984.

51. Hinton, op. cit.

52. Mark Bekoff, personal communication.

53. Cheney and Seyfarth 1990:131.

54. *The New York Times,* June 15, 1980. P. 28.

55. Corn 1978:21.

56. Goodall 1971, 1975, and personal communication.

57. The reader may object that these terms are "metaphoric," but that does not distinguish them sharply from other terms. Incipient metaphor is involved in all perception, since interpretation depends on categorization, and categorization asserts the identity of nonidentical phenomena. What we distinguish as metaphor is merely categorization across our normal categories.

58. Hobbes 1960:5.

59. Brown and Thouless (1965:33–42). W. Dennis (1953) reports similar findings.

60. Malcolm 1984:18.

61. In a recent movie about firefighting, *Backdraft,* a major character similarly tells a rookie that in order to defeat a fire, one must learn to think like one.

62. J. G. Miller 1978.

63. Aristotle, cited in Lloyd 1966:258.

64. Lovelock 1987:4.

65. François Jacob, *La Logique du Vivant,* p. 299, cited in Toulmin 1982:161.

66. Sebeok 1988:72.

67. James Gibson (1979) thinks animals differ from inanimate objects mainly in moving spontaneously, and A. N. Whitehead (1968:111, cited in Brown and Thouless, op. cit.) finds the distinction between animate and inanimate "vague and problematical." He says both animate and inanimate behave systematically in a way that is "perfectly general throughout nature, and represents no property peculiar to living bodies."

68. Gombrich (1969:107) suggests this as one example of artistic creation as "schema and correction." That is, the artist has a schema in mind, makes a tentative concrete representation of it, and corrects the representation. Gombrich also cites Leone Battista Alberti's 1430 treatise *De Statua,* on the origin of art: the earliest artists would observe "in tree trunks, clumps of earth, or other objects of

this sort certain lineaments which through some slight changes could be made to resemble a natural shape. They . . . tried, by adding or taking away here and there, to render the resemblance complete."

69. Ibid.

70. Ibid., p. 109. This image suggests yet another theory of cave art: that it served in part to form and reinforce search images, especially for neophyte hunters. Just as military training uses silhouettes of allied and enemy aircraft, briefly flashed on a screen, to foster rapid recognition, and as field guides to birds emphasize key features, so the hunter-artists may have said, this is how a horse may appear; this is how its features emerge from the background.

71. A modern version of the notion of growth, for instance, is the term "evolution," from the unfolding of a growing plant.

72. Frye 1968:6.

73. Lloyd 1966:233; see also chapter 6.

74. Ibid., pp. 233–234. Lloyd notes that it is unclear whether Thales took magnets and amber as typical or as atypical of other material objects.

75. Ibid., p. 237.

76. Ibid., p. 238.

77. Aristotle, *Mete.* 351a 26ff., cited in Lloyd, op. cit., p. 263. Brunschvicg (*L'Experience Humaine et La Causalité Physique,* livres V–VII, cited in Piaget 1929) also says that animism and artificialism are the two poles between which even Aristotle's sophisticated *Physics* still alternates. Frye (1968:6) similarly notes that Latin *natura* and Greek *physis* are linked etymologically to growth and to birth. We can see such linkage, for instance, in Lucretius's account in *De Rerum Natura* of the origin of animals and humans, in which they are born from wombs in the earth, rather as Egyptians thought frogs and mice were born each year by spontaneous generation from the Nile's mud.

78. Janson 1973.

79. John Donne, *A Nocturnal Upon Saint Lucies Day,* 11. 33–34, cited in Piper, op. cit., p. 9.

80. As chapter 6 shows, scientists may anthropomorphize as well.

81. K. Heim 1953, cited in Brown and Thouless, op. cit.

82. Eddington 1923:155.

83. Teilhard de Chardin 1959:55–56.

84. Haldane 1932:113.

85. Richter 1939, cited in Barkan 1975:43–44.

86. Eliade 1959:98.

87. Lovelock, op. cit.

88. Cited in Wolf 1988:752–761.

89. For a recent critical review of the concept, see Eric Wolf, op. cit.

90. One might also object that functionalist animism is only metaphor and therefore limited; but the functionalists take it more literally, and often more unconsciously, than that. It is such a fundamental model, in fact, that it is more often implicit than explicit. It is most explicit in Spencer, who compares societies to organisms in great detail, with massive correspondence in structure and function from the least-organized societies and organisms to the most organized. But less zealous functionalists as well depend on the same metaphor.

91. Piaget 1929.

92. *The Monthly Review,* LXVI, in Piper, op. cit., pp. 4–5.

93. In Piper, op. cit., p. 6.

94. Ibid., p. 9.

95. Ibid., p. 18.

96. Dugald Stewart, *Elements of the Philosophy of the Human Mind,* i, pp. 88–89. In Piper, op. cit., p. 18.

97. D. Diderot, *Oeuvres completes,* i, pp. 45–49 and 139–140, in Piper, op. cit., pp. 20 and 24.

98. J.B.R. Robinet, *Considerations Philosophiques de La Gradation Naturelle des Formes de L'Etre,* pp. 8–10, in Piper, op. cit., p. 24.

99. Piper, op. cit., p. 25.

100. Meier 1982.

101. *Barnaby Rudge,* p. 44, in Meier, op. cit., p. 36.

102. *David Copperfield,* p. 275, in Meier, op. cit., p. 37.

103. *Little Dorrit,* p. 71, in Meier, op. cit., p. 76.

104. *Dombey and Son,* p. 290, in Meier, op. cit.

105. *Hard Times,* p. 65, in Meier, op. cit., p. 146.

106. *David Copperfield,* p. 611, in Meier, op. cit., p. 39.

107. *Bleak House,* p. 482, in Meier, op. cit., p. 39.

108. *Nicholas Nickleby,* p. 763, in Meier, op. cit., p. 38.

109. Ibid., p. 77, in Meier, op. cit., p. 39.

110. *Martin Chuzzlewit,* p. 59, in Meier, op. cit., p. 46.

111. *Bleak House,* in Meier, op. cit., p. 49.

112. *Dombey and Son,* p. 149, in Meier, op. cit., p. 51.

113. *Martin Chuzzlewit,* p. 390, in Meier, op. cit., p. 51.

114. *Barnaby Rudge,* p. 314, in Meier, op. cit., p. 51.

115. *Our Mutual Friend,* p. 118, in Meier, op. cit., p. 51.

116. Van Camp 1988:59.

117. Treaster 1991:A9.

118. Eliot 1958:3–4.

119. Sze 1963:97.

120. Ibid.

121. Ibid., p. 89. Chapter 5 gives further examples.

Chapter 3

1. As George Stack (1983) shows, Friedrich Albert Lange (1866) and Friedrich Nietzsche (for example, 1966) do address it at some length. I discuss them later in this chapter. Many others, most notably Francis Bacon (1960) and Benedict de Spinoza (1955; see chapter 6 for Bacon and Spinoza), touch on or discuss it; but no one gives a thorough explanation.

2. Bacon 1960:52.

3. Spinoza 1955.

4. Hume 1957 [1757]:29.

5. Liebert 1909:1–22.

6. Nietzsche 1966:316.

7. Feuerbach 1967.

8. Ferré 1984:203–212.

9. Ribot, *L'Évolution des Idées Générales,* cited in Piaget 1929:234.

10. T. Percy Nunn (1927) finds anthropomorphism in physics, Norman Gary (1975) finds it in entomology, and William Adams (1981) finds it in archaeology.

11. See chapter 7.

12. Brandon 1970:86–87. Emphasis mine.

13. Tillich 1951:245.

14. A recent search of five data bases produced 344 abstracts mentioning anthropomorphism or personification.

15. The theologians are discussed primarily in chapter 7. The key anthropologists, discussed at several points, are White 1969, Horton 1960, 1967, Levi-Strauss 1966.

16. Bacon and Spinoza are discussed in chapter 6, on anthropomorphism in philosophy and science.

17. Vico 1725, 1744, par. 377, in Preus, op. cit., p. 70.

18. Vico, op. cit., pars. 186–87, in Preus, op. cit., p. 71.

19. Comte, in Preus, op. cit., p. 118.

20. Comte, op. cit., pp. 447, 446; in Preus, op. cit., p. 118.

21. Preus observes that Comte anticipates Freud in this idea. Op. cit., p. 118.

22. Comte 1974, in Preus, op. cit., p. 118.

23. Feuerbach 1957:198, 213.

24. Ibid., p. 116.

25. Ibid., p. 30n. For a modern reader, a problem with this third "reason" for religious anthropomorphism is that there is no apparent motive for people to seek this means to self-consciousness. Instead, it seems based on a Hegelian and nineteenth-century assumption that progress is inherent in the universe, an assumption which itself is teleological and hence anthropomorphic.

26. Ibid., p. 270.

27. My approach joins Feuerbach's and Durkheim's emphases on experience of self and of society and adds an emphasis on experience of the world in general. That is, God or gods are not simply experience of self or of society, or of both, projected onto the natural world but really referring only to humans. Rather they are, as religious believers think, an interpretation of the world in general, including humans. However, the interpretation uses a model originally constructed primarily of and for humans.

28. White 1949:64.

29. Ibid., p. 66. White cannot mean "in the beginning" literally, as one of his examples of people who confuse self with not-self is the Omaha of forty years earlier.

30. Ibid., p. 69.

31. Ibid., pp. 400–401.

32. Friedrich Albert Lange (1828–1875) was a philosopher at Zürich and Marburg. His *History of Materialism* maintains that anthropomorphism is fundamental and inescapable in our views of the world. Bernoulli, E. Hocks, Hans Vaihinger, Jörg Salaquarda (Stack 1983) and, most comprehensively, George Stack (1983) hold that Lange is a major source of Nietzsche's views on epistemology, philosophy of science, and anthropomorphism.

33. Stack 1980:41–71.

34. Lange sets out this thesis in *The History of Materialism,* and it subsequently runs through the works of Nietzsche.

35. For example Nietzsche, in an enthusiastic letter in 1866, quotes Lange's conclusions:

> 1. The world of the senses is the product of our organization. 2. Our visible (bodily) organs are, like all other parts of the phenomenal world, only images of an unknown object. 3. Our real organization is, therefore, as much un-

known to us as are real external things. We continually have before us nothing but the product of both (Stack 1983:10).

36. Nietzsche, *Morgenröte,* sect. 117.
37. Nietzsche 1968:263–264.
38. The evident predisposition of young infants to perceive faces and the predisposition of adults to see points of light attached to the joints of moving humans as whole humans are possible examples.
39. Nietzsche 1966:314.
40. Bernard le Bouvier de Fontenelle. Cited in Preus, op. cit., pp. 43–44.
41. This example is remarkably like the explanations of natural phenomena that Piaget (1923) finds among young children.
42. Bovier, op. cit., 16/35–36, quoted in Preus, op. cit., pp. 43–44.
43. Hume, op. cit., pp. 28–29. The subsequent seven citations from Hume are from the same publication, pp. 29–30 and p. 53.
44. Hume 1947:156.
45. Agassi 1973. For further discussion of Agassi on anthropomorphism, see chapter 6.
46. Barkan 1975:62.
47. Hume, op. cit., p. 31.
48. Horton 1960.
49. White 1949:111.
50. Ibid., p. 401.
51. Loukatos 1976:467–474.
52. Wayman 1982.
53. Freud 1964:20–21.
54. Ibid., pp. 22–23.
55. Ibid., p. 24.
56. Piaget 1929:189.
57. Wallace 1983:21.
58. Mendelson et al. 1978.
59. Ozick 1977:72.
60. *The New York Times,* July 11, 1977.
61. Loukatos, op. cit., p. 469.
62. Piaget, op. cit., p. 189.
63. Freedberg 1989:73.
64. Dickens 1956:4.
65. For example, many contemporary American children picture a God "consumed by rage and villainy," who "lashes out uncontrollably when angered. Sometimes this God acts sadistically, but always . . . arbitrarily" (Heller 1986:80).
66. Taussig 1980:149.
67. Vico, *The New Science,* par. 379, in Preus, op. cit., p. 71.
68. Hume, op. cit., p. 52.
69. Barkan, op. cit., p. 54.
70. Greenberg and Mitchell (1983; drawn upon in chapter 4) review Freud's notion of drives, and "object relations" as an alternative psychoanalytic view of motivation.
71. Zajonc (1984) thinks emotions may be primitive and have priority over cognition, but Lazarus (1984) persuasively denies this. Briggs's (1970) work at least implies emotions are learned and culturally variable, and Lutz (1988) says so

explicitly. Schachter and Singer (1962), investigating emotion as interpretation, administered the sympathetic hormone epinephrine to subjects, paired them with another person instructed to act out varying standard emotions, and asked them to report their emotions. The subjects interpreted their heightened sensations, such as pounding heart and shaking hands, as the emotions acted out by their companions. Kosslyn (1980:29) writes, a "physiological state (arousal) . . . is experienced radically differently depending on how the state is interpreted."

72. Lazarus 1984:126.

73. Zajonc (1984) and Lazarus (1984), though opposed on the relation of emotion to cognition, agree that an understanding of emotion awaits an understanding of consciousness.

74. Bickerton 1990:89.

75. Levi-Strauss 1963:69.

76. Lazarus, op. cit., p. 126.

77. Ibid., p. 125.

78. I heard this story on the radio and do not know its author or title.

79. Thoreau's phrase is set in the floor of the Poet's Corner in the Cathedral of St. John the Divine in New York City.

80. Donne, Meditation I, p. 8, cited in Barkan, op. cit., pp. 56–57.

81. For example, Lashley (1956), Schachter and Singer (1962), Nisbett and Wilson (1977), Dennett (1978), Kahneman and Tversky (1982a,b), Weiskrantz (1985), Wilson (1985), and Jackendoff (1987) in psychology; Lutz (1988) in anthropology; Bickerton (1990) in linguistics; and Cheney and Seyfarth (1990) in primatology.

82. Lutz 1988.

83. Cheney and Seyfarth 1990:241.

84. Fernandez 1986.

85. Penner, personal communication.

86. Piaget 1929:240.

87. Fernandez, op. cit.

88. Piaget, op. cit., p. 263.

89. Stern 1985:10.

90. Coy, op. cit., p. 80.

91. Cited in Arnheim 1974:51.

92. Arbib and Hanson 1987:1.

93. Evidence that young infants have a proclivity to see faces and that adults tend to see groupings of objects as social groupings seems at least partly to bear them out.

94. Mary Midgley and Frederick Ferré make points similar to mine regarding claims that we anthropomorphize animals. Midgley (1983:127) says that although human knowledge of the world must start from what is familiar, we can and do expand our understandings. In understanding other animals, one firm basis for expansion is our long history of living in a mixed community with them. Ferré (1984:211) continues Midgley's point: "In the mixed community there are many deep differences between the species, but it would take a weighty argument—and a difficult one to make in view of the evolutionary and physiological evidences— to show that these differences are absolute." Although we certainly do anthropomorphize animals, we do not do so merely by seeing them and ourselves as alike in some important ways. Ferré elsewhere (1980:31) remarks, however, with regard to the possibility of knowing God, that we cannot be completely cut off

from some "cognitive grasp of the realities that ultimately produced and surround us. If our mental capacities are the fine-tuned product of evolutionary interactions with our world, then it is not at all plausible that the fundamental structures and processes of reality are 'wholly other,' " But what Ferré means by wholly other is unclear.

95. Freud, Bovet (1928), and Piaget stress this formative experience as a source of anthropomorphism, and the object-relations analysts see this time as prototypical of human relations.

96. See chapter 7.

97. Frazer 1935:92. Frazer here implies that what sets gods off from magicians is invisibility; but we have seen that invisibility is not a reliable criterion.

98. Briggs 1970.

99. Cohen 1986.

100. Ibid., p. 12.

101. Ibid., p. 22.

102. Many people, including the well educated, still believe stories of wolf children and abominable snowmen. No tales of wolf children (or of snowmen), however, have been substantiated nor, given the needs of children and of wolves, are any likely to be. The notion that wolves might be able, and might wish, to raise human children is one more example of anthropomorphism. Abominable snowmen get a lengthy review from Napier (1973:181), who concludes they are a product of our "insatiable appetite for ghouls and bogles." The *exotiká* of modern Greece are discussed by Stewart (1991).

103. Clark (1988:31–32) answers that humanity is *not* a natural kind, and that the persistent Western view that it is rests in religious, ideological, and political commitments, not biological ones. He notes that

> Essentialist accounts of humankind are still very popular, in scientific as well as political contexts. Efforts to define humans as tool-making animals, or language-users, or food-sharers, or time-binders and 'promising primates' . . . all rest upon an unconscious assumption that there is some one feature which distinguishes 'human beings' from 'non-human beings.' Aristotle knew better than that: generic kinds such as Birds, Fishes, Quadrupeds and Humans, were characterized not by some one essential property, but by complexes of resemblances and homologous structures.

104. Hearne 1986:37.

105. Barkan, op. cit., p. 32.

106. Berkeley 1939.

107. *Maya* often is translated as "illusion" but (as Donald Crosby, personal communication, points out) has a broad range of meanings in Hinduism and Buddhism; see Deutsch (1969) for its meaning in Advaita Vedanta, where it is central.

108. Bacon 1960:50.

109. Nietzsche, though one of the great critics of anthropomorphism (with Bacon, Spinoza, and Lange), himself finally came to employ it for this reason in his philosophy of science, as Stack (1980) points out.

110. Campbell 1952:79.

111. Harman 1974:vii.

112. Piaget 1970:19.

113. Wittgenstein 1969.

Chapter 4

1. I use the term template not in the technical psychological sense of an exact and inflexible criterion for identification, but in the broader, dictionary sense: "a gauge, pattern, or mold . . . used as a guide to the form of a piece being made" (*Webster's New Collegiate Dictionary,* 1977:1200).

2. See chapter 6. Although a search for extraterrestrial life is not in itself anthropomorphic, the way it is done often is, and apparent intelligent signals heard so far have turned out to be.

3. Hans Penner, personal communication.

4. Fillipow 1977:5.

5. Diamond 1988:22–24.

6. Karl Scheibe and Margaret Erwin (1979:103) note that we may have "pseudo-conversations [with] pets, plants, machines, or gods."

7. Ibid.

8. Mark Mattson (personal communication) notes that if a program can be intelligent it probably can plan, that in fact there are planning programs, and hence that the students may not be anthropomorphizing in this regard. He continues, however, that "volition will have to wait until we understand consciousness."

9. Eibl-Eibesfeldt 1975:491–493.

10. Hearne 1986:44.

11. *Push Pin Graphic* 1979. [No author or pagination provided in original.]

12. Browne 1987.

13. McPhee 1990:58–59.

14. Heider and Simmel 1944:243–259.

15. Ibid., pp. 246–247.

16. In Straus 1956:213, cited in Sheibe and Erwin, op. cit.

17. Jansen 1973.

18. Alpers 1983:80–82. Chapter 5 further discusses this instance and reproduces the image.

19. Barkan 1975:41.

20. Chapter 5 elaborates.

21. Oatley 1978:159.

22. Ibid.; see also chapter 2.

23. Gregory 1973, Gombrich 1973, Neisser 1976, and Griffin 1984.

24. Arbib and Hanson 1987:35–36.

25. Roberts, in Oatley, op. cit.

26. The example is from Oatley, op. cit., pp. 1–2.

27. Johannson 1973.

28. Arnheim 1969:27. The term templates here again has a broad and flexible sense rather than the narrower one of contemporary psychology.

29. Oatley, op. cit., p. 193.

30. Griffin 1984:53.

31. Oatley, op. cit., pp. 189–191.

32. Ibid., p. 191.

33. Arbib and Hanson, op. cit., p. 43.

34. Rosch et al. 1976.

35. Oatley, op. cit., p. 209.

36. Rosch et al., op. cit., p. 384.

37. Ibid., p. 190.

38. Arnheim 1974:43.
39. Gombrich 1973:204–207.
40. Gregory 1973.
41. Gombrich 1956:103.
42. Reviews of over thirty years of research on infant face perception are in Field (1985), Maurer (1985), and Nelson (1985). See also Stern (1985) and Dodwell et al. (1987).
43. The disagreement may stem partly from differences in research methods. Media presented to infants include line drawings, photographs, films, video tapes, live faces, and holographs, which differ significantly. Their contents also vary, ranging from juxtapositions of normal and distorted schematic faces, to juxtapositions of the infant's mother and strangers, to moving facial expressions. The results cannot be directly compared. Another problem is that the results, consisting largely of attention spans, are ambiguous. For example, researchers usually interpret longer spans as showing preference; but when the picture is of a frown, they may interpret longer spans as indicating significance.
44. Field 1982.
45. Meltzoff 1985:27.
46. Field, op. cit., p. 31.
47. Bower and Wishart 1979.
48. Goren et al. 1975.
49. Ibid., p. 547, cited in Maurer, op. cit., p. 74.
50. The discrepancy might be explained by the emergence of other abilities, such as depth perception, not long after birth. Such abilities may interfere with a focus on patterns of expression. Maurer, op. cit., reviews her own work and that of others using similar techniques. For a review of infant perception of facial expressions in various media and in live faces, see Charles A. Nelson (1985).
51. Sackett 1966.
52. Desimone et al. 1984.
53. Mark Mattson, personal communication.
54. Maurer, op. cit., p. 97.
55. Ibid., p. 73.
56. Ellis 1981:1.
57. Greenberg and Mitchell (1983) provide a standard review of object-relations psychoanalysts and their relation to Freud, including Melaine Klein, Harry Stack Sullivan, Erich Fromm, W.R.D. Fairbairn, John Bowlby, D. W. Winnicott, Heinz Kohut, and others. Greenberg and Mitchell are my primary source on this topic.
58. Ibid., p. 131.
59. Klein, cited in Greenberg and Mitchell, op. cit., p. 132.
60. Sullivan 1953:233, in Greenberg and Mitchell, op. cit., p. 105.
61. Greenberg and Mitchell, op. cit., p. 80.
62. Ibid., p. 103, describing Sullivan's view of the self. His view, incidentally, resembles both Buddhist and Japanese concepts of the self, as an illusion and as composed of social relationships, respectively.
63. Ibid., p. 173. One is reminded of H. F. and M. K. Harlow's (1962) infant rhesus monkeys, which clung to terry-cloth-clad wire "mothers" even when these offered nothing but a shape and texture.
64. Ibid., p. 185.
65. Ibid.
66. Ibid., pp. 226–227.

67. Stern 1985:28.
68. Greenberg and Mitchell, op. cit., p. 227.
69. Ibid., pp. 360–361.
70. I owe the reference to the object-relations school to Robert Orsi (personal communication).
71. Greenberg and Mitchell, op. cit, pp. 405–406.
72. The object-relations and attachment views that sociality is central to us find support in some recent work on empathy and altruism. Although most contemporary psychologists (in the West, at least) assume people are selfish and ultimately care only about themselves, C. Daniel Batson (1990:336) thinks we are "very social animals indeed" not only in thought and action but also in motivation. His experimental questionnaires suggest "that not only do we care but also that when we feel empathy for others in need, we are capable of caring for them for their own sakes and not our own."

Batson's view would be less surprising in cultures other than our own individualistic one. In Japan, for example, humans are assumed fundamentally social, and a common view of individuals is that they essentially are nodes in networks. Hence Japanese psychotherapies, both secular and religious, tend to assume almost any problem may stem from a problem in social relationships (Reynolds 1976, 1980, 1983, Guthrie 1988).
73. Beck and Molish 1967. Elsewhere Beck (1968), Semeonoff (1976), and others say viewers of ink blots most commonly see them as animals other than humans. However, since the Rorschach category "animal" includes all animals other than humans—for example, amoebas, jellyfish, worms, insects, fishes, reptiles, birds, and all nonhuman mammals—its predominance is hardly surprising. As Klopfer (1942:214) notes, the animal kingdom has endless forms and shapes. Accordingly, it has endless versatility for interpreting blots. However, if we take *Homo sapiens* as one species among others, it is radically predominant, as an interpretation, over any other.
74. One might object that Rorschach interpretations are not unbiased, since the blots are bilaterally symmetrical and hence may prejudice interpreters to see humans and other animals, most of which also are bilaterally symmetrical. However, there also are other symmetries, such as those of plants and of crystals, which most viewers overlook. Moreover, many viewers do not see the symmetries of blots as individual persons or animals, but instead as pairs of people or animals. One still might say that the blots are prejudicial because people and animals often do come in pairs. But the couples that real people and animals form often are *not* symmetrical: for example, one of the pair often is larger or is shaped differently. (It may, for example, have antlers.) In daily life, we also often pair objects, such as salt and pepper, bottles, or watches, which are not in themselves symmetrical. Intrinsic symmetry is not necessary to the pairing toward which our thought tends. The symmetry of ink blots, then, does not explain why people usually interpret them as humans or parts of humans.
75. De Vos and Boyer 1989.
76. Piaget 1929. Modern critics of Piaget dispute aspects of the stages of development he asserts for children's conceptions. However, most developmental psychologists agree that animism, anthropocentrism, and anthropomorphism are prominent in children's thought, especially among younger children (Laurendeau and Pinard 1962, Keil 1979:132–133, Inagaki and Hatano 1987).
77. Ibid., p. 262.

78. Ibid., p. 212.

79. Ibid., p. 197.

80. Piaget's findings here seem to support Nietzsche's view of all human thought as anthropocentric and even Nietzsche's view that all our concepts of objects are anthropomorphic. Piaget also notes that the child tries to understand the entire world as the outcome of regular, coherent principles and laws but—again bearing out Nietzsche—that the laws invoked are not physical, but moral and social ones.

81. Piaget op. cit., p. 196. Although these responses are from an eight-and-a-half-year-old, they are typical of the first stage.

82. Ibid., p. 199.

83. Ibid., p. 200.

84. Ibid., p. 374.

85. Ibid., p. 375.

86. Donald Crosby (personal communication) says there is a difference: that Aristotle's natural ends usually are "not 'purposes' or 'goals' in the intentional sense. They are simply *termini* which usually characterize the career of a thing, e.g., acorns becoming oaks (but not with conscious purposes or because of divinely ordained purposes)."

87. For example, one informant recalled being nearly guillotined as a child by a falling window sash. He perceived the fall as intentional and for a long time harbored anger and suspicion toward the window.

88. Such parental omnipotence and omniscience encourage Bovet (1928), building on Piaget, to argue that children's conceptions of God are mainly extensions of their conceptions of their parents.

89. Some critics call his account culture-bound because he focuses on Swiss children, with some data from Parisian and Spanish ones. However, what little similar work has been done in other cultures (for example, Inagaki and Hatano 1987, Ciborowski and Price-Williams 1982, Dasen 1977) either supports Piaget's description or at least does not contradict it except in matters minor for us. A view that our orientation to humans begins even earlier comes from Freud, and still other evidence from a student of Merleau-Ponty, James Ostrow. Ostrow (1990: vii) devotes a recent book to the claim that "Human existence is inherently social by virtue of the sensitivity that immerses us within the world prior to the discrimination of objects of knowledge."

90. As noted earlier, Stern (1985) says there is no time when the self/other distinction is not made, and Coy (1988) writes that various social animals make it as well.

91. Inagaki and Hatano (op. cit., p. 1020), as noted in chapter 3, recently have written similarly about child animism that an "animistic or personifying tendency is not necessarily a sign of intellectual immaturity" because it may constitute an "educated guess" based on analogy.

92. One of these few is Edelgard Jessen's study of the perception of circles, squares, and triangles as male or female, in Germany and East Africa. Personal communication from Myrdene Anderson.

93. Much of the following material on folk literature comes from Thompson 1955.

94. Thompson, op. cit., pp. 269–277. In Piaget's terms, such explanations of animal characteristics as rewards or punishments would be "artificialist," as they imply a humanlike agent.

95. Ibid., pp. 395–423. In English literature, Kenneth Graham's *The Wind in*

the Willows is a famous example. George Orwell's *Animal Farm* and Beatrix Potter's work are others.

96. Jensen 1974:153.
97. "All Things Considered," National Public Radio, February 1, 1990.
98. David Miretsky, personal communication.
99. Thompson, op. cit., pp. 141–145.
100. Taussig 1980.
101. Thompson, op. cit., pp. 150–154.
102. Ibid., pp. 151–152.
103. *The New York Times,* Nov. 28, 1978.
104. National Public Radio, n. d.
105. Thompson, op. cit., pp. 155–159.
106. Ehnmark 1939:113.
107. Thompson, op. cit., pp. 160, 197–199.
108. Goldman 1977.
109. Davis 1980.
110. Taussig, op. cit., p. 157.
111. Ibid., pp. 165–166.
112. Middleton 1984.
113. Wilford 1987.
114. Simons 1986.
115. *The New York Times,* Feb. 29, 1984, editorial page.
116. *Time* 1980. April 7, p. 31.
117. Curtis 1984:C13.
118. Suro 1987 (no page number).
119. Bateson 1958:231.
120. Thompson, op. cit., p. 106.
121. *The New York Times,* Nov. 30, 1980.
122. Ponte 1977.
123. Broyard 1978:C16.
124. *Outside* magazine flyer 1977.
125. Raban 1988:16.
126. *The New York Times,* Jan. 7, 1981, p. C1.
127. *The New York Times,* April 17, 1986.
128. Brecher 1988:18–20.
129. David et al. 1988.
130. Wandibba 1988:740–741.
131. Brown 1989:B1.
132. "All Things Considered." 1981. National Public Radio, Dec. 18.
133. Taussig 1980:5.

Chapter 5

1. Barkan (op. cit., p. 61) writes, "The image of the human body and its pervasiveness in thought and literature are reminders that not only the proper but in fact the only study of mankind is man."
2. Aeschylus, *The Daughters of Danae,* in Wheelwright 1962:149.
3. Forster 1924:9.
4. "Embrowned itself," as Hecht (1985:489) notes, suggests the "landscape is purposively engaged in its own transmutations."

5. *Return of the Native,* in Hecht, op. cit., p. 489.

6. Bloomfield 1963:164, 161.

7. Bloomfield 1980:292.

8. Brock 1985:184.

9. Brock, op. cit., p. 193.

10. Waley 1958:172.

11. Hecht (1985:486, 491) and Miles (1965), for example, respectively think the pathetic fallacy concerns "inanimate objects" and the "natural world."

12. Hecht 1985.

13. Frye 1957:105.

14. Bloomfield 1963:161.

15. Addison, *Spectator,* no. 419, 1712. Cited in Knapp 1985:1.

16. Donald Davie (1981:94) calls it a "trick of language," and Lavinia Griffiths (1985:1) says it is a "strange rhetorical device." Nancy Goslee (1988:220) finds it exhausted, as a "fallen rhetorical mode, not a newly creative plastic form." Josephine Miles (1965:2) calls it a "trite device, representative of a past period."

17. These few are primarily Sharma (1987) and, to a degree, Bloomfield (1963) and Miles (1965).

18. Bloomfield 1963:161.

19. Ibid., p. 163.

20. Hedley 1982:55.

21. Bloomfield, op. cit., p. 161.

22. M. H. Abrams (1978), for instance, makes animation and humanity alternative features of personification, predicated either upon the inanimate or the abstract: "either an inanimate object or an abstract concept is spoken of as though it were endowed with life or with human attributes or feelings." Nelson Goodman (1976:76–77) thinks "personification may . . . echo aboriginal animism." For Oliver Goldsmith (Siskin 1982:377), personification predicates rationality and agency upon morality or the inanimate: it represents "moral virtues, or inanimate beings as rational agents." Leonard Barkan (op. cit.) and R. S. Sharma (op. cit.), in a minority opinion, regard personification as a form of anthropomorphism.

23. Griffiths, op. cit., pp. 1, 4.

24. Ibid., pp. 50–51.

25. Barnet et al. 1960:43.

26. Quintilian, *Institutio Oratoria* 8.6.9–12, ed. H.E. Butler (Loeb Library), III, pp. 304–307. Cited in Bloomfield 1980:290.

27. For Prudentius, for example, see *Psychomachia.*

28. Siskin (op. cit., pp. 375–376) says personification as ornament stems, as in eighteenth-century England, from a politically conservative society in which literature communicates a "finite set of immutable truths." In this milieu, personification prevents "imitation from becoming repetitious by ornamenting or dressing up thought."

29. Goslee 1988:219. Goslee cites Earl Wasserman, "The Inherent Values of Eighteenth-Century Personification," PMLA 65 (1950): 440ff.

30. Wordsworth 1959:20–21.

31. Ruskin 1987:364.

32. Ibid.

33. Ibid., p. 365. Ruskin is preceded by about a century by Johann Georg Hamann in his view that the pathetic fallacy is caused by violent feelings. Hamann writes, "Passion alone gives to abstractions . . . hands, feet, wings, to images, and

signs, spirit, life, and tongue" (from *Aesthetics in a Nutshell,* 1763, in Smith 1960: 199).

34. Ibid., p. 374.
35. Miles, op. cit., p. vii. She counts appearances of the fallacy in twenty-one poets from Collins to Eliot and in several anthologies and finds a steady decline since the early nineteenth century.
36. Griffiths 1985:1.
37. *The Chicago Manual of Style* 1982:194.
38. Boas 1932:10–11.
39. Miles, op. cit., p. 53.
40. Tate 1941:58.
41. Eliot 1958:3.
42. Miles, op. cit.
43. Sharma, op. cit., p. 262.
44. Ibid., p. 262.
45. Van Brunt 1977.
46. Storace 1987:34.
47. Bugeja 1984:106–115.
48. Joyce 1961:28. Other examples from the many in *Ulysses* are, "Listen: a four-worded wavespeech: seesoo, hrss, rsseiss, ooos. Vehement breath of waters . . . spent, its speech ceases" (p. 39), and "Under the upswelling tide he saw the writhing weeds lift languidly and sway reluctant arms, hising up their petticoats, in whispering water swaying and upturning coy silver fronds" (p. 49).
49. Barich 1984: n. p.
50. Some writers would say that computers are not personified but anthropomorphized, since they are concrete, not abstract. However, as I shall suggest, the traditional distinction between personification and anthropomorphism is unclear and probably unimportant.
51. Broege 1983:186. Broege finds a "universal tendency in human nature to personify machines and technological products" and quotes Robert Heinlein's view (which confuses anthropomorphism with animism) that "machines are human because they are made in our image . . . all machinery is animistic." Heinlein's remark is too narrow, since we see not only machinery, but everything, in our image. His suggestion that machinery is peculiar in this regard is like David et al.'s, claim (op. cit.) that pottery is peculiar in the same way. Since all domains of experience are anthropomorphic, both Heinlein and the archaeologists stop well short of an adequate description.
52. Robinson 1987:8.
53. *Phaedrus,* 275d 2ff. Cited in Feyerabend 1988:162.
54. Miles, op. cit., p. 30.
55. Hecht, op. cit.
56. Hinks 1939:108.
57. Abrams (1986) discusses this personification in detail.
58. Ruskin, op. cit., p. 459.
59. Ruskin 1882:83–85. Although the central topic of this book is Greek myths, Ruskin here gives his own views, not Greek ones.
60. Ibid., pp. 101–102. Ruskin's relations between air and earth here sound like a nineteenth-century Gaia, or Earth-as-organism (cf. Lovelock, op. cit.).
61. Griffiths, op. cit., p. 17.
62. de Man 1984:246–247.

63. Miles, op. cit., p. 55.

64. Ruskin does not say in his primary critique, however, why violent feelings should deceive us in this particular way. Elsewhere, in *The Queen of the Air*, he does hint at a version of the comfort theory: myths originate when the "sun, or sky, or cloud, or sea [becomes] a trusted and companionable deity, with whom you may walk hand in hand, as a child with its brother or its sister." Ruskin, op. cit., p. 7.

65. de Man 1984:247.

66. Sharma, op. cit., pp. 257–259; see also James 1937. Karl-Heinz Fingerhut (1969) also suggests a drive, an "Anthropomorphisierungstrieb," and William Anderson (1990:44–45) writes of an "instinctive human need to anthropomorphize."

67. Bloomfield 1980:292.

68. Turner 1987:21.

69. Griffiths, op. cit., p. 47. Rosemond Tuve (1966:177, cited in Griffiths, op. cit.) also says it is hard to tell the "proud or envious man [from] pride or envy personified. One talks for example of Chaucer's Pardoner as the 'very essence of Covetousness in a human form.' "

70. Caughey (1984) shows at book length that in popular culture, the line between real and fictional persons is indistinct.

71. Griffiths, op. cit., p. 63.

72. Gombrich 1973:202–203.

73. Our tendency, shared with other vertebrates (Eibl-Eibesfeldt 1975:98, 183, 492–493), to see eyes is similar to the innate inclination to see faces that Gombrich and some developmental psychologists think infants have. The minimal pattern for eyes—two adjacent dark dots—is simpler than the pattern for faces and simple enough to be easily built into perception. The diverse kinds of camouflage that have evolved to hide the eye pattern also suggest that our inclination to see it is innate.

74. Ibid., pp.204–207.

75. Ibid., p. 210.

76. Ibid.

77. Arnheim 1974:6.

78. Ibid.

79. Mankiewicz 1978:40.

80. Fingesten 1961, Freedberg 1989, Gombrich 1969, Möseneder 1986, Sze 1963, Tyler 1947, Griffiths 1985.

81. Ingemanson 1984:27.

82. I have found no publications on either covert or overt anthropomorphism in commercial art. Gombrich (1969) and Möseneder (1986) briefly discuss anthropomorphism in painting, and Fingesten (1961) discusses it in Gothic church architecture. Barkan (1975) discusses the human body as a model in Western literature, architecture, and philosophy.

83. Kanner 1989:35.

84. Ibid., p. 53.

85. Ibid., p. 39.

86. Miller 1982:C6.

87. Brown 1989.

88. Ibid.

89. Key 1973, 1976, 1980. In a picture of a bottle of liquor and a glass with

liquor and ice, for example, Key finds inverted sharks, demons, and erotic print messages, all in reflections within the ice cubes. He does not assess the glass or its companion bottle as characters, though they are the explicit subjects of the picture. Nor does Key specifically mention anthropomorphism in advertising, though he does find human anatomy there. Key's work has been largely rejected by researchers in perception and cognition, such as Schulman (1981), Moore (1982), and Vokey and Read (1985).

90. An ad campaign run several years ago for a brand of clothing showed a man standing vertically and a woman leaning against him, with the caption, "A man you can lean on. That's Klopman." Print advertisements such as those above duplicate with objects, again implicitly male and female, the postures of the Klopman ad and the subordination they represent.

91. Joyce 1961:39.

92. Cited in Freedberg 1989:78.

93. Hollie 1984 (n. p.). The advertising agency calls this film, which cost twice the normal price, a breakthrough.

94. Ibid.

95. Levy-Bruhl 1966.

96. Rice and Paterson 1988, Reed 1976.

97. Reed, op. cit., p. 136

98. David et al., op. cit. (See chapter 4.) Their suggestion that people in some cultures see pots as human seems unsurprising in light of the material I have presented. Nonetheless, several respondents to their article, including anthropologists and an art historian, doubt that suggestion.

99. Evers and Huffman 1988:739, who also cite Aschwanden 1982, among others.

100. Ibid., p. 739. This perception is not limited to the Shona. Arnheim, discussing an Ingres painting, *La Source,* in which a young woman pours water from a jug, says that the "jug with its uterine connotations rhymes also with the body" (Arnheim 1974:154).

101. Fingesten 1955.

102. Ibid., p. 356.

103. Evers and Huffman, op. cit., p. 739.

104. Freedberg 1989:56.

105. Charsley 1987.

106. Sheraton 1979:A16.

107. Nancy P. Hickerson, personal communication.

108. Hinks, op. cit., p. 94.

109. Ibid., p. 17.

110. Ibid., p. 29.

111. Ibid., pp. 34–35.

112. Ibid., p. 51.

113. Ibid., p. 67.

114. Ibid., p. 75.

115. Ibid., p. 105.

116. *The New Yorker,* Oct. 23, 1989.

117. Sze, 1963; see below.

118. Hinks, op. cit., p. 109.

119. Ibid., p. 111. Emphasis mine.

120. Möseneder (1986) gives a bibliography, and Gombrich (1969), cited below,

also comments briefly on anthropomorphism in art.

121. Arnheim 1969:165.

122. Ibid.

123. Ibid., p. 278.

124. Ibid., p. 165.

125. Ibid., p. 94.

126. Gombrich 1956:103.

127. Gombrich 1969:103–104. He continues, "And do not language and metaphor testify that the class of things which subjectively cluster around the ideas of eye, mouth, or face is much wider than the anatomist's concept? To our emotion, a window can be an eye and a jug can have a mouth. . . . The headlights of a car may look to us like a pair of glowing eyes."

128. Stokes 1972:117.

129. Harding, *Principles and Practice of Art*, p. 53 (1845, London), in Landow 1971:254.

130. *Meteorology* I, ii; *De Rerum Natura* IV, 129ff.; and *Apollonius of Tyana* II, 22, cited in Jansen 1973. Philostratus, in fact, uses chance images to question the distinction between perception and representation. He points out that in perceiving figures in clouds, we must be representing the figures to ourselves, using the clouds as medium.

131. Alberti writes, in *De Statua*, "I believe that the arts which aim at imitating the creations of nature originated in the following way: in a tree trunk, a lump of earth, or in some other thing were accidentally discovered one day certain contours that needed only a very slight change to look strikingly like some natural object. Noticing this, people tried to see if it were not possible . . . to complete what still was lacking." (in Gombrich 1969:105–106).

132. Janson 1973:341.

133. Ibid., pp. 342–343.

134. Ibid.

135. Ibid.

136. Ibid., pp. 343–344.

137. Möseneder 1986.

138. Abbeville Press 1987:287.

139. Alpers 1983:80–82.

140. Larson 1979.

141. Ibid., p. 38.

142. Broyard 1981.

143. Baer 1988.

144. Jean Etienne Liotard, *Traité des Principes et des Règles de La Peinture*, cited in Gombrich 1969, op. cit.

145. Tyler 1947:50.

146. Ibid., p. 60.

147. David Miretsky, 1988, personal communication.

148. Sze 1963:84.

149. Ibid., Vol. II, p. 54.

150. Ibid., Vol. I, p. 89.

151. Ibid., Vol. II, p. 129.

152. Ibid., p. 131.

153. Ibid., p. 155.

154. Ibid., p. 158.

155. Freedberg 1989. This conception of animism seems ambiguous but, like most, may be glossed as the attribution of life to the lifeless.
156. Wollheim 1987:315, 354.
157. Freedberg, op. cit., p. 55.
158. Ibid., pp. 160, 245, 436.
159. Stokes, op. cit., p. 84.
160. Barkan 1975:117.
161. Ibid.
162. Vitruvius, *De Architectura* 1:159, cited in Barkan, op. cit.
163. Barkan, op. cit., p. 142.
164. Vitruvius, op. cit., 4.1; 1:209, in Barkan, op. cit., p. 143.
165. Ibid.
166. Austin 1637:75–76, in Barkan, op. cit., p. 127.
167. *Gesta Abatum Trudonensium,* cited in Barkan, op. cit., p. 135. William Durandus, an allegorist of the thirteenth century, also says the "arrangement of a material church resembleth that of the human body: the chancel, or place where the altar is, representeth the head; the transepts, the hands and arms, and the remainder—towards the west—the rest of the body" (Fingesten 1961:13–14).
168. Lomazzo 1598:108, in Barkan, op. cit.
169. Lomazzo, op. cit., pp. 111–112, in Barkan, op. cit. Barkan says this attribution of bodily proportion to the ark goes back to Origen and Augustine.
170. Barkan, op. cit., p. 142.
171. Ibid., p. 139.
172. Ibid., p. 140.
173. In *Rerum Italicarum Scriptores* ed. Muratori (Florence), cited in Barkan, op. cit., p. 141.
174. Fingesten, op. cit., p. 14.
175. Ibid., p. 15.
176. Ibid., p. 20. Fingesten says another critic, Francis Bond, calls this ridge "the 'spine' of the cathedral, but without seeing its further implications."
177. Ibid., pp. 20–21.
178. Hirn 1912.
179. Ibid., p. 17.
180. Stokes, op. cit., pp. 68, 78.
181. Fernandez 1982.
182. Ibid., p. 383.
183. Ibid., p. 387.
184. Ibid., p. 398. Fernandez continues that this assimilation resembles the "traditional assimilation of the women's cook house to the woman's body."
185. Cunningham 1972.
186. Ibid., p. 122.
187. Starr 1982.
188. Champlin 1979.
189. Brown 1990:15.
190. Deitch, n.d.

Chapter 6

1. A sociologist of science, Barry Barnes (1974:45), finds a "strong aversion to anthropocentrism and anthropomorphism" among scientists in

many ways: *a priori* opposition to teleological argument and theorizing, aversion to anthropomorphic or animistic theoretical entities, an insistent differentiation of fact and value, a cosmology firmly denying man any special significance . . . [and] in the rites and customs of science, notably in the style and form of the scientific paper, where the passive tense is now *de rigeur* and verbs, wherever possible, are converted to nouns."

Animism seems less taboo than anthropomorphism, and has adherents among scientists from Kepler to Lovelock, and a few among philosophers. A few philosophers defend anthropomorphism as well.

2. For example, Brightman (1971), Agassi (1973), and Ferré (1984) think anthropomorphism often is justified, and Nietzsche in his late work yields to what he sees as its inevitability.

3. The Babylonians, for instance, also had seen the stars and planets as gods, and as consisting largely of fire (to them, the stuff of gods and souls). A classicist, G.E.R. Lloyd, similarly notes that the Greek philosophers anthropomorphized the universe. They depended on "man's own experience of his fellow beings, [for] social, political and technological images [and for] vitalist notions. . . . [They] considered man himself as the type or model of a living creature," and considered the cosmos such a creature.

4. Ibid., p. 297.

5. Ibid., p. 299.

6. Although many people now see these two kinds of images as mutually exclusive, the Greeks evidently did not.

7. Lloyd, op. cit., p. 212.

8. Ibid. Lloyd continues (p. 213) that Anaximander deals not with "supernatural, anthropomorphic deities, but with cosmological forces." But what Lloyd means is only that Anaximander's cosmological forces have neither human physical form nor well-developed personae. They do have legal relationships, and such relationships are characteristically human.

9. Ibid., p. 213.

10. Heraclitus, Fr. 94, cited in Lloyd, op. cit., p. 214.

11. *Republic,* Books II and III. Plato's attack is on both logical and moral grounds.

12. Plato, *Philebus,* 28c.

13. Aristotle, *Metaphysics,* in Lloyd, op. cit., p. 230.

14. Plato, *Grg.* 507e, f, in Lloyd, op. cit., p. 226.

15. Cornford 1957:55.

16. Lloyd, op. cit., p. 235.

17. Ibid., p. 253.

18. Cornford 1957, 30c, d.

19. Ibid., 33b.

20. Ibid., 33c, d.

21. Plato, *Timaeus,* 44D–45B. In Cornford, op. cit., pp. 150–151.

22. Randall 1960:160.

23. Plato, *Timaeus* 34A–B, in Cornford, op. cit., p. 58.

24. Plato, *Laws* 898D.

25. Cornford, op. cit., p. 108.

26. Ibid., pp. 108–109.

27. Ibid., 40B–C. in Cornford, op. cit., p. 120.

28. Plato, *Phaedo,* cited in Cornford, op. cit., p. 332.
29. Plato, *Timaeus* 40A, in Cornford, op. cit., p. 119.
30. Randall, op. cit., p. 149.
31. Plato, *Timaeus* 50C–D, in Cornford, op. cit., p. 185.
32. Anaximander, Heraclitus, Diogenes, and others also see it as piloted by some intelligent force, usually inherent in all matter (Lloyd, op. cit., pp. 272–273).
33. Lloyd, op. cit., pp. 277–278.
34. Plato, *Timaeus* 28C.
35. Lloyd, op. cit., pp. 285–286.
36. Aristotle, *De Caelo* II, Ch. 3:286a 8, 9; cited in Randall, op. cit. Here and elsewhere, as Piaget (1929, drawing on Brunschvig) notes, Aristotle's artificialism resembles that which is spontaneous in children. Everything that has some use exists for that use. Bacon and especially Spinoza, as we shall see, call attention to this same artificialist tendency in human thought.
37. Randall, op. cit., p. 286.
38. Ibid., p. 138. This army, Randall says, is in a

> continuous process of promotion . . . aiming at the General, and the whole army is kept going by the promotions that have actually been made. Nature is kept operating by. . . men begetting, hens laying, acorns oaking, and the rest. There must clearly be a General, an End toward which all the processes are directed.

Because of this urge to perfection, and because its ultimate motivation is attraction to the General—the Unmoved Mover—some later Christian philosophers saw Aristotle as religious and his Unmoved Mover as God. Randall (op. cit., p. 136) persuasively denies this equivalence. He says Aristotle is naturalistic and the Unmoved Mover is "not the 'creator' of anything, for the world is eternal, [nor] even the 'sustainer' of the world [for] the world does not need to be sustained." Moreover, the "Unmoved Mover exercises no providence, it has no 'will' and no 'purpose.' It does not 'know' the world: it does not 'know' anything. . . . [Rather,] it is an intelligible structure or order, a principle of intelligibility."
39. Ibid., pp. 138–139.
40. Randall finds Aristotle here a Platonist, following the "logic of the lover's discourse" rather than the logic of physics. Randall sees this choice of logics as a fallacy. His explanation of the fallacy is much the same as Ruskin's explanation of the pathetic fallacy, namely, that it is caused by strong feelings (Randall, op. cit., p. 140).
41. Barkan, op. cit., p. 71.
42. Fitting 1876:48, cited in Barkan, op. cit., p. 71.
43. Nicholas of Cusa, *De Concordantia Catholica,* in Barkan, op. cit., p. 74.
44. Cassirer 1963:110.
45. Barkan 1975:37.
46. Ibid., p. 41.
47. Richter 1939, cited in Barkan, op. cit., p. 43.
48. Willis 1847:3–4, cited in Barkan, op. cit., p. 44.
49. Agassi (1975:90), a modern philosopher of science, calls him the "*locus classicus* of the critique of anthropomorphism."
50. Bacon 1960:60.
51. Ibid., p. 52.
52. Ibid., pp. 51–52.

53. However, Bernard Gilligan (personal communication) points out that the pre-Socratic Atomists and the later Greek and Roman Epicureans also "emphasized a non-teleological view of nature."

54. Ibid., p. 47.

55. Ibid., p. 48. Subsequent quotations from Bacon are from Aphorisms XLII–XLV, pp. 48–50.

56. Bacon anticipates to some degree the modern linguists Edward Sapir and Benjamin Lee Whorf, who hold that the grammar and vocabulary of particular languages largely determine the world views of their speakers.

57. Ibid., pp. 64–65.

58. Galilei 1953:112.

59. Ibid., p. 113.

60. Ibid., p. 79. Galileo does seem to hesitate somewhat in attributing valor to the moon, qualifying the term with "as it were."

61. One might object that Galileo may be using metaphor self-consciously. Even if that is so, his metaphor still springs from the same source as unconscious anthropomorphism. Moreover, Galileo is in a tradition of anthropomorphizing astronomers. Copernicus wrote that the sun rules the solar system as God rules the universe, and "sits upon a royal throne ruling his children the planets which circle around him" (cited in Boas 1932, in turn cited in Tambiah 1990:17). Tambiah notes that Kepler also compared the sun to God, and even located God there.

62. Spinoza 1955.

63. Spinoza 1955:80. Subsequent quotations are from the same work, pp. 75–80 and p. 188.

64. Stack 1980.

65. Midgley 1983:127, in Ferré 1984:209–210. As it happens, Midgley also is discussing anthropomorphism. She points out that ascribing feelings to animals is not necessarily an instance, since they probably do have feelings.

66. Stack 1983:127.

67. Nietzsche 1901:XXIII, 55.

68. A contemporary American artist, James Turrell, shows this is true of our perception of light: we almost always see "objects," not light itself.

69. Stack, op. cit., p. 134. Stack's remark—that the notion of "thing" is a resting place for our thoughts—resembles Proudfoot's (op. cit.) assertion that in Schleiermacher the notion of God is an empty marker.

70. Ibid., p. 135.

71. Nietzsche (*Die Fröhliche Wissenshcaft*) in Stack 1980:57.

72. Stack, op. cit.

73. Stack (op. cit., p. 67) summarizes the lengthy circle of Nietzsche's critique of anthropomorphism: it

> moves from the human to the deanthropomorphic limits of the quantified world of dynamic physical theory back to the human standpoint. Neither our senses, nor our reason, nor our philosophical imagination can transcend the inevitability of a humanizing process that haunts our attempts to understand ourselves, the experiential world, the physical structure of reality and the nature of 'ultimate reality.'

74. Agassi 1973.

75. Although Agassi's view that anthropomorphism may be either valid or not is

unusual, it is not unique. For example, Ferré (1984:203), a philosopher of religion, calls anthropomorphism in general "inevitable and often justified," and Brightman (1965:314) writes,

> all knowledge—scientific, philosophical, or religious—must be based on human experience and reason; hence, anthropomorphism is unavoidable. The question should be: what kind of anthropomorphism, critical or uncritical? And the answer to this, it is said depends on the relations between human experience and reality: what human experience, if any, affords models of the real; what anthropomorphism is false, what true?

76. Agassi thinks anthropocentrism is the "idea that the universe is created for the benefit of man." But Lange, Nietzsche, and Spinoza show that anthropocentrism is not this idea, but consists in perceiving the world with human interests and human senses, whether or not we see the world as made for us.
77. Gould 1986:10.
78. Lloyd, op. cit., p. 270.
79. Ibid., p. 271.
80. Barnes, op. cit., p. viii.
81. Fedigan 1982:16–17.
82. Veblen 1908:35.
83. Planck 1925:7.
84. Nunn 1927:14.
85. Ibid., p. 15.
86. Ibid., p. 33.
87. Ibid., p. 35.
88. Grünbaum (1976:12) identifies one of the debaters as E. T. Jaynes (1965), who in turn attributes the remark, "Entropy is an anthropomorphic concept," to E. P. Wigner. This debate seems to merge anthropomorphism with anthropocentrism: Jaynes (op. cit., p. 398) says entropy is anthropomorphic as a "property, not of the physical system, but of the particular experiments you or I choose to perform on it."
89. 'Q & A,' in "Science Times," *The New York Times,* October 2, 1984.
90. Maddox 1990.
91. *The New York Times* 1981:C2.
92. Whitworth 1989:126.
93. Greene 1959:42.
94. Wright 1988.
95. Browne 1987a:C1.
96. National Public Radio, July 16, 1979.
97. Gelman et al. 1977:32. Sagan (op. cit.) seems to have high hopes: "The scientific, logical, cultural and ethical knowledge to be gained by tuning into galactic transmissions may be . . . the most profound single event in the history of our civilization."
98. Weston (1988) says humans in earlier times would have sent messages very different in form and content from modern ones, and he finds little reason to think any extraterrestrial beings might send messages in the forms now being looked for. He thinks the astronomers looking for such signals are anthropomorphizing wildly and says science-fiction writers do much better at reducing anthropomorphism.
99. Roberts 1989:2B.

100. Ibid., p. 2B.
101. Newton, *Opticks,* Query 31, and *Principia* ("General Scholium" to the 2nd ed.), respectively. Cited in Gaskin 1988:14–15.
102. Einstein 1934:28, cited in Gaskin 1988:11.
103. Earman (1987) reviews proponents of four forms of the anthropic principle: the weak, the strong, the participatory, and the final.
104. Earman (op. cit.) lists Robert H. Dicke, Brandon Carter, Steven Hawking, G.F.R. Ellis, John D. Barrow, and others writing in scientific journals including *Nature, The Astrophysical Journal, Journal of the Royal Astronomical Society, Philosophical Transactons of the Royal Society,* and *Observatory,* as well as in more popular ones including *Sky and Telescope, Psychology Today,* and *Scientific American.*
105. Carter 1974:293, cited in Earman 1987. What "taking account" means here, however, remains unclear.
106. Tipler 1982:37, in Earman, op. cit.
107. John Barrow (1983:149) writes that the "universe must contain life," and Barrow and Tipler (1986:22) that "observers are necessary to bring the universe into being."
108. Carter 1974; Earman, op. cit.; and Barrow and Tipler 1986, who, in a compendious book, wish, for example, to "highlight a number of extraordinarily finely tuned coincidences upon which the possible evolution of observers appears to hinge."
109. Barrow and Tipler, op. cit., p. 15. However, they cheerfully continue, "rather, astronomers seem to like to leave a little flexibility in its formulation perhaps in the hope that its significance may thereby . . . emerge in the future."
110. F. Dyson (in *Disturbing the Universe,* cited in Earman, op. cit., p. 307), for example, writes,

> I conclude from these accidents of physics and astronomy that the universe is an unexpectedly hospitable place for living creatures to make their home in. Being a scientist . . . I do not claim that the architecture of the universe proves the existence of God. I claim only that the architecture of the universe is consistent with the hypothesis that the mind plays an essential role in its functioning.

111. Earman, op. cit., pp. 309, 315.
112. Pagels 1985:34–38, cited in Earman, op. cit.
113. John Wheeler (1986:vii) writes in a single short paragraph, for example, "Meaning is important, is even central . . . The universe is adapted to man . . . a life-giving factor lies at the centre of the whole machinery and design of the world." Little appears to connect these claims but anthropomorphism and anthropocentrism.
114. Gary 1975:185.
115. Ibid., p. 186.
116. Hubbell 1988:56.
117. Virgil, cited in Hubbell, op. cit., p. 69.
118. Ibid., p. 70. Butler's anthropomorphism here doubtless is self-conscious; but self-conscious anthropomorphism, like other metaphors, still springs from the same source as naive anthropomorphism.
119. Gould, op. cit., p. 10. Gould says this prejudice pervades our attitudes toward larvae, but can be weakened by considering the glowworm, *Arachnocampa*

luminosa, of New Zealand. The glowworm larva is far more imposing, by its luminescence, complex nesting and feeding habits, and carnivory, than the smaller and shorter-lived adult. Gould's point is that the human adult/child contrast is a misleading model for understanding insects.

120. Seger 1989:741–742.
121. Caplan 1978.
122. Allen 1978, Burian 1978.
123. Burian, op. cit., p. 378.
124. Malone 1986:421. Malone says Wilson's attempt to 'biologicize' ethics is "nothing but the bad arguments, straw men, bogus distinctions, and other types of confusions many philosophers have noted."
125. Dusheck 1985:253.
126. Miller 1985:297.
127. Hellerstein 1984:77.
128. Dawkins 1978.
129. Judson 1978:98.
130. Bernstein 1979:34.
131. Wills 1989, cited in Lewin 1989:26.
132. Silberner 1986:254.
133. Lovelock 1990:100. Lovelock and a colleague, Lynn Margulis, reached this formulation in 1973, but he reendorses it in the later article.
134. Lovelock 1987: xii, 9.
135. Ibid., p. 49.
136. Young 1985:87.
137. Ibid., p. 87.
138. Ibid., p. 92.
139. Ibid., p. 93.
140. Ibid., p. 94.
141. Ibid., p. 100.
142. Ibid., p. 125.
143. Asquith 1984, 1986, Fedigan 1982.
144. Those who think anthropomorphism may be useful mean by that not the mistaken attribution of specifically human characteristics to nonhuman animals but the attribution to animals of human features generally, some of which may turn out to be shared.
145. Asquith 1984.
146. Asquith 1986.
147. Fedigan 1982:18.
148. Freud (1964:90) even anthropomorphizes science itself: "Science has many open enemies . . . who cannot forgive her for having weakened religious faith. . . . She is reproached for the smallness of the amount she has taught us [but] in this, people forget how young she is."
149. Freud 1923:25.
150. Sullivan 1924:9.
151. Angier 1990:C1.
152. Powell 1969:116–117.
153. Aleksandrov, in Kelley 1988:155.
154. Glazkov, in Kelley, op. cit., p. 120.
155. Makarov, in Kelley, op. cit., Preface.
156. Bean, in Kelley, op. cit., p. 72.

157. Overmyer, in Kelley, op. cit., p. 108.
158. Sevastyanov, in Kelley, op. cit., p. 146.
159. Volkov, in Kelley, op. cit., p. 5.

Chapter 7

1. That is, something like a "superhuman person . . . worshipped as having power over nature and the fortunes of mankind; a deity" (*Oxford Universal Dictionary* 1955:808). By this standard definition, gods are, first of all, persons. Correspondingly, worship is a social activity furthering a relationship between persons (human persons may be called "your worship," and gods conversely may be reviled) and not, for example, to relations between persons and things. I construe the term superhuman here as relative not absolute, because gods may be only marginally superior to humans, and may grade into spirits, ghosts, and demons, which may be inferior to humans.

Some scholars of religion (for example, Spiro 1966 and Penner 1989) prefer the phrase "superhuman being" to the term "god." But this phrase—unless one specifies that the being is a person—might include such beings as the sun, whose power and influence on the Earth are superior to those of humans, but which is not necessarily a religious object. On the other hand, "superhuman being" seems (since the vagueness of "being" shifts emphasis to "superhuman") to exclude varied spirits, etc., which often are part of religious systems, but which in important ways are inferior to humans. Lawson and McCauley (1990) usefully suggest action and intention with their entry, "superhuman agent." Another possible alternative is "nonhuman person." This still should suit Penner, for example, since he says (1989:9), "I mean someone who does things we cannot do." On the question of whether all religions do have gods (Buddhism often is claimed as an exception), chapter 2 reviews Durkheim's rejection of this claim.

2. Some people (for example J. Samuel Preus, personal communication) find mysticism problematic for any definition of religion that depends on the religious object, since mystics may deny that *their* object can be defined. Hume (1947) gives one response to this problem: such mystics really are skeptics or atheists in disguise. Penner (1989:9–10) gives another: mysticism never is freestanding but always is part of some larger religious system, the objects of which are more amenable to description. I suggest a third response: that even the "wholly other" may be viewed (as we have seen even inanimate objects are) unconsciously or implicitly as a person.

3. Penner (1989:11) understatedly calls these beings "one of the major unresolved puzzles in the study of religion."

4. Nilsson 1949:144.

5. Murray 1955:9.

6. Boas 1935:94; White 1949. Neither Boas nor White gives a satisfying account of anthropomorphism, however. White, as we saw, gives what I have called the confusion explanation. Boas offers no explicit explanation but seems to hold the familiarity view. However, his position that anthropomorphism is not a "rationalization but . . . an automatic reaction" agrees with mine.

7. Levi-Strauss 1966:221; emphasis his.

8. Evans-Pritchard (1970:7) writes that, though anthropomorphism in the Nuer God is "very weak," still "man's relationship to him is, as it is among other peoples, on the model of a human social relationship." Malefijt (1968:149) says

that although deities do not always have human form, they always have some human characteristics. Spiro (1966:96–98) describes gods as superhuman beings who can be influenced by ritual or symbolic actions. Jarvie and Agassi (1967:58, respectively a philosophical anthropologist and a philosopher) say anthropomorphism, together with revelation, distinguishes religion from magic and science.

Those anthropologists who do not acknowledge the anthropomorphism of religion are largely the symbolists, who see religion as doing something especially encoded and covert, rather than what it is doing on the surface. For the symbolists religion does not anthropomorphize, because it really concerns *only* human society.

9. Spencer 1870:442.
10. Feuerbach 1957 [1841]:17, 19.
11. Werblowsky 1987:317.
12. Idowu 1973:59.
13. As S. J. Tambiah (1990:6, drawing on Yehezkel Kauffmann, 1972) remarks, Israelite monotheism not only has but one God, but also has "no realm, primordial or otherwise, to limit his sovereignty. Such a supreme God therefore cannot be the focus of any mythology."
14. Ibid.
15. In Tambiah's (op. cit., pp. 7–8) words, "Judeo-Christian monotheism is honour bound to declare any conception of a cosmos, in which man and transcendental entities share certain similar properties and capacities . . . magical and pagan."
16. Freeman 1966:22.
17. Marmorstein 1927.
18. Stroumsa 1983:269.
19. Buber 1952:14–15, cited in Krasner, 1975. Krasner (p. 12) agrees that encounter with God is "most adequately described in anthropomorphic terms."
20. Schorsch 1988:69, 66.
21. Neusner 1988:23.
22. Ibid., p. 28.
23. These stories (ibid., p. ix) depict him as "(1) corporeal; (2) exhibiting traits of emotions like those of human beings; (3) doing deeds that women and men do, in the way in which they do them."
24. Donald Crosby (personal communication) urges, however, that the *via negativa* remains an important theme in Judaism.
25. Aquinas, *Summa Theologica,* Q. 13, Art. 2, in Ferré 1980.
26. Duggan 1979:195.
27. Ferré 1980:32.
28. Jevons 1913:573–574.
29. Prestige 1952.
30. Clement of Alexandria, in Prestige 1952:9.
31. Prestige, op. cit., pp. 55–56.
32. Augustine, *De Moribus Ecclesiae* X, 17, cited in Teske 1986:255.
33. Prestige, op. cit. Augustine's view of God as a material object evidently reflected the popular Greek notion of spirit as material.
34. Newman 1870:5–6.
35. Ibid., pp. 3–4.
36. Newman's contemporaries, religious and secular, also remark on religious

anthropomorphism. Feuerbach (1957 [1873], 1967) is the leading secular writer of that era on the topic. William Whitney (1881) also writes that religion is essentially anthropomorphism, and reasonable but mistaken. Moses Phelps (1881) and A. H. Craufurd (1909) call religion "anthropomorphistic," but reasonable and true.

37. Gibb and Kramers (1953:583). Wagtendonk (1987) gives a more recent discussion.

38. Palmer 1973:36.

39. Brandon 1970:86.

40. Nielsen 1974:199.

41. Meynell 1977:42.

42. Gallus 1972:546.

43. Palmer (1973:xv), for example, writes, "if theologians use words in their ordinary sense, their theology will be anthropomorphic. If on the other hand a term is to mean something quite different when applied to God, then theology is incomprehensible." Ian Barbour (1974:19) says, "if familiar terms are predicated of God literally (univocally), one ends in anthropomorphism. But if no familiar terms can be predicated, except equivocally, one ends in agnosticism. (If divine love in no way resembles human love, the term is vacuous.)"

44. Feuerbach 1957:14–15.

45. Ferré 1984:203.

46. Ibid., pp. 206, 208–209. Emphasis his.

47. Tillich 1973:127.

48. Tillich 1951:245.

49. Tillich 1973:72.

50. Tillich 1948:63.

51. Williamson 1976:5–9.

52. Crosby 1981:226.

53. Pailin 1990:42.

54. Gaskin 1984:15, 16.

55. Werblowsky, op. cit., p. 319. Ferré (1980:31), for example, holds that the " 'otherness' of ultimate reality . . . can be pushed too far . . . theological stress on absolute incommensurability between man and God can become a baseless and misleading dogma." Pailin (1990:35) writes, "Those who state that God is 'utterly other' similarly make it impossible to justify, and even to apprehend, the meaning of their claim."

56. Swinburne 1977:1. The rest of the book tries to show that such belief is coherent.

57. Coles 1990:48. See also Piaget 1928, Bovet 1928, Heller 1986.

58. Braithwaite 1955, Phillips 1970, 1976.

59. Gaskin, op. cit., p. 108. See also Swinburne 1977, especially chapter 6, for an argument against the view that religion consists only of recommendations and values.

60. Ibid., p. 19. Elsewhere (1988:37), Gaskin refers to their "rarified eccentricities."

61. Freud 1964 [1927]:51–52. He continues, "Critics persist in describing as 'deeply religious' anyone who admits to a sense of man's insignificance in the face of the universe, although . . . the religious attitude is not this feeling but only the next step after it, the reaction to it."

62. Greenberg 1980:196.
63. Gaskin 1988:1 and Preus 1987:84, respectively.
64. Gaskin 1984:69. Gaskin points out that although the design argument often is associated with Christianity, it also appears independently. It probably appears universally.
65. Xenophon, *Memorabilia*, I, iv, 6–7, cited in Gaskin 1984:69.
66. Aquinas, in Gaskin 1984:70.
67. Gaskin 1988:11–15; see also chapter 6.
68. Swinburne 1979:136.
69. Gaskin 1988.
70. Ibid., pp. 43–44. Gaskin points out that Hume (*Dialogues*, 184–185) suggests that during an infinite time, chance will produce "some forms, whose parts and organs are so adjusted as to support the forms amidst a continued succession of matter," and that any animal "immediately perishes whenever this adjustment ceases, and . . . its matter corrupting trie[s] some new form." Hume's anticipation of Darwin, as Gaskin notes, explains structural order in organisms and "fatally weakens" the teleological argument for design.
71. Gaskin 1988:127, 6; emphasis his. In another apt remark, Gaskin (1988:6) says, "we have a strong . . . propensity to believe in god(s) from the fact of natural order: a propensity we misread as the soundness of the design argument." Seeing this propensity as an aspect of anthropomorphism may help mitigate the misreading.
72. Hume 1947:154f.
73. Hume 1932: I, 157.
74. Gaskin (1984:48) discusses these and other typical cosmic questions.
75. Feuerbach 1957:12.
76. Ibid.
77. Ibid.
78. Feuerbach (1957:xiii; originally in *Die Philosophie der Zukunft*, H. Ehrenberg, ed., in *Frommanns Philosophische Taschenbücher*, Stuttgart, 1992, p. 68) does note that anthropomorphism in general is primitive: "The idea of an object is originally nothing other than the idea of another I—thus in his childhood man thinks of all things as freely acting and arbitrary beings." His account of it, however, seems another version of the confusion theory.
79. Penner 1986, 1989.
80. Horton 1967:52. Penner also points out problems in Horton's positivist description of science. I agree that positivism is a weak account of science, as it is of other knowledge. However, it does not seem central to Horton's comparison of science and religion. Other accounts of science, such as probabilistic ones (for example, that of Suppe 1977), would do just as well or better.
81. Hume 1947:160–164.
82. Swinburne 1968:208.
83. Barkan (op. cit.) repeatedly says the human body is a popular and powerful model of the world because it accounts for great diversity within unity. True as Barkan's point is of the body, it is still truer of the human being as a whole.
84. Tambiah (1990:7) similarly notes that in "pagan" religion, including, for example, those of the Greeks, Persians, and Hindus, there are "no fixed bounds between gods and men."
85. Nilsson, op. cit., pp. 146–147, 156–157.
86. Guthrie 1950:118.

87. Lactantius 1964, cited in Saler 1983:4.

88. Ehnmark (1939:79) writes similarly that where ancestors are prominent, "no clear distinction can be maintained" between them and gods.

89. Guthrie 1988.

90. Kopytoff 1971.

91. Aiyappan 1976:140.

92. Ehnmark 1939:74.

93. Thompson 1955:99.

94. Ibid., pp. 146, 139.

95. Ehnmark 1939:74.

96. Aiyappan 1976:139.

97. Ibid., p. 146.

98. Thompson 1955:98–99.

99. Ibid., pp. 74–77, 100; also Ehnmark 1939:129 for the mortality of gods.

100. Ibid., pp. 88–89.

101. Wallace 1966:93–94.

102. Ehnmark 1939:73.

103. Holmberg, in Ehnmark, op. cit., p. 77.

104. Jochelson, *The Koryak,* p. 24, cited in Ehnmark, op. cit., p. 79.

105. Jenness, *The Life of the Copper Eskimos,* p. 188, in Ehnmark, op. cit., p. 79.

106. Ehnmark 1939:95n.

107. Ibid., pp. 94–97.

108. Bovet 1928.

109. Rizzuto 1979.

110. Coles 1990.

111. Ehnmark, op. cit., p. 99.

112. Singleton 1976.

113. Saler, n.d.

114. Caughey 1984.

115. Ibid., p. 7.

116. Ibid., p. 53.

117. Saler, n.d. Here the appelation "immortal" evidently is more than metaphoric.

118. National Public Radio, "All Things Considered," June 18, 1990. One might object that her comment is only metaphoric. But all language is metaphoric, if not self-consciously so; it depends on categorical perception, which decrees likeness among the unlike, making, for example, "cats" of the house cat and the tiger. Statements consciously meant "metaphorically" differ only in degree from those meant literally.

119. Durkheim 1965:85.

120. Goode (1951:43) also sees behavior as more important than appearance in gods, all of whom, he says, are "anthropopsychic," having the minds or psyches of humans. I prefer "anthropomorphic," used broadly to encompass both physical and psychical anthropomorphism, since both have the same source.

121. An anthropologist, Rodney Needham (1981:84), similarly doubts that "such typical activities as 'worship,' 'sacrifice,' 'prayer,' and so on are distinct modes of symbolic action and peculiar to religion . . . each case . . . is assimilable to some more general form of social action."

122. For example, Barbour (1971:1; emphasis his) says, "most writers today see science and religion as *strongly contrasting enterprises* which have essentially noth-

ing to do with each other." A psychologist, Paul Pruyser (1976:18, 47), alludes to a "profound but sublime irrationality of all religious propositions" and says "religious thought is unlike common sense [or] scientific thought." Philosophers Stuart Brown and Peter Winch (Brown 1977:254) agree that, unlike secular practices, "religious practices are not . . . informed by beliefs," and I. C. Jarvie and Joseph Agassi (1967:57, 71) find it "no longer controversial to regard religion as irrational" and say religion "defies most criteria of rational belief." The sociologist Talcott Parsons (1968:431) says ritual is "not to be measured by the standards of intrinsic rationality at all."

123. Proudfoot 1985, Horton 1982:201, and Gaskin 1984:31, among others, suggest that people who find religion incommensurable with secular thought and action are trying to defend it.

124. Anthropologists, for example, who identify religion with supernaturalism or nonempiricism include Goldenweiser 1922, Norbeck 1961, 1974, Wallace 1966, Spiro 1966, and Lowie 1970.

125. Durkheim 1965:477, Horton 1967, Barbour 1971, 1974.

126. Watts and Williams 1988:51.

127. Black 1962, Ortony 1979.

128. Watts and Williams, op. cit. Nonetheless, these writers continue (p. 52), "scientific disclosure doesn't have the same power to arouse feeling and commitment as religious experience." On my account, that is because it is not disclosing persons behind appearances.

129. Ibid., p. 58.

130. Ibid., p. 74.

131. Suppes 1977:283.

132. Lawson and McCauley 1990:162.

133. James (1902) argues, for instance, that religious phenomena are continuous with other phenomena.

134. Smith 1964.

135. Eire 1986:vii.

136. Saler, n.d.

137. Preus 1987:34.

138. Medin et al. (1987:256) do suggest that the "naturalness of family resemblance sorting might be tied to the idea of genetic variation." They tested the idea by telling subjects that a set of drawings of imaginary animals represented genetic relationships and asking them to sort the drawings. The assertion of genetic relationships had no apparent effect on the sorting.

139. These centers are the angular gyrus, Wernicke's area, and Broca's area. The first of these is less developed in our nearest relatives, the chimpanzees, than in humans, and the other two are absent. Other anatomical features crucial for speech, though not for symbolism, include aspects of the lips, tongue, teeth, pharynx, and larynx.

140. Pailin (1990:43) also sees a source of religion in an unconscious assumption of meaning: the "notion of God arises in part from people's . . . unconscious assumption . . . of meaning, purpose and value."

141. Merleau-Ponty 1962:xix. I owe reference to the quotation to Hans Penner, personal communication. In a common religious view, in contrast (and in that of Tambiah 1990:6), meaning stems not from a condemnation but from something "transcendent."

142. The phrase *"Homo semioticus"* appears in a review by Thomas Sebeok, although I do not know whether it is original there.

143. Ricoeur 1974:230.

144. Tambiah 1990:96.

145. Rorty 1979:189.

146. Rorty (1979:190) says that in our attitudes toward animals, any "sense of community [is] based on the imagined possibility of conversation."

147. Swinburne 1977:101. To the list of personal characteristics, Swinburne adds theories, moral judgments, and wanting to have, or not to have, other wants.

148. Buber 1960:35.

149. Krasner, op. cit., p. 9.

150. Padoux 1990.

151. S. J. Tambiah (1990:6) says that from a "general anthropological standpoint," the distinctive religious acts are those of symbolic communication. Raymond Firth (1967:12) and Frederik Barth (1975:11), also anthropologists, respectively call ritual a "formal set of procedures of a symbolic kind, involving a code for social communication" and a "mode of communication." Another anthropologist, Edward Norbeck (1974:12), writes that although some gods are not physically anthropomorphic, "all share traits that are necessary for comprehension by and communication with human beings." Benjamin Ray (1973), a historian of religion, sees language as the central element in ritual. Paul Ricoeur (1974:71) says religion can be "identified . . . as a kind of discourse." Ehnmark (op. cit., p. 103) notes that Earthmaker, the Creator of the Winnebagos, is formless and invisible, but nonetheless reveals himself as a voice and hence is "anthropomorphic in so far as he speaks." And Feuerbach (1957:193) says the "essential act of religion . . . is prayer."

152. James 1902:465.

153. Ibid.

154. For example, Hume (1954:13) writes, "we can make use of no Expression . . . in Prayers & Entreaties, which does not imply that these Prayers have an Influence [on God]." Jevons (1913:573), writing on anthropomorphism in religion, begins, "[man] has felt it not only desirable, but possible, to enter into communication with [powers other than and greater than he;] he has taken it as a fact that they can understand him when he addresses himself to them." In the Judaism Neusner (1988:22–23) describes, God is a "person who receives prayer," who speaks, and who may simply be called the Word. Watts and Williams (1988:113) agree prayer is not mere soliloquy; people praying believe they "are not merely talking to themselves." Hewes (1989) links an upper paleolithic expansion of religion to fully phonemic speech, which made possible hallucinatory vocal communications from gods.

155. Werblowsky 1987:320.

156. Geertz 1966:4.

157. Observers in varied disciplines ask why religious beliefs persist in the face of science, and so far have no good answer. Penner (1989:115, 122–123), for example, says "historians and phenomenologists of religion have abandoned [this question and] left it to . . . anthropology, clinical psychology and philosophy." But these fields have had no more luck. Penner (p. 116) also names "three stubborn problems; the problem of the rationality of religious beliefs, the problem of the truth of religious beliefs and . . . the persistence of religious beliefs."

158. Wittgenstein 1969, Campbell 1952:79, and Harman 1974:vii, respectively.
159. Durkheim 1965:477.
160. This controversy still is pursued, for instance, in Brown (1977), Horton and Finnegan (1982), and Penner (1986, 1989).
161. Goodall 1975:163–164.
162. Durkheim 1965:237.
163. *Webster's New Collegiate Dictionary* 1977:1000.
164. Horton 1960.
165. Lawson and McCauley (1990) see religious ritual as distinguished from other ritual only by its postulation of "superhuman agents," and the scholar of religion Frits Staal (1979) sees religious and other ritual as indistinguishable. Freud even thinks ritual occurs in solitary secular behavior. On still other accounts, virtually *all* cultural behavior is "ritualistic," in that it consists of performances that are predictable, communicative, and highly patterned.
166. Otto 1950. Swinburne (1977:293) summarizes Otto's "numinous being" as "one on whom we depend, something fearful, overpowering, vital, wholly other, and attractively fascinating." Freud would say these are just the features a father has for a young child. I would say they are part of any human social relationship. Feuerbach (1957:281) writes, "Man feels nothing towards God which he does not also feel towards man."

References

"Car Grilles." 1979. *Push Pin Graphic*. No. 77. [No author or pagination in original.]

"Cleaver's Confession." 1978. *The New York Times*. November 28. P. C6.

"Cloakroom Problem: A Place for Down." 1981. *The New York Times*. January 7. P. C1–10.

"Dragons of Winter." 1984. *The New York Times*, February 29. Op-Ed page.

"Hard Trip Ends in Welcome by Eritreans." 1977. *The New York Times*, July 11. P. 8.

"Mother Nature Exposed as Polluter." 1980. *The New York Times*, November 30. Op-Ed page.

"Science Watch: A Really Big Syzygy." 1981. *The New York Times*. March 31. P. C2.

"Tale of a Whale a Lot of Trash." 1980. *The New York Times*, June 15. P. 28.

"The Call Went Through; Umbrella Was Disconnected." 1986. *The New York Times*, April 17.

"Tupperware Party." 1981. "All Things Considered." *National Public Radio*. December 18.

'Q & A,' in "Science Times." 1984. *The New York Times*, October 2. P. C6.

"Will She Spit Thunder Eggs?" 1980. *Time* magazine, April 7. P. 31.

Abbeville Press. 1987. *The Arcimboldo Effect*. Gruppo Editoriale Fabbri S.A., Milano. New York: Abbeville Press.

Abrams, M. H. 1978. *A Glossary of Literary Terms*. 3rd ed. Delhi: Macmillan.

Abrams, Richard. 1986. "Rumor's Reign in 2 Henry IV: The Scope of a Personification." *English Literary Renaissance* 16(3):467–495.

Adams, William Y. 1981. "On Guthrie's Theory of Religion." *Current Anthropology* 22:84–85.

Agassi, Joseph. 1973. "Anthropomorphism in Science." In *Dictionary of the History of Ideas*. Philip P. Wiener, editor in chief. New York: Charles Scribner's Sons.

Aiyappan, A. 1976. "Deified Men and Humanized Gods: Some Folk Bases of Hindu Theology." In *The Realm of the Extra-Human: Agents and Audiences*. Agehananda Bharati, ed. Pp. 139–148. The Hague: Mouton Publishers.

Allen, Elizabeth, et. al. 1978. "Against Sociobiology." In *The Sociobiology Debate*. Arthur Caplan, ed. New York: Harper and Row. Pp. 259–264.

Allport, Gordon W. 1950. *The Individual and His Religion*. New York: MacMillan.

Alpers, Svetlana. 1983. *The Art of Describing: Dutch Art in the Seventeenth Century*. Chicago: The University of Chicago Press.

Anderson, William. 1990. *Green Man: The Archetype of Our Oneness with the Earth*. Photography by Clive Hicks. London and San Francisco: HarperCollins.

Angier, Natalie. 1990. "Nature May Fashion All Cell's Proteins From a Few Primordial Parts." *The New York Times*, Tuesday, Dec. 11. P. C1.

Arbib, Michael A. and Allen R. Hanson. 1987. "Vision, Brain, and Cooperative Computation: An Overview." In *Vision, Brain, and Cooperative Computation*. Michael Arbib and Allen Hanson, eds. Cambridge: MIT Press. Pp. 1–83.

Arbib, Michael A., and Allen R. Hanson, eds. 1987. *Vision, Brain, and Cooperative Computation*. Cambridge: MIT Press.

Arnheim, Rudolf. 1969. *Visual Thinking*. Berkeley: University of California Press.

Arnheim, Rudolf. 1974. *Art and Visual Perception: The New Version*. Berkeley: University of California Press.

Aschwanden, H. 1982. *Symbols of Life*. Gweru: Mambo Press.

Asquith, Pamela J. 1984. "The inevitability and utility of anthropomorphism in description of primate behavior." In *The Meaning of Primate Signals*. Rom Harré and Vernon Reynolds, eds. Cambridge: Cambridge University Press. Pp. 138–176.

Asquith, Pamela J. 1986. "Anthropomorphism and the Japanese and Western traditions in primatology." In *Primate Ontogeny, Cognition and Social Behaviour*. James G. Else and Phyllis C. Lee, eds. Cambridge: Cambridge University Press. Pp. 61–71.

Bacon, Francis. 1960. *The New Organon and Related Writings*. Fulton H. Anderson, ed. New York: Liberal Arts Press.

Baer, Brigitte. 1988. "Donald Sultan's Black Lemons." The Museum of Modern Art, New York (exhibition leaflet). February 4–May 3.

Bambrough, Renford. 1977. "Introduction." In *Reason and Religion*. Stuart C. Brown, ed. Ithaca: Cornell University Press. Pp. 13–19.

Banton, Michael, ed. 1966. *Anthropological Approaches to the Study of Religion*. London: Tavistock Publications.

Barbour, Ian G. 1971. *Issues in Science and Religion*. New York: Harper and Row.

Barbour, Ian G. 1976. *Myths, Models, and Paradigms: A Comparative Study in Science and Religion*. New York: Harper and Row.

Barich, Bill. 1984. *Traveling Light*. New York: Viking.

Barkan, Leonard. 1975. *Nature's Work of Art: The Human Body as Image of the World*. New Haven: Yale University Press.

Barnes, Barry. 1974. *Scientific Knowledge and Sociological Theory*. London: Routledge and Kegan Paul.

Barnet, Sylvan, Morton Berman, and William Burto. 1960. *A Dictionary of Literary Terms*. Boston: Little, Brown, and Company.

Barrow, John D. 1983. "Anthropic Definitions." *Quarterly Journal of the Royal Astronomical Society* 24:146–153.

Barrow, John D., and Frank J. Tipler. 1986. *The Anthropic Cosmological Principle*. Oxford: Oxford University Press.

Barth, Fredrik. 1975. *Ritual and Knowledge Among the Baktaman of New Guinea*. New Haven: Yale University Press.

Barthelme, Donald. 1978. "The Leap." *The New Yorker*. July 31. Pp. 27–29.

Bateson, Gregory. 1958. *Naven*. 2nd ed. Stanford: Stanford University Press.

Bateson, Gregory. 1972. *Steps to an Ecology of Mind*. New York: Ballantine Books.

Bateson, Gregory, and Mary Catherine Bateson. 1988. *Angels Fear: Toward an Epistemology of the Sacred*. Toronto: Bantam Books.

Batson, C. Daniel. 1990. "How Social an Animal? The Human Capacity for Caring." *American Psychologist* 45:336–346.

Beck, Samuel J. 1968. "Reality, Rorschach and Perceptual Theory." In *Projective Techniques in Personality Assessment*. A. I. Rabin, ed. New York: Springer Publishing Company. Pp. 115–135.

Beck, Samuel, and Herman B. Molish. 1967. *Rorschach's Test. Vol. 2. A Variety of Personality Pictures*. 2nd ed. New York: Grune and Stratton.

Bellah, Robert. 1967. "Civil Religion in America." *Daedalus* 96:1–21.

Bergson, H. 1935. *The Two Sources of Morality and Religion*. New York: Henry Holt.

Berkeley, George. 1939. *A Treatise Concerning the Principles of Human Knowledge*. In *The English Philosophers from Bacon to Mill*. Edwin A. Burtt, ed. New York: Modern Library. Pp. 506–579.

Bernstein, Jeremy. 1979. "How Life Works." *The New York Times Book Review*. April 8. Pp. 1, 34.

Bickerton, Derek. 1990. *Language and Species*. Chicago: University of Chicago Press.

Black, Max. 1962. *Models and Metaphors*. Ithaca, N.Y.: Cornell University Press.

Bloch, Maurice. 1985. "Religion and Ritual." In *The Social Science Encyclopedia*. Adam Kuper and Jessica Kuper, eds. London: Routledge and Kegan Paul. Pp. 698–701.

Bloomfield, Morton. 1963. "A Grammatical Approach to Personification Allegory." *Modern Philology* 60(3):161–171.

Bloomfield, Morton. 1980. "Personification-metaphors." *The Chaucer Review* 14(4):287–297.

Boas, Franz. 1935. "Anthropology." In *Encyclopaedia of the Social Sciences*. New York: The MacMillan Company.

Boas, George. 1932. *Philosophy and Poetry*. Norton, Mass.: Wheaton College Press.

Boon, James A. 1987. "Anthropology, Ethnology, and Religion." In *The Encyclopedia of Religion*. Vol. 1. Mircea Eliade, editor in chief. New York: MacMillan Publishing Company. Pp. 308–316.

Bovet, Pierre. 1928. *The Child's Religion*. New York: E. P. Dutton.

Bower, T.G.R., and J.G. Wishart. 1979. "Towards a Unitary Theory of Development." In *Origins of the Infant's Social Responsiveness*. E. B. Thompson, ed. Hillsdale, N.J.: Erlbaum.

Bowker, J. W. 1976. "Information Process, Systems Behavior, and the Study of Religion." *Zygon* 2:361–79.

Braithwaite, R. B. 1955. *An Empiricist's View of the Nature of Religion*. Cambridge: Cambridge University Press.

Brandon, S.G.F. 1970. "Anthropomorphism." In *Dictionary of Comparative Religion*. S.G.F. Brandon, ed. New York: Scribner. Pp. 86–87.

Brecher, Kenneth S. 1988. "Samuel Beckett: Private in Public." *The New York Times Book Review*, June 12. Pp. 18–20.

Briggs, Jean L. 1970. *Never in Anger: Portrait of an Eskimo Family*. Cambridge: Harvard University Press.

Brightman, Edgar S. 1965. "Anthropomorphism." *Collier's Encyclopedia*. New York: Crowell-Collier Educational Corporation. P. 314.

Brock, S. P. 1985. "A Dispute of the Months and Some Related Syriac Texts." In *Journal of Semitic Studies* XXX/2:181–.

Broege, Valeri. 1983. "Electric Eve: Images of Female Computers in Science Fiction." In *Clockwork Worlds: Mechanized Environments in SF*. Richard D. Erlich and Thomas P. Dunn, eds. Westport, Conn.: Greenwood Press Pp. 183–194.

Brown, L. B., and R. H. Thouless. 1965. "Animistic Thought in Civilized Adults." *The Journal of Genetic Psychology* 107:33–42.

Brown, Patricia Leigh. 1989. "Soft Tech: The Feel of Things to Come." *The New York Times*. Nov. 2. P. B5.

Brown, Patricia Leigh. 1990. "The House that Fell to Earth." *The New York Times*. Jan. 4. Pp. 15–20.

Brown, Stuart C. 1977. *Reason and Religion*. Ithaca: Cornell University Press.

Browne, Malcolm W. 1987a. "Physicist Aims to Create a Universe, Literally." *The New York Times*. April 14. Pp. C1–4.

Browne, Malcolm W. 1987b. "Old Planes Restored for a Journey into the Past." *The New York Times*. Nov. 17. Pp. C1, C5.

Broyard, Anatole. 1978. "Books of the Times." *The New York Times*. June 19. P. C16

Broyard, Anatole. 1981. "Books of the Times." (Review of *Camera Lucida,* by Roland Barthes. Hill and Wang/Farrar, Straus and Giroux.) *The New York Times*. Oct. 14. N. P.

Bruner, Jerome S. 1977. "Early Social Interaction and Language Acquisition." In *Studies in Mother-Infant Interaction*. H. R. Schaffer, ed. London: Academic Press.

Buber, Martin. 1952. "Religion and Reality." In *Eclipse of God*. New York: Harper and Brothers.

Buber, Martin. 1960. *The Prophetic Faith*. New York: Harper and Brothers.

Bugeja, Michael. 1984. "James Wright: The Mastery of Personification in *This Journey*." *Mid-American Review* IV(2):106–115.

Burian, Richard M. 1978. "A Methodological Critique of Sociobiology." In *The Sociobiology Debate*. Arthur Caplan, ed. New York: Harper and Row. Pp. 376–395.

Campbell, Norman. 1952. *What is Science?* New York: Dover.

Caplan, Arthur L., ed. 1978. *The Sociobiology Debate: Readings on Ethical and Scientific Issues*. New York: Harper and Row.

Carter, Brandon. 1974. "The Anthropic Principle and Large Number Coincidences." In *Confrontation of Cosmological Theories with Observation*. Dordrecht: D. Reidel.

Cassirer, Ernst. 1963. *The Individual and the Cosmos in Renaissance Philosophy*. Oxford: Clarendon Press.

Caughey, John L. 1984. *Imaginary Social Worlds: A Cultural Approach*. Lincoln, Nebr.: University of Nebraska Press.

Champlin, Charles. 1979. Review of "The Amityville Horror." *Los Angeles Times*. [no exact date or page.]

Charsley, Simon. 1987. "Interpretation and Custom: The Case of the Wedding Cake." *Man* 22:93–110.

Cheney, Dorothy L., and Robert M. Seyfarth. 1990. *How Monkeys See the World*. Chicago: University of Chicago Press.

Cherbonnier, Edmond L. 1978. "In Defense of Anthropomorphism." In *Reflections on Mormonism*. T. G. Madsen, ed. Provo, Utah: Religious Studies Center, Brigham University Press.

Chicago Manual of Style, The. 1982. 13th ed., revised and expanded. Chicago: University of Chicago Press.

Churchland, P. M. 1979. *Scientific Realism and the Plasticity of Mind*. Cambridge: Cambridge University Press.

Churchland, P. M. 1988. *Matter and Consciousness: A Contemporary Introduction to the Philosophy of Mind*. 2nd ed. Cambridge: MIT Press.

Ciborowski, Tom, and Douglass Price-Williams. 1982. "Animistic Cognition: Some Cultural, Conceptual and Methodological Questions for Piagetian Research." In *Cultural Perspectives on Child Development*. Daniel A. Wagner and Harold W. Stevenson, eds. San Francisco: W. H. Freeman and Company. Pp. 166–180.

Clark, Stephen. 1988. "Is Humanity a Natural Kind?" In Tim Ingold, ed. *What is an Animal?* London: Unwin Hyman.

Clark, W. H. 1958. *The Psychology of Religion*. New York: The Macmillan Co.

Clowes, M. B. 1973. "Man the Creative Machine: A Perspective From Artificial Intelligence Research." In E. J. Benthall, ed. *The Limits of Human Nature*. London: Allen Lane. Pp. 192–207.

Cohen, Esther. "Law, Folklore and Animal Lore." *Past and Present: A Journal of Historical Studies* no. 110 (1986):6–37.

Cohn, Norman. 1961. *The Pursuit of the Millennium*. New York: Oxford University Press.

Coles, Robert. 1990. *The Spiritual Life of Children*. Boston: Houghton Mifflin Company.

Comte, Auguste. 1974. "Plan for the Scientific Operations Necessary for Reorganizing Society." In Ronald Fletcher, ed. *The Crisis of Industrial Civilization: The Early Essays of Auguste Comte*. Engl. transl. by H.D. Hutton, 1877. London: Heinemann. Pp. 214–245.

Conklin, Harold. 1969. "An Ethnoecological Approach to Shifting Agriculture." In *Environmental and Cultural Behavior*. Andrew P. Vayda, ed. Garden City, N.Y.: Natural History Press. Pp. 221–233.

Corn, Charles P. 1978. "Running in Kenya." *The New York Times*, March 19. P. 21.

Cornford, Francis MacDonald. 1957. *Plato's Cosmology: The Timaeus of Plato Translated With a Running Commentary*. New York: The Liberal Arts Press.

Cott, H. B. 1940. *Adaptive Coloration in Animals.* London: Methuen and Co., Ltd.

Coy, Jenny. 1988. "Animals' Attitudes to People." In *What is an Animal?* Tim Ingold, ed. London: Unwin Hyman. Pp. 77–83.

Craufurd, A. H. 1909. *The Religion of H. G. Wells and Other Essays.* London: T. Fisher Unwin.

Crick, Francis. 1988. "Lessons From Biology," *Natural History* 97(11) 32–39. [Excerpted from *What Mad Pursuit: A Personal View of Scientific Discovery,* by F. Crick.]

Crick, Francis. 1988. *What Mad Pursuit: A Personal View of Scientific Discovery.* New York: Basic Books.

Crosby, Donald. 1981. *Interpretive Theories of Religion.* The Hague: Mouton Publishers.

Cunningham, Clark. 1972. "Order in the Atoni House." In *Reader in Comparative Religion: An Anthropological Approach.* William Lessa and Evon Z. Vogt, eds. New York: Harper and Row. Pp. 116–135.

Curtis, Charlotte. 1984. "The Fading, Dying Sea." *The New York Times,* October 2.

Dasen, P. 1977. *Piagetian Psychology: Cross-cultural Contributions.* New York: Gardner Press.

David, Nicholas, Judy Sterner, and Kodzo Gavua. 1988. "Why Pots Are Decorated." *Current Anthropology* 29:365–79.

Davie, Donald. 1981. "Personification." *Essays in Criticism* 31:91–104.

Davis, Allan J. 1980. "Weathercasters: Mostly Cloudy." Letter to *Time* magazine, April 7.

Dawkins, Richard. 1978. *The Selfish Gene.* New York: Oxford University Press.

de Man, Paul. 1984. "Anthropomorphism and Trope in Lyric." In *The Rhetoric of Romanticism.* New York: Columbia University Press. Pp. 239–262.

De Vos, George A. and L. Bryce Boyer. 1989. *Symbolic Analysis Cross-Culturally.* Berkeley: University of California Press.

Deitch, Edward. n. d., n. t. *The New York Times.*

Dennett, D. C. 1978. *Brainstorms.* Cambridge: MIT/Bradford Books.

Dennis, W. 1953. "Animistic Thinking Among College and University Students." *Science Monthly* 76:247–249.

Desimone, R., T. D. Albright, C. G. Gross, and C. Bruce. 1984. "Stimulus-Selective Properties of Inferior Temporal Neurons in the Macaque." *Journal of Neuroscience* 4:2051–2062.

Deutsch, Eliot. 1969. *Advaita Vedanta: A Philosophical Reconstruction.* Honolulu: East-West Center Press.

Diamond, Jared. 1988. "Strange Traveling Companions," *Natural History,* 97(12):22–24.

Dickens, Charles. 1956. "A Christmas Tree." In *Christmas Stories.* London: Oxford University Press.

Dickinson, J., trans. 1927. *The Statesman's Book of John of Salisbury.* New York: Knopf.

Dodwell, Peter C., G. Keith Humphrey, and Darwin W. Muir. 1987. "Shape and Pattern Perception." In *Handbook of Infant Perception, Vol. 2: From Perception to Cognition.* Philip Salapatek and Leslie Cohen, eds. New York: Academic Press, Inc. Pp. 1–77.

Douglas, Mary, and Edmund Perry. 1985. "Anthropology and Comparative Religion." *Theology Today* 41(4):410–427.

Dresser, H. W. 1929. *Outlines of the Psychology of Religion*. New York: Thomas Y. Crowell.

Duggan, W. J. 1979. "Anthropomorphism." In *Encyclopedic Dictionary of Religion*. Paul Kevin Meagher, Thomas C. O'Brien, and Sister Consuelo Maria Aherne, eds. Washington, D.C.: Corpus Publications. Pp. 195–196.

Durkheim, Emile. 1965 [1915]. *The Elementary Forms of the Religious Life*. New York: The Free Press.

Dusheck, Jennie. 1985. "Fish, Fatty Acids and Physiology." *Science News* 128: 252–254.

Earman, John. 1987. "The SAP Also Rises: A Critical Examination of the Anthropic Principle." *American Philosophical Quarterly* 24(4):307–317.

Eddington, A. S. 1923. *The Mathematical Theory of Relativity*. Cambridge: Cambridge University Press.

Ehnmark, Erland. 1939. *Anthropomorphism and Miracle*. Uppsala: Amqvist & Wiksells Boktryckeri -A.-B. Uppsala Universitets Årsskrift 1939:12. (Recueil de Travaux Publié par L'Université D'Uppsala.)

Eibl-Eibesfeldt, Irenäus. 1975. *Ethology: The Biology of Behavior*. 2nd ed. Translated by Erich Klinghammer. New York: Holt, Rinehart and Winston, Inc.

Einstein, Albert. 1934. *The World as I See It*. New York: Covici Friede.

Eire, Carlos M. N. 1986. *War Against the Idols: The Reformation of Worship from Erasmus to Calvin*. Cambridge: Cambridge University Press.

Eister, Alan. 1974. *Changing Perspectives in the Scientific Study of Religion*. New York: Wiley.

Eliade, Mircea. 1961. *The Sacred and the Profane: The Nature of Religion*. Translated from the French by Willard R. Trask. New York: Harper and Row.

Eliade, Mircea. 1959. "Methodological Remarks on the Study of Religious Symbolism." In M. Eliade and J. Kitagawa, eds. *The History of Religions*. Chicago: University of Chicago Press. Pp. 86–107.

Eliot, T. S. 1958. "The Love Song of J. Alfred Prufrock." In *The Waste Land and Other Poems*. New York: Harcourt, Brace and Company.

Ellis, Hadyn D. 1981. "Introduction." In *Perceiving and Remembering Faces*. Graham Davies, Hadyn Ellis and John Shepherd, eds. London: Academic Press.

Evans-Pritchard, E. E. 1950. *Witchcraft, Oracles and Magic Among the Azande*. 2nd ed. Oxford: Clarendon Press.

Evans-Pritchard, E. E. 1965. *Theories of Primitive Religion*. London: Oxford University Press.

Evans-Pritchard, E. E. 1970. *Nuer Religion*. London: Oxford University Press.

Evers, T. M. and T. N. Huffman. 1988. "On Why Pots are Decorated the Way They Are." *Current Anthropology* 29(5):739–740.

Fedigan, Linda Marie. 1982. *Primate Paradigms: Sex Roles and Social Bonds*. Montreal: Eden Press.

Fernandez, James W. 1982. *Bwiti: An Ethnography of the Religious Imagination in Africa*. Princeton: Princeton University Press.

Fernandez, James W. 1986. *Persuasions and Performances: The Play of Tropes in Culture*. Bloomington: Indiana University Press.

Ferré, Frederick. 1980. "Theodicy and the Status of Animals." *American Philosophical Quarterly* 23:23–34.

Ferré, Frederick. 1984. "In Praise of Anthropomorphism." *International Journal for Philosophy of Religion* 16(3):203–212.

Feuerbach, Ludwig. 1957 [1873]. *The Essence of Christianity*. George Eliot, trans. New York: Harper and Row.

Feuerbach, Ludwig. 1967. *Lectures on the Essence of Religion*. Ralph Manheim, trans. New York: Harper and Row.

Feyerabend, Paul. 1988. "Knowledge and the Role of Theories." *Philosophy and Social Science* 18:157–178.

Field, T. M., R. Woodson, R. Greenberg, and D. Cohen. 1982. "Discrimination and Imitation of Facial Expressions by Neonates." *Science* 207: 323–324.

Field, Tiffany M. 1985. "Neonatal Perception of People: Maturational and Individual Differences." In *Social Perception in Infancy*. Tiffany M. Field and Nathan A. Fox, eds. Norwood, N.J.: Ablex Publishing Corporation. Pp. 31–52.

Fillipow, Lilly. 1977. "Taxi." *Push Pin Graphic* 5:5.

Fingerhut, Karl-Heinz. 1969. *Die Funktion der Tierfiguren im Werke Franz Kafkas*. Bonn: H. Bouvier u. Co.

Fingesten, Peter. 1955. "An Anthropomorphous Vessel from Luristan and the Western Tradition." *The Art Quarterly* 18(4):351–361.

Fingesten, Peter. 1961. "Topographical and Anatomical Aspects of the Gothic Cathedral." *The Journal of Aesthetics and Art Criticism* 20(1):3–23.

Firth, Raymond. 1967. *Tikopia Ritual and Belief*. Boston: Beacon Press.

Fischler, Martin A., and Oscar Firschein. 1987. *Intelligence: The Eye, the Brain, and the Computer*. Reading, Mass.: Addison-Wesley.

Fitting, H. 1876. *Juristische Schriften des Früheren Mittelalters*. Halle: Weisenhause.

Flew, Antony, ed. 1951 and 1955 (First and Second Series). *Logic and Language*. Oxford: Basil Blackwell.

Flew, Antony, and Alasdair MacIntyre, eds. 1955. *New Essays in Philosophical Theology*. London: SCM Press.

Forster, E.M. 1924. *A Passage to India*. New York: Harcourt, Brace and World.

Frazer, Sir James. 1935 [1890]. *The Golden Bough: A Study in Magic and Religion*. New York: MacMillan.

Freedberg, David. 1989. *The Power of Images: Studies in the History and Theory of Response*. Chicago: University of Chicago Press.

Freeman, Kathleen. 1966. *Ancilla to the Pre-Socratic Philosophers*. A complete translation of the Fragments in Diels, *Fragmente der Vorsokratiker*. Oxford: Basil Blackwell.

Freud, Sigmund. 1955 [1913]. *Totem and Taboo*. New York: W. W. Norton.

Freud, Sigmund. 1953–1974 [1923] "The Ego and the Id." In *The Standard Edition of the Complete Psychological Works of Sigmund Freud*. Vol. 19. London: Hogarth Press. Pp. 1–66.

Freud, Sigmund. 1964 [1927]. *The Future of an Illusion*. Garden City: Anchor Books.

Freud, Sigmund. 1962. *Civilization and Its Discontents*. Translated and edited by James Strachey. New York: W. W. Norton.

Frye, Northrop. 1957. *Anatomy of Criticism*. Princeton: Princeton University Press.

Frye, Northrop. 1968. *A Study of English Romanticism*. New York and Toronto: Random House.

Galilei, Galileo. 1953. *Dialogue on the Great World Systems*. In the Salusbury translation. Revised, annotated, and with an introduction by Giorgio de Santillana. Chicago: University of Chicago Press.

Gallus, Alexander. 1972. "A Biofunctional Theory of Religion." *Current Anthropology* 13:543–558.

Gary, Norman E. 1975. "Activities and Behavior of Honey Bees." In *The Hive and the Honey Bee*. Dadant and Sons, eds. Hamilton, Illinois: Dadant. Pp. 185–264.

Gaskin, J.C.A. 1984. *The Quest for Eternity*. New York: Penguin Books.

Gaskin, J.C.A. 1988. *Hume's Philosophy of Religion*. 2nd ed. Atlantic Highlands, N.J.: Humanities Press International.

Geertz, Clifford. 1966. "Religion as a Cultural System." In *Anthropological Approaches to the Study of Religion*. Michael Banton, ed. London: Tavistock Publications. Pp. 1–46.

Geertz, Clifford. 1973. "Ethos, World View, and the Analysis of Sacred Symbols." In *The Interpretation of Cultures*. New York: Basic Books. Pp. 126–141.

Gelman, David, Sharon Begley, Dewey Gram, and Evert Clark. 1977. "In Search of Other Worlds." *Review*. November. Pp. 29–33.

Gerth, H., and C. Wright Mills. 1948. *From Max Weber: Essays in Sociology*. London: Routledge & Kegan Paul.

Gibb, H.A.R., and J. H. Kramers, eds. 1953. *Shorter Encyclopaedia of Islam*. Leiden: E.J. Brill.

Gibson, James J. 1966. *The Senses Considered as a Perceptual System*. Boston: Houghton Mifflin.

Gibson, James J. 1979. *The Ecological Approach to Visual Perception*. Boston: Houghton-Mifflin.

Goldenweiser, Alexander A. 1922. *Early Civilization*. New York: Knopf.

Goldman, Ari. L. 1977. "Shelter Island Plagued by Ice . . . " *The New York Times*, Sunday, Feb. 20.

Gombrich, Ernst H. 1969. *Art and Illusion: A Study in the Psychology of Pictorial Representation*. 2nd ed. The A. W. Mellon Lectures in the Fine Arts. National Gallery of Art, Washington. Bollingen Series XXXV.5. Princeton: Princeton University Press.

Gombrich, Ernst. H. 1973. "Illusion and Art." In *Illusion in Nature and Art*. R. L. Gregory and E. H. Gombrich, eds. London: Gerald Duckworth.

Goodall, Jane. 1971. *In the Shadow of Man*. Boston: Houghton Mifflin.

Goodall, Jane. 1975. "The Chimpanzee." In *The Quest for Man*. Vanne Goodall, ed. New York: Praeger. Pp. 131–170.

Goode, William. 1951. *Religion Among the Primitives*. New York: The Free Press.

Goodman, Nelson. 1976. *Languages of Art*. Indianapolis: Hackett.

Goren, C., M. Sarty, and P. Wu. 1975. "Visual Following and Pattern Discrimination of Face-like Stimuli by Newborn Infants." *Pediatrics* 56: 544–549.

Gorsuch, Richard L. 1988. "Psychology of Religion." *Annual Reviews in Psychology* 39:201–221.

Goslee, Nancy Moore. 1988. " 'Promethean Art': Personification and Sculptural Imagery After Milton." In *Milton's Legacy in the Arts*. Albert C. Labriola and Edward Sichi, Jr., eds. University Park and London: The Pennsylvania State University Press. Pp. 219–236.

Gould, Stephen Jay. 1986. "This View of Life: Glow, Big Glowworm." *Natural History*, 95(12):10–16.

Greenberg, Jay R., and Stephen A. Mitchell. 1983. *Object Relations in Psycho-analytic Theory*. Cambridge: Harvard University Press.

Greenberg, Moshe. 1980. "Comments" [on "A Cognitive Theory of Religion" by Stewart Guthrie]. *Current Anthropology* 21:196.

Greene, John. 1959. *The Death of Adam*. Ames, Iowa: Iowa State University Press.

Gregory, R. L. 1973. "The Confounded Eye." In R. L. Gregory and E. H. Gombrich, eds. *Illusion in Nature and Art*. London: Duckworth.

Griaule, Marcel. 1980. *Conversations With Ogotemmeli*. London: Oxford University Press.

Griffin, Donald R. 1984. *Animal Thinking*. Cambridge: Harvard University Press.

Griffin, Jasper. 1985. "From Killer to Thinker" [review of *Greek Religion*, by Walter Burkert]. *The New York Review of Books*. June 27. Pp. 30–32.

Griffiths, Lavinia. 1985. *Personification in Piers Plowman*. Cambridge: D.S. Brewer.

Grünbaum, Adolf. 1976. "Is the Coarse-grained Entropy of Classical Statistical Mechanics an Anthropomorphism?" In *Vistas in Physical Reality: Festschrift for Henry Margenau*. Ervin Laszlo and Emily B. Sellon, eds. New York and London: Plenum Press. Pp. 11–29.

Guthrie, Stewart. 1980. "A Cognitive Theory of Religion." *Current Anthropology* 21(2):181–203.

Guthrie, Stewart Elliott. 1988. *A Japanese New Religion: Risshō Kōsei-kai in a Mountain Hamlet*. Ann Arbor, Michigan: University of Michigan Center for Japanese Studies.

Guthrie, W.K.C. 1950. *The Greeks and Their Gods*. Boston: Beacon Press.

Haldane, J.B.S. 1932. *The Inequality of Man and other Essays*. London: Chatto.

Hallowell, A. Irving. 1960. "Ojibwa Ontology, Behavior, and World View." In *Culture in History: Essays in Honor of Paul Radin*. Stanley Diamond, ed. New York: Columbia University Press. Pp. 20–52.

Hardy, Thomas. 1965. *Return of the Native*. New York: Scribner.

Harlow, H. F., and M. K. Harlow. 1962. "Social Deprivation in Monkeys." *Scientific American* 207:137–146.

Harman, Gilbert. 1974. *Thought*. Princeton: Princeton University Press.

Harnad, Stevan, ed. 1987. *Categorical Perception*. Cambridge: Cambridge University Press.

Hearne, Vicki. 1986. "Questions about Language." *The New Yorker*. Aug 18. P. 44.

Hecht, Antony. 1985. "The Pathetic Fallacy." *The Yale Review* 74(4):481–499.

Hedley, Jane. 1982. "What Price Energeia: Personification in the Poetry of Sidney and Greville." *Studies in the Literary Imagination* 15(1):49–66.

Hegel, Georg Wilhelm Friedrich. 1942. *Philosophy of Right*. T. M. Knox, trans. and ed. Oxford: Clarendon Press.

Heider, Fritz and Marianne Simmel. 1944. "An Experimental Study of Apparent Behavior." *The American Journal of Psychology* 57:243–259.

Heim, K. 1953. *Christian Faith and Natural Science*. London: S.C.M.

Heller, David. 1986. *The Children's God*. Chicago: The University of Chicago Press.

Hellerstein, David. 1984. "The Muse of Medicine." *Esquire*. March. Pp. 72–77.

Hewes, Gordon W. 1989. "The Upper Paleolithic Expansion of Supernaturalism and the Advent of Fully Developed Spoken Language." In *Language Origins* (papers of the Oxford meeting of the Language Origins Society, 1986). J. Wind, ed. Amsterdam: John Benjamin. n. p.

Hinks, Roger. 1939. *Myth and Allegory in Ancient Art*. London: Warburg Institute.

Hinton, H. E. 1973. "Natural Deception." In *Illusion in Art and Nature*. Richard Gregory and Ernst Gombrich, eds. London: Gerald Duckworth.

Hirn, Y. 1912. *The Sacred Vessel*. London: Macmillan.

Hobbes, Thomas. 1960. *Leviathan*. Michael Oakeshott, ed. Oxford: Blackwell.

Hollie, Pamela G. 1984. "Advertising: Encore Ads Go a Step Further." *The New York Times*. Friday, August 31.

Horton, Robin. 1960. "A Definition of Religion, and its Uses." *Journal of the Royal Anthropological Institute* 90:201–226.

Horton, Robin. 1967. "African Traditional Thought and Western Science." *Africa* 37:50–71, 155–187.

Horton, Robin. 1973. "Lévy-Bruhl, Durkheim, and the Scientific Revolution." In *Modes of Thought*. Robin Horton and Ruth Finnegan, eds. London: Faber and Faber. Pp. 249–305.

Horton, Robin. 1982. "Tradition and Modernity Revisited." In *Rationality and Relativism*. Martin Hollis and Steven Lukes, eds. Cambridge: MIT Press. Pp. 201–260.

Huang, I. 1943. "Children's Conception of Physical Causality: A Critical Summary." *Journal of Genetic Psychology* 63:71–121.

Hubbell, Sue. 1988. "Annals of Husbandry: The Sweet Bees." *The New Yorker*. May 9. Pp. 45–76.

Hume, David. 1932. *The Letters of David Hume*. J. Y. T. Greig, ed. Two volumes. Oxford: Clarendon Press.

Hume, David. 1947. *Dialogues Concerning Natural Religion*. 2nd ed. N. Kemp Smith, ed. New York: Library of Liberal Arts.

Hume, David. 1954. *New Letters of David Hume*. R. Klibansky and E. C. Mossner. Oxford: Clarendon Press.

Hume, David. 1957 [1757]. *The Natural History of Religion*. H. E. Root, ed. Stanford: Stanford University Press.

Idowu, E. Bolaji. 1973. *African Traditional Religion: A Definition*. London: SCM Press.

Inagaki, Kayoko and Giyoo Hatano. 1987. "Young Children's Spontaneous Personification as Analogy." *Child Development* 58:1013–1020.

Ingemanson, Birgitta. 1984. "The Screenplays of Ingmar Bergman: Personification and Olfactory Detail." *Literature/Film Quarterly*. 12(1):26–33.

Jackendoff, R. S. 1987. *Consciousness and the Computational Mind*. Cambridge: MIT/Bradford Books.

James, D. G. 1937. *Scepticism and Poetry: an Essay on the Poetic Imagination*. London: Allen and Unwin.

James, William. 1890. *The Principles of Psychology*. New York: Henry Holt.

James, William. 1902. *The Varieties of Religious Experience*. London: Longmans, Green & Co.

Jansen, H. W. 1973. "Chance Images." In *Dictionary of the History of Ideas: Studies of Selected Pivotal Ideas*. Vol. 1. Philip P. Wiener, editor in chief. New York: Charles Scribner's Sons. Pp. 340–353.

Jarvie, I. C., and Joseph Agassi. 1967. "The Problem of the Rationality of Magic." *British Journal of Sociology* 18:55–74.

Jaynes, E. T. 1965. "Gibbs vs. Boltzmann Entropies." *American Journal of Physics* 33:398.

Jensen, Erik. 1974. *The Iban and their Religion*. London: Oxford University Press.

Jevons, F. B. 1913. "Anthropomorphism." In *Encyclopaedia of Religion and Ethics*. James Hastings, ed. New York: Charles Scribner's Sons. Edinburgh: T. & T. Clark. Pp. 573–578.

Johansson, Gunnar. 1973. "Visual perception of Biological Motion and a Model for its Analysis." *Perception & Psychophysics* 14:201–211.

Joyce, James. 1961. *Ulysses*. New edition, corrected and reset. New York: The Modern Library.

Judson, Horace Freeland. 1978. "DNA—Part 2." *The New Yorker*. Dec. 4. Pp. 89–191.

Julesz, B., and J. R. Bergen. 1983. "Textons, the Fundamental Elements in Preattentive Vision and Perception of Textures." *Bell System Technical Journal* 62: 1619–1645.

Kahneman, Daniel and Amos Tversky. 1982a. "Variants of Uncertainty." In *Judgment Under Uncertainty: Heuristics and Biases*. D. Kahneman, Paul Slovic and A. Tversky, eds. Cambridge and New York: Cambridge University Press.

Kahneman, Daniel and Amos Tversky. 1982b. "The Psychology of Preferences." *Scientific American* 246(1):160–173.

Kanner, Bernice. 1989. "Mind Games." *New York Magazine*, May 8.

Kauffmann, Yehezkel. 1972. *The Religion of Israel from its Beginning to the Babylonian Exile*. Translated and abridged by Moshe Greenberg. New York: Schocken Books.

Keil, Frank C. 1979. *Semantic and Conceptual Development: An Ontological Perspective*. Cambridge: Harvard University Press.

Kelley, Kevin W., ed. 1988. *The Home Planet*. Reading, Massachussetts: Addison-Wesley Publishing Company.

Key, Wilson Bryan. 1973. *Subliminal Seduction*. Englewood Cliffs, N.J.: Signet.

Key, Wilson Bryan. 1976. *Media Sexploitation*. Englewood Cliffs, N.J.: Prentice-Hall.

Key, Wilson Bryan. 1980. *The Clam-Plate Orgy*. New York: New American Library.

Klingberg, G. 1957. "The Distinction Between Living and Non-living among 7–10-Year-Old Children, With Some Remarks Concerning the Animism Controversy." *Journal of Genetic Psychology* 90:227–238.

Klopfer, Bruno. 1942. *The Rorschach Technique: A Manual for a Projective Method of Personality Diagnosis*. Yonkers-on-Hudson, New York: World Book Company.

Knapp, Steven. 1985. *Personification and the Sublime: Milton to Coleridge*. Cambridge: Harvard University Press.

Kopytoff, Igor. 1971. "Ancestors and Elders in Africa." *Africa* 41(2):129–142.

Kosslyn, Stephen Michael. 1980. *Image and Mind*. Cambridge: Harvard University Press.

Krasner, Barbara R. 1975. " 'Sublime Anthropomorphism:' The Significance of Jewish Mysticism for Personal and Communal Existence." Ph.D. Dissertation, Temple University [Ann Arbor, Michigan: University Microfilms International, 1980].

Kuhn, Thomas. 1970. *The Structure of Scientific Revolutions,* enlarged edition. Chicago: University of Chicago Press.

La Barre, Weston. 1964. "Animism (Also Animatism)." In *A Dictionary of the Social Sciences.* Julius Gould and William L. Kolb, eds. New York: The Free Press. Pp. 26–29.

La Barre, Weston. 1972. *The Ghost Dance: Origins of Religion.* New York: Dell Publishing Company.

Lactantius (Lucius Caelius Firmianus). 1964. *The Divine Institutes.* Washington, D.C.: The Catholic University of America Press.

Ladendorf, Heinz. 1960. *Mouseion, Studien . . . für Otto Förster.* Cologne: M. DuMont Schauberg.

Landow, George P. 1971. *The Aesthetic and Critical Theories of John Ruskin.* Princeton, N.J.: Princeton University Press.

Lange, Friedrich Albert. 1866. *Geschichte des Materialismus und Kritik seiner Bedeutung in der Gegenwart.* Iserlohn: J. Baedeker Verlag.

Langer, Susanne K. 1962. *Philosophical Sketches.* Baltimore: Johns Hopkins University Press.

Larson, Kay. 1979. "New Landscapes in Art." *The New York Times Magazine.* May 13. Pp. 21–38.

Lashley, K. 1956. "Cerebral Organization and Behavior." In *The Brain and Human Behavior.* H. Solomon, S. Cobb, and W. Penfield, eds. Baltimore: Williams and Wilkins.

Laurendeau, M., and Pinard, A. 1962. *Causal Thinking in the Child: A Genetic and Experimental Approach.* New York: International Universities Press.

Lawson, E. Thomas, and Robert N. McCauley. 1990. *Rethinking Religion: Connecting Cognition and Culture.* Cambridge: Cambridge University Press.

Lazarus, Richard S. 1984. "On the Primacy of Cognition." *American Psychologist* 39 (2):124–129.

Leach, Edmund R. 1968. "Introduction." In *Dialectic in Practical Religion.* Edmund R. Leach, ed. Cambridge: Cambridge University Press. Pp. 1–6.

Lee, Richard B. 1979. *The !Kung San: Men, Women, and Work in a Foraging Society.* Cambridge: Cambridge University Press.

Levi-Strauss, Claude. 1963. *Totemism.* Rodney Needham, trans. Boston: Beacon Press.

Levi-Strauss, Claude. 1966. *The Savage Mind.* Chicago: University of Chicago Press.

Levy-Bruhl, Lucien. 1966. *How Natives Think.* Lilian Clare, trans. New York: Washington Square Press.

Lewin, Roger. 1989. "Is DNA Getting Smarter?" *The New York Times Book Review.* November 19. P. 26.

Liebert, Arthur. 1909. "Der Anthropomorphismus der Wissenschaft." *Zeitschrift für Philosophie und Philosophische Kritik* 136:1–22.

Lloyd, G.E.R. 1966. *Polarity and Analogy: Two Types of Argumentation in Early Greek Thought.* Cambridge: Cambridge University Press.

Lomazzo, Giovanni Paolo. 1598. *Tract Containing the Artes of Curious Painting, Caruing, Buildinge.* Richard Haydock, trans. London. [No publisher listed.]

Loukatos, Demetrious. 1976. "Personifications of Capes and Rocks in the Hellenic Seas." In *The Realm of the Extra-Human: Agents and Audiences.* Agehananda Bharati, ed. The Hague: Mouton Publishers. Pp. 467–474.

Lovelock, James E. 1987. *Gaia: A New Look at Life on Earth*. Oxford: Oxford University Press.

Lovelock, James E. 1990. "Hands Up for the Gaia Hypothesis." *Nature* 344: 100–102.

Lowie, Robert. 1970 [1924]. *Primitive Religion*. New York: Liveright.

Lutz, Catherine A. 1988. *Unnatural Emotions: Everyday Sentiments on a Micronesian Atoll and Their Challenge to Western Theory*. Chicago: University of Chicago Press.

Machalek, Richard. 1977. "Definitional Strategies in the Study of Religion." *Journal for the Scientific Study of Religion* 16:395–401.

Maddox, John. 1990. "Maxwell's Demon Flourishes." *Nature* 345:109.

Malcolm, Andrew H. 1984. "Contained Montana Fire Leaves an Eerie World." *The New York Times,* Sunday, Sept. 2. P. 18.

Malcolm, Norman. 1977. "The Groundlessness of Belief." In *Reason and Religion,* Stuart C. Brown, ed. Ithaca: Cornell University Press.

Malefijt, Annemarie de Waal. 1968. *Religion and Culture: An Introduction to Anthropology of Religion*. New York: The Macmillan Company.

Malinowski, Bronislaw. 1948. *Magic, Science and Religion and Other Essays*. Garden City, N.Y.: Doubleday and Company.

Malinowski, Bronislaw. 1979. "The Role of Magic and Religion." In *Reader in Comparative Religion: An Anthropological Approach*. 4th ed. William A. Lessa and Evon Z. Vogt, eds. New York: Harper and Row. Pp. 37–46.

Malone, Michael E. 1986. "From up Here They Look Like Ants." *Inquiry* 29: 407–422.

Mankiewicz, Jane. 1978. "Wooden Nickels." *The New Yorker*. May 8. Pp. 40–47.

Margand, N. A. 1977. "Perceptual and Semantic Features in the Young Child: Evidence for the Development of Semantic Feature Systems." *Developmental Psychology* 23:7–77.

Margolis, Howard. 1987. *Patterns, Thinking, and Cognition: A Theory of Judgment*. Chicago: University Of Chicago Press.

Marmorstein, A. 1927. *The Old Rabbinic Doctrine of God*. London: Oxford University Press.

Marx, Karl, and Friedrich Engels. 1957. *On Religion*. Moscow: Progress.

Maurer, Daphne. 1985. "Infants' Perception of Facedness." In *Social Perception in Infancy*. Tiffany M. Field and Nathan A. Fox, eds. Norwood, N.J.: Ablex Publishing. Pp. 73–100.

McPhee, John. 1990. *Looking for a Ship*. New York: Farrar Straus Giroux.

Medin, Douglas L., William Wattenmaker, and Sarah Hampson. 1987. "Family Resemblance, Conceptual Cohesiveness, and Category Construction." *Cognitive Psychology* 19:242–279.

Meier, Stephanie. 1982. *Animation and Mechanization in the Novels of Charles Dickens*. Bern: Francke Verlag.

Meltzoff, Andrew N. 1985. "The Roots of Social and Cognitive Development: Models of Man's Original Nature." In *Social Perception in Infants*. Tiffany M. Field and Nathan A. Fox, eds. Norwood, N.J.: Ablex Publishing Corporation. Pp. 1–30.

Mendelson, M. J., M. M. Haith, and S. Goldman. 1978. "Scanning of Faces and Responsiveness to Social Cues in Infant Rhesus Monkeys." Paper presented at the International Conference on Infant Studies, Providence, R.I.

Merleau-Ponty, M. 1962. *Phenomenology of Perception.* New York: The Humanities Press.

Meynell, Hugo. 1977. "The Intelligibility of the Universe." In *Reason and Religion.* Stuart C. Brown, ed. Ithaca: Cornell University Press. Pp. 23–43.

Middleton, Drew. 1984. "Israelis Tense at Post Near Syrians." *The New York Times,* February 23. N. P.

Midgley, Mary. 1983. *Animals and Why They Matter.* Athens, Georgia: The University of Georgia Press.

Miles, Josephine. 1965. *Pathetic Fallacy in the Nineteenth Century: A Study of a Changing Relation Between Object and Emotion.* New York: Octagon Books.

Miller, Bryan. 1982. "Successes in Food Packaging." *The New York Times.* April 14. Pp. C1–6.

Miller, David, ed. 1985. *Popper Selections.* Princeton: Princeton University Press.

Miller, J. G. 1978. *Living Systems.* New York: McGraw-Hill.

Miller, Jonathan, ed. 1983. *States of Mind.* New York: Pantheon.

Miller, Julie Ann. 1985. "Beyond Brain Circuitry." *Science News* 128:297.

Milton, John. 1957. *Complete Poems and Major Prose.* Merritt Y. Hughes, ed. New York: Odyssey.

Moore, Timothy E. 1982. "Subliminal Advertising: What You See Is What You Get." *Journal of Marketing* 46(Spring):38–47.

More, Henry. 1653. *An Antidote Against Atheism.* London.

Morioka, Kiyomi. 1977. "The Appearance of 'Ancestor Religion' in Modern Japan: The Years of Transition from the Meiji to the Taishô Periods." *Japanese Journal of Religious Studies* 4:183–212.

Morris, Brian. 1987. *Anthropological Studies of Religion: An Introductory Text.* Cambridge: Cambridge University Press.

Möseneder, Karl. 1986. "Blickende Dinge: Anthropomorphes bei Albrecht Dürer." *Pantheon: Internationale Jahreszeitschrift für Kunst.* Jahrgang XLIV. Pp. 15–23.

Mundkur, Balaji. 1988. "Human Animality, the Mental Imagery of Fear, and Religiosity." In *What is an Animal?* Tim Ingold, ed. London: Unwin Hyman. Pp. 141–184.

Munson, Henry, Jr. 1986. "Geertz on Religion: The Theory and the Practice." *Religion* 16:19–32.

Murray, Gilbert. 1955. *Five Stages of Greek Religion.* Garden City, N.Y.: Doubleday.

Nadel, S. F. 1954. *Nupe Religion.* London: Routledge and Kegan Paul.

Napier, John. 1973. *Bigfoot: The Yeti and Sasquatch in Myth and Reality.* New York: E. P. Dutton.

National Public Radio. 1979. "The Violent Universe." Originally produced by the Public Broadcast Laboratory in conjunction with the British Broadcasting Corporation. July 16.

Needham, Rodney. 1981. "Characteristics of Religion." Chapter 4 in *Circumstantial Deliveries,* by Rodney Needham. Berkeley: University of California Press. Pp. 72–90.

Neisser, Ulric, ed. 1987. *Concepts and Conceptual Development: Ecological and Intellectual Factors in Categorization.* Cambridge: Cambridge University Press.

Nelson, Charles A. 1985. "The Perception and Recognition of Facial Expressions in Infancy." In *Social Perception in Infancy.* Tiffany M. Field and Nathan A.

Fox, eds. Norwood, N.J.: Ablex Publishing Corporation. Pp. 101–125.

Neusner, Jacob. 1988. *The Incarnation of God: The Character of Divinity in Formative Judaism*. Philadelphia: Fortress Press.

The New Yorker. 1989. October 23. Cover.

Newman, F. W. 1870. *Anthropomorphism: A Comment*. Mount Pleasant, Ramsgate, England: Thomas Scott.

Nielsen, Kai. 1973. *Scepticism*. London: St. Martin's Press.

Nielsen, Kai. 1974. "Empiricism, Theoretical Constructs, and God." *Journal of Religion* 54:199–217.

Nielsen, Kai. 1982. "Wittgensteinian Fideism." In *Contemporary Philosophy of Religion*. Steven M. Cahn and David Shatz, eds. New York: Oxford University Press. Pp. 237–254.

Nielsen, Kai. 1984. "On Mucking Around About God: Some Methodological Animadversions." *International Journal for the Philosophy of Religion* 16: 111–122.

Nietzsche, Friedrich. 1901. *Werke*. Leipzig.

Nietzsche, Friedrich. 1966. *Werke in Drei Bänder*. Vol. 3. Karl Schlechter, ed. Munich: Carl Hanser.

Nietzsche, Friedrich. 1968. *The Will to Power*, trans. W. Kaufmann and R. J. Hollingdale. New York: Vintage Press.

Nilsson, Martin P. 1949. *A History of Greek Religion*. Translated from the Swedish by F. J. Fielden. Oxford: Clarendon Press.

Nisbett, Richard. E., and Timothy Wilson. 1977. "Telling More Than We Can Know: Verbal Reports on Mental Processes." *Psychological Review* 84:231–259.

Norbeck, Edward. 1961. *Religion in Primitive Society*. New York: Harper and Row.

Norbeck, Edward. 1974. *Religion in Human Life*. New York: Holt, Rinehart, and Winston.

Nunn, T. Percy. 1927. "Anthropomorphism in Physics." Annual Philosophical Lecture, Henriette Hertz Trust. In *Proceedings of the British Academy*. London: Oxford University Press.

Oatley, Keith. 1978. *Perceptions and Representations: The Theoretical Bases of Brain Research and Psychology*. New York: The Free Press. P. 159.

Ortony, Andrew. 1979. *Metaphor and Thought*. Cambridge: Cambridge University Press.

Ostrow, James M. 1990. *Social Sensitivity: A Study of Habit and Experience*. SUNY Series in The Philosophy of the Social Sciences. Lenore Langsdorf, ed. Albany, New York: State University of New York Press.

Otto, Rudolf. 1950. *The Idea of the Holy*. 2nd ed. New York: Oxford University Press.

Outside magazine flyer. 1977.

Oxford Universal Dictionary. 1955. 3rd ed. C. T. Onions, ed. Oxford: Clarendon Press.

Ozick, Cynthia. 1977. "Passage to the New World." *Ms.* 6:70–81.

Padoux, André. 1990. *Vac: The Concept of the Word in Selected Hindu Tantras*. Ithaca, N.Y.: State University of New York Press.

Pagels, Heinz. 1985. "A Cozy Cosmology," in *Sciences* 25(2):34–38.

Pailin, David A. 1990. *The Anthropological Character of Theology: Conditioning Theological Understanding*. Cambridge: Cambridge University Press.

Palmer, Humphrey. 1973. *Analogy*. London: MacMillan.

Parsons, Talcott. 1949. *The Structure of Social Action*. 2nd ed. New York: MacMillan.

Penner, Hans H. 1986. "Rationality and Religion: Problems in the Comparison of Modes of Thought." *Journal of the American Academy of Religion* 54: 645–671.

Penner, Hans H. 1989. *Impasse and Resolution: A Critique of the Study of Religion*. Toronto Studies in Religion, Donald Wiebe, general editor. Vol. 8. New York: Peter Lang.

Phelps, Moses Stuart. 1881. "Anthropomorphism." *Princeton Review*, 4th Series 8:120–144.

Phillips, D. Z. 1970. *Death and Immortality*. London: Macmillan.

Phillips, D. Z. 1976. *Religion Without Explanation*. Oxford: Blackwell.

Piaget, Jean. 1929. *The Child's Conception of the World*. London: Routledge and Kegan Paul.

Piaget, Jean. 1933. "Children's Philosophies." In *A Handbook of Child Psychology*, 2nd ed. C. Murchison, ed. Worcester: Clark University. Pp. 534–547.

Piaget, Jean. 1970. *Genetic Epistemology*. New York: Norton.

Piper, H. L. 1962. *The Active Universe: Pantheism and the Concept of Imagination in the English Romantic Poets*. London: Athlone Press.

Planck, Max. 1960 [1925]. *A Survey of Physical Theory* (formerly titled *A Survey of Physics*). New York: Dover Publications.

Ponte, Lowell. 1977. "Who Did It?" *The New York Times*. March 8.

Poole, Fitz John Porter. 1986. "Metaphors and Maps: Towards Comparison in the Anthropology of Religion." *Journal of the American Academy of Religion* 54(3):411–457.

Powell, John Wesley. 1969. *Down the Colorado: Diary of the First Trip Through the Grand Canyon 1869*. Eliot Porter, Photographs and Epilogue. Foreword and Notes by Don D. Fowler. New York: E. P. Dutton.

Prestige, George Leonard. 1952. *God in Patristic Thought*. London: SPCK.

Preus, J. Samuel. 1987. *Explaining Religion: Criticism and Theory from Bodin to Freud*. New Haven: Yale University Press.

Proudfoot, Wayne. 1985. *Religious Experience*. Berkeley: University of California Press.

Pruyser, Paul. 1976. *A Dynamic Psychology of Religion*. New York: Harper and Row.

Raban, Jonathan. 1988. *Coasting*. New York: Penguin Books.

Radcliffe-Brown, Alfred Reginald. 1922. *The Andaman Islanders*. New York and Cambridge: Cambridge University Press.

Radcliffe-Brown, Alfred Reginald. 1979 [1939]. "Taboo." ["The Frazer Lecture," 1939.] In *Reader in Comparative Religion: An Anthropological Approach*. William A. Lessa and Evon Z. Vogt, eds. New York: Harper and Row. Pp. 46–56.

Radcliffe-Brown, Alfred Reginald. 1945. "Religion and Society," *Journal of the Royal Anthropological Institute* LXXV:33–43.

Randall, John Herman, Jr. 1960. *Aristotle*. New York: Columbia University Press.

Raschke, Carl A. 1986. "Religious Studies and the Default of Critical Intelligence." *Journal of the American Academy of Religion* LIV/I:131–138.

Ray, Benjamin. 1973. " 'Performative Utterances' in African Rituals." *History of Religions* 13:16–35.

Reed, Robert C. 1976. "An Interpretation of Some 'Anthropomorphic' Representations From the Upper Paleolithic." *Current Anthropology* 17(1):136–138.

Reynolds, David K. 1976. *Morita Psychotherapy.* Berkeley: University of California Press.

Reynolds, David K. 1980. *The Quiet Therapies.* Honolulu: University of Hawaii Press.

Reynolds, David K. 1983. *Naikan Psychotherapy.* Chicago: University of Chicago Press.

Rhys Davids, T. W., trans. 1899. *Dialogues of the Buddha* (Sacred Books of the Buddhists, Vol. II). London: Henry Frowde.

Rhys Davids, T. W., and C.A.F., trans. 1957. *Dialogues of the Buddha, Translated From the Digha Nikaya,* Part 3 (Sacred Books of the Buddhists, Vol. 4). London: Luzac.

Rice, Patricia C., and Ann L. Paterson. 1988. "Anthropomorphs in Cave Art: An Empirical Assessment." *American Anthropologist* 90(3):664–674.

Richardson, Alan, ed. 1951. *A Theological Word Book of the Bible.* New York: Macmillan.

Richter, Jean Paul. 1939. *The Literary Works of Leonardo Da Vinci.* London: Oxford University Press.

Ricoeur, Paul. 1974. "Philosophy and Religious Language." *Journal of Religion* 54:71–85.

Rizzuto, Ana-Maria. 1979. *The Birth of the Living God.* Chicago: University of Chicago Press.

Roberts, Walter Orr. 1989. "Thoughts on Science: Is Anyone Sending Us Messages from Space?" Boulder, Colorado, *Daily Camera.* June 1. P. 2B.

Robinson, Marilynne. 1987. "Language is Smarter Than We Are." *New York Times Book Review.* Jan. 11. P. 8.

Rorty, Richard. 1979. *Philosophy and the Mirror of Nature.* Princeton: Princeton University Press.

Rorty, Richard. 1982. *Consequences of Pragmatism.* Minneapolis: University of Minnesota Press.

Rosch, Eleanor, and Carolyn B. Mervis, Wayne D. Gray, David M. Johnson, and Penny Boyes-Braem. 1976. "Basic Objects in Natural Categories." *Cognitive Psychology* 8:382–439.

Ruskin, John. 1882. *The Queen of the Air: Being a Study of the Greek Myths of Cloud and Storm.* New York: John Wiley & Sons.

Ruskin, John. 1987. *Modern Painters.* Edited and abridged by David Barrie. New York: Alfred A. Knopf.

Sackett, G. P. 1966. "Monkeys Reared in Isolation with Pictures as Visual Input: Evidence for an Innate Releasing Mechanism." *Science* 154:1468–1473.

Saler, Benson. 1977. "Supernatural as a Western Category." *Ethos* 5:31–53.

Saler, Benson. 1983. "Anthropomorphism and Theomorphism." Paper presented at the 82nd Annual Meeting of the American Anthropological Association, Chicago. Nov. 17.

Saler, Benson. n.d. "Theomorphism and the Homeric Gods." Extract from *Religion and the Supernatural.* Unpublished manuscript.

Saliba, John A. 1976. "Religion and the Anthropologists." *Anthropologica* 18:179–213.

Schachter, Stanley, and J. E. Singer. 1962. "Cognitive, Social, and Physiological Determinants of Emotional State." *Psychological Review* 69:379–399.

Scheibe, Karl E., and Margaret Erwin. 1979. "The Computer as Alter." *The Journal of Social Psychology* 108:103–109.

Schleiermacher, Friedrich. 1988. *On Religion.* New York: Cambridge University Press.

Schorsch, Ismar. 1988. "Poetry and Pietism: The 'Hymn of Glory.' " *Judaism* 145:67–72.

Schrödinger, Erwin. 1945. *What is Life?* Cambridge: Cambridge University Press.

Schulman, M. 1981. "The Great Conspiracy." *Journal of Communications* 31(2): 209.

Schutz, Alfred. 1962. *Collected Papers 1. The Problem of Social Reality.* Maurice Natanson, ed. The Hague: Martinus Nijhoff.

Sebeok, Thomas. 1988. " 'Animal' in Biological and Semiotic Perspective." In *What is an Animal?* Tim Ingold, ed. London: Unwin Hyman. P. 72.

Seger, Jon. 1989. "Who are the Drone Police?" *Nature* 342:741–742.

Semeonoff, Boris. 1976. *Projective Techniques.* London: John Wiley and Sons.

Sharma, R. S. 1987. "Anthropomorphism and the Language of Poetry." *Language and Style,* 20(3):257–267.

Sheldrake, Rupert. 1988. *The Presence of the Past.* New York: Times Books.

Sheraton, Mimi. 1979. "A New York Pastry Chef Moves to the White House." *The New York Times.* Jan. 15. P. A16.

Silberner, J. 1986. "Metaphor in Immunology." *Science News* 130:254.

Simons, Marlise. 1986. "In Haiti, the Land Is Worn Nearly to the Bone." *The New York Times,* June 15. P. E3.

Singer, Isaac Bashevis. 1979. "What is God to do—Discuss His Book With Every Reader?" (Excerpts from an address, "A Personal Concept of Religion," delivered at New York University.) *The New York Times.* May 18. P. A29.

Singleton, M. 1976. "Smallpox in Person: Personification or Personalization (Africa)?" *Anthropos* 71:169–179.

Siskin, Clifford. 1982. "Personification and Community: Literary Change in the Mid and Late Eighteenth Century." *Eighteenth-Century Studies* 15(4):371–401.

Skorupski, John. 1976. *Symbol and Theory: A Philosophical Study of Theories of Religion in Social Anthropology.* Cambridge: Cambridge University Press.

Smart, Ninian. 1976. *The Religious Experience of Mankind.* 2nd ed. New York: Charles Scribner's & Sons.

Smith, Ronald Gregor. 1960. *J.G. Hamann, A Study in Christian Existence, With Selections From His Writings.* London: Collins.

Smith, Wilfred Cantwell. 1962. *The Meaning and End of Religion.* New York: The New American Library.

Snaith, Norman H. 1962 [1944]. *The Distinctive Ideas of the Old Testament.* London: Epworth Press.

Spencer, Herbert. 1870. *Illustrations of Universal Progress.* New York: D. Appleton and Company.

Sperber, Dan. 1975. *Rethinking Symbolism.* A. Morton, trans. Cambridge: Cambridge University Press.

Spilka, Bernard, Ralph W. Hood, Jr., and Richard L. Gorsuch. 1985. *The Psychology of Religion: An Empirical Approach.* Englewood Cliffs, N.J.: Prentice-Hall.

Spinoza, Benedict de. 1951 [1670]. *A Theologico-Political Treatise.* R.H.M. Elwes, ed. New York: Dover.

Spinoza, Benedict de. 1955. *The Chief Works of Benedict de Spinoza: On the Improvement of the Understanding; The Ethics; Correspondence.* Translated from the Latin With an Introduction by R.H.M. Elwes. New York: Dover.

Spiro, Melford. 1966. "Religion: Problems of Definition and Meaning." *Anthropological Approaches to the Study of Religion.* Michael Banton, ed. London: Tavistock. Pp. 85–126.

Staal, Frits. 1979. "The Meaninglessness of Ritual." *Numen* 26:2–22.

Stack, George J. 1980. "Nietzsche and Anthropomorphism." *Critica: Revista Hispanoamerica de Filosofia.* 12:41–71.

Stack, George J. 1983. *Lange and Nietzsche.* Berlin: Walter de Gruyter.

Stark, Rodney, and William Sims Bainbridge. 1987. *A Theory of Religion.* Toronto Studies in Religion, Vol. 2. New York: Peter Lang.

Starr, Roger. 1982. "The Editorial Notebook: Seals of Approval." *The New York Times.* (no date). Editorial page.

Stern, Daniel N. 1985. *The Interpersonal World of the Infant: A View from Psychoanalysis and Developmental Psychology.* New York: Basic Books.

Stewart, Charles. 1991. *Demons and the Devil: Moral Imagination in Modern Greek Culture.* Princeton, N. J.: Princeton University Press.

Stokes, Adrian. 1972. *The Image in Form: Selected Writings of Adrian Stokes.* Edited and with an introduction by Richard Wollheim. New York: Harper and Row.

Storace, Patricia. 1987. "Song of Salt and Pepper." *The New Yorker,* March 9. P. 34.

Straus, A., ed. 1956. *The Social Psychology of George Herbert Mead.* Chicago: University of Chicago Press.

Stroumsa, Gedaliahu G. 1983. "Form(s) of God: Some Notes on Metatron and Christ." *Harvard Theological Review* 76:3, 269–288.

Sullivan, Harry Stack. 1962 [1924]. "Schizophrenia: Its Conservative and Malignant Features." In *Schizophrenia as a Human Process.* New York: Norton. N. P.

Sullivan, Harry Stack. 1953. *The Interpersonal Theory of Psychiatry.* New York: Norton.

Suppe, Frederick. 1977. *The Structure of Scientific Theories.* 2nd ed. Urbana: University of Illinois Press.

Suppes, Patrick. 1977. "The Structure of Theories and the Analysis of Data." In *The Structure of Scientific Theories.* Frederick Suppe, ed. Urbana: University of Illinois Press. Pp. 266–283.

Suro, Robert. 1987. "The Waters, Befouled, 'Cry out for Vengeance.'" *The New York Times,* October 20. N. P.

Swanson, Guy. 1960. *The Birth of the Gods: The Origin of Primitive Beliefs.* Ann Arbor: The University of Michigan Press.

Swinburne, Richard G. 1968. "The Argument from Design." *Philosophy* 43:199–212.

Swinburne, Richard G. 1977. *The Coherence of Theism.* Oxford: Clarendon Press.

Swinburne, Richard G. 1979. *The Existence of God.* Oxford: Clarendon Press.

Sze, Mai-mai. 1963. *The Tao of Painting: A Study of the Ritual Disposition of Chinese Painting.* With a translation of the *Chieh Tzu Yüan Hua Chuan* or *Mustard Seed Garden Manual of Painting* 1679–1701. Bollingen Series 49. New York: Pantheon Books.

Tagore, Rabindranath. 1961. *The Religions of Man.* Boston: Beacon Press.

Tambiah, Stanley Jeyaraja. 1970. *Buddhism and the Spirit Cults in North-east Thailand.* Cambridge: Cambridge University Press.

Tambiah, Stanley Jeyaraja. 1990. *Magic, Science, Religion, and the Scope of Rationality.* Cambridge: Cambridge University Press.

Tate, Allen. 1941. *Reason in Madness: Critical Essays.* New York: Putnam.

Taussig, Michael T. 1980. *The Devil and Commodity Fetishism in South America.* Chapel Hill: The University of North Carolina Press.

Teilhard de Chardin, P. 1959. *The Phenomenon of Man.* London: Collins.

Teske, Roland J., S. J. 1986. "The Aim of Augustine's Proof that God Truly Is." *International Philosophical Quarterly.* 26:253–268.

Thomas, Keith. 1971. *Religion and the Decline of Magic.* New York: Charles Scribner's Sons.

Thomas, Lewis. 1989. "Beyond the Moon's Horizon—Our Home." *The New York Times.* July 15, Op-Ed page.

Thompson, Stith. 1955. *Motif-Index of Folk-Literature.* Revised and Enlarged Edition. Bloomington, Ind.: Indiana University Press.

Tillich, Paul. 1948. *The Shaking of the Foundations.* New York: Charles Scribner's Sons.

Tillich, Paul. 1951. *Systematic Theology.* Vol. I. Chicago: University of Chicago Press.

Tillich, Paul. 1973. *What is Religion?* James L. Adams, trans. New York: Harper and Row.

Tipler, Frank J. 1982. "Anthropic-Principle Arguments Against Steady-State Cosmological Theories." *Observatory* 102:36–39.

Toulmin, Stephen. 1982. *The Return to Cosmology: Postmodern Science and the Theology of Nature.* Berkeley: University of California Press.

Treaster, Jospeh B. 1991. "Giant B-52 Grows Old Virulently." *The New York Times,* January 22, P. A9.

Turner, Mark. 1987. *Death is the Mother of Beauty: Mind, Metaphor, Criticism.* Chicago: University of Chicago Press.

Tuve, Rosemond. 1966. *Allegorical Imagery.* Princeton: Princeton University Press.

Tyler, Parker. 1947. "The Humanism of Abstract Art." *Gazette des Beaux-Arts.* 6th series. 31:47–60.

Tylor, Edward B. 1873. *Primitive Culture: Researches Into the Development of Mythology, Philosophy, Religion, Language, Art, and Custom.* 2nd ed. 2 vols. London: John Murray.

Tylor, Edward B. 1979 [1873]. "Animism." In *Reader in Comparative Religion: An Anthropological Approach.* 4th ed. William A. Lessa and Evon Z. Vogt, eds. New York: Harper and Row. Pp. 9–19.

Unamuno, Miguel de. *The Tragic Sense of Life in Men and Nations.* Translated by Anthony Kerrigan. Princeton, N. J.: Princeton University Press.

Van Brunt, H. L. 1977. "Ossabaw Suite." In *Poems 1962–1977.* Pittsburgh, Pa.: Carnegie-Mellon University Press.

Van Camp, Mike. 1988. "How to Adjust Your Bottom Bracket." In *Mountain Bike Action.* October. P. 59.

Vico, Giambattista. 1725, 1744. *The New Science.* Thomas G. Bergin and Max H. Fisch, trans. Rev. ed. Ithaca: Cornell University Press.

Vokey, John R., and J. Don Read. 1985. "Subliminal Messages: Between the Devil and the Media." *American Psychologist* 40:1231–1239.

Wagtendonk, Kees. 1987. "Images in Islam: Discussion of a Paradox." In *Effigies Dei: Essays on the History of Religions.* D. Plas, ed. New York: Brill. Pp. 112–129.

Waley, Arthur. 1958. *The Way and Its Power.* New York: Evergreen.

Wallace, Anthony F. C. 1956. "Revitalization Movements." *American Anthropologist,* 58:264–281.

Wallace, Anthony F. C. 1966. *Religion: An Anthropological View.* New York: Random House.

Wallace, David Rains. 1983. *The Klamath Knot: Explorations of Myth and Evolution.* San Francisco: Sierra Club Books.

Wandibba, Simiyu. 1988. "On Why Pots Are Decorated the Way They Are." *Current Anthropology* 29:740–741.

Watts, Fraser, and Mark Williams. 1988. *The Psychology of Religious Knowing.* Cambridge and New York: Cambridge University Press.

Wax, Murray L. 1984. "*Religion* as Universal: Tribulations of an Anthropological Enterprise." *Zygon: Journal of Religion and Science* 19(1):5–20.

Wayman, Alex. 1982. "The Human Body as Microcosm in India, Greek Cosmology, and Sixteenth-Century Europe." *History of Religions* 22(2):172–190.

Webster's New Collegiate Dictionary. 1977. Henry Bosley Woolf, editor in chief. Springfield, Mass.: G. & C. Merriam Company.

Weiskrantz, L. 1985. "Categorization, Cleverness and Consciousness." In *Animal Intelligence.* L. Weiskrantz, ed. Oxford: Clarendon Press. N. P.

Werblowsky, R. J. Zwi. 1987. "Anthropomorphism." In *The Encyclopedia of Religion.* Mircea Eliade, editor in chief. New York: Macmillan. Pp. 316–320.

Weston, Anthony. 1988. "Radio Astronomy as Epistemology: Some Philosophical Reflections on the Contemporary Search for Extraterrestrial Intelligence." *The Monist: An International Quarterly of General Philosophical Inquiry* 71(1):88–100.

Wheeler, John A. 1986. "Foreword." In *The Anthropic Cosmological Principle,* by John D. Barrow and Frank J. Tipler. Oxford: Oxford University Press. N. P.

Wheelwright, Philip 1962. *Metaphor and Reality.* Bloomington: Indiana University Press.

White, Leslie. 1949. *The Science of Culture.* New York: Farrar, Straus.

Whitehead, A. N. 1968. *Science and the Modern World.* Cambridge: Cambridge University Press.

Whitney, William D. 1881. "On the So-called Science of Religion." *Princeton Review,* 4th Series 7:429–452.

Whitworth, A. P. 1989. "When Protostars Cease Trading." *Nature* 342:126–127.

Wiebe, Donald. 1984. "The Failure of Nerve in the Academic Study of Religion." *Studies in Religion/Sciences Religieuses* 13:401–422.

Wilczek, Frank, and B. Devine. 1988. *Longing for the Harmonies.* New York: Norton.

Wilford, John Noble. 1987. "Everest, the Old Champion, Is Crowned Anew." *The New York Times,* October 20. P. 1 of "Science Times."

Williamson, René de Visme. 1976. *Politics and Protestant Theology: A Interpretation of Tillich, Barth, Bonhoeffer, and Brunner.* Baton Rouge: Louisiana State University Press.

Willis, Robert, trans. 1847. *The Works of William Harvey.* London.

Wills, Christopher. 1989. *The Wisdom of the Genes: New Pathways in Evolution.* New York: Basic Books.

Wilson, Bryan. 1982. *Religion in Sociological Perspective.* Oxford and New York: Oxford University Press.

Wilson, Timothy. 1985. "Strangers to Ourselves: The Origins and Accuracy of Beliefs About One's Own Mental States." In *Attribution: Basic Issues and Applications.* J. H. Harvey and G. Weary, eds. Orlando, Fl.: Academic Press. N. P.

Winch, Peter. 1958. *The Idea of a Social Science and Its Relation to Philosophy.* London: Routledge.

Winch, Peter. 1964. "Understanding a Primitive Society." *American Philosophical Quarterly* 1:307–325.

Winch, Peter. 1977. "Meaning and Religious Language." In *Reason and Religion.* Stuart C. Brown, ed. Ithaca: Cornell University Press. Pp. 193–221.

Wittgenstein, Ludwig. 1969. *Blue and Brown Books.* 2nd ed. Oxford: Basil Blackwell.

Wolf, Arthur P. 1978. "Gods, Ghosts, and Ancestors." In *Studies in Chinese Society.* Arthur P. Wolf, ed. Stanford: Stanford University Press. Pp. 131–182.

Wolf, Eric R. 1988. "Inventing Society." *American Ethnologist* 15(4):752–61.

Wollheim, Richard. 1964. *Hume on Religion.* Cleveland and New York: Meridian Books.

Wollheim, Richard. 1987. *Painting as an Art.* Bollingen Series XXXV. 33. Princeton: Princeton University Press.

Wordsworth, William. 1959. "Preface to the Second Edition of the Foregoing Poems, Published, with an Additional Volume, Under the Title of *Lyrical Ballads.*" In *Major British Poets.* Enlarged Edition, Vol. 2. G. B. Harrison, general editor. New York: Harcourt, Brace & World. Pp. 18–29.

Worsley, Peter. 1957. *The Trumpet Shall Sound.* London: Paladin.

Wright, Robert. 1988. "Did the Universe Just Happen?" *The Atlantic Monthly.* April. Pp. 29–44.

Young, Robert M. 1985. *Darwin's Metaphor: Nature's Place in Victorian Culture.* Cambridge: Cambridge University Press.

Zajonc, R. B. 1984. "On the Primacy of Affect." *American Psychologist* 39(2): 117–123.

Zucker, Stephen W. 1987. "The Diversity of Perceptual Grouping." In *Vision, Brain, and Cooperative Computation.* Michael A. Arbib and Allen R. Hanson, eds. Cambridge: MIT Press. Pp. 231–261.

Figure Credits

1. Frontispiece. Drawing by Ross; © 1989. The New Yorker Magazine, Inc.
2-1. Rabbit or duck? Line drawing by the author, after Jastrow.
2-2. Protective mimicry. Photo © 1987 by Donald Perry, from *Life above the Jungle Floor: A Biologist Explores a Strange and Hidden Treetop World.* Simon and Schuster. Used with the permission of International Creative Management, Inc.
3-1. Old Man of the Mountains. Stamp design © 1988 U.S. Postal Service.
3-2. Bacardi advertisement by permission of Bacardi Imports, Inc.
4-1. The Far Side Cartoon by Gary Larson is reprinted by permission of Chronicle Features, San Francisco, CA.
4-2. Michelob advertisement by permission of Fleishman-Hillard Inc.
4-3. *Lincoln Grid* by permission of the Estate of Leon D. Harmon.
4-4. Ronald C. James, *The Dalmation*, photo by permission of Van Nostrand Reinhold ©.
4-5. Hallucinatory cube by David Miretsky, after Max Clowes.
4-6. Face-like designs reproduced by permission of *Pediatrics.*
4-7. Drawing by Handelsman; © 1989. The New Yorker Magazine, Inc.
4-8. American postcard.
5-1. *Cruising around Manhattan*, Hudson Talbott ©.
5-2. Mr. Automatic advertisement reprinted with the permission of Tetley Inc.
5-3. Telecommunications advertisement. OKI® is a registered trademark of Oki Electric Industry Company, Limited. Copyright © 1984 by OKI America, Inc. All Rights Reserved.
5-4. Macayo advertisement by permission of Macayo Mexican Restaurants, Phoenix, AZ.
5-5. British postcard.
5-6. *Time* cover, copyright 1956 Time Warner Inc. Reprinted by permission.

5–7. Chrysler advertisement by permission of Bozell 1000.

5–8. Illustration, copyright © 1981 by The New York Times Company. Reprinted by permission.

5–9. Illustration, copyright © 1978 by The New York Times Company. Reprinted by permission.

5–10. Vodka advertisement created by TBWA Advertising and Carillon Importers Ltd.

5–11. Liqueur advertisement created by TBWA Advertising and Carillon Importers Ltd.

5–12. Beer advertisement by permission of Coors Brewing Company.

5–13. Rum advertisement by permission of Bacardi Imports, Inc.

5–14. Vodka advertisement created by TBWA Advertising and Carillon Importers Ltd.

5–15. Advertisement by IBM Corporation.

5–16. Liqueur advertisement created by TBWA Advertising and Carillon Importers Ltd.

5–17––5–24. Pottery vases, figurines, jars, pots, and bowl. Negative numbers 123187, 122892, 319339, 326195, 315911, 120638, 332641, and 328532 courtesy Library Services Department, American Museum of Natural History.

5–25. German New Year's Card.

5–26. Chwast, *Bestial Bold*. Push Pin Group, Inc., New York.

5–27. Arcimboldo, *Winter*. Kunsthistoriches Museum, Vienna.

5–28. Foliage Mask. Temple of Bacchus at Baalbek.

5–29. Grave Stele. Epigraphic Museum, Athens.

5–30. Figurines. Landesmuseum, Schleswig.

5–31. Foliage Mask. Marburg/Art Resource, New York.

5–32. De Gheyn, *Rocks Overrun by Plants Forming Grotesque Heads*. Institute Néerlandais, Paris.

5–33. Dürer, *Ruined Alpine Hut* (Detail). Biblioteca Ambrosiana, Milan.

5–34. Dali, *Paranoic Visage*. Musée Nationale D'Art Moderne, Paris.

5–35. *Enigmatic Landscape*. Dr. Gunter Bohmer Collection, Munich.

5–36. Figures from the trunk of an apple tree. Municipal Archives, Haarlem.

5–37. Spaghetti Christ. © Associated Press.

5–38. Martian apparition. National Aeronautics and Space Administration.

5–39. Roerich, *Warrior of Light*. © Nicholas Roerich Museum, New York.

5–40. Flower ballet. Copyright Kjell B. Sandved.

5–41. Coupling. John Walter Baybay and Emanuele Ames.

5–42. Anthropomorphic animals. Grandville.

5–43. Baron Ernst von Maydell, *A-Climbing We Will Go* (detail), ca 1941. Courtesy Art Resource/ Cooper-Hewitt Museum, The Smithsonian Institution's National Museum of Design.

5–44. Kawanabe, *Mice Transcribing a Book* (detail). Arthur M. Sackler Gallery, Washington, D.C.

5–45. Palazetto Zuccari. Art Resource, New York.

Index

Abrahamic God, 179, 187. *See also*
  Christianity; Islam; Judaism
Abstractions, personified, 59, 75, 120,
  123–30, 132, 136–39, 153,
  240*n.148.*
Addison, Joseph, 124
Advertising, 96–97, 131, 132–33, 134,
  232*n.90*
Aeschylus, 123, 125
Afanasyev, Viktor, 56
Africa, 190, 192
  architecture, 149, 150
  art, 120, 135–36, 138
  literature, 114–18
  religion, 17, 26, 34, 71, 190, 191, 192
"African Traditional Thought and Western
  Science" (Horton), 34
Afterlife. *See* Death; Spirits
Agassi, Joseph, 70–71, 164, 237–38*nn.75,
  76,* 241–42*n.8,* 245–46*n.122*
Airplanes. *See* Anthropomorphized or
  animated things and events
Alberti, Leone Battista, 141, 217*n.68,*
  233*n.131*
Albertus Magnus, 142
Allegory, 124, 125, 136–37, 139. *See also*
  Personification
Allport, Gordon, 23, 206*n.5*
Ambiguity. *See* Perceptual uncertainty
American Indians. *See* Native Americans

Analogy, 200–201. *See also* Metaphor
  animism and, 215*n.9*
  anthropomorphism and, 64, 65, 68–71,
    78, 98, 182, 183, 186
  cognition and perception, 21, 26, 34,
    46–47, 54, 69, 70, 71
  in literature, 129–30
  mythology and, 68–69, 70
  in religion. *See* Religion, analogy
Anaxagoras, 153
Anaximander, 55, 153, 235*n.8*
Anaximenes, 55, 154
Ancestor worship, 16, 23, 86–87, 190
Animals. *See also* Chimpanzees
  animism in, 6, 39, 47–48, 51, 52, 54,
    188, 202
  anthropomorphism in, 82, 83–84, 92,
    101, 104, 112, 113, 116
  anthropomorphism of, 41, 81, 87–88, 93–
    94, 113, 114, 127, 132, 134–35, 138,
    144, 145, 170, 171, 183, 193–94
  as continuous with humans, 82, 87–88,
    138, 193, 197, 222–23*n.94*
  as continuous with inanimate nature, 53,
    174, 217*n.67*
  deception and, 48–54, 185, 217*n.48*
  perception and, 21, 45, 74, 80, 81, 82,
    101, 104, 140, 202
  in philosophy and science, 170–71, 174
  and religion, 177, 183, 193, 197, 202

Animation, 125, 229*n.22*
Animatism, 25
Animism. *See also* Personification
  as analogy, 215*n.9*
  in animals. *See* Animals, animism in
  anthropomorphism compared with, 39–
    40, 62–63, 65, 66, 67, 70, 71, 83,
    112, 189, 230*n.51*
  and art, 54, 55, 75, 133, 136, 145–46
  as belief in souls, 70
  as belief in spirits, 21–22, 39, 40, 48
  in children. *See* Children, animism
  in daily life, 6, 25, 39, 40, 44, 45, 47,
    51, 53, 60–61, 116
  definitions, 4, 5, 22, 39–40, 41, 233*n.155*
  diffuse, 110
  evolution of, 214*n.3*, 218*n.77*, 231*n.73*
  as innate, 66, 110, 231*n.73*
  intellectualist theories, 21–25, 35
  in literature, 57–60, 75, 113–20, 123–
    30
  as metaphor, 218*n.90*
  in nature, 9, 25, 52, 57, 58–60, 107–9,
    123–26, 218*n.77*
  perception and, 39–41, 46, 47–48, 52–
    54, 61, 107, 110–11, 189, 200,
    214*n.1*, 231*n.73*
  in philosophy, 55–56, 153, 218*n.77*
  in religion. *See* Religion, animism
  in science, 25, 41, 55–56, 57, 165, 167,
    197, 234–35*n.1*,
  social functionalist theories, 18, 56–57,
    218*n.90*
  sources of, 6, 41, 52–54, 110–11
  systematic 110
Anthropic principle, 169–70, 239*nn.103,*
  104, 107, 108, 109, 110, 113
Anthropocentrism
  and anthropomorphism, 63, 81, 82,
    107–8, 110, 111, 144, 161–65, 170,
    178
  in art, 144
  as perception, 83, 107, 159, 160, 161–
    65, 238*n.76*
  in philosophy and science, 160, 161,
    162, 169–70, 234–35*n.1*, 238*n.76*
Anthropology, 187, 206*n.5*, 247*n.151*. *See*
  also specific anthropologists, e.g.,
  Horton
  anthropomorphism as central to religion,
    67, 178, 220*n.15*
  anthropomorphism and cultural
    differences, 174
  anthropomorphism as a cultural
    universal, 63, 64–65

attitude toward religion, 26, 178,
  211*n.116*, 246 *n.124*
culture as purposive, 175
familiarity theory, 78–79
intellectualist theories, 33, 40, 214*n.167*
symbolic communication, 247*n.151*
Anthropomorphism. *See also topics generally*
  accidental, 96. *See also* Chance images
  as analogy, 64–65, 68–71, 78, 98, 182,
    183, 186, 235*n.3*
  animals and. *See* Animals,
    anthropomorphism
  animism compared with, 39–40, 62–63,
    65, 66, 67, 70, 71, 83, 112, 189,
    230*n.51*
  in architecture, 132, 146–50,
    234*n.167*
  in art, 43–44, 64, 75, 120, 122, 130–
    46, 151, 231*n.82*
  in children. *See* Children,
    anthropomorphism
  as confusion, 65–68, 79–82, 161–62,
    244*n.70*
  in daily life, 40, 74, 80, 84, 92, 95, 116,
    117–19, 143, 233*n.127*
  definitions of, 3–4, 6, 62, 81, 82–83,
    240*n.144*
  familiarity theory, 64–71, 73, 78–82,
    185
  forms, 92–98, 132, 142, 208*n.54*
  gods. *See* Deities
  hidden, 132, 142, 151
  immediate, 153, 167
  implicit, 129, 133, 143, 144
  as innate, 66, 77, 103–6, 141, 144,
    216*n.41*, 231*n.66*, 233*n.127*
  intellectualist theories of, 22, 24, 34–37,
    214*n.16*
  literal, 70, 92–93, 96, 182
  in literature, 75, 113–20, 123–30, 132,
    134, 139, 150, 158, 229*n.16*,
    230*n.48*
  of nature, 62, 137, 138, 144, 161. *See*
    also Anthropomorphized or animated
    things and events
  origin of, 6, 37, 62, 65–66, 72, 82–83,
    89–90, 131, 216*n.41*
  as perceptual strategy, 62, 64, 68, 69,
    81, 90, 98, 101–03, 121, 141, 187,
    189, 202, 214*n.1*
  in philosophy, 62, 63, 70, 153–58, 161–
    64, 235*n.3*
  religion and. *See* Religion
  religious and secular compared, 112,
    139, 188, 197–201

in science, 65, 75, 122, 163–70, 174, 175, 176, 234–35*n.1* 237*n.61*, 238*n.88*, 240*nn.124, 148*
warnings against, 91–92, 159–60, 161–63, 164–65, 176, 182–83
wish-fulfillment theory, 63, 65, 66, 67, 70, 72–78
Anthropomorphized or animated things and events (specific examples)
abstractions. *See* Abstractions, personified
air, 153
airplanes, 59, 60, 94–95, 192
automobiles, 39, 60, 92, 94, 132, 134
bags, 39
bells, 44
bicycles, 59
boats and ships, 60, 95, 127
books, 127, 136
bottles, 58, 85, 97, 132–33, 133–34, 231–32*n.89*
buildings, 132, 142, 146, 149, 150. *See also* houses, *below*
celestial bodies, 41, 132, 137, 153, 155, 156, 235*n.3. See also specific bodies*, e.g., Moon
cities, 137, 138
clothing, 47, 58, 119
clouds, 40, 55, 62, 69, 142, 143, 175, 233*n.130*
computers, 63, 93, 127, 167, 192
doors, 47
earth, 55, 56, 57, 58, 60, 77, 118, 123, 132, 137, 153, 155–56, 161, 172–73, 175, 176
earthquakes, 118
fire, 53, 55, 58, 114, 138, 153, 217*n.61*
fire hydrants, 6
fog, 59
food, 113, 115, 127, 132, 134, 136, 139, 143–44, 145
furniture, 58,
garbage, 51, 74, 80, 92
hat, 47
handbag, 58
houses, 58, 60, 132, 149, 150, 234*n.184*
hurricane, 25
insects, 170–71, 239–40*n.119*
instruments, musical, 144
jar, 133
lakes, 40
landscapes, 59, 62, 83, 96, 117, 123, 125, 142, 143, 144–45, 228*n.4. See also specific parts of landscapes*, e.g, mountains

leaves, 6, 39, 58–59, 144
letter *and* numerals, 127, 132, 136
logs, 9, 45
machinery, 58, 60, 92, 94–96, 127, 132, 133, 192, 230*n.51*
mailboxes, 92, 119–20, 132, 204
moon, 62, 69, 114, 115, 116, 132, 155, 161
mountains, 40, 60, 84, 117–18, 124, 128, 132, 142, 145
paper, 6, 39
pens, 58
plants, 50, 52, 60, 113, 124, 127, 128, 132, 141–42, 144–45, 193
pottery, 120, 135–36, 230*n.51*, 232*n.98*
rain, 124
rivers, 58, 68, 83, 92, 128
rocks, 25, 39, 51, 55, 60, 72, 74, 77, 128, 141, 144, 145
sea, 58, 62, 72, 74, 75, 118, 132, 137, 139, 151
sirens, 39
sky, 123, 137
smoke, 59
stars and planets, 41, 55, 56, 112, 114, 115, 132, 137, 153, 155, 156, 167
sun, 114–15, 155, 161, 237*n.61. See also* stars and planets, above
swords, 123
tools, 6, 60
toys, 75
trains, 58
trees, 60, 74, 80, 83, 92, 96, 122, 128, 132, 142, 143, 144, 145
volcanoes, 118, 119
walls, 44, 142
water, 138
weather, 47, 51, 52, 58, 68, 75, 114, 116, 117, 132
wind, 58, 62, 74, 92, 114, 124, 132, 137
Anthropomorphs (in Paleolithic art), 134–35
Anxiety, 10–14, 41, 72–74, 105–7. *See also* Wish-fulfillment theory
Aquinas, Thomas, 63, 181
Arbib, Michael, 81, 99
Architecture, 132, 146–50, 234*nn.167, 184. See also* Anthropomorphized or animated things and events, buildings
Arcimboldo, 138, 151
Aristotle
animism and perception, 53, 55
artificialism, 155–56, 165, 167, 236n.36
chance images, 141
cosmology, 55, 153–57, 172

Aristotle (*continued*)
    criticized by Bacon, 159
    immediate anthropomorphism, 153, 167
    Umoved Mover, 55, 156–57, 236*n.38*
Arnheim, Rudolf, 143
    anthropomorphism in art, 232*n.100*
    perception as interpretation 43, 47, 131,
        140
    predisposition to see human form, 101,
        103
Art. *See also* Animism, art;
        Anthropomorphism, art; Architecture;
        Literature; Visual art
    commercial, 131–34, 136, 231*n.82*,
        232 *n.90. See also* Advertising
    fine, 43–44, 75, 122, 130, 131, 132,
        136–46, 151, 232*n.100*
    folk, 54, 131, 134, 135, 136, 143,
        146
    origin of, 233*n.131*
    tribal, 54–55, 131, 134–36, 143. *See also*
        Computers
Artificial intelligence, 48, 98, 121. *See also*
        Computers
Artificialism, 40, 55, 57, 153, 167,
        218*n.77*, 236*n.36*
    child, 107, 109–10, 111, 112, 236*n.36*
    definition, 40, 153, 214*n.4*
Astronauts. *See* Space exploration
Astronomy, 41, 43, 56, 167–68, 237*n.61*,
        238*n.98*, 239*n.109. See also* Space
        exploration
Astrophysics. *See* Physics
Atheism, 32, 178, 184, 210*n.81*,
        241*n.2*
Atheistic religion, 7, 20, 182, 184, 191–
        92, 210*n.81*
Attachment theory, 226*n.72*
Augustine, 24, 134, 181, 214*n.161*
Austin, William, 147
Automobiles. *See* Anthropomorphized or
        animated things and events

Bacon, Francis
    on anthropomorphism, 62, 63, 65, 158–
        61, 165, 172, 176
    anticipates Sapir, Whorf, 237*n.56*
    goals unique to humans, 175
    human mind exaggerates order, 89
Bainbridge, William, 206*n.16*, 207*n.40*
Bali, 14, 23
Barbour, Ian, 26–27, 30, 195, 243*n.43*,
        245–46*n.122*
Barkan, Leonard, 71, 146, 148, 228*n.1*,
        244*n.83*
Barnes, Barry, 165, 234–35*n.1*

Barrow, John, 169
Barth, Frederik, 247*n.151*
Barthelme, Donald, 122
Barthes, Roland, 143
Basil, 181
Bateson, Gregory, 25
Batson, C. Daniel, 226*n.72*
Baudelaire, Charles, 129
Bekoff, Mark, 51
Believers' theories of religion, 5, 8–10,
        199. *See also* Religion
Bell, Jocelyn, 168
Bellah, Robert, 27, 32, 199
Bergman, Ingmar, 132
Bergson, Henri, 210*n.94*
Bible, 24, 30, 123, 124, 135, 136, 177,
        179, 180, 181, 192, 203
Bickerton, Derek, 76, 206*n.9*
Biology, 25, 53, 56, 57, 168, 170–74,
        208*n.54. See also specific biologists*, e.g.,
        Gould
Bishop Berkeley, 89
Blake, William, 128
Bloch, Maurice, 205*n.1*
Bloomfield, Morton, 123, 124, 125,
        129
Boas, Franz, 178, 216*n.41*, 241*n.6*
Bodin, Jean, 16
Body image as microcosm, 71, 72, 141,
        146–50, 154–55, 157–58, 234*n.167*
Body/mind dualism. *See* Dualism
Bohr, Niels, 166
Bolton, John, 167–68
Botticelli, 138
Bottles. *See* Anthropomorphized or
        animated things and events
Bovet, Pierre, 192, 227*n.88*
Bowker, J. W. 205*n.1*
Bowlby, John, 106
Braithwaite, R. B., 184, 211*n.122*
Brandon, S.G.F., 63, 182, 215*n.13*
Breughel, 142, 151
Brightman, Edgar, 237–38*n.75*
Brown, L. B., 53, 56
Brown, Stuart, 245–46*n.122*
Broyard, Anatole, 143
Bruner, Jerome, 15
Brunschvicg, 218*n.77*
Buber, Martin, 180, 198–99
Buddhism, 146, 210*n.81*, 212*n.137*
    anthropomorphism in, 89, 187, 191–92,
        209–10*n.80*, 210*n.81*
    art, 146
    demythologized, 7, 20, 191–92
    detachment in, 212*n.137*

gods, 17, 18, 19–20, 89, 192,
    209nn.76, 77, 80
  self-concepts, 225n.62
Buildings. *See* Anthropomorphized or
    animated things and events
Butler, Charles, 170

Camouflage, 48–50, 83, 86, 185 *See also*
    Deception
Campbell, Norman, 90
Cargo cults, 12
Carter, Brandon, 169
Categorical perception. *See* Pattern
    Recognition
Caughey, John, 193, 231n.70
Causation concept, 163
Celestial bodies. *See* Cosmology
Chance images, 55, 62, 96, 141–43,
    233nn.130, 131
Chatham, Russell, 143
Cheney, Dorothy, 51
Children. *See also* Infants; Parent/child
    relationship; Piaget
  animism 40, 47, 53–54, 56–57, 107–9,
    214–15n.5, 215 nn.9, 10
  anthropomorphism, 65, 66, 73, 74, 91,
    104, 110–11, 184, 187, 192
  artificialism, 40, 107, 109–10
  religion and, 184, 192, 221n.65,
    227n.88
Chimpanzees
  aggression, 74
  continuity with humans, 80, 82, 87, 88,
    223n.103
  storm threats, 52, 88, 188, 202,
    210n.90
China
  animism and anthropomorphism, 60,
    116–17, 124
  art, 60, 124, 135, 138, 144–45
  gods, 86, 190. *See also* Confucius
  religion, 12, 16, 17, 190
Ch'i spirit, 60, 145
Chomsky, Noam, 77
Christianity, 7, 12
  animal/people separation in, 87, 174
  animism and perception, 55
  anthropomorphism and, 24–25, 31, 63,
    139, 151, 179, 180–82, 185, 188,
    191–92, 196
  arts and, 139, 143, 147–50, 151
  demythologized, 7, 19, 191–92
  faith and 30, 31
  God in, 13, 24, 25, 31, 75, 174, 179–
    81, 183–84, 185. *See also* Bible

intellectualist theory and, 24, 30, 31
philosophy, science, and, 174, 196,
    236n.38
social functionalist theory and, 17, 18,
    19
theologians, 139, 179–82 *See also specific
    theologians*, e.g., Tillich
wish-fulfillment theory and, 12, 13, 63,
    75, 207n.40
Churches, 146–50, 234n.167
Churchland, P. M., 214n.166
Cleaver, Eldridge, 116
Clement of Alexandria, 180–81
Clothing
  anthropomorphized and animated, 47,
    58, 119
  camouflage, 86
Clouds. *See* Anthropomorphized or
    animated things and events
Cognition. *See also* Intellectualist and
    eclectic theories of religion
  and anthropomorphism, 64, 66, 68,
  and emotions, 76–77
  and perception, 37, 42–43, 47
Coherence and perception, 43, 102
Coleridge, Samuel, 57
Coles, Robert, 184, 192
Comfort theory. *See* Wish-fulfillment
    theory
Commercial art. *See* Art, commercial
Commitment. *See* Faith
Common sense, 29, 30, 34, 36–37, 178,
    194, 214nn.165, 166
Communication *See* Language; Religious
    symbolism
Computers
  anthropomorphized, 63, 93, 94, 127,
    166, 167, 192
  scanning, 98, 99, 100, 101, 230n.50
Comte, Auguste, 16, 65, 66, 80, 178,
    208n.62
Confucius, 16, 86, 124, 190, 193,
    208n.56
Confusion theory. *See* Familiarity theory
Conklin, Harold, 23
Consciousness, stages of (Piaget), 108–9,
    226n.76
Corbusier, Charles Le, 150
Cosmology. *See also* Anthropomorphized
    or animated things and events,
    celestial bodies; Astronomy; Space
    exploration
  animism in, 41, 55–56
  anthropomorphism in, 67, 75, 137,
    153–57, 166, 167, 235n.8

Cosmology (*continued*)
    arts and, 148, 153–58, 168–69
    religion and, 187, 200, 209*n.76*
Courbet, Gustave, 144, 151
Coy, Jenny, 80, 111
Crick, Francis, 19, 33, 44, 172
Crosby, Donald, 184, 227*n.86*

Dali, Salvador, 142
Darwin, Charles, 19, 57, 173–74, 194
Darwin, Erasmus, 57
David, Nicholas, 120
Dawkins, Richard, 171
Death
    afterlife and, 13, 193
    animism and perception, 40, 48, 50
    as departure of spirit, 22, 24, 40, 48
    personified, 75, 120, 128, 139
    wish-fulfillment theory and, 11, 12, 13,
        73
Deception. *See also* Camouflage
    as characteristic of gods, 48, 50, 51,
        185
    as characteristic of humans, 48, 50, 83–
        86, 185
    natural, 48–54, 217*n.48*
"Definition of Religion, and Its Uses, A"
    (Horton), 33
Deities. *See also* Greece, ancient, gods;
    Religion; Tribal religions; *specific*
    religions, e.g., Judaism
    animism and perception, 40, 45, 51, 57
    arts and, 137, 139, 146, 151
    anxiety and, 10–14, 72, 75, 220*n.65*
    continuous with humans, 18–20, 22,
        24–25, 40, 86–87, 112, 138, 177–85,
        189–94, 196, 198–201, 203,
        209*n.80*, 211*n.110*, 221*n.65*, 241*n.1*,
        242*n.23*, 243*n.55*, 244*n.84*, 245*n.88*
        See also Meaning, humanlike models as
        basis for
    continuous with lesser beings, 75, 177,
        192, 193
    definition, 177–78, 241*n.1*
    design and universal order, 19, 21–22,
        166, 168, 186–87, 204, 210*n.91*,
        244*nn.64, 70, 71*
    encounter, 30, 31, 242*n.19*
    familiarity theory, 66, 67, 70
    origin of, 72, 209*n.64*, 220*n.27*
    in popular belief, 34, 64, 75, 178, 189–
        93, 195, 209*n.76*, 235*n.3*. *See also*
        Mythology; Folk literature
    revelation of, 8
    superhuman, 212–13*n.144*, 241*n.1*

symbolic action, 7, 38, 177, 178, 198–
    200. *See also* Religious symbolism
as transformation, 83
wish-fulfillment theory, 14, 72, 75,
    207*n.40*, 220*n.65*
De Man, Paul, 129
Democritus, 165
Descartes, René, 24, 57, 174
Design, argument from. *See* Deities, design
    and universal order
Detachment, religious. 212*n.137*
Dialogue on the Great World Systems
    (Galileo), 161
Dickens, Charles, 58–59, 75
Diderot, Denis, 58
Diogenes, 153, 157
Dissatisfaction. *See* Anxiety
Doctrine of Signatures, 96, 158
Donne, John, 55, 75, 78, 128
Douglas, Mary, 26, 33
Drake, Frank, 168
Dreams, 22, 24, 40, 48, *See also* Spirits
Dualism, 22, 24, 25, 57, 126
Duggan, W. J., 181
Durandus, William, 234*n.167*
Dürer, Albrecht, 142, 151
Durkheim, Emile, 62, 175
    denies religion anthropomorphizes, 17,
        19, 20, 191, 193
    intellectualist theory, 22, 23
    religion as encoded morality, 17
    religion no illusion, 204
    religion and science similar, 20, 21, 38,
        195, 201, 210*n.84*
    sacred and profane, 17, 18, 20, 203
    social solidarity theory, 17–21, 28, 38,
        56, 67, 209*n.64*
    totemism as original religion, 17, 18,
        209*n.64*

Earman, John, 169
Earth. *See* Anthropomorphized or animated
    things and events
Eddington, Arthur, 56
Egocentrism. *See* Anthropocentrism
Ehnmark, Erland, 191, 192, 245*n.88*,
    247*n.151*
Eibl-Eibesfeldt, Irenäus, 231*n.73*
Einstein, Albert, 166, 168, 186
Eliade, Mircea, 9, 31, 37, 56
Eliot, Charles, 19
Eliot, T. S., 59, 127
Emotions,
    and art, 124, 126, 129, 132, 133, 229–
        30*n.33*

as compound states, 76–77, 79, 206nn.8, 9, 221–22n.71
perception and, 9, 31, 76–77, 126, 160, 203
and religion, 9, 12, 33, 203, 204, 205–06n.5
as source of anthropomorphism 75–77, 126
Encounter. *See* Deities
Entomology, 170, 171
Entropy, 166, 167, 238n.88
Erwin, Margaret, 93, 96
Eskimos, 18, 72, 84, 86, 116, 138, 191
Essence of Christianity (Feuerbach), 188
Ethical religions. *See* Religion
Ethnography, 4, 63, 98, 112, 120–21, 145
Ethology, 25, 48, 51, 54, 77, 101, 106, 174
Euhemerus, 86, 190
Euhemerism, 190
Euripides, 11
Evans–Pritchard, E. E., 10, 26, 210n.81, 211nn.106, 116, 241n.8
Explanation, 42–43, 215n.17. *See also* Interpretation; Meaning

Face perception, 77, 103–5, 141, 143, 221n.38, 231n.73. *See also* Infants
Fairbairn, W.R.D., 106
Faith, 29, 30, 31, 35–36, 183, 196, 202–03
False warning, 49–50
Familiarity theory, 65–71, 73, 78–82
analogy, 64, 65, 68–71, 78–79, 215n.9
confusion, 65–68, 79–82, 161–62
problems with, 73, 78–79, 79–80, 81–82, 185
Family resemblances concept, 197–98
Fear. *See* Anxiety
Fechner, Gustav, 56
Fedigan, Linda, 165
Fernandez, James W., 79, 234n.184
Ferré, Frederick, 63, 181, 183, 212n.144, 222–23n.94, 237–38n.75, 243n.55
Fetishism, 66
Feuerbach, Ludwig
anthropomorphism primitive, 244n.78
familiarity theory, 65, 66–67, 80
on religion, 179, 182–83, 187–88, 200, 209n.64
religion as anthropomorphism, 66, 179, 185, 187–88, 200, 248n.166
religion as prayer, 247n.151
wish-fulfillment theory, 10, 13, 63, 72, 163

Ficino, Marsilio, 158
Film, 132, 150
Fine art. *See* Art, fine
Fingesten, Peter, 148–49
Finster, Howard, 143
Fire. *See* Anthropomorphized or animated things and events
Firth, Raymond, 247n.151
Folk art. *See* Art, folk
Folk literature, 48, 111–21, 144, 146, 223n.102
Fontenelle, Bernard, 21, 68–69, 178, 210n.90
Food. *See* Anthropomorphized or animated things and events
Forster, E. M., 106, 123
Frazer, James, 87
Fredkin, Edward, 167
Free will, 203
Freedberg, David, 75, 145–46
Freud, Sigmund
animism, 65, 214n.3
anthropmorphizes ego and id, 175
anthropomorphizes science, 240n.148
familiarity theory, 65, 66, 78, 80
human drives, 14, 37–38, 105, 106, 107, 208n.49
humanization of nature, 15, 37–38, 72–73
on religion, 15, 179, 184–85, 190, 193, 206n.13, 243n.61
religion based in feelings toward father, 248n.166
secular ritual, 248n.165
social functionalist theory, 16
wish-fulfillment theory, 10, 11, 12, 14–15, 28, 75, 76, 78
Fright. *See* Anxiety
Fromm, Erich, 106
Frye, Northrop, 55, 124
Functionalism, 208n.54, 212n.141. *See also* Social functionalist theories

Gaia, 56, 172, 230n.60. *See also* Lovelock, James
Galileo, 161, 194, 237n.61
Gallus, Alexander, 182
Gaskin, J.C.A., 12, 184, 186, 205n.3, 212n.140, 244nn.64, 70, 71
Gavua, Kodzo, 120
Geertz, Clifford, 10, 14, 15, 23, 38, 199, 201, 211n.128, 212n.143
religion and meaning, 213n.145
"Religion as a Cultural System," 27–32
Gell-Mann, Murray, 167

Genesis, 203
Geology, 172, 175
Gheyn, Jacques de II, 142
Gibb, H.A.R., 182
Gibson, J. J., 215*n.15*, 217*n.67*
God and gods. *See* Deities
Goethe, Johann, 63
Gombrich, Ernst, 143
    animism, 54–55
    art as schema and correction, 217*n.68*
    perception as betting, 42, 98, 130–31
    perception and biological interests, 80–
        81, 103, 141
    predisposition of humans to see humans,
        91, 103, 141, 233*n.127*
Goodall, Jane, 52, 65, 202, 210*n.90*
Goodman, Nelson, 216*n.39*, 229*n.22*
Gorsuch, Richard L., 215*n.13*
Gould, Stephen Jay, 164–65, 239–
    40*n.119*
Grandville, 144
Graphic art. *See* Visual art
Greece, ancient. *See also individual Greeks*,
        e.g., Aristotle
    animism, 43, 55, 59, 153
    anthropomorphism 21, 72, 135, 136,
        137, 139, 178, 235*n.3*
    art and architecture, 128, 136, 137,
        139, 141, 144, 147, 153
    gods, 11, 18, 24, 51, 86, 126, 137,
        139, 178, 179, 189–90, 191, 193,
        195, 242*n.33*. *See also* Homer
    mythology, 135–36, 195
    philosophy, 21, 55–56, 153–57, 235*n.3*
    religion, 11, 16, 139, 153, 157, 242*n.33*
    science, 165
    spirit as material, 242*n.33*
Greece, modern, 88
Greenberg, Jay, 105, 106, 211*n.114*
Greenberg, Moshe, 185
Gregory, Richard, 98, 103
Gregory of Nazianzus, 181
Griaule, Marcel, 23
Griffin, Donald, 98, 101
Griffiths, Lavinia, 125, 129–30
Grünbaum, Adolf, 166
Guth, Alan, 167
Guthrie, W.K.C., 190

Haldane, J.B.S., 56
Hamann, Johan Georg, 229–30*n.33*
Hanson, Allen, 81, 99
Harding, J. D., 141
Hardy, Thomas, 123
Harman, Gilbert, 90, 102

Harvey, William, 158
Hatano, Giyoo, 215*n.9*, 227*n.91*
Hearne, Vicki, 93
Hebrew Bible. *See Bible*
Hecht, Anthony, 127
Hedley, Jane, 125
Hegel, Georg, 8, 12, 56
Heider, Fritz, 95
Heinlein, Robert, 230*n.51*
Heller, David, 220*n.65*
Helmholtz, Hermann von, 99, 163
Heraclitus, 55, 153
Hermits, 18, 83
Herschel, William, 167
Hewes, Gordon W. 247*n.154*
Hierarchies of perceptual interests, 44–45,
        101–3. *See also* Pattern recognition
Hinduism,
    as atheistic, 19, 20
    gods, 75, 89, 187, 190–91, 192, 199
    hermits, 18
    Shaiva, 199
Hinks, Roger, 136–37, 138, 139
Hinton, H. E., 51
Hippocrates, 154
Hobbes, Thomas, 53
Homer, 123, 125, 127, 137, 139, 153,
        178, 185, 189
Horton, Robin, 213*n.155*
    familiarity theory, 63, 67, 68, 71, 72
    intellectualist theories, 23, 26, 33–37,
        214*n.163*
    personalism, 33–34, 36, 178, 188
    as rationalist, 214*n.163*
    on religion, 178, 185, 188, 195, 200,
        203
    on ritual, 203
    science and religion, 34–35, 37, 71,
        188, 195, 205*n.3*, 214*n.65*
    traditional societies, 213*n.159*
    wish-fulfillment theory, 72, 75
Human classification. *See also* Deities
    continuity of human and nonhuman,
        18–20, 24–25, 40–41, 79–80, 86–89,
        112, 130, 134, 136, 146, 192, 193,
        222–23*n.94*, 223*n.103*, 231*n.70*
    discontinuity of humans, 24, 79, 87, 88,
        151, 174, 179, 188, 193–94
Humanistic theories of religion, 5, 10,
        199. *See also specific theorists*, e.g.,
        Hume
    intellectualist, 10, 21–37, 38
    reviews of, 207*n.18*, 213*n.154*
    social functionalist, 10, 16–21, 28, 33,
        208*n.54*

wish-fulfillment, 10–16, 28, 34, 37–38, 207n.40
Humanlike models. *See* Meaning, humanlike models as basis for
Humboldt, Wilhelm von, 198
Hume, David, 191, 195, 200, 210n.91
  animism and perception, 39, 48
  anticipates Darwin, 186, 244n.70
  design argument, 21–22, 48, 186–87, 189, 244n.70
  familiarity theory, 62, 63, 68, 69, 70, 72, 79, 162, 185–87
  intellectualist theory, 21–22, 38
  mystics as atheists, 177, 241n.2
  prayer as communication with God, 247n.154
  social functionalist theory, 18
  wish-fulfillment theory, 10, 11, 13, 63, 72, 75
Hutton, James, 57, 172
Hypothesis levels in perception, 101–3. *See also* Perception

Iban people, 113
I Ching, 60
Idowu, E. Bolaji, 179, 206n.13
Illusions, 51–52, 82, 89, 111
Imagism, 126–27
Impersonalism, 35
Inagaki, Kayako, 215n.9, 227n.91
India, 114–18, 190–91
Indians, American. *See* Native Americans
Infants, 14, 17, 80, 231n.73. *See also* Children; Face perception; Parent/child relationship
"In Praise of Anthropomorphism" (Ferré), 183
Intellectualist and eclectic theories of religion, 10. *See also specific theorists*, e.g., Horton
  eclectic, 27–33
  intellectualist, 10, 21–27, 33–38, 214n.163
Interpretation, 43, 90, 215n.17. *See also* Pattern recognition; Perception; Perceptual uncertainty
  as betting, 4–5, 6, 38, 42, 45, 46, 47, 48, 204, 215n.9, 216n.31, 227n.91
  and desire for meaning, 15, 21, 23, 101–3. *See also* Meaning
Inuit, 18, 138. *See also* Eskimo
Invisibility, 48–51, 185, 189
Irrationalist theory. *See* Wish-fulfillment theory

Islam, 146, 151, 179, 180, 182, 185, 187
Isolation, 18, 106
Isomorphism, 81–82

Jainism, 18, 19, 210n.81
James, William, 18, 23, 28, 37, 42, 199, 206n.5, 210n.82, 246n.133
Janson, H. W., 141, 142
Japan
  ancestors, 16, 23, 190
  art, 135, 145
  kami, 86, 190, 192
  psychotherapy, 226n.72
  religion, 12, 16, 17, 18, 23, 190. *See also* Buddhism; Shinto
  science, 174
  self-concepts, 225n.62
Jarvie, Ian, 26, 241–42n.8, 245–46n.122
Jaspers, Karl, 182
Java, 15, 23, 30
Jesus, 30, 143, 148, 149
Jevons, F. B., 181, 247n.154
Jews, 87–88. *See also* Judaism
Job (biblical character), 28, 30–31, 180
John of Damascus, 181
Journalism, 59, 62, 112, 117, 118, 120, 175
Joyce, James, 127, 133–34, 230n.48
Judaism
  anthropomorphism in, 20, 115, 116, 135, 146, 151, 179, 180, 185, 191–92, 199
  art and, 136, 139, 146, 151
  demythologized, 19, 191–92
  God, nature of, 28, 30–31, 75, 174, 179, 180, 185, 187, 199. *See also* Bible
  theologians, 139, 179–80. *See also specific theologians*, e.g. Maimonides

Kalabari people, 34, 71
Kant, Immanuel, 17, 68, 162–63, 203
Keats, John, 128
Keil, Frank C., 214n.5, 215n.6
Kepler, Johannes, 56
Key, Wilson Bryan, 133, 231–32n.89
Kipling, Rudyard, 48, 113
Klein, Melanie, 105
Kollwitz, Käthe, 138
Koran, 179, 182. *See also* Islam
Kramers, J. H., 182
Krasner, Barbara, 199
Kroeber, A. L., 175
Kumin, Albert, 136

La Barre, Weston, 12, 207*n.40*
Ladendorf, Heinz, 141
Landscapes. *See* Anthropomorphized or
    animated things and events
Lang, Andrew, 24
Lange, F. A., 68, 80, 220*nn.32, 34, 35*
Language, 27, 127, 163, 245*n.118*. *See
    also* Religious symbolism; Symbolic
    interaction
    as basis of human community with
        animals, 81, 224*n.6*, 247*n.146*
    central to religion, 177, 198–200,
        247*n.154*
    as human capacity, 197–98, 224*n.6*,
        246*n.139*
Lawson, E. Thomas, 196, 208*n.55*
    common sense as theoretical, 214*n.166*
    gods as superhuman agents, 241*n.1*
    interpretation vs. explanation, 215*n.17*
    religion has gods, 213*n.144*, 248*n.165*
Lazarus, Richard, 206*n.7*
Lee, Richard B., 23, 210*n.96*
Leibnitz, G. W., 25
Lenin, V. I., 56
Leonardo da Vinci, 43–44, 56, 158
Levi-Strauss, Claude, 23, 26, 63, 76, 178,
    211*n.120*
Levy-Bruhl, Lucien, 134
Lichtenberg, Georg, 163
Linguists, 78
Linnaeus, 171
Literature. *See also* Folk literature;
    Personification; *individual writers*
    animism in, 57–60, 75, 123–30
    anthropomorphism in, 75, 122–30, 132,
        134, 139, 150, 158, 230*n.48*
Lloyd, G.E.R., 154, 165, 235*nn.3, 8*
Lomazzo, Giovanni, 148
Lorenz, Konrad, 92
Loukatos, Demetrious, 72, 73
Lovelock, James, 53, 56, 172–73, 230*n.60*
Lowie, Robert, 23, 25, 210*n.101*
Lucretius, 55, 118, 141, 217*n.77*
Lutz, Catherine, 206*n.9*

Machinery. *See* Anthropomorphized or
    animated things and events;
    Computers
Magic
    and religion, 11, 12–13, 14, 20, 26, 48,
        74, 87, 89, 112, 210*n.82*
    Malinowski on, 11, 12–13
Maimonides, Moses ben, 180, 181
Makeup. *See* Camouflage
Malcolm, Norman, 13

Malefijt, Annemarie de Waal, 241–42*n.8*
Malinowski, Bronislaw, 10, 11, 12–13, 16,
    28, 193, 207*n.34*
Mandela, Nelson, 193
Manetti, Gianozzo, 148
Mantegna, Andrea, 142
Mao Tse-Tung, 193
Marett, Robert, 25
Margolis, Howard, 33, 42, 213*n.150*
Marmorstein, Arthur, 180
Mars, 168, 172
Martinet, François-Nicholas, 144
Marx, Karl, 10, 13
Materialism, 22, 24, 35. *See also* Dualism
Maxwell, James Clerk, 167
Maya, 89
Maydell, Ernst von, 144
McCauley, Robert, 196, 208*n.55*,
    common sense as theoretical, 214*n.166*
    gods as superhuman agents, 241*n.1*
    interpretation vs. explanation, 215*n.17*
    religion has gods, 213*n.144*, 248*n.165*
McPhee, John, 95
Mead, G. H., 96
Meaning. *See also* Interpretation;
    Perception
    humanlike models as basis for, 14–15,
        21, 33, 35–36, 38, 82–83, 89, 98,
        103, 130, 140, 151, 153, 187, 188–
        89, 201, 220*n.27*, 228*n.1*, 231*n.82*,
        234*n.167*, 244*n.83*. *See also* Deities,
        continuous with humans
    and perception, 41–48, 61
    primacy of search for, 23, 32, 33, 64,
        76, 77–78, 90, 198, 204
    search for, as basis of religion, 27–28,
        32, 33, 34, 198, 213*n.145*, 246*n.140*
Melanesia, 11, 12, 138
Melothesia, 158
Melville, Herman, 25
Merleau-Ponty, M., 198
Metaphor. *See also* Analogy
    art, 54, 134, 138
    literature, 54, 123–30, 216*n.39*
    language, 245*n.118*
    mythology, 155
    perception, 13–14, 21, 47, 64, 68, 79,
        92, 98, 134, 216*n.39*, 217*n.57*
    philosophy and science, 13, 19, 21, 27,
        54, 71, 166, 171, 194, 195, 218*n.90*
    religion, 13, 19, 21, 27, 71, 112, 181,
        182, 194, 195
Meynell, Hugo, 182, 183
Midgley, Mary, 163, 222–23*n.94*
Millennial movements, 11, 12, 17

Milton, John, 128, 139
Mimetic characters, 129–30
Mimicry. *See* Camouflage
Mind/body dualism. *See* Dualism
Mitchell, Stephen, 105, 106, 211*n.114*
Models, 27, 35, 43–44, 51, 54, 82, 140, 204. *See also* Meaning, humanlike models as basis for; Pattern recognition; Perception; Scanning; Schemata; Template
Momper, Josse de, 142
Monarchy as cosmic principle, 153–54
Moon, 62, 69, 114, 115, 116, 132, 155, 161
Morality, 18, 111
Mormons, 25, 182
Morris, Brian, 205.*n5*
Möseneder, Karl, 231*n.82*, 232*n.120*
Moslems. *See* Islam
Mountains, 40, 60, 117–18, 124, 128, 132, 142, 145
Munson, Henry, 211*n.128*
Murray, Gilbert, 178
Mustard Seed Garden Manual of Painting, 60, 138, 144
Mysticism, 11, 18, 177, 184–85, 196, 241*n.2*
Mythology, 68–70, 109, 135, 136, 137, 195. *See also* Folk literature
as explanation, 21, 55, 68
origin of anthropomorphism, 68–69, 70
religion and, 187, 190–91, 192, 195
as social charter, 207*n.34*

Native Americans
Central and South America, 18, 87, 114–18, 135, 138, 192
North America, 17, 18, 25, 86, 113, 115–18, 138, 150
Nativistic movements, 11, 12
Natural deception. *See* Deception, natural
Natural History of Religion (Hume), 69, 210*n.91*
Naturalism, 40
Natural selection, 19, 48, 52, 106, 173–74, 186
Nature, 40, 57, 58–59, 60, 72, 118–19, 203. *See also* Animism, in nature; Anthropomorphism, of nature; Anthropomorphized or animated things and events; *specific natural phenomena*, e.g., Moon
Nazi, 88, 132
Needham, Rodney, 245*n.121*
Neisser, Ulrich, 98, 101

Neo-Tylorian. *See* Intellectualist theories
Neusner, Jacob, 180, 247*n.154*
Newman, F. W., 181–82
New Testament, 30. *See also* Bible
Newton, Isaac, 55–56, 57, 166, 168, 186
Nicholas of Cusa, 158
Nielsen, Kai, 9–10, 182, 206*n.12*
Nietzsche, Friedrich, 237*n.73*
animism, 25
anthropocentrism, 63, 81–82, 83, 163
anthropomorphism intrinsic to perception, 65, 68, 78, 80, 144, 163–64, 176, 204, 220–21*n.35*, 223*n.109*
and Lange, 220*nn.32, 34, 35.*
meaning, 213*n.145*
perception and biological interests, 68, 78, 80, 81–82, 163–164, 187
perceptual uncertainty, 44, 68
and Piaget, 227*n.80*
Nilsson, Martin, 178, 189–90
Nonbelievers' theories. *See* Humanistic theories of religion
Norbeck, Edward, 247*n.151*
Norm image, 140
Norse mythology, 116, 123
Numinous. *See* Religious experience
Nunn, T. Percy, 165–66

Oatley, Keith, 101–2, 103
Object constancy, 43
Object-relations theory, 15, 77, 105–7, 121, 208*n.49*, 226*n.72*
On the Origin of Species (Darwin), 173
Ortner, Sherry, 211*n.128*
Otto, Rudolf, 9, 18, 23, 37, 203, 248*n.166*

Pagels, Heinz, 169
Pailin, David, 184, 205.*n5*, 243*n.55*, 246*n.140*
Paleolithic art, 54–55, 134, 135
Paley, William, 186
Palmer, Humphrey, 182, 243*n.43*
Parent/child relationship, 14, 15, 77, 106, 110–11, 215*n.10*
Parmenides, 154
Parsons, Talcott, 245–46*n.122*
Pascal, Blaise, 4, 6, 45
Pathetic fallacy, 123, 124, 125, 126–27, 128, 150, 229–30*n.33* 236*n.40*. *See also* Anthropomorphism in literature
Pattern recognition, 42, 44–47, 53, 64, 71, 90, 160, 163–64, 218*n.70*, 233*nn.130, 131. See also* Models; Perception; Scanning; Schemata
Pauling, Linus, 171–72

Pei, T'ing C., 150
Penner, Hans, 79, 207*n.17*,
    functionalism, 208*n.54*, 212*n.141*,
    God as ineffable, 205*n.5*,
    on Horton, 188–89, 213*n.154*,
        214*n.162*, 244*n.80*
    on persistence of religion, 247*n.157*
    religion and superhuman beings,
        213*n.144*, 241*nn.1-3*
    symbolist theory, 208*n.55*, 213*n.154*
    on ultimacy, 213*n.149*
Perception. *See also* Animals, perception;
    Animism, perception;
    Anthropomorphism, as perceptual
    strategy; Interpretation; Models;
    Pattern recognition; Perceptual
    uncertainty; Scanning; Schemata
    Arnheim on, 43–47, 101, 103, 131, 140
    in art, 140, 141, 146
    biological interests and, 54–55, 68, 78,
        80–81, 103, 141, 161–62, 187–88
    definition, 37, 47
    as direct apprehension, 215*n.15*
    emotions and, 9, 31, 76–77, 126, 160,
        203
    Gombrich on, 42, 80–81, 103, 130–31,
        141
    as interpretation, 37, 38, 41–48, 101–3,
        162–63, 188, 196, 204
    metaphor and, 13–14, 21, 47, 64, 68,
        79, 92, 98, 134, 216*n39*, 217*n.57*
    as representation, 233*n.130*
Perceptual uncertainty, 3, 4, 38, 40–41,
    44, 46, 50–51, 52–54, 69, 197
Perry, Edmund, 33
Persaeus, 190
Personalism, 22, 34–36, 37, 178, 188
Personification, 150. *See also* Animism;
    Perception
    in art, 136–40. *See also*
        Anthropomorphism, in art
    in literature 123–30, 139, 229*nn.16, 22,
        28. See also* Anthropomorphism, in
        literature
    as rhetoric, 229*n.16*
Perspective, 144
Phillips, D. Z., 184, 211*n.122*,
Philosophy. *See also specific philosophers*,
    e.g., Plato
    animism and, 55–56, 153, 218*n.77*
    anthropomorphism and, 62, 63, 70,
        152–58, 161, 165–66, 178, 183–85,
        235*n.3*
    criticism of anthropomorphism, 152,
        161, 162–63, 164, 179, 182

Philostratus, 141, 233*n.130*
Photography, 11, 132, 142, 143, 168
Physics, 25, 34, 56, 163, 165–69.
Piaget, Jean
    animism, 40–41, 47, 48, 53, 55, 56–57,
        65, 107–9, 214*n.3*, 215*n.8*
    anthropomorphism, 65, 73, 74, 79, 80,
        90, 91, 107, 110–11
    artificialism, 40, 55, 107, 109–10,
    criticism of, 227*n.89*
    interpretation as structure, 101–2
    and Nietzsche, 227*n.80*
    self-other distinction, 215*n.9*
    vs. Tylor on animism, 215*n.8*
Piper, H. L., 44
Planck, Max, 165
Plants. *See* Anthropomorphized or
    animated things and events
Plath, Sylvia, 127
Plato, 55, 56, 98, 153–55, 156, 172,
    187
Pliny, 55, 141
Poetry, 125–27, 128, 129, 138. *See also*
    Pathetic fallacy; *individual poets*, e.g.,
    Shakespeare
Polybius, 16
Poole, Fitz John Porter, 205*n.1*
Popper, Sir Karl, 207*n.47*
Popular science, 175
Postmodernism, 215–16*n.17*
Pottery, 120, 135–36, 230*n.51*,
    232*n.98*
Powell, John Wesley, 175
Prayer, 199, 200, 212*n.138*, 245*n.121*,
    247*n.154*. *See also* Language;
    Symbolic action; Religious symbolism
    central to religion, 247*n.154*
Preus, J. S., 10, 197, 207*n.17*, 208*n.62*,
    241*n.2*
Priestly, Joseph, 57
Primates and primatologists, 51, 78, 104,
    165, 174, 193, 225*n.63*. *See also*
    Chimpanzees; *specific primatologists*,
    e.g., Goodall
Primitive Culture (Tylor), 22
Primitive peoples, 210*n.82*. *See also* Art,
    folk, tribal; Tribal religions
Principles of Sociology, The (Spencer), 22
Prodicus of Ceos, 190
Profane, sacred and, 17, 18, 20
Proudfoot, Wayne, 9, 31, 37, 76, 202,
    205*n.3*, 212*n.140*
Prud'hon, 138
Pruyser, Paul, 245–46*n.122*
Psellus, Michael, 142

Psychoanalysis, 15, 78, 98, 105–7, 192, 207*n.47*, 211*n.114*, 226*n.72. See also* Object-relations theory

Psychology. *See also* Cognition; Object-relations theory; Perception; Psychoanalysis; Rorschach Test
  animism, 39, 40, 41, 53, 54, 226*n.76*
  anthropomorphism, 63, 65, 66, 175, 226*n.76*
  perception, 39, 41–45, 47, 78, 98, 101, 107, 121
  and religion, 41, 106–07, 192, 196, 212*n.140*, 215*n.13*
  self-other distinction, 80
  social relations, 37–38, 187, 193
  wish-fulfillment theory, 63, 65, 66, 76, 77

Radcliffe-Brown, A. R., 14, 16, 56, 175
Randall, J. H., 157
Raschke, Theodor, 211*n.115*
Rationalists. *See* Intellectualist theories
Ray, Benjamin, 247*n.151*
Religion. *See also* Deities; Theology; Tribal religion; *specific religions,* e.g., Christianity
  analogy and, 65, 69–72, 182, 183, 195, 200–201
  animism in, 18, 40, 55–56, 57, 66, 189
  as anthropomorphism, 7, 38, 66–67, 70, 112, 178, 185–204, 208*n.62*, 242–43*n.36*
  anthropomorphism, secular, compared with, 112, 139, 188, 197–201
  anthropomorphism as inevitable in, 63–64, 70, 178–85, 212*n.144*, 242–43*n.36*, 243*n.43*
  anxiety and, 10–14, 72, 75
  art and, 30, 139, 143, 147–50, 178, 234*n.167*
  atheistic, 7, 20, 182, 184, 191–92, 210*n.81*
  believers' theories, 5, 8–10, 199
  children and, 184, 192, 221*n.65*, 227*n.88*
    common sense and, 29, 30, 34, 36–37, 178, 194, 214*nn.165, 166*
  continuous with other thought and action, 20, 26, 112, 178, 193, 194–97, 200–01, 209*n.75*, 245*n.121*, 246*n.133*, 248*n.165*
  definition, 8, 15–16, 27–28, 33, 178, 182, 185, 197, 199, 200, 205*n.1*, 207*n.40*, 215*n.13*
  as disease of mind, 206*n.13*
  ethical/non-ethical, 13, 17–18, 177, 209*n.67*

faith and, 29, 30–31, 35–36, 183, 196, 202–03
God and gods. *See* Deities
humanistic theories, 10–38, 199
metaphor and, 13, 19, 21, 27, 71, 112, 181, 182, 194, 195
nonempirical, 205–6*n.5*, 246*n.124*
origin of, 11–12, 15, 21, 65–67, 72, 211*n.106*, 210*n.91*
persistent, 206*n.13*, 247*n.157*
philosophy and, 163, 168, 172, 188–89, 195–96, 201, 210*n.84*, 236*n.38. See also specific philosophers,* e.g., Proudfoot
popular, 11, 34, 64, 70, 190–93
psychology and, 41, 106–07, 192, 196, 212*n.140*, 215*n.13*
reason and, 210*nn.91, 94*, 211*n.116*
science and, 20–21, 27, 29, 30, 34–35, 36–37, 38, 71, 178, 194, 195–96, 201, 210*n.84*, 245–46*n.122. See also specific scientists,* e.g., Newton
  as search for meaning, 27–28, 32, 33, 34, 198, 213*n.145*, 246*n.140*
  secular, 32, 212*n.143*
  as symbolic communication, 247*nn.151, 154*
  theories of, 8–10, 205*n.1*, 206*n.16 See also* Intellectualist and eclectic theories; Social functionalist theories; Wish-fulfillment theories
"Religion as a Cultural System," (Geertz), 27–29
Religious emotions, 9, 12, 23, 203, 204, 205–06*n.5*, 211*n.122*
Religious experience, 4, 9–10, 26, 30, 31, 37, 187–88, 194, 195, 200, 201, 203, 214*n.163*
Religious and secular anthropomorphism compared, 112, 139, 188, 197–201
Religious symbolism, 16, 27–28, 29, 31, 32, 177, 178, 198–200, 247*n.151*
Revitalization movement, 5, 11
Reynolds, David K., 226*n.72*
Ribot, Théodule, 63
Richardson, Alan, 30
Ricoeur, Paul, 198, 247*n.151*
Ritual, 29, 149, 200, 203, 213*n.144*, 248*n.165*
Rizzuto, Ana–Maria, 192
Robinet, J.B.R., 58
Rocks. *See* Anthropomorphized or animated things and events
Roerich, Nicholas, 143

Romans, 12, 55, 75, 116, 125, 136–37, 139, 141
Romanticism, 57, 58, 59
Rorschach test, 96, 107, 226*nn.73, 74*
Rorty, Richard, 198, *215n.17, 247n.146*
Rosch, Eleanor, 101, 102, 216*n.31*
Ruskin, John, 13, 126, 127, 128, 129, 141, 231*n.64*
Rutherford, Ernest, 166

Sacred and profane, 17, 18, 20, 202, 203, 209*n.69*
Saenredam, Pieter, 143
Sagan, Carl, 168, 238*n.97*
Saler, Benson, 193, 197
Saliba, John, 205*n.1*
San, 18, 116
Scanning, 44, 62, 76, 90, 99, 100, 131, 203–4. *See also* Pattern recognition; Schemata
Scheibe, Karl, 93, 96
Schemata, 51, 78–80, 98–103, 140, 150–51, 188, 217*n.68. See also* Pattern recognition; Scanning; Template
Schleiermacher, Friedrich, 9, 10, 18, 23, 26, 37, 66, 67, 194, 203
Schorsch, Ismar, 180
Schrödinger, Erwin, 45
Science. *See also specific scientists*, e.g., Einstein, and *specific disciplines*, e.g., Physics
  animism and, 25, 41, 55–56, 57, 165, 167, 197, 234–35*n.1*
  anthropomorphism and, 65, 75, 122, 163–70, 174, 175–76, 234–35*n.1*, 237*n.61*, 238*n.88*, 240*nn.124, 148*
  criticism of anthropomorphism, 35, 151, 152, 159–61, 165
  nonempirical, 211*nn.114, 115*
  religion and, 20–21, 27, 29–30, 34–35, 38, 71, 178, 194, 195–96
Science fiction, 77, 89, 192
Sea. *See* Anthropomorphized or animated things and events
Searching image, 51, 98, 101, 217*n.70*. *See also* Pattern recognition; Scanning; Schemata; Template
Seascapes, human scale in, 151
Sebeok, Thomas, 53
"Seeing as," 6, 37, 42, 47. *See also* Interpretation; Perception
Self-knowledge. *See also* Familiarity theory
  anthropomorphism as perception, 110, 111
  not reliable, 78–79

origin of anthropomorphism, 66–67, 78–79, 80–81, 215*n.9*, 220*n.25*
  in philosophy and science, 160, 163
Sensory organization, 68
Sexual imagery, 150–51
Seyfarth, Robert, 51
Shakespeare, William, 83, 128, 193
Shamans and shamnanism, 11, 87, 89, 134, 194
Sharma, R. S., 127, 129
Shelley, Percy Bysshe, 128
Shinto, 16, 18, 192
Siculus, Diodorus, 11
Signatures, doctrine of, 96, 158
Significance. *See* Meaning
Simmel, Marianne, 95
Singleton, M., 192
Siskin, Clifford, 229*nn.22, 28*
Skorupski, John, 208*n.55*, 210*n.83*, 212*n.140*
Smart, Ninian, 31, 209*n.69*
Smith, Wilfred Cantwell, 203*n.1*, 214*n.167*
Sociability, 77, 202–3
Social functionalist theories, 28, 33, 208*n.54*, 212*n.141. See also specific theorists*, e.g., Durkheim
  animism and, 18, 56–57, 218*n.90*
  anthropomorphism and, 175, 178
  definition, 16
  problems with, 17–20
  of religion, 10, 16–21, 38, 199, 213*n.150*
Social sciences, 13, 31, 56, 57, 174–75, 208*n.54. See also specific disciplines*, e.g., Anthropology, and *individual social scientists*, e.g., Horton
Social solidarity. *See* Social functionalist theories
Sociobiology, 171, 240*n.124*
Sociology, 16, 17, 65, 175
Socrates, 127, 154, 186
Solidarity. *See* Social functionalist theories
Souls. *See also* Spirits
  animism, 22, 24, 57, 58, 70, 71
  Christianity, 87, 134
  Greek cosmology, 55, 154, 155, 156
Space exploration, 168, 175–76
Spencer, Herbert, 22, 56, 175, 178–79, 190, 218*n.90*
Spender, Stephen, 127
Sperber, Dan, 208*n.55*
Spilka, Bernard, 205*n.1*, 212*n.140*, 215*n.13*

Spinoza, Benedict de, 152
  anthropocentrism, 63, 65, 161–62, 172, 175
  wish-fulfillment theory, 10, 11
Spirits
  animism and, 5–6, 18, 25, 40, 48, 50–51, 57, 67, 87
  in art, 138
  intellectualist theories, 22, 24, 25, 40
  as material, 242*n.33*
Spiro, Melford, 20, 213*nn.149, 150,* 241*n.1,* 241–42*n.8*
Staal, Frits, 248*n.165*
Stack, George, 163, 164, 219*n.1,* 237*n.73*
Stalin, Joseph, 193
Stark, Rodney, 206*n.16,* 207*n.40*
Stars and planets. *See* Anthropomorphized or animated things and events
Stern, Daniel, 15, 80, 106, 111
Sterner, Judy, 120
Stewart, Dugald, 57
Stokes, Adrian, 141, 146, 149
Storace, Patrice, 127
Stroumsa, Gedaliahu, 180
Structural-functionalists, 16. *See also* Social functionalist theories
Suffering and religion, 10–11, 12, 72, 207*n.28. See also* Wish-fulfillment theory of religion
Sullivan, Harry Stack, 105, 106, 175
Sultan, Donald, 143
Sun, 114–15, 155, 161, 237*n.61*
Superhuman, 212–13*n.144,* 241*n.1*
Supernatural, 174, 203, 209*n.76,* 217*n.49*
Superstition, 11, 16
Suppes, Patrick, 196
Swanson, Guy, 209*n.67*
Swinburne, Richard, 184, 186, 189, 198, 248*n.166*
Symbolic action, 7, 38, 62–63, 193, 197–200. *See also* Religious Symbolism; Symbolism, as human characteristic
Symbolism, 199, 202
  and functionalist school, 16, 17, 28, 31, 199, 208*n.55,* 241–42*n.8*
  as human characteristic, 38, 62–63, 90, 93, 112, 172, 177, 193, 197–98, 199, 202

Tagore, Rabindranath, 177
Tambiah, S. J., 26,
  Buddhism, 209*nn.76, 77*
  Horton, 213*nn.155, 159*
  intellectualism, 214*n.167*

Israelite God, 242*nn.13, 15*
  pagan gods continuous with humans, 244*n.84*
  religion as symbolic communication, 247*n.151*
  religion as transcendental, 206*n.5*
  Tylor, 206*n.13*
Taoism, 18
Tao te Ching, 60, 124
Tate, Allen, 126–27
Taussig, Michael, 120, 221*n.66*
Teilhard de Chardin, Pierre, 56
Teleology, 159, 172, 220*n.25,* 236*n.38,* 244*n.70*
Template, 91, 101, 140, 188, 224*nn.1, 28. See also* Model; Pattern recognition; Scanning; Searching image; Schemata
Terhune, Albert Payson, 93–94
Thales, 55
Theodoret, 181
Theology, 37, 62–64, 139, 178, 179–82, 183–85, 199–200. *See also specific religions,* e.g., Christianity; *specific theologians,* e.g., Tillich
Theories of Primitive Religion (Evans-Pritchard), 26
Theories of religion. *See* Religion, theories of
Theravada Buddhism, 20, 209*nn.76, 77*
Theriomorphism and theriomorphic forms, 193
Thomas, Keith, 210*n.82*
Thomas, Lewis, 171
Thompson, Ernest Seton, 93
Thoreau, Henry David, 78, 123
Thouless, R. H., 53, 56
Threat behavior
  in animals, 52, 74, 88, 202, 210*n.90*
  gods, 75
Tillich, Paul, 32, 63, 64, 120, 183–84, 205*n.2,* 212*n.140*
Timaeus (Plato), 56, 153–54, 156
Tipler, Frank, 169
Totemism, 17, 18, 29, 209*n.64*
Toulmin, Stephen, 41, 53
Trees. *See* Anthropomorphized or animated things and events
Tribal art. *See* Art, tribal
Tribal religions, 11, 21–23, 26, 34–35, 65–66, 159–60, 187, 193, 209*n.69,* 241*n.8*
Turner, Mark, 129
Turrell, James, 143
Twain, Mark, 18
Tyler, Parker, 144

Tylor, E. B.
  and animism, 22, 40, 48, 190,
    215*n.8*
  criticism of, 22–25, 206*n.13*
  intellectualist theories and, 21–26, 28,
    33, 35, 38
  vs. Piaget on animism, 40, 215*n.8*

Ultimacy, 27–29, 32, 204, 212*n.130*,
  213*n.149*
Unamuno, Miguel de, 15
Universe. *See* Cosmology

Van Brunt, H. L., 127
Veblen, Thorstein, 165
Via negativa, 180, 181, 182
Vico, Giambattista, 16, 65–66, 72, 75, 80,
  178
Violent feelings (and animism and pathetic
  fallacy), 126, 129, 229–30*n.33*,
  231*n.64*, 236*n.40*
Virgil, 170
Vision quests, 18
Visual art, 75, 122, 130, 150. *See also* Art,
  commercial, fine, folk, tribal
Vitruvius, 147

Waley, Arthur, 124
Wallace, A.F.C., 12, 191
Wallace, A. R., 173–74
Wandibba, Simiyu, 120
Watts, Frazer, 196, 206*nn.11, 16*,
  212*n.140*, 246*n.128*, 247*n.154*
Wax, Murray, 10, 206*n.16*
Wayman, Alex, 72
Weather. *See* Anthropomorphized and
  animated things and events
Weber, Max, 28, 207*n.28*
Werblowsky, R. J. Z., 179, 200

White, Leslie, 65, 67, 72, 80, 178, 241*n.6*
Whitehead, A. N., 217*n.67*
Wiebe, Donald, 207*n.17*
Williams, Mark, 19, 206*n.11*, 212*n.140*,
  246*n.128*, 247*n.154*
Williamson, René, 184
Wilson, E. O., 171
Winch, Peter, 206*n.12*, 245–46*n.122*
Wind. *See* Anthropomorphized or animated
    things and events
Winnicott, D. W., 106
Wish-fulfillment theory
  of animism, 41
  of anthropomorphism, 65, 66, 72–78,
    106–7
  in art, 132, 140, 231*n.64*
  in mythology, 231*n.64*
  origin of anthropomorphism, 63, 65, 66,
    67, 70, 72–78
  in philosophy and science, 163, 176
  problems with, 13–14, 59, 74–75, 106–
    7, 132, 162
  of religion, 10–16, 28, 34, 66, 72–
    75
Wittgenstein, Ludwig, 42, 90, 102, 197,
  199
Wolf children, 88, 223*n.102*
Wollheim, Richard, 145–46
Wordsworth, William, 57, 126, 128
Wright, James, 127
Writers. *See* Literature; *specific names*, e.g.,
    Joyce

Xenophanes, 63, 179, 186

Yin and *yang*, 60
Young, Robert, 173, 174

Zoomorphism, 144, 193, 202

Printed in the United States
791100003B